Creating Canadian En

MW01227585

This lively account of the making of Canadian English traces the variety's conceptual, social, and linguistic developments through the twentieth century to the present. This book is not just another history of Canadian English; it is a history of the variety's discovery, codification, and eventual acceptance, as well as the contribution of the linguists behind it. Written by an active research linguist focussing on Canadian English, this book is an archive-based biography on multiple levels. Through a combination of new data and reinterpretations of existing studies, a new voice is given to earlier generations of Canadian linguists who, generally forgotten today, shaped the variety and how we think about it. Exploring topics such as linguistic description and codification, dictionary making, linguistic imperialism, linguistic attitudes, language and Canadian identity, or the threat of Americanization, Dollinger presents a coherent, integrated, and balanced account of developments spanning almost a century.

STEFAN DOLLINGER is Associate Professor at the University of British Columbia's Department of English Language and Literatures, specializing in Canadian English and linguistic border studies. He is the author of *New-Dialect Formation in Canada* (2008) and *The Written Questionnaire in Social Dialectology* (2015), and, of particular interest for the present book, Chief Editor of the new edition of the *Dictionary of Canadianisms on Historical Principles* – www.dchp.ca/dchp2 (2017).

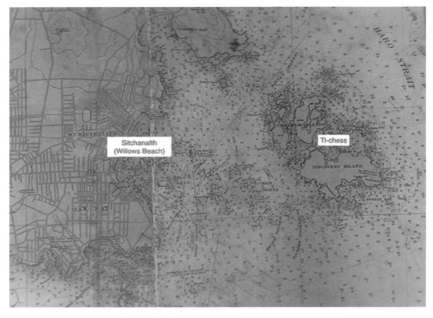

Figure 1 Early twentieth-century map (1920–23) of Oak Bay
and Tl-chess – colonial names Discovery and Chatham Islands
(Oak Bay Archives, used by permission)

Creating Canadian English

*The Professor, the Mountaineer, and
a National Variety of English*

Stefan Dollinger

University of British Columbia, Vancouver

CAMBRIDGE
UNIVERSITY PRESS

CAMBRIDGE
UNIVERSITY PRESS

University Printing House, Cambridge CB2 8BS, United Kingdom

One Liberty Plaza, 20th Floor, New York, NY 10006, USA

477 Williamstown Road, Port Melbourne, VIC 3207, Australia

314–321, 3rd Floor, Plot 3, Splendor Forum, Jasola District Centre,
New Delhi – 110025, India

79 Anson Road, #06–04/06, Singapore 079906

Cambridge University Press is part of the University of Cambridge.

It furthers the University's mission by disseminating knowledge in the pursuit of
education, learning, and research at the highest international levels of excellence.

www.cambridge.org
Information on this title: www.cambridge.org/9781108497718
DOI: 10.1017/9781108596862

First published 2019

Printed in the United Kingdom by TJ International Ltd. Padstow Cornwall

A catalogue record for this publication is available from the British Library.

Library of Congress Cataloging-in-Publication Data
Names: Dollinger, Stefan, author.
Title: Creating Canadian English : the professor, the mountaineer,
    and a national variety of English / Stefan Dollinger.
Description: New York : Cambridge University Press, 2019. |
    Includes bibliographical references and index.
Identifiers: LCCN 2018057998 | ISBN 9781108497718 (hardback) |
    ISBN 9781108708753 (paperback)
Subjects: LCSH: English language–Canada–History. | English language–Dialects–
    Canada. | English language–Variation–Canada.
Classification: LCC PE3208.8 .D65 2019 | DDC 427.9/71–dc23
LC record available at https://lccn.loc.gov/2018057998

ISBN 978-1-108-49771-8 Hardback
ISBN 978-1-108-70875-3 Paperback

To my most brilliant teachers in Upper Austria,
Vienna,
Ontario,
and
British Columbia

Contents

Figures

Tables

Preface

The intellectual history of individuals in the field of Canadian English is to a considerable degree also the history of the development of linguistics in Canada. This book is based on archival work, retracing and reconstructing the creation of a Canadian variety of English – against the odds – by descriptive linguists from the 1940s to the 1990s. A synthesis of new data and reinterpretations of older studies reveal that Canadian English appears to have finally solidified as an accepted concept only as late as the 2000s, after a period of prolonged debate.

It is hoped that the present account may start a conversation in Canada and perhaps in the fields of sociolinguistics and English linguistics in general. This is desirable in the light of linguists holding competing beliefs and often making contradictory theoretical assumptions about the nature of language and how it should be studied. The differences in opinion, however, have generally not resulted in increased exchanges redressing incompatibilities, but in the formation of intellectual silos.

Any discipline that forgets its past is bound to repeat errors and add some new ones. In the frenzy of linguistic inquiry today, which includes the relentless and sometimes ruthless battle for funding, we have seen more and more ahistorical perspectives taking hold, so much so that the "founders" of Canadian English need to be written back into linguistic history. I have aimed to present a balanced account of the developments over the past eighty years. While I hope that my interpretations will meet with my colleagues' approval – by and large, at least – I also hope that any disagreements will be constructively discussed in future exchanges.

I believe that linguistic findings should be made widely accessible, which is why the present book has been written with the general-interest reader in mind. It is geared towards anyone with an interest in language and presumes no advance knowledge.

Historical interpretations are bound to a given place, time, and interpreter. In this light, this book is more personal than any of my previous linguistic texts. While I strove to keep anecdotes to a minimum – hence the focus on 1940 to 1998 – I also felt that readers ought to know where this book's language historian positions himself.

Acknowledgements

Thanks are owed to many. Without David Friend (formerly of Nelson Ltd and, later, Oxford University Press Canada) and Terry Pratt (Professor Emeritus at the University of Prince Edward Island), I would never have gotten in the position to write this book. They are also the reason I got the opportunity to try my hand on the second edition of the *Dictionary of Canadianisms on Historical Principles* (*DCHP-2*).

My Viennese teachers were the start of it all as far as linguistics is concerned: Herbert Schendl (Ph.D. supervisor), Nikolaus Ritt (MA supervisor), Barbara Seidlhofer (first introductory seminar in linguistics), Henry G. Widdowson (first seminar in linguistics), Dieter Kastovsky, Monika Seidl (two language proficiency courses), Lisa Nazarenko (one language proficiency course), Karin Lach (first University of Vienna English teacher), Margarete Rubik (seminar lecture), Otto Rauchbauer (literature seminar), Richard Schrodt (introductory seminar in new High German grammar), Wendelin Schmidt-Dengler (many lecture courses on Austrian literature), Konstanze Fliedl (introductory seminar on literature, and a lecture on Austrian literature), Wynfrid Kriegleder (introductory seminar on German literature), as well as the late Klaus Häusler (English pedagogy seminar) and the late Patricia Häusler-Greenfield. It's been a great privilege learning from all of you.

A number of people made all the difference in secondary school, including the four "-bauers" in engineering school: Mag. Draxlbauer, who was the prime reason for me, English student at electrical engineering high school, trying the odd choice of an English–German major at university; Dipl. Ing. Rauchbauer; Mag. Ruckerbauer; and Ing. Kothbauer. Dipl. Ing. Jörg Haßlacher modelled an appealing kind of humanity for all of us. Much earlier, I accumulated debts to teachers Liselotte Schermaier, Sister Brigitte, Sister Ariane, and Sister Hamurabi.

More closely related to the present project, Professor Leslie Saxon is thanked not just for assistance with my affiliate-faculty status at the University of Victoria, but above all for spotting mistakes in an early draft of Chapter 1; and Alexandra D'Arcy for giving me the opportunity to present the book.

A debt of gratitude is owed to the many colleagues who provided answers on things long past: Paddy Drysdale (Oxfordshire, UK), Charles Boberg (Montreal), Jack Chambers (Toronto), Sandra Clarke (Newfoundland), Gerard Van Herk (Newfoundland), Anastasia Riehl (Kingston, Strathy Language Unit), and Judith Nylvek (Victoria). Anastasia is especially thanked for last-minute archival hunts in Kingston, Ontario. I would like to thank Margery Fee for her typical encouragement, her critical comments, and her stylistic improvements of Chapter 1. Special thanks must go to the Lovell family, especially to Bonnie Lovell, the late Charles J. Lovell's daughter (the "lexicographer's daughter"), and Charles M. Lovell, his son, for their uplifting assistance with this project. I hope the book will do justice to their remarkable father.

Paddy Drysdale is owed special thanks for inviting me to visit his Oxfordshire home in March 2017, for his willingness to mine his impressive memory, and for being a great host with his wife, Olwen – a *DCHP-1* tradition, Paddy informs me, that Faith and Wally Avis cultivated to perfection in their Kingston home. Paddy read full-length versions of the manuscript, offering factual corrections that always turned out to be correct. Olwen Drysdale saved the day with her picture of Walter Avis, thus putting a face to this book's professor that would otherwise have been missing. Victoria Neufeldt is credited for connecting the *DCHP-2* team with the last surviving member of the *DCHP-1* team, the "Big Six". Hayley Wickenheiser was so kind to provide a photo of herself in action for Team Canada; Jack (J. K.) Chambers granted permission to use his spectacular photo of the Quebec–Vermont border in Chapter 6.

University of Victoria Archives was the central research location for this book. Thanks must go to archivist Lara Wilson, who has never stopped humouring my requests, whether in 2006, 2017/18, or since. Thank you to Lawrence Hong for lugging *DCHP* boxes from special storage across campus and back, including the wild-goose chase for Box 4, which had already been sitting on my cart for weeks; and to John Fredrick, Jaqui Thompson, and Jane Morrisson for assisting when Lawrence was off. The staff at British Columbia Archives, I thank for help with my work on Douglas Leechman; Oak Bay Community Archives and archivist Caroline Duncan helped with the Douglas Treaties, historical image location, and rights clearances.

Helen Barton and Brian Stone of Cambridge University Press assisted in very different but equally important ways to make this book a reality; Frances Peck taught me some of the basics of trade publishing.

Tim Stewart, Rebecca Shapiro, and members of the DSNA Facebook group are thanked for taking the time to comment on the book's structure and the opening paragraph. *Kiitos/thanks* to: Sharon Pasivirta for her close reading of Chapter 1; Dina Al Kassim, Laura Moss, Barbara Dancygier, Anne Dragemark-Oscarsson, Gerard Van Herk, Alexander Rauscher, and Nancy

Tinari for their input on Facebook queries revolving around this book; Liz Hodgson for the decisive tip regarding the subtitle; Lynn Slobogian for believing in the project and improving the text's flow in so many ways; and copy-editor Leigh Mueller for catching what I missed.

Debbie Sherwood is owed thanks for feedback on Chapter 1 and a late version of Chapters 1–7. To Mrs Taylor, librarian at St Patrick's Elementary, I say thanks for reading an early version of the manuscript and for offering encouraging feedback.

The fact that a person's name is listed here does not imply the approval of any part of the book. While I got help from many, all faults and misrepresentations remain entirely my own.

Vielen Dank & *Daungschee* (in Upper Austrian traditional dialect), y'all

A Note to the International Reader

The use of the term *American* is in line with Canadian usage: *American* is always the adjective/noun for the United States; *North American* refers to both Canada and the USA. Referring to the southern parts of the Americas, we'd use *Central*, *Latin*, or *South America*, respectively. While I use Canadian terminology throughout, e.g. *hockey* but never *ice hockey*, I explain every aspect of it – if not in the main text, then in a note.

Figure 2 The staff at Ivy's Bookshop, Oak Bay Avenue, 12 Jan. 2018 (Shirley – left; Jessica – right)

Figure 3 The mystery novel section at Ivy's
(Photos: S. Dollinger, 2018)

1   What is Canadian English?

Until quite recently . . . few Canadians were interested enough in their speech to undertake the gigantic task of finding out about it. Consequently, there were no Canadian dictionaries worthy of the name; and our imported dictionaries virtually ignored Canadian usage. After all, British dictionaries are primarily intended for Britons and American dictionaries for Americans; no reputable editor claims anything more.

(Walter S. Avis)[1]

Murder he must have read often. Professor Scargill was a man who loved English whodunnit novels. From the 1960s until well into the 1990s, Scargill used to get his weekly fix of crime novels at Ivy's Bookshop, which today is a local Victoria institution in the heart of lovely Oak Bay Village. The friendly staff at Ivy's remember Scargill, the Yorkshire–Canadian gentleman, habitually browsing the mystery section (opposite). Bookseller Shirley St. Pierre tells me that staff knew Scargill as a linguistics professor at the then small University of Victoria, but that they did not fathom his importance as a key figure in the making of Canadian English – in the creation of a national variety of English, lifting it and its speakers from ridicule and linguistic insecurity to some prominence and pride. The way that Scargill, who was formally Director of the Lexicographical Centre for Canadian English, and his many associates achieved this monumental task was by writing a series of high-quality dictionaries. The flagship of the resulting four-volume series called Dictionary of Canadian English was the scholarly *Dictionary of Canadianisms on Historical Principles (DCHP-1)*,[2] which was published in Canada's centennial year of 1967 (Avis *et al.* 1967). Between the late 1950s and, basically, their deaths – just one of the main players is alive today – Scargill and his team members were continuously banging the drum for Canadian English. They were tooting their own horn, but not primarily for their own sake.

Dictionary writing is, surprisingly perhaps, a lot like crime solving. Do you remember *Columbo*, the detective show with Peter Falk? I know *Columbo* because it attained a cult status when I was studying in Austria, running in the Sunday 10 p.m. slot for years, long after no other station would buy it. That's a bit how I imagine Scargill going about establishing the correct etymology of

1

toque – invariably pronounced "tooke" in Canada – or *Canuck*: cigar in hand and the like, much like Inspector Columbo. It's not really how Margery Fee, our team, and I proceeded half a century later on the second edition, but the basic Sherlock-Holmesian principles have remained unchanged: data, data, and more data; facts; plausible chains of events; historical knowledge; linguistic knowledge; logic; and a good helping of Occam's razor as explained in Chapter 4. These are the eternal tools of the word sleuth.

So far in the story, people are usually with me. I tell them about what I did this past dozen years, at least some of the time, and they get it: writing a dictionary. Boring, perhaps, because folks know what a dictionary is. But "Canadian English"? This phrase people often repeat after me with a little bewilderment and usually, if not always, a rising intonation, as if to question whether such work could possibly be a real job. Their final intonation gets particularly raised if they detected the colourful notes in my English accent.

So what, then, is Canadian English? By Canadian English we mean the English language as used in Canada. Canadian English is therefore not a monolithic thing but an assembly of the varieties of English that are spoken, written, texted, dreamed, and occasionally sung in the country. Later, I will introduce a more technical definition of what Canadian English is – or, to be precise, what Standard Canadian English is, which is the English we hear from George Strombolopolous, Canada's news anchors, the prime minister, Avril Lavigne, and Shawn Mendes, for the most part. But for now the very loose definition provided will do.

When it comes to language in Canada, English is just one of many languages, of course. Besides French, the other former colonial language in the federal domain, English is only 1 of at least 263 languages spoken in the country.[3] English is the most widely used language in the country, but there are quite a few oddities about English in Canada that we will need to explore later. About 60 of the 263+ languages are the languages of the original population of Canada. I say "about" because it is not universally agreed upon what counts as a particular language and as a dialect of a given language. This should not be surprising, as the concept of language is paradoxically not so much a linguistic one as primarily a social one.[4] Like all things social, the concept of language is subject to debate and as many opinions as there are colours in the rainbow.

Where scholars do agree, however, is that the five dozen or so aboriginal languages are divided into no fewer than ten language families,[5] and some fifty of them are spoken in the province of British Columbia (BC) alone. This is one reason why some researchers think that BC is something like the cradle of Indigenous languages in (northern) North America, as it is possible that the rest of the (northern half of the) continent was settled, via Asia, from BC. This was long before the Europeans made a showing with their Indo-European languages, which they turned, through their actions, into colonial languages.

The linguistic diversity of BC is indeed special in the North American context. Picture this diversity in comparison with the European Union, which is often taken as the epitome of linguistic tolerance and multilingualism in western culture. One can quickly see that more than twice as many Indigenous languages are spoken in BC, a Canadian province of just 5 million inhabitants (Jan. 2019), as in the European Union, a 512-million-strong economical unit, with twenty-four official languages at present. English is also, it needs to be said at the outset, the offshoot of the language of the most "effective" colonizers. This "efficiency" has brought a number of negative effects that anyone living in Canada is still confronted with today. This far-reaching fact means that we need to consider the consequences of colonization, in particular by English-speaking colonizers, throughout the entire book, in one way or another. It's therefore a good idea to start with the basics before we turn to the story of the making of Canadian English.

First Nations Beginnings and Canadian English

The problems that are the result of colonialism are linguistic, cultural, and social – in other words, they affect every area and cut through every aspect of life. If you live in Canada, whether you're aware of it or not, you're without exception affected by this colonial legacy.

Flashback to just a century before Professor Scargill's browsing in the crime-novel section at Ivy's. Residential schools had not yet established their steady grip on the First Nations peoples in the far west. *Residential school* is a historical euphemism for colonial schools whose primary goal was to "take", by any legal and illegal means, "the Indian out of the child", resulting in cultural genocide that almost completely wiped out entire Indigenous cultures and languages. These institutions were nothing other than inhumane places of neglect, terror, and abuse: anything but places of learning. In 1897, a century before Scargill's death, a host of First Nations languages would have been heard in the meadows, woods, and soft slopes through which Oak Bay Avenue cuts today. While English – by which we mean forms of British English, some American English, with some speakers starting to show early Canadian English features – would have been firmly rooted by then, the Indigenous languages that had been exclusively heard for thousands of years in this land were still dominant in some locations. The first sizeable in-migration of settlers happened in the wake of the Fraser River and Cariboo Gold Rushes of the late 1850s and 1860s; before then, the settlers were outnumbered by and depended on the goodwill of the First Nations. Migration from the Canadian East in considerable numbers only occurred after the completion of the trans-Canadian railway in 1885, a generation after the big BC Gold Rush.

The First Nations languages of the region are the languages of Coast Salish peoples. Today these languages are frequently called Salishan, to distinguish them from their linguistic relatives of the same name in Eastern Washington

Figure 4 View in 1896 from Oak Bay
(Gonzales Hill) to Tl-chess (Discovery Island)
(Photo: Oak Bay Archives, Image number 2012–001-018, used by permission)

State (Salish languages). The languages in and around Victoria belong to an extensive array of Salishan and upriver varieties that are quite closely related. It would be any dialectologist's or sociolinguist's dream to study these languages and their relationships, yet most of them are either sleeping – what used to be called *dead* – or on the brink of extinction with only a handful of native speakers left. (In linguistics today, we prefer the term *sleeping language* over *dead language* – by which is meant a language awaiting revitalization based on archived material. Revived languages include Modern Hebrew and, in fact, the Musqueam language that is now taught to dozens of people at the University of British Columbia.) Ivy's Bookshop is located on traditional Chilcowitch territory, referring to the family or "band" of Songhee Lekwungen speakers that are the traditional custodians – in western parlance, "owners" – of that part of Oak Bay. The Chekonein Lekwungen dialects would be heard as well, in addition to nearby Esquimalt Lekwungen and Saanich Lekwungen dialects.[6]

Indigenous heritage is written all over Oak Bay and Greater Victoria – all across Canada, actually, yet we have forgotten much about it. The islands off Oak Bay, for instance, are in plain sight of Willows Beach, a popular Victoria location that is visited by many locals and visitors alike. When you look out to sea from Willows Beach, it's impossible to miss them. This book's cover photo shows the islands in the foreground. They have a story that is not so widely known, however, and today the two biggest ones are still most often referred to by their colonial names of Chatham and Discovery Islands, named after Captain Vancouver's two ships. The real name, from the local Lekwungen dialect of Salishan, is of course another one – so much so that it looks different at one glance: ƛ̓čés. This word may be transcribed in English letters as something like *tl-chess*, which is pronounced close to *til-chess* with stress or emphasis on *chess*. ƛ̓čés is an interesting case because it is a particular place name in Lekwungen culture but also the general word for 'island' – any island. Tim Montler from the University of North Texas, one of the experts in Coastal Salish informs us that ƛ̓čés

is both the word for 'island' and the proper name of Discovery Island in Lkwungen, SENĆOŦEN (spelled T̸ĆÁS), and in Klallam, which has a direct relative [a so-called "cognate"], ƛ̓čás. The word for 'island' in Hul'q'umin'um' [spoken from Saanich to Nanaimo and over to the southern Gulf Islands] is not [related], but it is in Upriver Halkomelem [Fraser Valley, Chilliwack, Harrison Lake], tl'chá:s, which has no proper name for Discovery Island. Other smaller islands have their own names and the generic word used is typically the diminutive of ƛ̓čés, ƛ̓əƛ̓éčəs. (Tim Montler: pers. correspondence, April 2018)

The non-colonial, actual name for the island reveals an astonishing amount of cultural knowledge *and* the connections via the Salish Sea among the Coast Salish First Nations. Why, for instance, is one island's name in the Lekwungen language also the word for 'island' in general? It is as if it were a kind of archetypal island, as Tim suggests.

Part of ƛ̓čés is today legally known as Chatham Islands Indian Reserve No. 4 and still owned by the Songhees and Esquimalt First Nations.[7] Having largely remained in Native hands, ƛ̓čés – which from now on I shall render as *Tl-chess* to help readers remember it[8] – is sadly a rare exception to the rule of colonial land grab on more or less outrageous terms, if any terms were offered. It is a sad fact that British Columbia as a province has been exceptionally intransigent in refusing to negotiate treaties, which means that almost all lands were seized illegally from their Native custodians (see Mawani 2009; Barman 2007). Today, we also have good evidence that even disease, against which the First Nations had no immune response, was used as a means of conquest (Swanky 2012: 70–97).

As the legal names make clear in almost all cases, it was the colonizers who bestowed their names on everything, which had, among other things, the effect that even today it is not easy to unearth the traditional, original names. Although the land was usually taken from the First Nations by force or, less often, by some sort of shady agreement, on Tl-chess the original custodians managed, against all odds, to hold on to it until this day.

Who are the Songhees, then? (Today we usually speak of the Songhee, Saanich, and Esquimalt First Nations.) Chief trader Charles Ross, put in charge of Fort Victoria by Governor James Douglas, appears to be the first to spell

Songhees in 1844, when he referred to the aboriginal people "encamped near the fort" and added "whose lands we occupy".[9] Prior to this spelling being standardized in English, the name had many variants, including *Songish*, *Samose*, *Stsamis*, *Tsomass*, *Tchanmus*, or *Etzamish*, depending on which Coastal Salishan dialect speaker's version was rendered in English and by whom. For the people as such, spellings were utterly irrelevant, as their tradition was predominantly oral, with spelling questions playing no role whatsoever. So by asking about the "right" spelling, we are already enacting colonial routines and expectations on another culture that had more important things to deal with, such as the co-existence with nature, sustainability, and fostering respect for all things, living or not, but definitely not with spelling.

There are two contracts between Governor James Douglas and the Songhees that are relevant for the land that the village of Oak Bay is located on, though the interpretation of the vague terms is not agreed on. How could it be? The territories were partly overlapping and somewhat fluid, as was the make-up of families. On that, James Douglas tried to tease out definitions for his western-style contracts that did not exist; asking for boundaries, he got descriptions that had worked for centuries but that were not the down-to-the-inch measurements he wanted to hear. It is like fitting square pegs into round holes: the exercise was bound to fail and we are living with its negative ramifications to this day.

The "Purchase of Land" from the Chilcowitch, dated 30 April 1850, is one of fourteen treaties that James Douglas signed between 1850 and 1854. Collectively, they cover only a minuscule part of BC's vast landmass. In the Chilcowitch case, the Crown agreed to pay "Thirty pounds sterling" for the treaty that includes the location of Ivy's Bookshop. While the Chilcowitch Lekwungen agreed to share some of their lands, the alleged surrendering part is overly explicit, as they

do consent to surrender, entirely and for ever, to James Douglas, the agent of the Hudson's Bay Company in Vancouver Island, that is to say, for the Governor, Deputy Governor, and Committee of the same, the whole of the lands situate [*sic*] and lying between the Sandy Bay east of Clover Point, at the termination of the Whengwhung [*sic*] line to Point Gonzalez, and thence north to a line of equal extent passing through the north side of Minies Plan.

What is less clear is the purchase price beyond the 30 pounds sterling – a bargain, truly, though it was not even paid in coins, but merely in blankets. And here it comes: for the entire lands in the Victoria region 371 blankets were paid.[10] I would call that a rip-off. What comes with that purchase is stated in the next paragraph:

The condition of or understanding of this sale is this, that our village sites and enclosed field are to be kept for our own use, for the use of our children, and for those who may follow after us; and the land shall be properly surveyed hereafter. It is understood, however, that the land itself, with these small exceptions, becomes the entire property of the white people for ever; it is also understood that we are at liberty to hunt over the unoccupied lands, and to carry on our fisheries as formerly.[11]

Any western lawyer would object to such formulation of benefits, "for ever" or not, which includes a diminishing resource in hunting over "unoccupied" land. It is clear that the Lekwungen could have no idea of just how many "white people" would come and how little land would eventually be left. It was not communicated to them. So many would come that soon nothing would be left "to hunt over".

The dice were heavily loaded against the First Nations. Speaking of "small exceptions", for instance, can easily be used to reduce the size of reserves later on; after all, small is relative. What is clear is that "the content of that treaty is not at all clear".[12] What makes matters worse is that the treaty above was only agreed on orally, together with most other ones on Vancouver Island. Douglas collected the signatures and marks of the chiefs on a *blank sheet of paper* and, after consultation with London a few months later, filled in the sheet post hoc (*ibid.*: 5). Any lawyer at the time would have argued that a people cannot sign away their land with a *carte blanche*, an empty slate of conditions, to be filled in post hoc unilaterally by only one party. Clearly, informed consent was not given.

Languages, Cultures, and Reconciliation

Recent research at the University of Victoria's Faculty of Law states that what the First Nations thought they'd signed was a sharing agreement, not a treaty handing over land in perpetuity; the former is fully in line with traditional practices and Indigenous lines of thought. Such misunderstanding had profound consequences; as it was both culturally and linguistically caused, it calls for reconciliation. The First Nations evidence is clear. The oral traditions of the five participating First Nations on 30 April 1850, in combination,

provide a strong denial of the cession or surrender of their land in favour of the HBC [Hudson's Bay Company] or the Crown. The pieces of the puzzle contributed by each account add up to a convincing argument that the oral agreements included the following terms: compensation for land already occupied and resources previously harvested by non-First Nation residents; continuation of the terms of their existing joint occupation and enjoyment of land and resources; and, agreement to negotiate expansion of non-First Nation establishments and activities, provided it did not interfere with the existing way of life of the First Nations. In sum, the First Nation negotiators likely agreed to share, not surrender, their land and its resources. (Vallance 2015: 361)

While the Lekwungen and others came to sign a sharing and joint occupation contract with the Hudson's Bay Company for the benefit of all – the typical win-win that is so deeply rooted in First Nations culture – the Crown considered James Douglas to be signing a treaty and they probably thought, in line with early capitalist culture, that they'd won.

What is beyond doubt is that two very different cultures signed a contract in very concise English, laying out neither western assumptions, rights, and obligations nor Lekwungen assumptions, rights, and obligations. At that time, the First Nations were still more powerful than the settlers, yet they agreed to share a part of the land in exchange for some goods and services. As they were soon to find out, the "contract" would come to haunt them, with their original intention distorted and interpreted to their disadvantage. We can see what western culture brought to the table. The story about pretty much all of Oak Bay – with the exception of Tl-chess – is the sad story of how western legal traditions exploited the trust of First Nations in British Columbia and in Canada more generally.

The English language as used in Canada has enshrined many western misunderstandings of both the land and the culture the colonizers had burst into. It begins with the naming. Virtually all First Nation names known today, for places, flora, fauna, and people, have been replaced with western names. Take, for instance, Chatham and Discovery Islands, which are in reality not two islands but just one. What happened? They were named in 1846, when the western portions of the Canadian–US border were finalized, in honour of colonial explorer George Vancouver, who had sailed these waters briefly half a century earlier. The surveyors who named them saw what they thought were two islands. What they didn't know was that they saw two parts of one and the same island at high tide. (You can see it in the foreground of this book's cover, with Willows Beach behind it and towards the left.) We can safely assume that they were so busy surveying in the name of colonization and exploitation that they just didn't care to ask any First Nations member, who would have told them that they were looking at one and the same island.

This little example is a good illustration of how colonial eyes, and with it English and Canadian English, often construct the world differently from those who really know.[13] This upsetting legacy is part of the history of every (former) colonial language and needs to be dealt with. We will address this difficult aspect of linguistic "baggage" throughout, but with more focus in Chapter 8. It would be wrong to say that colonialism is a thing of the past, as its legacy is everywhere in one form or another. Consider the two totem poles in Figure 5, both found in Victoria and both commissioned by non-Indigenous people.

In terms of awareness of the colonial processes, the plaques indicate some progress between 1966 and 1997, when the two poles were erected. It is striking that in the 1966 plaque (left), the donor of the log was given ample space and acknowledgement: "Log donated by Macmillan, Bloedel and Powell

Figure 5 Two totem poles in Victoria, and their plaques
(Photos: S. Dollinger, 2018)

River, Limited" – a company that in effect took the pole from lands seized
from the First Nations. The 1997 plaque does much better, using Native names
and Lekwungen language, but offers no contextualization, which, however,
might have been a deliberate choice.[14] Today, more than twenty years after the
second pole was erected, we might be in the position to offer more than
symbolic improvements, which means legal settlement of the illegal Canadian
land grab from one or two centuries ago.

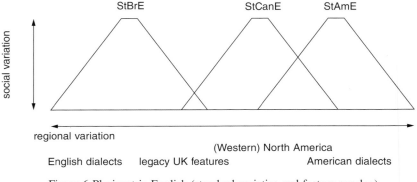

Figure 6 Pluricentric English (standard varieties and feature overlap)
(Dollinger in press: fig. 1)

Canadian English in the Slow Cooker

There are different types of Canadian English. There is Standard Canadian English, the type we teach in schools and the equivalent to Standard British English,[15] Standard American English, Standard Australian English, and so forth. A long time ago there was only one "standard English", but since about 1800, beginning with the political independence of the United States, the idea of just one standard in the language is a thing of the past. English has since been a "pluricentric language" (Clyne 1992), meaning that there is more than one linguistic centre and standard.

Language is co-determined by a host of social and regional (= location) features. The relationship between the standard varieties of English can be illustrated by expanding a classic pyramid that schematizes social and regional variation in language. The pyramid was originally published in 1974 by Peter Trudgill, one of the most famous linguists today. In Trudgill (1974: 42), the situation for English society is visualized, which has served as a direct input for Standard British English (StBrE) depicted in Figure 6 on the left. As a rule of thumb, the socially upwardly mobile and higher social strata speak the standard variety – in this context, Standard British English – while lower classes often speak more regional varieties. Note that *standard* refers to phonology/phonetics (the sounds of the language) as well as all other levels: syntax and morphology (often called grammar when combined), pragmatics (how language is used in concrete contexts), and more, such as spelling, etc. But there is more than standard and non-standard, as linguistically very interesting, intermediate, mixed forms exist. Do you know the Naked Chef? How does Jamie Oliver, the Naked Chef, speak, precisely? Standard or not?

You'll find his speech best characterized as some new in-between variety that some call "Estuary English", after the banks of the River Thames. (In German, such intermediate variety has been quite common; it is called *Umgangssprache*, meaning "colloquial language", and is the most frequently used kind of German.) Is British English developing a less formal standard, for lack of a better word, now? We need to revisit the question in a generation or two, but it looks as if it is.

Returning to the question of standard varieties, the introduced principles will lead us to make sense of the jungle of linguistic variation. As the schematization in Figure 6 shows, there is overlap in each of the three depicted Englishes: British, Canadian, and American. While there is more overlap with American and Canadian than with British, overlap is present in all. Each variety has its own standard represented by the peaks, while less standard forms are found farther down the pyramid. Besides Standard British, Standard Canadian, and Standard American English that are depicted in Figure 6, the graph could be extended with Standard Australian and Standard Jamaican English and many more Englishes [*sic*]. Because of this, we say that English is a pluricentric language, meaning it has more than one norm, just as is the case with German, Spanish, Portuguese, and many more languages (see Muhr *et al.* 2013 for an overview).

In contrast to the two national standards of the more powerful nations of the USA and the UK, Standard Canadian English is spoken by an astonishingly large portion of the Canadian society: close to 40 per cent of all Canadians – from a total of some 38 million speakers – use that Canadian standard habitually. That this figure is remarkable can only be seen in comparison to the other national standards. Standard British English, for instance, is spoken by "probably not . . . more than about 15 per cent of the population of England".[16] For Standard American English no reliable estimates exist, but in all likelihood the US percentage would be situated somewhere between the UK and the Canadian values. Perhaps it's 20 or 25 per cent. For some reason, no linguist has yet put a figure on it. Indirectly, as we move along, we will explore possible reasons for the surprising fact that no American estimate seems to exist.

A Very Concise History of Canadian English

As this book is a biography of the makers of Canadian English and their time, we cannot discuss the development of the linguistic features of this national variety without going beyond the bounds of this book. That is not a big problem today, however. Fortunately, for the past decade or so we have had a number of texts added to the very young field of historical Canadian English. There is Chambers' (2010) introductory text; Chapter 2 in Boberg's book

(2010: 55–105) stands out in sociohistorical detail. Dollinger (2008a) was the first monograph on early Canadian English, using eighteenth- and nineteenth-century data from Ontario; Reuter (2017) is a recent addition on early newspaper language in Ontario, while Tagliamonte (2013) traces grammatical features in Canada back to Scotland, Northern England, and Ireland. More recently, work on Victoria English and Manitoba English has begun. Even the pragmatic marker *like* is traced back in time in Canadian English (D'Arcy 2017) and there is, of course, a wealth of information on Newfoundland English (start with Clarke 2010). A recent summary of work on historical Canadian English is available in Dollinger (2017a), while both Schneider's and Trudgill's approaches are discussed for their strengths and weaknesses in the Canadian context in Dollinger (2015a: 200–208).

It seems a good idea at this point to provide a developmental sketch of Canadian English, the variety we are dealing with throughout this book. As a linguistic variety that developed in a settler colony (see Denis and D'Arcy 2018), Canadian English has come about through dialect contact (different dialects of English combine and form a new one) and language contact (English takes up influences from other languages). These mixing processes are followed by the formation of a new variety per se; this is called the new-dialect formation or koinéization process.

We can organize the immigration that shaped the variety over the past three centuries in five waves, as shown in Table 1. Ontario plays a central role in the settlement of the country. While the Maritimes received a good number of English speakers early on, they did not become the pivot point for the settlement of the west, which happened from Ontario. Accepted opinion is that the first wave of immigration, which was almost exclusively composed of US immigration in the wake of the American Revolution in 1776, was responsible for establishing the basic character of Canadian English. Bloomfield (1948) called this scenario the Loyalist Base Theory, named after the United

Table 1 *Canada's five major immigration waves*

1776–1812	Wave I	American immigration (United Empire Loyalists)
1815–1867	Wave II	British and Irish immigration ("British Isles")
1890–1914	Wave III	Continental European immigration (Germany, Italy, Scandinavia, Ukraine) and British immigration
1945–70s Post World War II	Wave IV	Highly diverse immigration populations, including from Europe, Asia (Korea, China, Vietnam, India, Pakistan), Latin America, and the USA
1990s–Present	Wave V	Diverse immigration continues, with Chinese immigration now peaking

(Dollinger 2015a: 205, table 6.9), after Chambers (2010: 12–19, 28–32)

Empire Loyalists leaving the newly founded USA for Canada. Between the 1780s, when Ontario was bush land, and 1812, about 1 million people, four-fifths of them from the USA, moved to what is now Ontario. There was a sprinkling of Scots who came early and held important posts, as they were often literate because of their advanced school system; German, Dutch, and some other European nationalities complete the mix (Dollinger 2008a: 67–76). French speakers were the majority in the province of Quebec, but usually not, with the exception of the Catholic clergy, in positions of power.

Besides all of this, east of the Maritimes on the island of Newfoundland were – aside from the local First Nations, of course – speakers of English, French, Spanish, and Portuguese, who, from the sixteenth century, carried out a summer fishery and returned in the fall to Europe. In the late eighteenth century, the English and Irish speakers eventually decided to settle in what would remain an independent colony until 1949, when Newfoundland and Labrador joined the Canadian Confederation. An Irish component is very strong to this day in parts of Newfoundland and an essential part of the heritage. With permanent colonization, the settlers developed varieties of English that they formed and developed from Southwest England and South-east Ireland varieties. Newfoundland Englishes represent to this day, despite influence from the mainland, a unique set of varieties that are Canada's most distinct linguistic enclave varieties (see Clarke 2010). Newfoundland Englishes are so unique that an entire academic research unit has been studying them, and nothing but them, for more than sixty years, and is still going strong. In the Canadian context, however, the Newfoundland varieties have not had much influence on the formation of Standard Canadian English, as a result of location, settlement streams and, important in new-dialect formation, numbers of speakers.

Before we move on to describe what came to be the dominant speech patterns in Canada, a word or two is necessary on Maritimes English (from New Brunswick, Nova Scotia, and Prince Edward Island) and the Atlantic Englishes (from the Maritimes and Newfoundland). Atlantic Englishes are older than the varieties that would come to dominate later in Canada by virtue of speaker numbers. Historically and linguistically, however, they are immensely important in the Canadian context. If you travel to the Maritimes or to Newfoundland and you poke around a bit – i.e., go off the beaten tourist path – you'll be able to hear the unique Eastern Canadian patterns of speech, whether in Acadia (where French varieties and English co-exist and intermingle, as graduate student Kristan Newell (2019) has been researching), Lunenburg (founded by Germans in 1749 who left a trace of German substrate), Halifax (the capital of Nova Scotia), Saint John (the first city in New Brunswick), St John's (Newfoundland's capital), or, certainly, in Gander, Patty Harbour, and Carbonear (all in Newfoundland). This aspect is often forgotten in the big sea of millions of Canadians, who, due to a change in economical and political fortunes starting in the nineteenth century, often no longer have significant ties with the historically important Canadian Atlantic provinces.

We can see Canada is a beautifully complex place. If one aims to generalize the immigration to Canada, however, it might be summarily captured as in Table 1. Wave II followed in the wake of the War of 1812, when British subjects were brought in to rid Britain of its demobbed soldiers after the Napoleonic wars, and of its paupers, the first victims of the early Industrial Revolution. The idea was also to "dilute" the American base, which was – unjustly – suspected of potentially being disloyal towards the British Crown if hostilities with the USA were to break out again. The Irish came late in that period but in great numbers as of the late 1830s. Scargill (1957) identified this "swamping" with British Isles speakers (from Britain and Ireland) as the second important input to Canadian English. The British Isles immigrants were from non-southern locations in Britain and more than 90 per cent of them were probably non-standard speakers (Dollinger 2008a: 83). Tagliamonte (2013: 195–213) shows some of the present-day reflexes of Irish and non-standard British English in rural and urban Ontario English and re-focusses on the Atlantic link that was at the base of *The Linguistic Atlas of the United States and Canada* in the early twentieth century.

The British Isles migrants' strong numbers were responsible for foregrounding linguistic variables of British descent that speakers can consciously manipulate. In total, 1.25 million British immigrants came between 1815 and 1865 (Dollinger 2008a: 79). With them, they brought features such as *schedule* with a *sh* sound, *fill in a form* rather than *fill out a form*, *tap* instead of *faucet*, *colour* vs *color*, *centre* vs *center*, and first person *shall* instead of *will* for the future tense – all of which gained wide currency as the prestige forms in Canada. But the large numbers of British Isles migrants from 1815 to 1867 were not nearly enough to change the basically North American character of Canadian English.

Walter Avis, whom we'll hear lots about in Chapters 2 and 3, used to make the point in his teachings (reported in McConnell 1978: 47) that, in American English, *tire* is the dominant spelling, but *tyre* in Britain. In the USA, of course, *center* is the standard form today, while in Britain it is *centre*. What do Canadians do? As Figure 7 shows, Canadians combine the originally American *tire* with British *centre* and create something of their own. We just don't see it so often today, with brand names having taken over since the 1960s – Fountain Tire, Kal Tire, OK Tire, even Big O Tire, and the like – but Figure 7 is a photo from a Vancouver shop that meanwhile has given way to – you guessed it – more condominium housing in that city.

Today, there is a wide range of features that is characteristic of Canadian English. Vocabulary is only one – but an important and the most pervasive – part. Canadian English also sounds a little different, uses grammatical forms in

Figure 7 Tire centre sign in Vancouver on 2nd Avenue
(Photo: S. Dollinger, 2014)

different proportions than down in the USA and, very strikingly so, sometimes employs the same linguistic material in different ways in terms of politeness and language use more generally. It's impossible to introduce these features, many of which are very subtle, in the few words we have space for in this book. But to give you an idea, here is a short list of phonetic (sound) features that are found in Canadian English, often in contrast to the US dialects:

- a phenomenon called Canadian Raising, which is the "oot and aboot" pronunciation of *out and about* that is different from most places in the USA
- the Canadian Vowel Shift, now also found in California and other places and spreading quickly,[17] making *dress* sound more like "drass" and a host of related changes
- the pronunciation of "foreign a", which is the *a* in original loan words, such as *pasta*, *drama*, *Iraq*, or *Stefan*, where the *a* is usually pronounced "a" as in *cat* in Canadian English, rather than "ah" as in *father*.

The effects of the subsequent immigration waves, Waves III to V, are important. They have added a lot of spice to what might have been a less exciting linguistic broth. Of what we know now, the effects of these waves have been limited to cultural items, often loan words for various kinds of foods and other concepts. But we have started to look beyond such obvious features of language contact and have begun to explore how such interesting cultural mélanges is expressed linguistically and constructed and negotiated in the moment of speaking (e.g., Hoffman and Walker 2010; Hinrichs 2015, 2018; Boyd, Hoffman, and Walker 2015).

Speaking and Writing: a Primer

In our introduction to basic linguistic concepts, we next need to reflect on the roles of speaking vs writing. The overwhelming majority of writing in English happens in the respective national standards, while, in speaking, non-standard varieties have a very important part to play. The distinction between speaking and writing is important, because before 1700 *standard* generally referred to written English. In British English, we can still see some of that limitation, as you can speak Standard British English with a wide variety of accents (the Queen's or an upper-class accent, or with a Scottish accent – think Ewan McGregor – or with Jamie Oliver's trendy London-inspired accent).

While the notion of a written English standard is old and goes back to the Old English times of King Alfred the Great (who reigned AD 871–99), standard English had little effect on most people's lives until the early seventeenth century. At that point in time, scholars were beginning to promote spoken forms of varieties that were "approved" by one means or another. These approved forms, called "codified" forms, were as a rule the forms of the king/queen or the forms of the most economically or politically powerful speakers. These standardization processes were purely social processes, foregrounding the social acceptability of, for instance, "You and I are good friends" over the variant "You and me are good friends", which could both be heard and read in English roughly equally at the time.[18]

Linguistically speaking, the selected forms of a language, the forms that become the standard, are just one way of expressing an idea, like the *you-and-me* vs *you-and-I* example. These selected forms are linguistically no better or worse than the other ones, just different. Socially, however, the standard forms generally bestow respect on the user, while the other forms don't – at least, not in official or public settings. It's a bit like wearing black tie (a tuxedo) in formal settings: people notice such things favourably, often by not sticking out (but wear a *Canadian tuxedo*[19] and you're in trouble). The standard thus creates clear uses for itself (e.g., in official forms of address, treaties between heads of state, job negotiations, and other serious matters).

There are, however, also times when one would do better to avoid standard forms in order not to appear too posh, too formal, or too aloof. For instance, in a pub crawl with Liverpudlian (Liverpool), Haligonian (Halifax, NS), or

Bostonian friends on a Friday night. Someone sounding like Prince Charles would probably not be pub crawling for long on such a night unless they were in a royal pub crawl, so to speak. (But that would be a very different pub crawl altogether.) This is one of the downsides of speaking a standard variety: it creates distance on less formal occasions, while bestowing social power on its speakers in formal contexts. To keep with our attire analogy: wear a Canadian tuxedo with your hipster friends, not a real tuxedo – but, most important of all: know the difference.

In addition to the standard, many other varieties of English are used in Canada. There are non-standard Englishes that linguists call "varieties" of English or simply "dialects". It is important to know that the standard variety itself is also just another dialect, although a socially privileged one. In order not to confuse this use of the word *dialect* with the word's meaning of traditional, rural ways of speaking, linguists therefore often prefer the word *varieties*. As we said above, linguistically the standard dialect, or standard variety, is no better or worse than any other dialect or variety. In this respect, there is little to no semantic difference between the utterances A and B:

A: "Would you be so kind as to pass me the salt shaker, please?"
B: "Gimme the salt, eh!"

A and B are linguistically equivalent, in the strict sense of the word: they are both the speech act we call requests, and both would in their respective contexts be likely to get the job done of putting the speaker in temporary possession of the salt container.

Socially, however, the two sentences are anything but equivalent: the former is very conservative Standard Canadian English – or, perhaps more so, conservative Standard British English – while the latter is non-standard, more informal English. In this case, the latter is somewhat rude, but that assessment depends entirely on the utterance's context – that is, the concrete social and situational conditions. One can easily imagine a situation, for instance, in which sentence A would be very much out of place, even indeed wrong (e.g., in a biker gang's club house, but also during the lunch break of a group of Canadian high-school students).

Reading of salt and salt shakers, the reader might make a connection with a previous section's slow-cooker metaphor. The reason may not be obvious but is logical on second thought: like many things Canadian, Canadian English took its sweet time to materialize. Like the yummy stew people throw into the crockpot in the morning and let sit until the evening to come home to a ready meal, Canadian English has been sitting and simmering for a long, long time – centuries, actually, as the case of *beaver stone* will show us at the end of Chapter 4. And since the beginning, a most important ingredient that has turned an otherwise standard mix into a yummy broth with spunk has always been there. Sometimes more appreciated, sometimes not so much, this ingredient, coming in all shades and colours, may be called "linguistic immigrant spice".

Immigrant Spice: the Linguistic Flavour

There are many second language varieties of English around the world, and many of them are used in Canada. Linguists call second language varieties simply L2 varieties, to distinguish them from mother tongue or first language – L1 – varieties. The more immigration there is, the more second languages (or L2s, for short) are spoken, and Canada has been an immigrant destination for many centuries. Some say it's *the* immigrant destination *par excellence*.

English, indeed, is a bit of a strange language to begin with. It is the only originally European language that is spoken by more L2 speakers than L1 speakers. So, in other words, there are more second language speakers of English than there are first language (mother tongue) speakers.[20] Many more. As early as 2013, estimates deemed that for every native speaker of English there were five (!) non-native speakers of reasonable competence. So is it not reasonable to suggest that, as I am writing these lines in January 2018, we are at a ratio of 1:6, if not higher?[21] As that ratio has been shifting very dramatically in favour of L2 speakers over the past twenty years, we will continue to see that trend for a couple of decades or so. Simultaneously, we will be facing more and more debates over what is "acceptable" English. We will return to this interesting question about the "ownership of English" – who "owns" the language and who has the authority to decide what's acceptable and what is not – in Chapter 7 and in the last chapter, as we attempt to peer into the future.

For now, we only need to point out that, because of its many forms of L2 Englishes, Canada is a bit of an odd country – in the best sense of the word — among its peers, which are usually the USA, UK, Australia, and New Zealand. In a famous model of English in the world, the "Circle Model," Canada has traditionally been considered part of the "Inner Circle", just like the UK or the USA, while as a matter of fact Canada's demographic and linguistic make-up is surprisingly different from those countries. Many readers will be thinking of the role of French in Canada, but that is just the beginning of the story. Complementing the model, there is the "Outer Circle" of countries in which English plays an institutional role, such as in India or the Philippines, as well as the "Expanding Circle", which is the rest of the world where English has had no or only very limited functions, e.g., Austria, China, or Russia.[22]

So how is Canada a strange bird in the mix of Inner Circle countries? It is all linked to the gruesome days of overt and government-promoted colonialism, when European powers were colonizing the world. In that task, the English were outperforming the French, Spanish, Portuguese, Dutch, German, Swedish, Italian, and any other colonizing navies as the most successful colonizers – a most doubtful claim to fame. Clearly, having suppressed the most peoples in the world under the pretext of civilization is nothing to be proud of. But, as many authors have pointed out, the English language was passed on that way too. Once a language is in the hands of others, it is only a question of time before the colonized begin to mould the language the way they see fit, whether the colonizers like it or not. It's language change and a natural process. The fact that the English subjugated peoples, however, is not in any way natural but a matter of historical coincidence, disrespect of other cultures, and a western superiority complex and arrogance.[23] Edgar W. Schneider, an Austrian scholar in Germany, has devised an appealing universal model for the process of the creation of postcolonial Englishes that impresses both by its simplicity (five phases) and by its complexity (each phase has multiple processes), which we will introduce later in this chapter.[24]

Coming back to the Circle Model, we can define the Inner Circle as the English varieties around the world that go back to "settler" Englishes, varieties that sprang up in locations in which enough native speakers were present to ensure a steady transmission of English. Where this was not the case, in all places where English speakers were far outnumbered by speakers of other languages, the local languages played a very profound part in the formation of the new Englishes that would eventually develop in these locations. These new Englishes are the Outer Circle Englishes, such as those used in India, Pakistan, or the Philippines.

Here lies the reason why Canada is a bit of an oddball in the Inner Circle. When it comes to second language speakers among the Inner Circle countries, Canada is almost playing in a league of its own. The census figures speak clearly. According to the 2016 Canadian census, a mere 56 per cent of the population, or just over half of all residents in Canada, are native speakers of English. Compare this with any other Inner Circle country and you'll see Canada considerably lagging behind all others. This ratio has been decreasing as of late, down from 58 per cent in the 2011 census, which shows that today, somewhat counter-intuitively, Canada has fewer native speakers of English than five years ago. Immigration continues to be strong and is expected to shape Canadian English more than it has previously. Such facts make Canada special in the best sense of the word. Francophone English, the English spoken by the roughly 7 million Canadians who have French as their L1, is just one type of L2 English with certain features, as is the L2 English of the half a million L1 speakers of Punjabi, Chinese, and Arabic dialects. That is, half a million *each*. Beyond these four groups of L2 speakers is a long list of over 250 other groups of L2 speakers of Canadian English.

The Bias against Canadian English

With the basic terminology and the social setting covered, let's go back to the main theme. It is fair to say that, prior to the 1950s, no *positive* notion of Canadian English existed. True, the term *Canadian English* is attested as early as 1857, but it was a slur[25] and remained so for the first century of its existence. The situation of Canadian literature at that time simultaneously encapsulates the dominant verdict on Canadian English, with the variety being worse off than the literature. In a telling episode, the founding chair of the University of British Columbia's (UBC's) Department of English Language and Literatures, the locally celebrated Garnet G. Sedgewick, is a case in point. In the 1930s and 1940s, Sedgewick was considered by some of his peers as "the finest teacher of English in Canada",[26] but he viewed Canadian literature "as essentially insignificant and repeatedly refused to permit a course in it at U.B.C." (Akrigg 1980: 16). In 1959, a decade after the autocratic – yet also in many ways innovative – Sedgewick passed away, UBC would launch the prime journal in the field, *Canadian Literature*.

While Canadian literature is widely known today, Canadian English is still the Cinderella among the "Canadian disciplines", if there is such a thing. The reason people look at you with incredulity when they hear that you're researching Canadian English is because no one ever mentioned the concept to them during their schooling. If it was mentioned, it was in all likelihood a negative mention.

Chances are that if the label of Canadian English was used prior to the 1950s, it was used utterly negatively, as a slur: no one wanted to be told that they were speaking Canadian English. Sedgewick is once more a good example: born in rural Nova Scotia in 1882, he is reported as saying he had "spent forty years trying to smoke the Halifax dialect out of [his] speech" and that he successfully "tempered his raw Nova Scotian" (Akrigg 1980: 21). What needs to be eradicated like a bad habit is hardly a worthy object of study. Since people like Sedgewick, who fostered a love for languages, thought that way, there was little hope for Canadian English more generally at the time.

In this climate, the crime-novel-loving Matthew Harry Scargill from the first pages of this chapter was one of a handful of linguists on a mission. It is significant that he came to his object of study as an outsider, from England; distance increases the likelihood that local ways of speaking are taken seriously, as something organically grown over the generations. Scargill's mission was to work towards a description and appreciation of the varieties of Canadian English, and while he had important roles to play, Scargill was not the most widely known or the most prolific agent in a small group of scholars at the time. The most famous one of them was Walter Spencer Avis, English Professor at the Royal Military College in Kingston, though he should have worked at one of the big research universities. Avis died at the age of 60, at a time when most scholars are just about ready to publish the books that will form their legacies.

Another person might well have become more famous than Avis. This man, Charles J. Lovell, is the protagonist of the first couple of chapters of this book, but you will probably never have heard of him. He is the mountaineer in the subtitle. Like Avis, who is the subtitle's professor, Lovell died quite young in scholarly life, at age 52. With two early deaths of main figures, from the perspective of the early 1980s, Canadian English must have seemed like a most hazardous enterprise.

Scargill, Avis, and Lovell were members of a small group of scholars that I shall call the "Big Six". While their group was not at all diverse in gender and ethnicity, which reflects the academic biases (of gender) and cultural biases (of ethnicity) of the day, they were rather diverse by other social parameters, which makes them an interesting crowd to tell a story about. The Big Six were comprised of two native-born Canadians – Walter Avis and Charles Crate – and three individuals who came to Canada from Britain – Patrick Drysdale, Matthew Scargill, and Douglas Leechman – and one American working from the USA – Charles Lovell. Scargill was one of the many "immigrants" – better described as non-natively born Canadians – who kept explaining to everyone who cared to listen that there was something Canadian about the English that was spoken and written in Canada. Scargill was a Yorkshire man who migrated to Canada in 1948 – so, shortly after World War II. With a Ph.D. from the University of Leeds and a profound interest in languages – in those days, Leeds University was about to become the administering body for the first scientific study of the dialects of England – Scargill's career in academia seemed like a safe bet.

While the career seemed inevitable, his interest in Canadian English was a rather unlikely choice in the Canadian intellectual climate of the day. That climate has been labelled "Canadian Dainty".[27] Canadian Dainty refers to an attitude that was prevalent from at least the 1830s onwards, when immigrants from England first started to appear in bigger numbers with what we called Wave II, until the last quarter of the twentieth century. That attitude put everything English on a pedestal: not Scottish, not Irish, not Welsh, but English.

At its tail end in the 1950s, funny man Irving Layton put his finger on the upper-middle-class phenomenon of Canadian Dainty in a wonderfully amusing three-stanza poem. The poem portrays a man of an old Canadian lineage, a man who had lived all his life in Kingston, Ontario, as did his parents and grandparents. After spending three years as a young adult at Oxford University in England, however, we are informed he began to speak the purest Canadian Dainty accent, an English that out-Englished the English,

beating them on their linguistic home turf. How's that for a dubious achievement and exercise in identity formation? Garnett Sedgewick displayed certain
traits of Canadian Dainty, when he "could not understand how people could
endure living with poorly enunciated, imprecise, or ugly speech", which
included in his mind "a horrible harsh flat Ontario 'a'" (Akrigg 1980: 21).
(So, *can't* with the vowel sound from *cat* rather than from *father*.) Unpreten-
tious, unaltered, and originally grown Canadian speech was not up to scratch
for Sedgewick (who had – so much is certain – other qualities that he put to
good use for his university). In Layton's poignant words from the poem's third
and last stanza, we see a more extreme form of Canadian Dainty than Sedgewick's. A complete denial of his upbringing is found in the poem's protagonist
and Kingston native:

> *Now his* [the Kingston man's] *accent*
> *makes even Englishmen*
> *wince, and feel*
> *unspeakably colonial.*[28]

In this climate, Scargill, who was educated in England and clearly using
Standard British English, likely with northern English traits, had a different
take on Canadian English than one might expect to find in early postwar
Canadian academia: rather than ridiculing it, like so many before him, he
chose to research and promote it, something Sedgewick would not have
appreciated.

Scargill's choice of Canadian English over the languages that carried a lot of
academic prestige in those days was even the more remarkable as Canadian
English was derided and attacked from Day 1, as it were. Called "a corrupt
dialect" by the nineteenth-century Scottish Presbyterian minister Reverend
A. Constable Geikie, the variety was off to a bad start. Geikie, who was posted
to the small town of Berlin, Ontario (now Kitchener), for a few years in the
1850s, coined the term *Canadian English* as a slur in a lecture read before a
Toronto learned society, a lecture that by today's standards is better classified
as a rant against all things Canadian, for the simple reason that Canadian
English was different from the King's or the Queen's English.[29]

Lexicographer and linguist John Considine from the University of Alberta
has come up with the most convincing reason for Geikie's astonishingly
dismissive lecture. Why should the small-town minister, giving a talk in the
Ontarian capital, vilify the language variety of the land? Considine speaks in
this context of Geikie's "linguistic anxiety", an anxiety

of someone triply remote from the norms of the metropolitan [in this case, London,
England] elite: as a Scot, as a resident of Canada, and as a resident of a town with a very
substantial German-speaking population [at the time, hence the name Berlin].
(Considine 2003: 251)

It all makes perfect sense: if you might be attacked for not coming from the "right" background, offence is the best defence, which gives us Geikie's rant. It was, after all, the heyday of colonialism and no one seemed to question Geikie's thesis. On the contrary, the Ontario learned men (we don't know of any women) must have approved the talk, as they published the lecture in their 1857 proceedings – fortunately so, because that's how we know about it.[30]

Scargill was a scholar who loved to forge alliances and make projects happen. His alliances went beyond the typical reach of the academic, which in those days often meant confinement to one's office only to emerge many years later with a hefty manuscript in one's name. While Scargill wrote books as well, he seems to have enjoyed the brokering aspect of inquiry as much as the research itself, if not more. In German you would have called Scargill a *Macher*, a 'maker', someone who makes things happen. He provided the Lexicographical Centre for Canadian English – first at two universities in Alberta and, as of 1964, at the newly founded University of Victoria in Saanich, BC – with an organizational frame that would allow a small group of scholars to create what is today known as Canadian English.

The Big Six: Face-lifting the Idea of Canadian English

The group of scholars working on Canadian English was on one level shockingly homogeneous: they were, without exception, white males. This fact has led more than one student to see a narrative of colonization in their work. While this is a fair assumption, I think it is paramount to measure any achievement against the sociohistorical backdrop of the period. From that angle, that group was not as colonial as one would expect, and might even be considered something of an establishment vanguard of *de*colonization at the time. Maybe this was because, on some level, the group was a motley crew of individuals who actively became involved with First Nations matters, long before others would.

What strikes the eye is that many key players had not been socialized in Canada. There were three men who hailed from England; besides Scargill, there was Patrick "Paddy" Drysdale, who came from Oxfordshire with an MA from prestigious Oxford University. (In those days, an Oxford BA was automatically "transformed" into an MA after a little while.) Drysdale was the youngest of them all, about 10–15 years the junior of the others. The most pivotal of the group while he was alive was Charles Julien Lovell. Lovell was a writer and researcher with a most diverse past, a story that deserves treatment in its own right.[31] Orphaned at a very young age, Lovell grew up in various foster homes in Massachusetts, before walking out the door in his Sunday best one morning "at around 18", never to return.[32]

During the 1920s and 1930s, it is unclear precisely how Lovell spent his time, but at some point he made his way across the USA to Pasadena, California. Along the way, he surely met all sorts of characters and their languages, lingo, and linguistic varieties. This was the time of the Great Depression, so he was not alone on the roads. In a touching memoir about her lexicographer father, Bonnie Lovell can only speculate about the two decades between her father running away from home and his marrying her mother in his late 30s in 1945. Daughter Lovell "became convinced Daddy [Lovell] had been a hobo, riding the rails and camping in hobo jungles during the Depression years when countless thousands of men did just that" (B. Lovell 2011: 48). As it turns out, Lovell preferred to *walk* across the USA. He was a mountaineer, after all: "A gentleman will walk but never run" was not just a line in Sting's post-The Police smash hit, but apparently also Lovell's motto.

Despite having only a high school education, Lovell became perhaps the most central figure in the making of Canadian English. These three "newcomers" to Canada, all of whom arrived in the early years after World War II, were pivotal in the "construction" of Canadian English. Perhaps their roles only prove a more general pattern, a pattern that makes the outsider see what's special about a particular linguistic variety they are not native to. There are some famous examples that prove the rule. James A. H. Murray (1837–1915), the primary and, to date, the longest-serving editor of the *Oxford English Dictionary* (*OED*), hailed from Scotland and was therefore not exactly an English gent by lineage. Yet, as the defining Chief Editor of the *Oxford English Dictionary*, Murray described the language of the English for posterity, and – this point is important – not the language(s) of the Scots. Fredric G. Cassidy, another giant in dialectology and lexicography, was instrumental in the documentation of the English of Jamaica, the island of his birth. As he left the Caribbean state at the age of 11, he too returned to it with an outsider's perspective, at least to some degree.[33] Lovell, like Murray and Cassidy, was also a linguistic outsider, which is no coincidence either.

Beyond Lovell, Drysdale, and Scargill, there was another "immigrant scholar" of Canadian English. That fourth newcomer was Douglas Leechman (FRSC), a man who was much older than the rest of them and whose "FRSC" suffix declares him to be a Fellow of the Royal Society of Canada. Now there is someone from the scholarly establishment. Born in 1890 in Coventry, England, and thus at least three decades senior to the other five in the Big Six, Leechman came to Canada as a young adult. In 1924, he joined the Division of Anthropology at the National Museum of Canada. In addition to a BA from the University of Washington in the early 1920s, he earned a Ph.D. in Ottawa in the early 1940s and became a decorated anthropologist, archeologist, museum curator, and, perhaps most lastingly, an artefact conservation scientist. In his day, Leechman was a prime authority on the lives of the

Canadian Inuit and northern First Nations. As he fought for three years with the 11th Mounted Rifles in World War I, much of that war's military slang was probably contributed to *DCHP-1* by Leechman; for World War II military slang, Avis and Scargill brought first-hand battle experience to the editorial board.

Besides the three Englishmen and one American, two native-born Canadians complete the group. There is Walter Spencer "Wally" Avis, who would, as Chief Editor, see to completion the defining dictionary of Canadian English. As a recent graduate with a Ph.D. in Linguistics from the University of Michigan, a leading school in the field since at least the 1920s, Avis was part of the first generation of academically trained linguists in Canada. Avis brought a unique skill set to the table. The second native-born Canadian was Charles Brandel "Chuck" Crate. Crate was a university-educated man of many trades and, during the dictionary days, a high school teacher in Alert Bay, BC – an island community off the north coast of Vancouver Island with a majority First Nations population – and later in Quesnel, BC, located in the old Cariboo gold-digging Eldorado of northern British Columbia. Crate took an avid interest in the Canadian north, thus contributing special expertise that was otherwise hard to come by.

These six men – Lovell, Avis, Scargill, Drysdale, Leechman, and Crate – comprised the editorial team that would write and publish the first significant landmark in the study of Canadian English: a historical dictionary that would document, through the historical record, about 10,000 terms with some 13,000 meanings and Canadian usages. This book, entitled *A Dictionary of Canadianisms on Historical Principles* (*DCHP-1*), was published to much acclaim in November 1967, as a contribution to the Canadian centennial celebrations. The *A* in the title is overly modest: it is not just *a* historical dictionary of Canadian English – it is *the* historical dictionary of the variety. It is the only one there is. It also reflects, however, the intent of the group to produce more than just one historical dictionary, plans that didn't materialize.

As all six men are listed on the dictionary's masthead, we will place their paths and contributions to *DCHP-1* at the centre of the present book. We will also look at the roles of women in that process, who were, more often than not, in positions that were not sufficiently acknowledged. Without the Big Six, the study of Canadian English would have developed very differently, if it had developed at all.

The lion's share of the present book aims to retrace and reconstruct how this group of men managed to define, document, and propel Canadian English based on the way Canadians use English, an idea that was nothing less than ridiculous at the time. Canadian English was developed from a vague hunch to a fully fledged theoretical concept with ample empirical proof in one and a half decades. The Big Six must be credited for *inventing* or *creating* Canadian

English. Their idea was not just backed up with scholarly articles, but with a most impressive "proof of concept" in life size, so to speak: a complete set of dictionaries, comprised of the scholarly historical *DCHP-1*, the "flagship" dictionary as they called it, and a set of three graded school dictionaries (from elementary to middle to high school).

Some Canadian readers may be familiar with the *Gage Canadian Dictionary* from their own or their children's school years. The *Gage Canadian*, first published in 1967 as *The Senior Dictionary*, was the high school and lower undergraduate dictionary. Together with *The Intermediate Dictionary* (1963, with Scargill in charge), *The Beginning Dictionary* (1962, with Avis in charge), and *The Senior* (1967, which was the responsibility of University of British Columbia linguist Robert J. Gregg) formed the graded school dictionaries. These three and *DCHP-1* comprised, by 1967, the complete dictionary series, which was called, collectively, the Dictionary of Canadian English – so no single book was called this as such, only the collection of the four dictionaries.

Rounded off with a host of academic papers, some of which we'll discuss in the next chapter, and with a steady supply of press coverage that spread the word, the Big Six ensured that no one would be able to escape their "face-lift" of Canadian English – that is, the Big Six plus Robert J. Gregg, who would turn them into the Magnificent Seven. At the end of 1967, Canadians would for the first time be proudly proclaiming that they spoke Canadian English, and there were four dictionaries to prove it, which is a far cry from the origins of the term in Reverend Geikie's mid-nineteenth-century mouth.

"Face-lifting" (Codification) in the Big Picture

Now that we know roughly what the Big Six did, let us look at their achievement in the bigger linguistic and historical contexts. Historical linguists – those who study the development of languages over time – and sociolinguists – who study the social correlations of language – have been very productive in the theoretical modelling of new linguistic varieties over the past decade and a half, so that today we have three models that together cover the process of new-dialect formation in great detail. What we called informally the "face-lifting" process is in the literature referred to as the *new-dialect formation* process, the *koinéization* process, or the *standardization* process, depending on the particular theoretical stance taken.

There are two models that can be applied to the development of the dominant or colonial language in colonial settings: Edgar Schneider's *Dynamic Model* and Peter Trudgill's *New-Dialect Formation Model*. Both are useful in the Canadian context. A noteworthy development of the Dynamic Model is Buschfeld, Kautzsch, and Schneider (2018), in which some of Schneider's former students are taking the model further.

Table 2 *Dynamic Model phases (Schneider 2007)*

I	Foundation (of the language in the new location)
II	Exo-normative stabilization
III	Nativization
IV	Endo-normative stabilization
V	Diversification

The most general model in this area is Edgar Schneider's *Dynamic Model* (Table 2). First published in 2003, and after in – recommendable – book form (Schneider 2007), the model does not make any firm predictions, but instead charts a sequence of five general phases that are required for a new language variety to be formed out of an older variety or several older ones. Originally developed for postcolonial Englishes, this model is of immediate relevance as well for other languages in which writing plays a role.

Schneider's scenario can be explained with the following thought experiment: suppose you transplant a language – say, German – to another part of the world – say, Peru – in the 1850s. Provided that enough speakers followed (which was not the case in the real-world Peruvian town of Pozuzo, which inspired this example), sooner or later the imported German would develop into a kind of Peruvian German that might attain public functions (which it didn't – today, Peruvian German, to the extent it is still spoken in the 8,000-people town, is merely a language enclave). Suppose more and more German speakers, from different parts of the German-speaking areas in Germany, Austria, Switzerland, Northern Italy, East Belgium, Luxembourg, Liechtenstein, parts of Romania, and the Czech and Slovak Republics followed. Today, we might have a Standard Peruvian German.

To use Schneider's model, this development of a new standard variety would have occurred in five successive phases (see Table 2). In Pozuzo, Peru, the first settlement of German speakers arrived in 1859 and was comprised of families with a total of 170 members from Austria (Tyrol) and Germany (the Rhineland). This would have been Phase I: Foundation. In the Canadian example, the scenario is more complex, as the speakers of English were to arrive in what is now Canada in bigger numbers after 1714 in the Maritimes (Nova Scotia), but only after 1763 in Montreal and Quebec, and after 1776 in what was to become Ontario. The west of Canada, however, was not settled until the mid and late 1800s. Before 1846, the area west of the Rockies and north of the Columbia River, comprising what are today Oregon and Washington states, was, moreover, still in British-Canadian hands. The provinces of Saskatchewan and Alberta were not settled until the early twentieth century.

Following this foundation phase, the settlement stabilizes and it becomes clear that the immigrants are here to stay. Their identities are tied to the motherland. They are *Motherland plus*, so, in the Peruvian case, *German plus Peruvian*. Culturally and linguistically, the settlers take their cues from German-speaking Europe – hence exo-normative stabilization (from "exo" meaning 'outside of') – for their norms. In the Pozuzo case, the Rhineland influences were given up early in favour of the Tyrolean customs, so that today you have a Spanish-speaking Tyrolean town in the remote South American mountains. Phase III is the really interesting phase, when a creative combination of Old World German and New World linguistic features creates a kind of language that is new. In Phase III, the settlers begin to identify with their Peruvian-German identity for the first time. In this phase, something really new happens, culturally and linguistically.

At this point, it's a good idea to halt for a moment, because what Schneider summarizes under Phases I, II, and perhaps also III, is spelled out in Peter Trudgill's New-Dialect Formation Theory (2004) in greater detail and with testable claims. (Schneider's model does not offer such testability, is rather descriptive after the fact, and doesn't allow much in the way of prediction.) For the development of Canadian English, I applied Trudgill's theory to eighteenth- and nineteenth-century Ontario a few years back and found it very useful (Dollinger 2008a). While it needs to be said that a lot of colleagues see opposition between Schneider and Trudgill, I see much more common ground. I won't focus on their differences here beyond the general statement that Trudgill, the sociolinguist *par excellence*, sees social factors as non-applicable in certain, well-defined situations in which the group sizes of language speakers over-ride other aspects (for more, see, e.g., Dollinger 2015a: 200–208 and references therein), with Schneider objecting to that aspect.

Returning to Schneider's model, Phase IV is when the country has stabilized as an entity in its own right rather than a colony and is in the process of gaining a new sense of self. It is then when, linguistically, the focus is transferred to the country rather than the motherland. This is the time when dictionaries and grammars are composed and the country's new norms, which solidified over Phases I–III, are now codified into a new standard. In this phase the Big Six were instrumental in Canada. The Big Six basically invented Canadian English in that they undertook the "endo-normative stabilization" of Canadian English. This chapter's epigraph is taken from a little-known publication by Avis a year before the major dictionaries, *DCHP-1* (today at www.dchp.ca/dchp1) and *The Senior Dictionary*, were published. Haugen's (1966) classic model on the standardization process of language, which he developed in the 1960s, deals first and foremost with Schneider's Phase IV. Together, the three models cover the entire process admirably well.

Phase V is then characterized by the period of post-nationalist zeal. The country is long established and its linguistic standard is a given. In the formation of Standard Austrian German (AutG), this phase would have been in the 1990s, when AutG was more or less accepted. It is now – when other forms of social organization trump the "national" story and other "affiliations" are foregrounded, such as certain music styles, philosophies, perhaps professional memberships, and any other group construction markers – that more cultural and linguistic diversification ensues.

This Book's Scope: 1940 to 1998

Establishing cut-off points is usually a tricky issue, especially when it comes to the creation of ideas or concepts. Think about Middle English, the language of Chaucer. When did it start? We can offer political dates, such as 1066, the date of the Norman Conquest, as the defining moment turning English from a fully Germanic language into a mongrel of a Germanic legacy, which has been swamped with Romance-type language varieties. So, 1066, right? On Christmas Day, to be precise, the last English king of that period, Harold, was killed (by an arrow straight into his eye!). But did Middle English then start on Boxing Day 1066, or even on New Year's Day 1067? Hardly, as nothing much had changed on the ground by then. This is why some scholars prefer 1100 as a reasonable delimiter between Old English (think *Beowulf*) and Middle English (think *Canterbury Tales*). Others still, though less often, set 1154 as a cut-off, because it was the last year that an important Old English document, the *Peterborough Chronicle*, was maintained. You can see this is the stuff that the worst academic debates, those devoid of solution, are made of!

Periodization is a tough call, as you can see, and the call is not any less tough in the case of Canadian English. So, when is the period of Canadian English? A possible start date is in 1867 with Confederation, the Canadian "independence day" of 1 July 1867. But what about 1917 and the date of the often-quoted battle of Vimy Ridge, in which Canadian units won a victory on the international stage paid in blood? Or 1926 with the Balfour Declaration that rendered all colonies of Britain as *de jure* equal with Britain, at least on paper? Perhaps later? What about 1945, when World War II was over and Canada was finally, with newly found confidence, looking towards the future? Or how about 1947, when the first Canadian passports and Canadian rather than British citizenship certificates were issued? Or maybe as late as 1982, when the original Canadian constitution – the British North America Act – was brought home from Westminster, London, so it could be altered by the Canadian rather than the British parliament? Perhaps a date in the future? After all, we could argue that Canada is not yet fully "completed", because the Meech Lake Accord,[34] an important fix in the Canadian constitution revolving around Quebec, failed in 1990? I think we'd all agree that 1982 would be too late and the last date nonsensical. But which date would it be?

I have chosen none of the above, because this book is not so much about the political events as the language variety. While the former influence the latter, I looked for a date that would be more language-related. And what better cut-off date than the publication of the first book that dealt in an empirical way with Canadian English, even though (very Canadian perhaps) it didn't high-light its Canadian content? This content was not advertised at all, so much so that I have never seen it even mentioned in any of the works on Canadian English. I therefore consider the book's "rediscovery" an exciting event that is important enough to mark the beginning of the scope of the present book.

So when does this book's story start? In 1940. In that year, Queen's University Professor of English Henry Alexander, an Oxford-educated man whom in the next chapter we will call "the grandfather of Canadian English", published a textbook on the history of English. He called it, revealingly and somewhat imposingly – and, I'm sorry to say, certainly colonially – *The Story of Our Language*. You can see why Hugh MacLennan felt the need to write *Two Solitudes*, the novel about English-speaking and French-speaking Canadians, just five years later: French was not part of "our" story according to the anglophone Alexander.

More interesting for our purposes, Alexander's table of contents reveals nothing about Canadian English. It only mentions – quite modern for the time – British and American English and, in the later parts of the book, their differences. Moreover, neither Canada nor any of its parts even makes the index. Unless you read it from cover to cover, you won't be able to appreciate that this book, read by many a student (a new edition was published in 1962), seems to be the first book that took Canadian English seriously, sprinkling interesting tidbits of information on it into the chapters on British and American English, here and there.

It is clear that Alexander knew what he was writing about and that he had first-hand experience (and data) on what he was adding to the book. So, in other words, he added "Canadian spice" in what would otherwise have been a more routine broth on the history of English. Here's an example of that spice concerning the word for what is often called a *see-saw* today in many Englishes and is found on playgrounds:

But in certain regions, especially in and near Cape Cod [MA, USA], *tilt, tiltin board* and *tilter* are found. *Tilter* seems to be a "blend" of *tilt* and *teeter*. There are also quite different expressions such as *dandle*, and *dandle board* and the picturesque *tippety-bounce*. The word *seesaw* itself is also generally known, but is often felt to be somewhat literary. In Nova Scotia most of these words are heard and in addition *tippin board* and *sawman*. It is interesting to note that the form *teeter-totter*, which is very common in Ontario, is rare in New England and Nova Scotia. (Alexander 1962 [1940]: 224)

Teeter-totters, as a potentially Canadian form from Quebec westwards, was new information at the time and extended the view of English, long overdue, to north of the Canada–US border. We'd probably still be using *teeter-totter* these days in most parts of Canada had the equipment not been banned from Canadian playgrounds for being considered as excessively dangerous for Canadian kids. Now only kids in other parts of the world can enjoy and experiment with teeter-totters, see-saws, or tilting boards, so that Canada has little use for the word.

Alexander's book appeared two years before Martin Joos, a University of Toronto linguist, would first describe what has since become known as Canadian Raising, the particularly Canadian vowel pronunciations of *out* and *about* or *wife* and *life*.[35] Alexander must have felt that the time was not yet ripe to mention the phrase "Canadian English", but he managed to sneak a lot of information into his textbook (a strategy that, more conspicuously and much more directly, was continued by J. K. Chambers' very readable textbook *Sociolinguistic Theory*, first published in 1995; see Chambers 2009a for the latest edition).

Having clarified the starting date of 1940, we note that this book formally stops in 1998, with the occasional glimpse beyond. There are a number of reasons for that second cut-off. First, any historian will tell you that it's always good to write with the benefit of hindsight – after the dust has settled, so to speak. That's the reason for not taking this book up to 2015 or so. Another, more profound reason is that, as of 2002, I have had a role (and stake) in the field myself and my involvement in it would certainly endanger the historian's balanced point of view. As of 2006, when I was appointed Editor of the second edition of the *Dictionary of Canadianisms*, I would stand in a potential conflict of interest, writing on the history of my own project. Some things are better left to others.

So far, so good. But why 1998? That was the year of publication of the *Canadian Oxford Dictionary*, which, for about a decade, was a game changer in the public perception of Canadian English. The year 1998 is also the height of the Canadian dictionary war, in which three new dictionaries and editions were competing in the small Canadian market, together with some older editions. For a time it looked as if there was one clear winner – there certainly was one big loser, the *ITP Nelson Dictionary*, and one not-so-big loser, the *Gage Canadian Dictionary*. Since 2008, when the *Canadian Oxford Dictionary* shut down its operations in Canada, we have known that this desk dictionary war knew only losers. So, in a word, 1998 seemed like a good cut-off.

But why not the year 2000 – perhaps just for the sake of being a bit different? Canadians do things slightly differently at times, and this is perhaps symbolized by the difference between 1998 and 2000: almost the same, but not quite. Linguistically, it is often just like this: Canadian is almost the same as American English, but not quite. (We could say, of course, that American English is almost the same as Canadian English too.) Our Canadian linguistic ride is therefore set for 1940 to 1998.

What to Expect from this Book

This book consists of nine chapters, of which the last one builds on the previous chapters to make a number of suggestions and recommendations – perhaps even something coming close to a call to action. Before that conclusion, Chapter 8 looks at what colonial bias there may be in *DCHP-1* and what can possibly be done about it. Chapter 7 is about the 1990s when a dictionary war was raging behind the scenes in Canada, not unlike the one among American dictionary publishers in the 1860s. It was the time of the *Canadian Oxford Dictionary*, but there is so much more to it – for instance, the legacy of the *Gage Canadian Dictionary*, which established the field of Canadian English reference and which was not appreciated for what it was. Chapter 6 explains the business constraints behind dictionary publishing and how the new discipline of sociolinguistics affected the study of Canadian English, which, after the success of the 1970s (Chapter 5) had to re-orient itself, with the old guard gone (or on their way out) and the new one not yet ready to take over.

The earlier chapters, notably Chapters 3 and 4, are dedicated to the making of the first edition of the *Dictionary of Canadianisms*, *DCHP-1*, which was arguably the galvanizing project that put not just dictionaries but the entire field of Canadian English into the mind of the public. Chapter 2 is on the American lexicographer Charles Lovell, the person who was poised to lead the field but died of a heart attack only days after having received the necessary funding from the Canada Council that would have allowed him to lead the project. The story of how this American "convinced" the Canadians that there was something noteworthy about their English, and how it came to be that he knew so much about it, will be the start of explaining how Canadian English was first envisaged, documented, conceptualized, and, ultimately, codified and promoted.

This is the story of the making of Canadian English, which was an early working title for this book. Another, more provocative, title that did not make the cut was *Canadian English, American Made* – American made because Charles J. Lovell was American. Another reading of this title arises from the historical relevance of American English for Canadian English, which emerged out of late eighteenth- and early nineteenth-century American English (mostly from the mid-Atlantic and New England). American English is for Canadian English what British English is for American English: its immediate and most important parent variety.[36] A most accessible history of American

English is Bailey (2012), while Mencken (1936) is still worth a read (after almost a century!).

The Big Six were what early British Columbian settlers might have called *prairie chickens*, which the *Dictionary of Canadianisms* defines in meaning 3 as "a newcomer, especially a farmer from the prairies" and labels it "especially B.C.". For the Songhees people, it must have felt odd that the newcomers would, within a generation or two, develop their own words for *newcomers*, or rather the "newcomers' newcomers". Language is meaningful only in relation to the people who use it and their experiences. It is made just for them.

I wonder which words the Songhees and Esquimalt used for the Europeans who showed up on their shores and who were quite dependent on them. What is the *prairie chicken*, or *greenhorn*, equivalent in the Lekwungen language? There are indeed many other words for *newcomers*: *cheechakos*, also from BC and the west more generally, were newcomers, not nearly as smart as the *sourdoughs*, those who had already survived a winter in the wilderness. While all these words are in *DCHP-1*, both *DCHP-1* and *DCHP-2* are quiet on the Lekwungen terms for *newcomers*. The words in *DCHP-1* are the product of a settler society. Although the makers tried, both in the 1960s and half a century later for the new edition, to do justice to the Indigenous experience, this endeavour is bound to fail: only Indigenous people can speak for Indigenous people, and in neither project was there an aboriginal core member. We will need to keep in mind that entire nations and cultures are vastly under-represented in Canadian English lexicography as we read on.

Figure 8 Charles J. Lovell, *c.* 1946
(Photo courtesy of the Charles J. Lovell family, reproduced by kind permission)

2 The Heritage of Canadian English

> I very much doubt that the average Canadian could pick out an average of
> 10 different terms [that are Canadian] from any given newspaper picked at
> random. . . .
>   [They] wouldn't be familiar enough with the overall picture to notice the
> difference.
> (Lovell to Avis, 16 Jan. 1954; University of Victoria Archives, 90–66, Box 4 File 6)

Academic inquiry and knowledge creation are, like other social activities,
intricately complex – so much so that it is possible only in hindsight to identify
events of significance. In the past ten or fifteen years, for instance, the field of
historical sociolinguistics has been blossoming, a field that has taken shape by
combining the social-science methods developed by William Labov and his
followers from the 1960s with the philological approaches that have their roots
with the Grimm Brothers in the early nineteenth century. With philological
study, an appreciation of old, and mostly dead, languages and varieties holds
sway in much of historical linguistics, which is something most Labovians are
not too keen on. Historical sociolinguistics has now managed to combine the
two approaches with success. There were, as often, predecessors of the
"buzz" – predecessors that were ahead of their time.[1]

Resistance to innovation too advanced for the established professionals and
academics is quite a general phenomenon that even the most prominent minds
had to overcome. This resistance is generally formidable and usually requires
help. To his great luck, Albert Einstein, then a German clerk in a Swiss patent
office, had in Max Planck a powerful ally on his side. Planck, one of the most
highly respected professors of physics at the time, knew that Einstein's outrageous theories – theories of a nobody (young Einstein) – would be faced with
fierce opposition. Planck wrote to Einstein after the latter had submitted the
first draft of his theory of relativity saying that "we need to stick together"
against the opposition.[2] Without Planck, Einstein's findings would not have
had much of a chance to be discussed. Planck was in his late 40s, at a point
when most scholars would have locked themselves into the particular intellectual positions that they would choose to defend, come what may – and often,
quite literally, to their deaths. It is to Planck's credit that he promoted talent

whenever he saw it – as only true scholars do – no matter what this might mean for their own work.

Summarizing the above, we can say: fields emerge – at times, against fierce opposition. While new fields may sometimes be suppressed, or more often held back, they are hardly ever "engineered": they are not created and, if they are, they are created differently from how their "creators" would wish. The name *sociolinguistics* is a case in point. While Labov used the name for his type of approach to language variation and change – a profoundly quantitative, science-based method with a much narrower focus than had previously been common in language studies – other linguists studied social and linguistic uses by *qualitative* means, or a combination of quantitative with qualitative means. The qualitative linguists were in the position to consider linguistic phenomena in relation with social variables that were disregarded by the Labovian paradigm, so they had advantages in their overall perspectives. They, too, called themselves sociolinguists so that today *sociolinguistics* is a very wide term, perhaps as wide a term as *school medicine*. Labov's subtype of sociolinguistics is therefore called *variationist sociolinguistics*, though not all variationists – all those who deal with variation in language – are Labovians or use the methodological preferences that have come to be characteristic of Labov's approach.

In the case of Canadian English, I will show in this chapter that the work around the *Dictionary of Canadianisms on Historical Principles* (*DCHP-1*) was a decisive moment for the development of the variety, perhaps *the* decisive moment, *the* catalyst that crystallized previous work and made future work possible, if only by putting the concept as an intellectually viable one into administrators', politicians', and university stakeholders' minds. This awareness-creation process with the "big cheese" (administration) is a very important process, without which no field can gain a lasting foothold. This is one of the unfortunate parts of academic inquiry: you may do the best, the most innovative, the most cutting-edge work by a long shot, but the next generation may just not be interested in that aspect of language.

In this sense, the story of Canadian English deserves a corrective that I hope to provide with this book. The names of Alexander, Lovell, Avis, Scargill, all of whom were instrumental in the founding of the field, are all but forgotten today, despite their great achievement. During the time of the Big Six (Avis, Crate, Drysdale, Leechman, Lovell, and Scargill), the odds were stacked against "inventing" Canadian English, as Lovell's quote at this chapter's beginning testifies to; Canadians lacked the overall picture of how Canadians spoke and how they differed from the Americans and the British.

It is impossible simply to pick up on the fly how Canadians talk, especially if you live in Canada; most features are more easily detected if you move to

Canada from elsewhere. The example of *take up* is a case in point. One particular meaning of *take up* is based in school settings in which the teacher takes up a test or exam, meaning that, usually on returning the marked sheets, teachers go over the answers and detail what the students did wrong and what worked well and what needs improving. *Take up* is a particularly good example for the complexity we're talking about in Canadian English: it took six years and multiple data collections to figure out the regional and social distribution and to show that this meaning of *take up* was indeed a *bona fide* Canadianism.

Take up in this sense emanates out of Ontario, where Jack Chambers, one of the most widely known Canadian linguists and a native of Stony Creek, Ontario, recalls using it in the 1940s. The hint to study *take up* in detail did not come from Chambers but from a Canadian math teacher and friend of Chambers working in the USA, who noticed that his students didn't fully understand him when *he was taking up the exam*. A summary of the full story of what is now called "*take up* #9" is the entry in the newly updated *Dictionary of Canadianisms on Historical Principles, Second Edition* (*DCHP-2*), which is freely available at www.dchp.ca/dchp2. (Search for *take up* or enter the entry's URL directly: www.dchp.ca/dchp2/Entries/view/take%252520up.) We will revisit *take up* #9 in Chapter 7. In memory of Lovell, the unsung hero of Canadian English, we launched *DCHP-2* on the 57th anniversary of his "death day", 17 March 2017. What you'll read in *DCHP-2* is, in more than one way, just another beginning, because what we know about Canadian English today is far from complete.

Returning to our theme of catalysts in academic inquiry, we can say that, had *DCHP-1* not become the driving force behind Canadian English, it's possible, indeed likely, that some other project would have taken that role. Perhaps we would instead now have had the traditional dialect survey of English in Canada that never materialized: a linguistic atlas of Canada, which would have been based on travels and trips with old VW camping vans, fully loaded with recording equipment, a tiny bed, and a kitchenette, on their way from coast to coast to coast. (For the north coast, it would have been by plane unless one dared to go in the winter on an *ice road* (see www.dchp.ca/dchp2[3]).) The daredevil choosing ice roads would also have driven over the *muskeg* 'northern area consisting of organic bog and frozen in the winter' (also in *DCHP-2*). For such an ice-road trip, everyone in their right minds would have wanted to use a 4 x 4 off-road truck rather than an old VW bus!

In the United States, two big fieldwork projects were indeed carried out in such a way. After the founding of the American linguistic atlas in 1928, Hans Kurath, a Carinthian emigrant from Austria to the USA (yes, again a new-comer), did more for the empirical study of American English than anyone else. His atlas and its subatlases were the first of those big projects, while the fieldwork for the "American *OED*", the *Dictionary of American Regional English* (*DARE*), was the second project. *DARE* was organized by Fred Cassidy, whom we recall from Chapter 1, with fieldwork running from 1965 to 1970. In Canada, however, the time of fieldworker-based dialect geography has unfortunately passed us by. Imagine, a Great Canadian Road Trip in the name of science!

Originally, the American linguistic atlas was envisaged as covering Canada as well, as the full name of Kurath's project reveals: *The Linguistic Atlas of the United States and Canada*. The addition *Canada*, however, stands there only in name, with very little fieldwork undertaken in that country, amounting to little more than baby steps in the 1930s and early 1950s.[4] What we do have in Canadian linguistic atlas data, however, has informed important insights, such as the dating to the 1880s of Canadian Raising, the "oot and aboot" pronunciation of *out and about* and other words.[5] As a lasting consequence of the focus on vocabulary (lexis), we do not know nearly as much as we would like about the geographical variation of the English language in Canada,[6] but we know a good deal about the historical vocabulary that has shaped Canadian English.

On the flip side, the profound knowledge of the vocabulary of Canadian English can be linked back directly to one man: Charles Julien Lovell. Lovell's dedication to words and his passion have left a more profound legacy than most linguists working in the field today may realize. It is one of the ironies of research that today's experts on Canadian English generally do not work very much on vocabulary, as it is seen – I'm guessing here – perhaps as too unsystematic, too "cultural", and as too much part of folklore and social customs rather than of linguistics. It's a point of view I don't agree with, as it expresses biases that are rooted in the social dimension of academia and are not objective, but this point of view is in the clear minority at present and may be the topic of another book. Such slighting of lexis, of "open class" vocabulary – open class, because words can be added basically at will if the need arises – is a real pity, and not just because the public are very much interested in words.

Canadian English, B. L. (Before Lovell)

Many things in English vocabulary studies, which include in not insignificant ways *DCHP-1*, go back to the *Oxford English Dictionary* (*OED*). But before we report on the forgotten connection between *DCHP-1* and *OED*, mention must be made of the first pioneer of Canadian English dictionary making. While the details are more complex (see Considine 2003: 250–53), it is fair to say that John Sandilands' *Western Canadian Phrasebook and Dictionary*, first published in 1912, is the first dictionary of Canadian English. That inspiring pioneer endeavour listed some 800 entries, and in a revised version the following year expanded to 1,500. The entries explained the Canadian West, the *last best West*, to the newcomer, the greenhorn, who, as we know from Chapter 1, was in Canada called *cheechako*. You didn't know what *making the grade* meant (to succeed, pass)? Sandilands was the first to spell it out for you, among other useful things.

After Sandilands, and after the West was settled (that is, colonized), it got quiet again around Canadian English. In 1937, English Professor Henry Alexander set to the task of Canadianizing an American dictionary, so that for the first time Canadian English speakers had a general-purpose dictionary of their own. Alexander did so in very subtle ways – some might say in very traditionally Canadian ways – but his almost non-detectable Canadianization leads me to speculate that he did not have much freedom to change the expensive printing plates that such dictionaries were made from. So Alexander chose the only feasible option and adapted the spelling – and only the spelling – from American to what today is perceived as Canadian. In other words, the 1937 *Winston Simplified Dictionary: For Home, School and Office* (*WSD*), printed in Toronto, managed to exert an influence on Canadian spelling. The Canadian *WSD* was not huge, but with 35,000 entries as big as the literati's ad-hoc vocabularies without looking words up or guessing from the context. To give you a benchmark for comparison, however, the three dictionaries at the centre of the Great Canadian Dictionary War in Chapter 7 each include upwards of 120,000 entries.

What did the Canadian *Winston Simplified* look like? If you look for *chesterfield*, *tap*, *eh*, or other Canadianisms of long standing (or of former standing in the case of *chesterfield*, as this term has been on its way out for more than a generation), you won't find them listed. To see the Canadian character of the *WSD*, one needs to know what to look for. Alexander, for instance, listed only *honour* (not *honor*) but included "*theatre* or *theater*", while *centre* and *metre* are the main entries, as is *colour*, listing some very Canadian choices by today's standards. Interestingly, *color* is referred to, quite remarkably for the time, as "an American spelling of colour" (Brown and Alexander 1937, s.v. "color"). Alexander lists with "American" *apologize*, *systematize* (no *-ise* endings) and *fufilment* (one *l*) and "British" *levelling* (two *l*'s), the mix that to this day characterizes Canadian English spelling (see Pratt 1993: 47–49).

That, however, was it. Sandilands (1977 [1913])[7] and Brown and Alexander (1937) comprise the full list of Canadian dictionaries B. L. – before Lovell entered the scene – a thin "hard word" dictionary of "hard" or difficult terms for the western newcomer and an intermediate dictionary you'd give to someone in Grade 5 today. While a start, these two titles – both of them one-offs – could not provide what would be needed to document, define, reveal, or create a national variety: a full series of dictionaries, from elementary to scholarly dictionaries, Canadian-made.

So on came Lovell to the dictionary scene, shortly after World War II, probably in 1946, as the tiniest cog in the then-mighty North American dictionary-publishing industry. It's little known that Lovell's lexicographic career can be traced back in its beginning to Sir William A. Craigie (1867–1957), who succeeded James Murray as one of four co-editors of the *Oxford English Dictionary*. Craigie was, like Murray, a Scot (once more, newcomer alert) and, like Murray, he became a prominent figure in Oxford philological circles. Craigie is also the indirect but clear connection between *DCHP-1* and the *OED*.

When Craigie was appointed Professor of English at the University of Chicago in 1925, one of his tasks was to edit a kind of American *OED* or, as some put it, an American *answer* to the *OED*. In 1934, after about a decade of data collection,[8] Craigie and his helpers were finally in the position to edit entries for the *Dictionary of American English on Historical Principles*. Then the question arose "of what to do with the relatively small amount of Canadian material found among what was available" (Mathews 1969: 90). It was decided – perhaps somewhat typically of the colonial feelings that were still widespread in the mid-1930s – to treat the Canadian material as if it was American: as one and the same, without any discrimination.

Given the complexity of creating an American historical dictionary, the choice may at first glance seem understandable. Craigie, his co-editor James R. Hulbert, and their team would work for the next decade on their four-volume dictionary. The bulk of Craigie's work would eventually be done remotely from England, as he would give up his Chicago linguistics chair in the mid-1930s. The decision to treat American and Canadian evidence indiscriminately is a clear breach of one of the major rules in lexicography, which is to keep your database – in those days, your citation file – clean: when you write on British English, use only British citations, and when you write on American English, only American ones, and so forth.[9] To be fair to Craigie, one of the greats of lexicography, in those days the idea of Canadian English was still quite ridiculous to most, if not all.

Including Canadian material in an American dictionary was a poor choice in hindsight, something like the linguistic annexation of Canada to the United States, carried out by a Brit – a Scot, for that matter! In this sense, Craigie's outsider status may have worked against him. It is telling that, of all people, Craigie, who has been called "the ablest and most productive lexicographer of his time" by Scottish linguist A. J. Aitken, and who had, as a Scot, a "fellow-feeling for simple folk and small nations" (Aitken 2004), would discard the evidence from "small nation" Canada. Canadian English clearly was not on the radar even to those sympathetic to the idea of new national standards in budding nations.

It is fair to assume that both Lovell, who kept a separate private file of Canadian data as early as 1946, and Avis, who about a decade later would embark on his MA thesis on the (Canadian) patterns of speech in a famous nineteenth-century novel (see Avis 1950), would probably have opted differently in Craigie's position. This is hypothetical, of course, because neither Lovell nor Avis were quite old or experienced enough to make such a call before the editing of the *Dictionary of American English on Historical Principles* began in 1934 (Craigie and Hulbert 1968 [1938–44]). Avis was by then a lad of only 15, and Lovell was a young man of 27, with probably an interest in words but not the required expertise and skill just yet.

A decade later, Craigie might have made a different decision himself. World War II was another catalyst in the long road towards statehood in Canada, which finds an early linguistic expression in Henry Alexander's trial fieldwork in the Maritimes as part of *The Linguistic Atlas of the US and Canada*. Alexander's 1940 textbook is another indicator that the linguistic times were a-changin'. It is relevant in this context that Lovell started his private Canadian quotation file shortly after World War II, which became the nucleus for *DCHP-1*'s file. By 1949, Avis was writing on early Canadian English in what appears to be the first graduate work on a Canadian English topic.[10]

In short, within a decade of completion of Craigie and Hulbert's American dictionary, the practice of lumping Canadian quotations with American ones was no longer state-of-the-art. ("Quotations" are what dictionaries are built from: they are attestations of actually used language, traditionally copied out on "slips", as we will learn in more detail in Chapter 4.) During these years, the field was moving quickly. Those were days of rapid theoretical innovations in lexicography and the pace of development was very fast. By the mid-1950s, Avis would critique Craigie's practice of using Canadian evidence as American to launch his attack against American lexicography.[11] At the end of the process, Avis had come to the conclusion that Canadian lexicography must follow a process that was "clearly quite different from that of lexicographers in the United States" (Avis 1967: xiii), and I can add from personal experience that this holds true today: there is so much more work that is required for a Canadian entry in comparison to an American one, as one needs to look at other varieties of English as well. This requirement is usually ignored in American dictionaries, due to the sheer size and relevance of their variety. Avis' assessment of differences in the Canadian and American lexicographical traditions is worded very strongly for a Canadian who depended on US academic discourse communities for international recognition. Avis clearly wasn't out to please his peers but to do the methodologically right thing – an attitude that was respected in the scholarly societies of the time, as proven by his invited talk on *DCHP-1* at the Modern Language Association conference in 1969.

Before moving on to Avis' and Lovell's most important predecessor, I will add a word on Craigie's problematic choice concerning Canadian material.

Craigie, of course, would have had a way to deal easily with his Canadian "problem" without getting distracted with the Canadian angle too much, an angle that was not part of his mandate. It would have been entirely do-able, in fact easily so, to add a little *C* or something in front of any Canadian attestations that were used, which would have served well not just his dictionary but the entire twentieth-century American school of lexicography. One of the most important Canadian lexicographers, Terry Pratt, pointed out the general problem in a review of the (wonderful) *Dictionary of American Regional English* (*DARE*). *DARE* is, hands down, the dictionary that treats geographical variation in English – perhaps in any language – the best. And still, Pratt finds fault in *DARE* for its (very, very occasional) use of Canadian quotations for the documentation of American English, such as the first quotation, from a 1906 British Columbia magazine, in the entry for *skid road / skid row* 'logging road; derelict part of town'.[12] An Austrian linguist might sense a kind of inadvertent "linguistic Anschluss" of Canada to the USA. Surely, we must do better than that.

"Godfather" and "Father" of Canadian English

To understand the connection of early work on Canadian English with American English, one needs to know that in North American scholarly circles, the American component has always been very important due to its geographical proximity to Canada and its much bigger size. While Canada has its own learned societies, sooner or later one needs to connect to American circles, in which Canada has traditionally been the "add-on". In the American Dialect Society (ADS), one of the oldest such groups, founded in 1889, Canadians have always been present and active. The same can be said of the younger Linguistic Society of America (LSA), founded in 1924, or the Modern Language Association (MLA), founded in 1883.

All of these important groups are – sometimes with member ratios of nine out of ten – fair and square in American hands. This means, if one wishes to be heard, one had better aim at making the Canadian findings relevant to American audiences. Sometimes this can be a tough sell, which was the point in Morton W. Bloomfield's early (and very nice) paper. Published in 1948, Bloomfield's paper speaks of Canadian English as, "of course, a subject of intrinsic interest", but he hastily adds that an understanding of English in North America (which he calls, in the old fashion, simply "America") will be beneficial to all American dialectologists with "the enlargement of the boundaries of American English" towards Canada.[13] What held true for Morton Bloomfield (not to be confused with Leonard Bloomfield) is still a good idea for the modern-day researcher. In more than one way, Bloomfield exercised in his paper what every scholar anywhere needs to aim to achieve: to be accepted by the key players in the field. In Canadian linguistics these key players used to be, predominantly, located in the USA, which is of relevance when one is aiming to construct a Canadian variety of English out of what used to be considered an American – or, perhaps occasionally, a North American – variety. Fortunately, today, American colleagues readily realize the relevance of Canadian English for their own stories as well – e.g., Zimmer (2010) on the use of *optics* in political discourse. On the other side of the Atlantic Ocean, where *American* is often used meaning *North*, *Central*, and *South American* (hence my "Note to the International Reader"), the idea of a North American English that is comprised of American and Canadian English has also been taking hold (see Kytö and Siebers in press).

This is not the place to go into the politics of twentieth-century linguistics, but we should briefly look into the work on Canadian English prior to 1945: there was not much. As we learned earlier, the most distinguished researcher prior to World War II was Henry Alexander, an English Professor at Queen's University in Kingston, Ontario. If we call Lovell the father of Canadian English, it would be apt to call Henry Alexander its grandfather, godfather, or perhaps "über" or "ur" father. Educated in Liverpool and at Oxford University, Alexander took on the task of linguistic fieldwork on Canadian English in the 1930s, as the first person ever. His work, carried out in the Maritimes for the *Linguistic Atlas*, was never published and we know about its existence today from general reports from the late 1930s. Alexander, like many in the day, was not the most prolific writer in his later professional career.

Most importantly, however, Alexander was educating and supporting a new generation of linguists, the first generation of North-American-trained Canadian linguists. The most prolific one of them all was Wally Avis, who would see Lovell's idea of a historical dictionary to completion after the latter's early death. When taking over *DCHP-1* from Lovell in 1960, Avis had already had extensive experience in cross-border empirical work – he had published three groundbreaking papers on cross-border varieties as early as 1954,[14] long before the European tradition of cross-border linguistic studies would come to the fore in the late 1970s and 1980s. It seems plausible to suggest that Alexander, the only fieldworker in Canadian English at the time, planted empirical ideas into Avis' mind that informed the latter's work throughout his entire career.

There is, moreover, a very good chance that Henry Alexander had a role to play in getting Avis into the position that would allow him to move a lot of things as one of the first Canadians with a Ph.D. in linguistics. In Avis' case, the Ph.D. was from the University of Michigan, a real powerhouse in English linguistics and dialectology to this day and simply *the* place to be for cutting-edge approaches at the time. The first major step in Avis' career was his MA thesis, which, as we know from Avis' (1950) preface, was suggested and supervised by Alexander. Never published and only available on microfiche (of terrible quality) today, the thesis still is, to great surprise, as inspiring and fresh for its clear treatment of historical letter-sound representations and phonetic reconstruction as it must have been half a century ago. It is indeed rare that graduate work remains current over half a century. The only comparable case I know of is guitar hero Bryan May's Ph.D. thesis in astronomy, which was interrupted in the early 1970s to allow a full-time career with his band Queen, together with Freddie Mercury, and was only completed thirty-five years later in 2006 without starting all over again, as "not much" had developed in that particular subfield in the interim. Similar things may be said of the use of literary depictions in historical phonology, which Avis worked on. (In other subareas in historical phonology, however, great achievements have been made since.)

When the famous Massey Report,[15] which was important in the intellectual development of Canada, was commissioned in the late 1940s, it included a section of academic-paper length on Canadian English by the one person who was in the position to write it: Henry Alexander. Published in 1951, the subsection on the "English language in Canada" is not a wonderful piece, mostly because the field was too young, with almost nothing to build on. Alva Davis' 1948/49 unpublished Ph.D. thesis on Great Lakes English[16] is noted as the only tenable piece of fieldwork evidence and shows the profound empirical stance that Alexander took. Above all, however, Alexander's Massey Report section proved one thing: the impossible task of writing an overview of Canadian English before the late 1960s.[17]

What has been lost entirely today is that Alexander is, as a matter of fact, the godfather of all Canadian sociolinguists and historical linguists. Alexander's student Avis was to move on to establish the field of Canadian English firmly and for good. In the 1970s, Avis would be in touch with a new generation of linguists, who were the first wave of Canadian variationist sociolinguists to use the new paradigm founded by William Labov and, shortly after, Peter Trudgill in England. One of this new generation was J. K. Chambers at the University of Toronto, who would go on to become one of the leading Canadian socio-linguists. Chambers, as a young scholar in Toronto, corresponded with Avis in Kingston, and I remember vividly Chambers' sign-off in a 1976 letter to Avis, which offers a glimpse into the Flower Power age. Chambers closed the letter to Avis with "Peace", followed by his signature.[18] No more "Sincerely" or perhaps "Cordially"; it was all "Peace", man!

Sadly, Avis had a heart condition that had been plaguing him for close to twenty years, which meant that all through the editing of *DCHP-1* he was forced to deal with compromised health. Beyond *DCHP-1*, Avis simply did not have time to write his own monograph on Canadian English, as he died before retirement. We know, however, Avis' appreciation of the first university textbook on the study of Canadian English, written by Ruth E. McConnell at the University of British Columbia Education department (McConnell 1978).[19]

So far, I've been writing a lot about the paternal lineage of Canadian English: man after man after man. So much so that there remains one question: if Lovell is the father of Canadian English, who's the mother? While today we have many highly decorated female linguists working on Canadian English (e.g., Sandra Clarke from Memorial University and Sali Tagliamonte at the University of Toronto, but also Alexandra d'Arcy at the University of Victoria) and many of them leading the field, the situation was very different in the 1950s and 1960s. As a matter of fact, at that time there was not a single woman in a prominent position (Ph.D. holder, MA holder, or professor) working on the variety, at least not until Ruth McConnell in the 1970s. Such imbalance clearly produced a blind spot that the old boys' club comprising the field had no means to counterbalance.

Were There Really No Women? The Enigma of Helen C. Munroe

Is it true that no women were working on Canadian English before Ruth E. McConnell entered the scene with her brilliant textbook in 1978? While there were some women in the field, you have to know where to look and you have to look hard. It is unfortunately true that the founding of Canadian English was an entirely male affair at first glance; there are no archival records from the early decades showing any female authors or researchers in Canadian English. There was a female scholar, Helen C. Munroe, however, who in the late 1920s and early 1930s wrote a number of articles on Montreal and Canadian English in *American Speech*: a short note (Munroe 1929) on Montreal English, a paper on bilingual signage that somewhat foreshadows the linguistic landscape approach of the 2000s (Munroe 1930), and a usage point that Munroe tackles from an applied linguistic perspective (Munroe 1931) – very cutting-edge indeed.

Concluding contradictory evidence, Munroe states that, while almost no one admits to the form *raise in pay* rather than *rise*, it is in popular use in Canadian English. "Yet such is undoubtedly the case", she writes (Munroe 1931: 410). Munroe then raises the question whether the majority of objections to *raise in pay* are the opinion of "a certain group lean[ing] backward in its determination to speak correct English, or are the ultra-conservative letters from persons not Canadian-born?" Munroe is therefore one of the earliest champions of Canadian English. That we don't know much else about her is surely the result of her being female. She received her BA at the University of Illinois in 1927. Figure 9 shows Helen C. Munroe in her 1926 all-women junior class at the University of Illinois in Urbana-Champaign. Munroe is in the second row from the front, fourth from the right, wearing glasses.

Fellow linguist McLay (1930: 328) commented on Munroe's (1929) half-page note on "the cultivated circles of Montreal in which she moves". Was she

Top Row: WENBAN, HERSHMAN, DAVIS, L. MITCHELL, E. NICKOLLS, PRIDEAUX.
Third Row: HUMPHREY, O. BOWTON, HANSEN, CHEESMAN, MARLOWE, DAY, R. BOWTON.
Second Row: R. MITCHELL, STROUP, DICKINSON, TUCKER, MUNROE, COCKE, McCAULEY, FABRI.
Bottom Row: H. NICHOLS, PAISLEY, TONEY, FOSTER, LAKE, BOTELER, BURNS, MYERS.

Figure 9 Helen C. Munroe's junior-year photo, University of Illinois (1926).
Helen is the bespectacled woman, second row.
(Photo: 1926 issue of *The Illio Yearbook*, p. 466. Used by kind permission of
Preservation Services at Urbana-Champaign)[20]

someone from a well-to-do house, who did not go to finishing school but instead
to a real school? Someone who had the leisure to engage in linguistic inquiry?

Her three papers had quite an effect. For instance, she is extensively quoted
in Mencken's last edition of *The American Language* (e.g., 1936: 371). After
1931, the trail ends, however. Munroe would be an interesting case study that
is beyond the scope of this book. In any case, there seem to have been no
female Ph.D. students working on Canadian English until well into the 1970s.
A real feminist linguist trailblazer was, of course, Louise Pound, who was
working in the USA a full half-century ahead of the (female) pack.[21]

This does not mean, however, that no women were *working* with the topic.
They did, but they usually did not get academic recognition for it. There are
many examples scattered throughout the record that attest to this sad fact. Avis,
for instance, thanked his wife in his MA thesis for "typing and re-typing" his
manuscript and for proofreading it. It seems that Faith (Eileen) Avis, *née*
Hutchison, a strong and intelligent woman with a BA degree to her name, was
at times nothing short of an editor for her husband. While I had the chance to
correspond with Ms Avis a couple of years before her death in February 2010,
I never had the pleasure of meeting her. She approached Queen's University in
2006 with her late husband's personal collection and granted us permission to
transcribe her husband's quotation slips for *DCHP-2*, collected after the publication of *DCHP-1* in 1967 until his untimely death in 1979, with the help of the
Strathy Language Unit of Canadian English at Queen's University.[22]

In those days, the men operated in public, while the women, all too often,
operated behind the scenes for no or little credit. For instance, novelist
Margaret Atwood, born in 1938, writes about her parents' adoption of what

seems to have been the usual split of tasks in writing: "My mother had typed my father's PhD thesis on [a portable Remington from the 1930s]: she'd taught herself how to write in order to do so."[23] Indeed, women in post-World War II Canada were at a significant disadvantage in academia. Legally, they had the right to study, but socially it was made clear that something else was preferable – so much so that Atwood's early manuscripts were sent out to publishers as "M. E. Atwood", as she writes, "because I didn't want anyone to know I was a girl".[24] In short, there weren't many women around; if there was one, she was somewhat exotic and at a significant disadvantage.

Ms Faith Avis

Faith Avis was a highly educated woman, graduating in 1946 with a BA in journalism from Carleton in Ottawa. She is shown in Figure 10 at a reception from 1945/46 (left to right, facing the reader: Faith Avis, Wally Avis, and H. M. Tory), greeting people as they enter the building for a social gathering.

Faith Avis may have played a more major role in Canadian English than first meets the eye, though we can only surmise about it. She certainly knew Douglas Leechman before Wally Avis, as Leechman is a signee on Faith Avis'

Figure 10 Faith Avis (far left) and Wally Avis (third from left) at a 1945/46 Carleton University reception
(Photo from the Heritage Photograph Collection, Archives and Research Collections, Carleton University Library. Donated by Faith Avis. Used by kind permission)[25]

BA graduation certificate. At that time, Wally had not even started his BA degree. While it is possible that Faith Hutchison (Avis) may have introduced Leechman, probably one of her teachers, to Wally when he took on the editorship of *DCHP-1*, Leechman was to play, as we will see in later chapters, an important role in *DCHP-1* and – which is little known – in the *OED* supplements by Robert Burchfield in the 1960s and 1970s.

So, in a nutshell, the earliest phase of Canadian English studies was a very traditional, almost colonial, affair: while the men worked in the public sphere, the women assisted in less prominent roles. The gentleman scholars went to conferences, meetings of the Canadian Linguistic Association (CLA) – of which Avis, Lovell, and Scargill were founding members – Canadian Congresses of the Humanities and Social Sciences – the 1958 Edmonton Congress was lexicographically most important (Drysdale: personal correspondence, 2 April 2018) – and MLA meetings, of which the one in 1969 is well documented for Avis' keynote. The men would engage there, amidst cigarette smoke (smoking was ubiquitous, like coffee breaks today) and a glass of the (hard) liquor of their choice, in scholarly discussions far away from their wives and significant others.

Times have changed considerably since then. Younger areas in linguistics, such as historical sociolinguistics, with which we started the present chapter, were to a great degree founded by women: Ingrid Tieken-Boon van Ostade in Leiden (the Netherlands), Anita Auer in Lausanne (Switzerland), and Marina Dossena (Italy) are but three of them. Another young field, English as a Lingua Franca (ELF), devised in the early 2000s and developed in the past ten years or so, has three female scholars who have been called the "three mothers" of the field[26] – no fathers this time, only mothers. ELF is the immensely important and quickly growing field of the study of English among non-native speakers. As ELF speakers become self-affirmative, claiming a form of English as "theirs" and no longer willing to put up with labels such as "learner English" or "non-native Englishes", research into ELF is becoming more important by the day. One ELF "mother", Barbara Seidlhofer, is very clear about ELF's relevance, when she writes that ELF is perhaps the most widely used variety of English world-wide[27] – not American English, not British English, and certainly not Canadian English.

Ms Joan Hall

While women were not given the opportunity to play a critical role in the foundation of Canadian English, evidence of their involvement lies hidden in the files of the Lexicographical Centre in the Archives of the University of Victoria. In the 1960s, the Centre's administrative assistant Joan Hall clearly played an important role in the making of *DCHP-1*. It was she who corresponded with Wally Avis prior to the publication, as of 1964. As Avis was editing the dictionary from Kingston, Ontario, at the time, relying on most information being sent to him by mail, including the appropriate range of quotation slips, Ms Hall made it all happen on a secretarial salary. She was paid by the University of Victoria Centre of Lexicography, which was directed by Scargill, who brings us back to the beginning of Chapter 1.

Avis usually replied with precise answers and often quite intricate queries to Ms Hall's letters, but always in a light and entertaining way, a congenial way. In the exchange from a letter sent by Avis to Hall on 21 September 1964 (received on 5 October), we can see that Joan Hall was more than a secretary. Avis responded to Hall's letter by hand, rendered in bold below, writing on Hall's original. Avis was, decades before email became available, answering to Hall's updates in an email style that he called "Avis-Type" answers, which suggests that his timesaving style was anything but usual. The following exchange shows the kind of professional relationship that the professor and the so-called "editorial assistant" (slash student, slash person eager to learn) built:

Dr. Leechman and Dr. Scargill are both checking the files now. Dr. Leechman has finished the A file, and is now working on the C's. Dr. Scargill is doing the B file. **Good.**

Mr. Crate has written and assures me that he will be sending in more cite slips. **I have no doubt.**

The shorthand lessons have come to a complete halt. **Tsk! tsk!**

I typed up the envelopes for you some time ago but didn't send them to you. However, here they are. I hope that will save you some time. **Good girl.**

P.S. Which dictionary would you recommend for the personal library of a student in an M.A. programme? **I think the best bet is Funk and Wagnalls (no apostrophe) Standard College Dictionary (Canadian Ed.), Longman's Canada, 1963. This book is the most recent and is excellent in many ways. ... Moreover, it does make a gesture towards Canadian English. Finally, it ... reflects a good dictionary philosophy. We'll have the Senior out some day, I hope. But it is a long job.** (Sept./Oct. 1964 Hall and **Avis**; University of Victoria Archives, 90–66, Box 4)

It is clear from the many exchanges such as the one above that Avis greatly depended on MA student Joan Hall to get work on *DCHP-1* done. She is acknowledged in *DCHP-1* as editorial assistant of the Lexicographical Centre (see *DCHP-1* inner cover).[28] One wonders, however, whether Joan might have been offered more attractive roles, by default if you will, had she been a male. We won't know for sure, but the thought shows how strange (to be nice) or how discriminatory (more to the point) societies are: we only see what we are used to seeing, unless we make the effort to see past the usual limitations.

We can also see in their business correspondence a caring, professional relationship with humour (Avis' "Tsk! tsk!" from above, as a mild but understanding form of critique) and the time-bound "Good girl", in the fashion of the day, for a job done well, which generally stopped being perceived as a compliment at some point in the early 1980s. There is also advice-seeking by Hall, which means that the boss–employee relationship must have been a good one. Avis' advice, to be sure, is most interesting, but there are also other questions that one might wonder about. Why not ask Scargill, who was her immediate boss and present at the University of Victoria, as a professor of linguistics? Why ask Avis, who was sitting thousands of miles to the east, for the "best" dictionary of Canadian English? It seems Ms Hall trusted Wally Avis. It also indicates that Scargill was, perhaps, not as often in the Lexico-graphical Centre and as easily reachable as an employee would wish for. Since the Gage dictionaries had not been completed at the time (*The Senior Diction-ary* would not appear until late in 1967, a little before *DCHP-1*), Avis offers his best alternative with a Funk & Wagnalls title, whose *s*, as Avis alerts his reader, is not a genitive *'s* but part of the name (as in Chambers or Ross).

Let's take stock of the roles women played in *DCHP-1*. So, here we are: a bunch of men, all white, from a range of walks of life, and very few women, themselves all white but in lesser roles, of whom Faith Avis and Joan Hall can be connected to the project. Both were, exclusively, in lesser supporting roles with their potential not fully tapped, it seems, and in any case with no significant credit given to them. This, too, is the legacy of *DCHP-1*. But does this fact sabotage the project as a biased and skewed effort to document the variety, to invent and create Canadian English? Only to the degree that it would also render useless the *Oxford English Dictionary*, the *Dictionary of American Regional English*, and other works of the period. In any case, the lack of women and the lack of ethnic diversity is certainly the dark spot, a very dark spot, in the history of *DCHP-1* – a dark spot that would remain with the history of linguistics well into the latter half of the twentieth century.[29]

The Pioneer Collector

The year 1960 was key for *DCHP-1*, when the high hopes since 1958 were quashed by a blow that almost killed the entire project. The extant correspond-ence from that fateful year of 1960 began on 11 January with a long letter in search of funding to Dr Trueman, the Chair of the Canada Council, which is the predecessor organization of the Social Science and Humanities Research Council of Canada (SSHRC), which funds most humanities research in the country. SSHRC is the taxpayer's research branch in that area, so to speak, offering astonishing and outstanding returns for comparatively little money.[30]

In early March came the extraordinary news of substantial funding being granted to Charles Lovell to work a full year on *DCHP-1* in Calgary. Lovell, the pioneer collector of Canadian data ("quotations", as Chapter 4 will make clear) had done it, and secured research funding. However, what promised to be an excitingly good year for *DCHP-1* had turned into its *annus horribilis* by mid-March. On 17 March, just about two weeks after the funding letter arrived, all plans fell apart with Lovell's sudden death. The 1960 volume of the *Canadian Journal of Linguistics* testifies to the death of *DCHP-1*'s founding editor in a page-long note in volume 6, issue 2, page 98, set in the wide black box typical of death notices.

The obituary was laudatory but a bit odd at the same time, perhaps as odd as Lovell's ascension as the champion of Canadian English. In it, the reader is told that Lovell was afflicted by "a slight deafness" that "may have caused him to appear rather withdrawn", but we are assured that "those of his colleagues in the Association who got to know him well found him to be a very humorous and kindly man". Perhaps an atypical career deserves an atypical obituary. The most significant part of the short obit showed, however, the high standing Lovell had achieved among the linguists:

> From our knowledge of Mr. Lovell and of his work, we judge him to be the man whose name must always come first among those who have contributed to the lexicography of Canadian English. His work in the field of the lexicography of American English is there for all to read. In Mr. Lovell's death, the Association has lost an outstanding colleague and a good friend. (*Canadian Journal of Linguistics*, 6(2): 98)

Lovell's daughter, Bonnie Lovell, was 9 years old when her father collapsed and passed away. Decades later, she retraces her memory of that day in a recent memoir about her father:

> Just days before a letter had arrived with news that was going to change all of our lives: He had won a grant to conduct research in Canada on a proposed Canadian dictionary. We were moving to Canada for a year, and there was a lot to do to set the wheels in motion. That afternoon, he was tired and took a nap. That evening, after cooking supper, he told my mother, when she came home from work, that he had been so out of breath coming back up the hill from the post office that he had had to sit down and rest before coming home. (B. Lovell 2011: 36)

That night, Charles Lovell died of a heart attack. He was whisked away by an ambulance without the knowledge of his 9-year-old daughter, who was upstairs sound asleep. As a result, no one went to Canada and no research was conducted that year on what was to become *DCHP-1*. As secretary of the Canadian Linguistic Association, Avis (1960: 103) put the blow for the field in the strongest words that the academic administrator role would allow him, writing that "the [dictionary] Committee and the CLA have been seriously crippled by this development".

Scholar Without Degrees

Who was Mr Charles J. Lovell – Mr Lovell, not Dr Lovell – whom Avis, the most qualified academic in the area, paid tribute to in such a way? This was a time when a formal degree was, while still immensely useful, not the absolute entry requirement into academic activities it is today. It was not unheard of, actually, for academics to have neither a Ph.D. nor an MA. What is not known to many, for instance, is that James A. H. Murray, the most important editor of the *Oxford English Dictionary*, who is today the epitome of the highly intelligent, disciplined, knowledge-seeking Oxford don, was originally not a university graduate. Instead, Murray was a hands-on man with a curiosity and a zeal for learning, a man who distinguished himself as a school teacher, which, in nineteenth-century England, one could still become without a post-secondary degree.

In contrast to Murray, Lovell had no post-secondary education at all. Even in this respect, however, Lovell was not totally unlike Murray, whose first post-secondary degree was no more than a sober pass, as Murray had to attend to family duties and was therefore prevented from writing his exams, still triggering a pass in recognition of his talent. Yet Lovell, by contrast, never got that far, due to an utter lack of chances; signing up for post-secondary education and studying even some time at that level was surely his dream but, unfortunately, entirely beyond the reach of this talented man. Given that the first degree at university is often the most challenging one, because one has to figure out so many things beyond academia, especially for those who are the first-generation academic in a family or network, Lovell was socially *de facto* locked out of university. Intellectually, though, he would have been over-qualified and a boon for any department, as we know in hindsight.

Murray, on his part, was not an outsider in academic circles but an outsider in Oxford circles, which is another challenge altogether. Everyone who has seen an Inspector Morse episode has some sort of idea of where the challenges lie in the oldest institutions, and while this is not the place to go into any details, let's just say that the challenges at Oxford University and at, say, Johannes Kepler University in Linz, Upper Austria, which are both institutions of academic merit, could not be more different. Still, Murray's *OED* connections lobbied in his name for an honorary doctorate from Edinburgh University (Gilliver 2016: 81–82), which would be the degree that put the required check mark in terms of formal education with Murray's name. Murray was literally lobbied into the "right" degree. Lovell, for his industry and knowledge in lexicography and dialectology alone, would probably have deserved an honorary degree as well. I venture to guess that he might have actually received one had he been able to complete the dictionary himself.

Despite their different situations, the parallels between Murray and Lovell can even be pushed a wee bit further. As we know from the literature on Murray's and Lovell's correspondence, both men were fierce advocates for the highest quality in their work. This, as such, is not a given in academia, and where it does occur, it often does so in skewed ways – for instance, with a field that is defined overly narrowly. Just as Murray managed to enter an illustrious circle of perhaps 200 men (mostly) that formed the Philological Society of London, Lovell managed to garner the appreciation of Canada's and America's best linguists within the Canadian Linguistic Association and beyond.

It is here where the parallels stop. Murray grew old; Lovell didn't. A lot is known about Murray today, while Lovell remains a mysterious figure. I remember well reading Lovell's obituary in the *CLA Journal* – later to be renamed *Canadian Journal of Linguistics* –for the first time. What stuck in my mind were, paradoxically, not his achievements but Lovell's hearing problem and perceived aloofness. Born Charles Julien Steckiewich, Lovell changed his name, perhaps to leave his difficult foster years symbolically behind, years that ceased to know happiness as of Grade 7 when a family he was living with and that were planning to adopt him changed their mind overnight because of an unexpected pregnancy. There no longer was any "need" for little Charles, so he had to go: call that a moral 180! Overnight, the orphan with a bright and loving future was without a home, cut loose. As Lovell would discover only decades later, his foster mother, considered barren, became pregnant against all expectations (B. Lovell 2011: 103). So there was no place for Charles and he was "re-orphaned" at the age of 12, fully realizing what was going on. For some, such shock and humiliation might be enough to make them drift off into the darker corners of society. Not so Charles J. Lovell, who developed, perhaps in compensation for so much grief, a number of surprising talents, of which English usage and lexicography are the ones he will be most remembered for, paired with outstanding tenacity and perseverance. (Our knowledge of Lovell's life owes a great deal to Bonnie Lovell's Ph.D. thesis in creative non-fiction. Bonnie dug up a lot of material and wove it into an admirably fine story.)

After that apparent stroke of bad luck regarding plans for Lovell's adoption, the foster-home system showed his real character. In the mid-1920s, Lovell ran away from a foster home in which he was regularly forced to clean the house's fourteen rooms. On Sundays, he was given the afternoons off, when he roamed around learning about plants and plant names, the Latin names of which started to fascinate him. Later on, he became an unpaid carpenter's apprentice before switching to (badly) paid work in a plant nursery, where he could use his interest in plant names and biological terminology.

Running away in his Sunday best in search for a better life in the west, Lovell did *not* ride the railway hobo-style across the USA; he took the bus to Missouri and on to San Antonio, Texas, where his money ran out. Even then, he did not jump on railcars, like so many did in the day. No. Lovell stuck with his principles, which included no free rides, no matter what. Lovell started walking and would walk the entire 1,300 miles to Los Angeles, head held up high. Until he was presentable again and rested up, he bade his time at an LA mission, before walking the remaining 12 miles out of town to Coolidge Rare Plant Gardens, which he knew as a destination through a trade journal ad he had read at his nursery job out east.

Even then, early on, Lovell kept important information in safe places to redeem it when he needed it. Much like entries for his quotation file, as we will see in Chapter 4, Lovell kept such documentary treasures for years, readily available. Mr Coolidge, the plant nursery's owner, hired Lovell on the spot, which proves that he must have impressed his new boss, perhaps with Latin plant names – we will never know. As the Great Depression hit with full force, however, Coolidge had to let Lovell go. Bonnie Lovell recounts the following years:

Through the 1930s, my father worked odd jobs, lived in rented rooms and residential hotels, did some freelance writing – detective stories, humor, nature stories – until the war came along and he went to work in an airplane factory. Always, he would work a while, save his money, and then head for the mountains. (B. Lovell 2011: 103)

Lovell the mountaineer is a recurring theme and expresses an obsession with mountain hiking, effectively turning Lovell into someone with a drive that is not all that different from the drive of professional mountaineers. Had Lovell had the chance to explore this interest as a child rather than in his young adulthood, who knows? What if he had had the opportunities of someone like Reinhold Messner (born 1944), the South Tyrolean mountaineer who became famous as the first to climb all fourteen 8,000-metre summits on earth without oxygen?

Lovell's first loves were the outdoors and mountain hiking, starting with his afternoon ramblings in nature during his few hours of freedom each week. But when did the *word nerd* enter the scene? His daughter informs us:

Somewhere along the way [in the 1930s] his interest in words turned into scholarly research. In the spring of 1943, he had a contract to ghostwrite a biography of James Warren Nye, the first governor of the newly created Nevada Territory. He used the assignment as an excuse to conduct research at the Library of Congress, as interested in researching word history as in researching Governor Nye's history. Before returning to California, he swung by New Bedford [Massachusetts] to revisit his childhood tormentors. . . . He returned to California, continuing to make summer sojourns in the Canadian Rockies, which sustained him spiritually. (B. Lovell 2011: 103)

Working odd jobs, Lovell was carving out time for what grew into a profound interest in words, which he managed to foster continually against the odds. Here are the trappings of the true scholar, who is not after prestige or glory or money but after knowledge. While a love of plants and the outdoors were passions of someone who comes as close to being called the "father" of Canadian English as anyone, his love for words was developed under the most disprivileged conditions. He must have been a remarkable man, this Charles Julien Lovell, born Steckiewich.

Lovell seems to have made a virtue of necessity and embraced walking and hiking: at first across the western USA to get to Pasadena, chosen in part because of its "interesting name", then for leisure in the Canadian Rockies. Clearly, a word-geek in the best sense of the word was "making lemonade when given lemons", so to speak. Combining the Canadian context, originally foreign to Lovell, and his autodidactic skill set, adding initiative and a sheer unstoppable drive, Lovell would be in the position not only to contribute significantly to the field of Canadian English before too long, but to define it. Formally with just a high school degree, Lovell was a kind of educational wallflower who would turn into a scholarly giant in a field that didn't exist when Lovell caught his "Canadian English bug", as we might call it. First, however, he had to get some sort of credentials in lexicography and this he did by working for the University of Chicago lexicographical unit, which had been founded by Sir William Craigie. When Lovell worked at the unit, it was under Mitford Mathews, who was then the prime lexicographer of American English.

Lovell in Chicago

The question we need to address is how Lovell, the autodidact with no university education, managed to convince Mitford Mathews to give him a job. Mathews was, shortly after the end of World War II, in the process of writing a follow-up dictionary to Craigie and Hulbert's *Dictionary of American English*, which had been published between 1938 and 1944. How Lovell, a nobody in the field, managed to enrich Mathews' *Dictionary of Americanisms* with his "veritable avalanche" of quotations is a feat that demands respect. Bonnie Lovell's text again proves essential by offering insights into 1940s lexicographers' circles. Like Murray, who almost a century before impressed the Philological Society and the *OED*, Lovell impressed through outstanding autodidactic work. Hard to believe today, but there was a time when the skill counted more than the formal degree! Through correspondence, Lovell managed to impress another very important man in the field of American English: H. L. Mencken, who was probably sympathetic to Lovell's situation and recognized Lovell's talent. In 1919, Mencken had published a key book with a very provocative title, *The American Language*, meaning American English.[31] With this book, Mencken put American English as a national variety on the map, and Mencken turned out to be Lovell's key entry to academic work. In Bonnie Lovell's words:

Through the suggestion of and encouragement of Mencken my father ended up with his first professional lexicographical employment. My father told Mencken his idea about producing a dictionary of Americanisms; Mencken told him such a project was already underway at the University of Chicago and advised him to combine forces with its editor, Alabama-born and Harvard-educated Mitford M. Mathews. Mathews wrote my father, saying, "Come over into Macedonia and help us." It wasn't an easy decision. He called it a "bombshell." My father had recently embarked on another project, a guide to the trails of the national parks in the Canadian Rockies. Now he was being asked to choose between the woods and words. Yet he decided he must answer the call.

There it is again, the recurring mountaineering theme in Lovell's life. Bonnie Lovell continues:

And so, in November of 1946, he left Pasadena, his home base of twenty years, to join Mathews as his research and editorial assistant in the Dictionary Department of the University of Chicago Press, where Mathews headed work on *A Dictionary of Americanisms on Historical Principles*, an extension of the Press's earlier *Dictionary of American English on Historical Principles*. (B. Lovell 2011: 86)

Importantly, Lovell did not arrive empty-handed at his new job in Chicago but with, as Mathews wrote, a "veritable avalanche of some sixty pounds of 'slips,' including thousands of antedatings of the *DAE*" (B. Lovell 2011: 87). This is truly remarkable because it meant that Lovell must have spent hundreds of hours of his spare time, and on his own dime, building a collection that would not only impress the lexicographical professionals but elevate Mathews' dictionary to a whole new level. In a day of "big data", where some linguists would not even dream of collecting their own data (though many do, of course), I cannot stress enough the fact that Lovell, much like Avis and other greats, never shied away from doing the legwork himself.

Lovell burst on the scene not only with unique data of high quality and in unforeseen quantities but also with a kind of energy that is equally remarkable. The *OED* had W. C. Minor, the literal "madman" in the bestseller by Simon Winchester.[32] Minor would, sitting in his cell as a convicted murderer, read and excerpt entire bookshelves on index cards. When Murray needed help on a given word, Minor would look it up in his files and send him the antedate or answer. Minor supplied quotations, mostly precious antedatings, to no fewer than 1,000 problem cases, on queries for which the *OED* editors had come up empty-handed.[33] Note that Minor needed to be asked for every single item – he did not just send on a bunch of material to Oxford, like most other volunteers did. In contrast to Minor, Lovell was not mad, had no criminal record, but was equally obsessed with words, which he shared much more freely than Minor. Yet Lovell did not have nearly as much time on his hands. I therefore count Lovell's achievement for Mathew's dictionary as greater than Minor's for the *OED*.

The plan was to name Lovell as a co-editor of the *Dictionary of Americanisms*, besides Mathews. The University of Chicago Press stubbornly prevented that, arguing that Lovell had just been an employee, a paid hand. Mathews could say what he wanted, the Press bureaucrats would not listen.[34] Lovell's treatment is one of the substantial injustices in lexicography but, sadly and surely, neither the first nor the last. Lovell performed tasks that are generally given to the most competent team members. He read copy ahead of the actual copy-editor, improving the draft in many places, and he kept collecting material, again in his own time. Mathews confirmed that Lovell was "able, along with his other duties, to supply the project with a surprisingly large amount of further material" (Mathews, qtd in B. Lovell 2011: 88).

Lovell, the First Canadianist?

In those early Chicago days, Lovell had already cut his teeth on Canadian English. Right from the beginning of his time in Chicago in 1946, and perhaps earlier, Lovell treated the Canada–US border as a boundary of significance in utterly non-trivial ways. Avis' (1954) first paper on the issue, which was published almost a decade later, must have just confirmed Lovell's own thinking. This means that Lovell's practice of delineating Canadianisms, to what is sometimes, by gross misunderstanding, called an arbitrary political boundary of little linguistic significance, antedates the key work on pluricentric English varieties, which starts with Partridge and Clark's (1951 [1968]) essay collection on the topic. Even after publication of Mathews' dictionary, Lovell's mind did not rest. In his copy of the 1951 *Dictionary of American-isms*, Lovell "penciled in the margins, in red, blue, green and graphite, updates on words, earlier appearances in print, better examples, corrections, notations that words were 'Canadian!'" (B. Lovell 2011: 89).

How did Lovell get in the position to be so ahead of the curve? I think the answer is clear: as an autodidact he had all the disadvantages of doing and learning everything himself, but he could also draw from the single most important advantage of the autodidact, who is free to approach any topic without scholarly bias. This, and only this, is the explanation why Lovell did more exciting and more avant-garde work in Canadian English than, without exagger-ation, all academic scholars at the time. In that activity, his second lifetime hobby and vocation comes into play: hiking, walking, and mountaineering, which brought him in touch with what many Americans considered an unimportant, out-of-the-way place to the north of their country. This early Canadian connec-tion, Lovell never lost. Instead it became the catalyst for his later years' work:

In the field of Americanisms, my father had joined forces with Mathews. But he helped pioneer the field of Canadianisms. During his California years, he used to work for a while, save his money, and then quit and head for the mountains, often in Canada. He developed a love for the country and the warm, friendly people he met and, as always, found its distinctive words fascinating, and so in the 1940s he began collecting Canadianisms. (B. Lovell 2011: 91)

In one way this book should actually have been subtitled *The Mountaineer, the Professor* ... , rather than *The Professor, the Mountaineer* ... , because

Lovell was collecting Canadianisms even before Avis, the later professor, had begun his BA studies at Queen's.

There is a long tradition of how outsiders propose, carry out, and, more often than not, see to completion projects that are connected with the linguistic autonomy of a certain place. Murray, a Scot, was writing the *OED* for the English. Cassidy, with his Jamaican roots, was writing *DARE* for the Americans, and here, Lovell, the American mountain hiker and word lover, was ushering the Canadian professional linguists along in their meetings of the newly founded Canadian Linguistic Association (CLA):

> At the organization's first meeting in 1954 in Winnipeg, Manitoba, my father proposed a Canadian dictionary, following it up with an article about "Lexicographical Challenges of Canadian English" that appeared in the first issue of its journal. (B. Lovell 2011: 91)

I can somehow picture the Winnipeg meeting in 1954 vividly: the most highly decorated linguists and philologists assemble and a man with but a high-school degree gets up and suggests a rather grandiose task – Canadian dictionaries. Silence. Then some whispering and head-turning: who made this suggestion? Do you know the guy? Nope, never seen him before. Soon everyone could read in Lovell (1955a), the article that Bonnie talks about, that this newcomer was not just dead serious but also knew what he was talking about.

Why didn't the Canadian scholars think of the dictionary first, one wonders? Sure, Avis was quick to come aboard within a couple of years, as were Scargill and the others. But the impetus, the idea, came from this American man who was orphaned as a child. Given the advantage of outsiders in dialectology, that an American was to propose the dictionary is less the fault of the Canadians than of their disadvantaged position, as it's hard to hear what's special if Canadian English is your default variety. By 1957, Lovell had won the CLA over, securing the official backing of his idea and the seal of approval.

The Renaissance Man

It's hard to imagine what Lovell would have been capable of, had he not had to worry about making financial ends meet throughout his life, always working without support staff and most of the time on his own dime. Then again, financial windfall might not have helped his zeal, as some who are financially safe from the start fall for the dangers that come with this luxury and often become "coasters". Bob Dylan said the "coasting" that is the result of being pampered makes one "helpless like a rich man's child". Lovell was never coasting, for sure; he was trailblazing – always, it seems.

He was surely neither rich nor helpless but a man who surprised with many talents. And, unlike the linguist who is a good guitar player in private or at linguistic parties (a nice and ubiquitous talent among linguists), Lovell found a way to celebrate his talents in more than just one way. Consequently, his appellations are many: humourist – he published jokes in small journals – word-puzzle creator, stamp collector, and the like. The hobbies were something like smaller "vocations" with which he filled his time.

I like to imagine Lovell as a kind and driven "proto-hippie", long before the term came into use, yet without the slacker qualities that were all the rage in the grunge period of the early 1990s, when Nirvana, Soundgarden, the Lemonheads, Radiohead, and Blind Melon ruled youth subculture. Lovell's alter egos included the record-breaking blood donor, which impressed not only the nurses who attended to his regular donations, but also newspaper journalists who reported on the "one-man-blood-bank". He was once Cook of the Month in the *Chicago Tribune* – not exactly a small newspaper – in the 1950s. The child Bonnie reports of morning pancake odour regularly filling their house at weekends.

In his California years, Bonnie Lovell informs me, her father designed bookplates. Bookplates, just in case you don't remember them, are the pre-printed sheets that used to be glued on the inner cover of books, consisting of the following elements: the letters "Ex Libris" (Latin for "from the books"), then an ornament and a blank line for the name of the book owner to be – ideally, in calligraphy – filled in. In such bookplates Lovell hid his name in the design, a bit like some Anglo-Saxon monk who would do so and, as a rule, deliberately insert an error, because in medieval sentiment only the divine was perfect. Perfection is never to be attained but always to be striven for, in the medieval world and in Lovell's alike. Precisely this sentiment is what meets the biographer in Lovell's file and scholarly legacy. Like Avis, Lovell worked hard, questioned everyone, and was not too proud to stand corrected. Consequently, Lovell, like Avis, was a true scholar.

Considering Lovell's difficult childhood, I wonder whether he, given the chance to go through the best education channels, would still have gone to such lengths with so many things? This further leads me to wonder whether relative poverty is a requirement for success – meaningful success. Despite the odds – or possibly a bit as a result of them – we know that Lovell learned to love words. As Bonnie, perhaps surprisingly, informs us

he loved the woods more. In May of 1951, he was commuting seventeen miles into Chicago every day to work in his office in Wieboldt Hall. But on weekends and long summer nights, he had the forest preserve. (B. Lovell 2011: 91)

So there is yet another Lovell, the near-pro hiker and member of not only the Alpine Club of Canada but, personally more significantly, his most beloved Skyline Hikers of the Canadian Rockies. We read earlier that in his CLA obituary, Lovell was inadvertently presented as an aloof, hard-of-hearing geek – at least that was what stuck with me after first reading the obituary many years ago. Against all odds, Lovell had a remarkably full life – fuller than most. It is, in my mind, another example of how adversity at times brings out some of the best that humanity can proffer, as Bonnie Lovell makes clear about her papa:

My father was an orphan, living in brutal foster homes, treated abysmally, starved of affection. I pictured a small boy wearing rags and, under the rags, undergarments cut from the unmentionables of a stingy old woman, stuck in the scullery, never allowed out for swimming, sledding, photos, or hugs. (B. Lovell 2011: 116)

Undergarments cut from rags are a fact, so much so that Lovell's story is a version of an American dream from literally rags to lexicographical riches. Lovell from the scullery reminds me of Harry Potter under the staircase. Both let their magic work. As his daughter remembers today, while her father went "every May for a linguistics conference in Toronto" (B. Lovell 2011: 96) – which was in fact at rotating places in Canada – he pursued an agenda of freeing Canadians from their dependence on American and British reference works. To his young daughter, of course, it was much more important that her daddy would come home every time, and this was even sweeter when he came with a "suitcase stuffed with maple syrup and candy leaves spun of maple sugar, souvenirs of Canada" (B. Lovell 2011: 96). Lovell, the Canada-phile.

In case there is any question as to who was the driving force behind *DCHP-1*, who got it off the ground, who convinced the Canadian linguists about it being a good idea, the recollection of the daughter as a 9-year-old drives home that point once more:

We are in Cicero at Midway Airport, Mama, Charlie, and me, along with the Smiths, who have driven us to the airport in their green Studebaker, before us, a Trans-Canada airplane, red maple leaf emblazoned on its side. As Daddy climbs the steps to board the plane, he turns back and gives a jaunty wave. He is off to Toronto to give a talk at the Canadian Linguistic Association conference where he will once again promote his project: a Canadian dictionary based on historical principles. (B. Lovell 2011: 97)

Lovell, the Renaissance man, the uncredited champion behind Mathews' *Dictionary of Americanisms on Historical Principles*, and the inventor and creator of *DCHP-1* – "his project", not just in the words of his young daughter, but also in the words of the Chief Editor of the current edition (yours truly).

It's one of the strange twists of fate that Lovell was not given the chance to apply the principles of historical lexicography that he had worked out and adapted for Canada in four papers (C. Lovell 1955a, 1955b, 1956, 1958). Had Lovell died twenty years later than he did, he probably would have received more than one substantial obituary in scholarly journals. But being axed down before his most productive years, only two weeks after he was going to be fully funded for the first time in the academic year 1960–61 to pursue this work, all we got is the one-page obituary in the *Canadian Journal of Linguistics*.

Lovell, the Driven Linguist

The extent of debt that the field of Canadian English owes to Lovell is difficult to overstate. It's perhaps best to let Lovell recount his early years in Chicago in his own words from a letter that I found just after finishing the first draft of this book, incidentally on Christmas Eve 2017. This late discovery made clear that, despite having researched the making of Canadian English full-time for almost a year by then, I *still* had underestimated Lovell's role and dedication. This is the passage that made that point clear to me:

I [Lovell] worked for several years collecting thousands of antedatings of the DAE [*Dictionary of American English*]. My research carried me from coast to coast. I financed all that myself, from my slender resources. (When I got clues that "hobo" might have originated in the Pacific North-west, and went to Sacramento, Berkeley, Portland, and Seattle, tracking down 21 DAE antedatings from that area, hotel rooms were unobtainable, so that I had to sit up nights in bus stations, until I finished at each library. Two of my antedatings are in the DA; the rest are locked in its files, utterly unavailable to me.) At Chicago I passed up my 15-minute rest periods each morning and afternoon, amounting to one work day of time in each 14 days, over a period of seven years. (Lovell to Avis, 2 Dec. 1954, page 3 of 4, University of Victoria Archives, 90–66, Box 4 File 6)

This is better than a Dan Brown novel: Lovell, the imagined hobo (by his daughter Bonnie), actually becomes a hobo sleeping at the bus station to be able to research the word *hobo*! The letter continues from above:

Also, I put in from 10 to 20 minutes of my 30-minute lunch period on dictionary matters. In my hour of commuting each morning and evening, I spent most of the time reading papers, books, and magazines for the DA's [*Dictionary of Americanism's*] benefit. I bought a photostatic machine, and secured hundreds of reference materials, at my own expense. Yet with all that, when I collapsed [from a first heart attack in 1953], all too obvious from overwork, the powers that be [in Chicago, being the Press and the University] refused to give me even five minutes of their time for presentation of my case. Though I had a leave of absence that ostensibly lasted through March 31st, in January I was unceremoniously fired, with pious remarks that it was for my own good, etc. (*ibid.*)

In light of such evidence, which I find confirmed in the sheer number and scope of Lovell's quotations in the *DCHP-1* collection, I think that no one but Avis, Scargill, and Drysdale – perhaps also Leechman – would have known how much the field owes to Lovell. With all but Paddy Drysdale gone, he is the only one who may fully appreciate this fact. I hope my interpretations will meet with his approval, at least to a good degree. When it comes to Lovell, and likewise Avis, I think there was an element of utter dedication to the task that makes the Reinhold-Messner-world-record-mountaineering comparison appropriate – to do the job not just well but admirably so, nearly perfectly, as it were. Paddy told me when I visited him in Oxfordshire in the spring of 2017 that Avis wanted to get to the bottom of things, every time, with everything. From what I can tell, Lovell was alike: they were kindred spirits in that regard. They were the Lennon and McCartney of North American lexicography, the musically inclined linguist might say.

Lovell's and Avis' dedication to words is especially important as professional linguists have often been snobby about words as something uninteresting, unsystematic, or – worse, and equally snobby – about public outreach, so much so that *outreach* has become something of a slur in the field. When you hear that "someone's doing outreach", it's often code for "s/he can't do real work". That is, of course, utter nonsense, as David Crystal has proven to us, as the professor turned public educator who has done more for the field than a 1,000 of us professional linguists combined.[35]

It would help linguistics as a discipline if we started listening to what the people want – who, for the most part, fund our privileged research positions with their tax dollars (more like tax cents). I'm not saying we should or would surrender our research to public requests, but we should adequately consider them. The public, quite rightly, sees the importance of words. It is not a good idea to leave aside words because they may not be as systematic or as easy to study as, say, phonetics (which is a fun field). The disconnect between what the public needs and what the linguist is willing to provide was what Lovell started to bridge, long before anyone realized that there was such a gap. When I took on the job of editing *DCHP-2*, I got it, as an outsider to Canadian academe, merely because no one else wanted it: there were a dozen Canadian-born candidates, with a Ph.D. or close to it or better equipped than I was, but I was the only one, Terry Pratt tells me, who responded to his call for "a new Avis", which he uttered at Jack Chambers' retirement conference in January 2005. I knew then and know now that I was no new Avis, and would never be, but I hoped I would do a good enough job to warrant the trust that Terry Pratt, David Friend, Nelson Education – who funded some of my early research – and later the University of British Columbia and SSHRC placed in me.

My personal debt to Lovell is huge. The fact that I am now in the luxurious position to be able to write this thrilling story, I owe, at the bottom of it, to Lovell. Without Lovell, there would be no *DCHP-1*, no *DCHP-2*, no such academic career of mine – or at least it would look very different. So, it must be said: thanks, Charles Julien Lovell, "founding father" of Canadian English. Lovell's story is the story of an outsider with incredible drive, an American, telling Canadians that there was something special about their English. Lovell took this concept from a ridiculous idea to a real lexicographical project in the real world that Avis, the "co-father" of Canadian English, saw to a successful completion.

Figure 11 Walter S. Avis in 1978
(Photo from an album of P. and O. Drysdale, used by kind permission)

3   Avis Pulls It Off

To compare [Avis] with Webster and Mencken is no more than he deserves;
he will be remembered with them.

Raven I. McDavid[1]

Jack Chambers remembers Avis as "larger than life." Everything about this
"lumber jack" of a man was big: his body, his voice, even his white beard.
"He made a large impression," Chambers recalled. "When he entered a room,
people tended to look."

Steven High[2]

The obituary is a strange yet socially important genre. Denied to some by
historical coincidence, others' biographical details and achievements are made
widely known. While one should not speak ill of the dead, as the saying goes, a
good obituary would want a fair assessment of a person's life. Siding with the
proverb more than with facts, in some obituaries it is difficult to tell what kind
of praise is owed to the real ingenuity and qualities of the deceased and which
to the human condition that, understandably, at times seeks to find more praise
than is owed.

There have been linguists who, as practitioners in a small professional field,
went without public obituaries, and the fact that more than a few were published
in the wake of Walter S. Avis' passing on 11 December 1979 testifies to his
importance in the field and beyond. Avis was – this he shared with Lovell – a
word lover, and both joked around in their correspondence. As this chapter's
epigraph states, Avis was "larger than life" to at least one of the next generation
of Canadian linguists. Perhaps, for newcomers, he was too much to handle.
So it might have been an advantage that some, at first, only got to know Avis in
an epistolary manner through letters. Maybe this lack of information allowed
Lovell to be poking fun (scholarly and benevolently) at Avis:

It gives me an excuse to kill two birds with one stone – no, that's an unfortunate phrase
to use in the case of one with your surname, lest you gain the impression that I intend to
put you on the pan! (Lovell to Avis, 2 Dec. 1954, UVic 90–66, Box 4 File 6)

Since *avis* is the Latin word for 'bird', Lovell's joke is a word-nerd joke.
Lovell continues that he might "put" Avis "on the pan" (attack him) with "one

of the stones intended to be aimed at that bird, Avis!" That is humour of the literati type.

So who was Avis? Walter Spencer Avis was born on 4 June 1919 in Toronto. He received his BA in 1949 (Queen's University), MA in 1950 (Queen's University), and his Ph.D. from the University of Michigan in 1955. In 1952, he had already joined the teaching staff at the Royal Military College (RMC) in Kingston, thereby returning to the location of his under-graduate days after just two or three years at Ann Arbor. It was at RMC where Avis became a full professor of English and where he, ultimately, chose to remain, because, as "an outstanding scholar in the field of Canadian English",[3] he had choices. Avis was a founding member not only of the CLA – the Canadian Linguistic Association – but also of the Canadian Association for Applied Linguistics. He was a giant in both a figurative and, as Chambers' quote makes clear, quite a literal sense.

In mid-December 1979, Walter Avis died, leaving behind a long list of accomplishments but also an equally long list of unfinished projects – above all, his monograph on Canadian English. It would not be before 2010 when such a monograph would appear in Charles Boberg's very fine *The English Language in Canada: Status, History, and Comparative Analysis*. It's not a great overstatement to say that Avis' death delayed the field by some thirty years or so, at least in some respects.

Fast-forward to 2019: ask any Canadian graduate student of linguistics about Wally Avis and chances are that they will draw a complete blank. Wally who? This ignorance of the field's history we will address, among other things, in the present chapter. It will teach us about the advantages and problems of academic inquiry and will help us put into context the Big Six – Avis, Crate, Drysdale, Leechman, Lovell, and Scargill – and their relative obscurity in today's professional circles.

So Much To Do, So Little Time

Life is short, and sometimes much shorter than one prefers to think.[4] So the question must be how best to spend one's time. Among the host of obituaries for Avis, one of the most flattering, most factual, and most detailed ones was written by the then-director of *The Linguistic Atlas of the United States and Canada*, Raven I. McDavid. Remarkably, McDavid, in a text on the "spokesmen of linguistic autonomy" put Avis expressly in line with the greatest of the greats, Noah Webster and H. L. Mencken, the two towering figures in American English:

Noah Webster died as his 85th birthday approached; Mencken was permanently disabled shortly after his 68th ... Wally was cut off at sixty; he was still to complete his overview of Canadian English. (McDavid 1981: 125)

Avis' death was a serious setback for an academic field that had just found its first firm footing. It is indeed telling that a scholarly monograph overview of Canadian English would not materialize until half a lifetime after Avis. That the field switched around the same time from the humanities-driven modes of publication – books (the thicker, the better), essay collections, and the French *oisiveté*, roughly translated as the creative state of idleness – to the social-science preferences for journal papers, lab-driven competition, co-authored papers with long lists of authors, and the publish-or-perish mentality meant that no monograph, and thus no useful introduction, would be available till 2010.

We can only surmise how many capable students were not drawn to the field as a result. To say that no good book on Canadian English existed is not correct, however. A popular (and surprisingly good) text was available with Mark Orkin's (1970) *Speaking Canadian English*, but, despite its qualities – written by a lawyer and hobby linguist who did a remarkable job – it was generally not much appreciated by linguists, so it was of little use for introducing young students to the field. It virtually had no effect in the academic world.

The delay of some thirty years is suggestive of the setback in the field that came with Avis' untimely death. First Lovell was dead of a heart attack at 52, then Avis was dead of a heart attack at 60; given what we know about these two giants in Canadian English, it is also not much of a stretch to say that these two worked themselves to death, producing as much as they left unfinished. Avis was called "generous, tireless, dedicated, farseeing, and innovative" (Toon 1981: 142), all qualities that any scholar and human should strive for. Paddy Drysdale, then a tenure-track linguist, credits Avis for teaching him "to ask basic questions and to put them in practical terms" (Drysdale 1980: 117). As the statement suggests, this is paradoxically not a given in academia.

Lovell, because of his perennially precarious financial situation, was even a worse workaholic. By April 1959, Lovell and Avis had shared a four-year friendship. At that point in time, W. J. Gage and the Canadian Linguistic Association had agreed on four dictionaries produced by Gage, and all seemed set: Drysdale coordinated for Gage in Toronto, Robert J. Gregg from University of British Columbia Linguistics was working on *The Senior* (on letter *B* to be precise), Avis on *The Beginning Dictionary*, Scargill on *The Intermediate Dictionary*, and Lovell, as Editor-in-Chief, on *DCHP-1*. Not that Lovell had any staff: he was Editor-in-Chief and utterly alone, "staffless". At this crucial point, when all systems seemed to be "go", Avis and Lovell wrote about their respective worries and problems in the bigger context. The following exchange shows us how tenuous the situation was, even when everything was arranged and all contracts were signed.

Avis was worried that *DCHP-1* might be neglected, in the light of Lovell doing his "day job" for American lexicographer Barnhart. The better part of a year before Canadian Council funding was secured for Lovell, Avis writes:

I realize that the Barnhart job is your bread and butter, but you must not forget the D.C. [*DCHP-1*] for which you have already been advanced some money and which the publisher has been led to believe will be ready within a couple of years. Somewhere you must set aside collecting for this project and get on with the job of editing. (Avis to Lovell, 14 April 1959, University of Victoria Archives, 90–66, Box 4 File 6)

The main motivation behind these lines seems to come from Scargill and Avis' championing of Lovell in his role. As with many projects, once the rubber hits the ground, unforeseen worries surface. This seems to have happened to both Scargill and Avis, as Avis reminds Lovell that they had

done a great deal of promoting on your [Lovell's] behalf with regard to this project, and we [Avis and Scargill] are most anxious that everything possible be done to ensure satisfaction for Dr. Wees, who has been so generous with regard to our dictionary activities on several fronts. (Avis to Lovell, 14 April 1959, University of Victoria Archives 90–66, Box 4 File 6)

Wilf Wees was Vice-President (VP) of Publishing for Gage, and a major force on the publisher's side, wanting to make a Canadian dictionary happen. The reason for the professors' worries seems to derive from a year's delay in the overall planning, with Lovell having to sustain his day job.

Lovell replies three days later, on 17 April, which means he went to task the very same day he received Avis' letter in Illinois. Lovell, clearly annoyed, replies rather sternly:

I am having to work four 10-hour days a week for Barnhart in order to be able to put in three on my Canadian projects. I don't think you realize what a hell of a job I'm having. Using the DA [*Dictionary of Americanisms*] as a basis of comparison to my work, being 1/10 its size, I ought to have at least 17 months full time, and about $10,000 in salaries. I'm not getting anything like that and am really sorry I ever got involved in the business. I wish you'd get it through your head about the research that I need to do to complete my editing; it isn't a matter of getting further citations, but of getting the information necessary to defining a good many things concerning which I lack firsthand knowledge. (Lovell to Avis, 17 April 1959, University of Victoria Archives, 90–66, Box 4 File 6)

Lovell's reply suggests that Avis was himself not entirely clear what was required at this stage. Only Lovell knew and he was struggling to relay the situation to Avis. The clearest attribution of the disadvantages of coming to a field as an outsider follows a few lines down:

I received a certain amount of criticism when it was first announced [in the summer of 1958] that I was to do this work, it being resented that a Yankee should "pose as an authority upon Canadian English." Can't you imagine the ha!ha!s that will greet a first date of "dipsydoodle," [from 1954 in Lovell's files] from hockey fans who've known the term for 20, 30, or 40 years? People are most unreasonable, I tell you, and I don't want to have to apologize for such shortcomings. (Lovell to Avis, 17 April 1959, University of Victoria Archives, 90–66, Box 4 File 6)

Lovell, who apparently wanted to do a better job than Mathews was able to do in his American work, was beginning to feel the pressure of the outsider: nationality-related and, I have no doubt, as an academic outsider despite his accolades, lacking even a BA. This is the flip side of nationalism: some – if not many – would look at achievements from an ignorant nationalist angle, not an identity-confirming one. We can empathize with Lovell's position.

The way I read their exchange is that one workaholic reminds another workaholic not to forget about his second full-time job. (Seven days a week, ten hours a day: who can shoulder that?) The second workaholic replies to the former that he is not a Canadian and must work especially hard on this project to earn his keep.

Webster–Mencken, Lovell–Avis

In some ways, Webster–Mencken on the American side and Lovell–Avis on the Canadian side both "created" their respective varieties. At the risk of going too far, both teams were the Lennon–McCartney for their respective variety, though the Americans lived centuries apart. Despite the parallels, there are striking differences between Webster–Mencken and Avis–Lovell, of course – differences that seem of particular relevance in the Canadian context and for the route that academic inquiry has taken since the Big Six shaped the field. Mencken, as well as Webster, had others finishing their work. Avis finished some of Lovell's, but no one completed Avis' work. This fact may say more about the collegial and competitive spirit at the time than anything else. Whatever we do, we do on the shoulders of giants – giants who sometimes need to be written back into collective memory.

The rest of this chapter is about the man and about exploring the reasons that Avis' work was allowed to fall into relative oblivion, so that today it is only known by a few insiders. A frequent misconception about academia is that the "real" research is always happening at the biggest, "the best", and the most renowned universities. This is straight-out nonsense. Avis worked at the RMC in Kingston, Ontario, which to many seems an unlikely place for the foremost authority on Canadian English that Avis was from the 1950s to his death in 1979. Yet, RMC was the place to be for some unsuspecting reasons and, as McDavid makes convincingly clear, the RMC was indeed a good place for Avis:

For both Webster and Mencken linguistics was a part-time activity; each was a personage with whom one tangled at his peril. For Wally [Avis], linguistics was his vocation, deliberately chosen, and shared with his dedication to his classes at the Royal Military College. At no other institution could he have enriched his knowledge and love of Canada and the English spoken there with so broad an exposure to the variety of Canadian life and the many problems we from south of the border know largely by hearsay. The RMC perhaps comes as close as any institution can to putting into practice the philosophy of bilingualism and biculturalism. From institutional concerns Wally went on to provincial and national ones, and from the problems of French Canadians to those of the Inuit. (McDavid 1981: 122–23)

At the RMC, Avis was teaching members of the Canadian Forces who came from every nook and cranny of Canada. By a stroke of luck, he therefore had access to Canadians from every part of the nation that was simply unparallelled anywhere else. While other institutions might have been the more obvious choice for Avis, RMC was the best choice in this regard. Had he really wanted, there probably would have been a place in another university, Canadian or American. But such moves are not that easy to make, as the few suitable jobs might have been filled by others just before Avis entered the job market. But this is speculation beyond the evidence of one planned move that we'll discuss later in this chapter. In any case, it is *not always* the best in the field that are at the *most prestigious* universities, and senior brass at the big schools, or any school aspiring to play in the big leagues, would do well to acknowledge that fact.

The downside of the RMC would have been in the teaching and administrative loads, which would have been bigger than at institutions more used to research-heavy duties. Another downside – a considerable one in hindsight, given his early death – was that Avis did not have access to Ph.D. students. His pool of students was limited to those in the Canadian Forces, who generally left with their BA, which explains the lack of a younger generation to take up the torch. The next generation of linguists following Avis was instead formed by students from other linguistic paradigms, such as the Chomskyans or the budding sociolinguists of the Labovian school. These are, in short, the most important reasons why Avis has not become the lasting household name in Canadian linguistics that Webster and Mencken have become in America.

Avis' Early Years

Long before becoming a top-rate scholar, Avis was first a soldier. In 1935, at the age of 16, as Vincent *et al.* (1978) report, he joined the militia of the Canadian Armed Forces, entering "the war against Nazi Germany" in August 1939. In early 1940, Avis went to Europe with the Royal Canadian Artillery. As a result of "injuries received overseas", he was discharged and returned to Canada in 1942, which meant that he missed D-Day and, luckily, the carnage at Juno Beach during the D-Day landing. Working as an accountant during the remaining war years, he went to night school to finish his "Senior Matricula-tion" – his high school degree (Vincent, Parker, and Bonnycastle 1978: vi). At Carleton University in Ottawa, in 1945/46, he must have met Faith Hutch-inson, who was just about to graduate with her BA in journalism. At that point, it was Faith who had more education and all the connections, while her future husband strove to gain the privilege to enter university. Faith Hutchison was not just anyone. She was nothing less than one of the best-educated women in the country at that point in time. It showed: look at her beaming with confi-dence in Figure 10 in the previous chapter.

In 1946, Avis eventually transferred to Queen's University, where he would meet Murray Wanamaker. Both Avis and Wanamaker went on to become linguists; on their way to becoming professionals, they both "were army veterans gaining more knowledge at public expense" at Queen's University, thanks to what was the Canadian equivalent of the American GI Bill (Wana-maker 1981: 87). At Queen's, they studied with the best linguist of Canadian English at the time: Henry Alexander, whom we know from before. By now, you'll be asking yourself what's been happening in Canadian linguistic circles in the interim. This is another interesting story that cannot be told here, though I can refer you to a book called *Linguistics Wars*, which will give you an idea of what *may* have happened.[5]

Alexander was no nobody. He was, as we heard in Chapter 2, the sole participant in Canada in Hans Kurath's *Linguistic Atlas of the United States and Canada* at the time, and he would remain the Canadian with the closest connections to the project. By virtue of this alone, he was a trailblazer in the field of Canadian dialectology. In this regard, it is a pity that nothing of his data has been published – though, much to the credit of succeeding *Linguistic Atlas* directors Raven I. McDavid and William A. Kretzschmar, the materials from Maritime Canada can now be accessed online among the questionnaires and recordings that were collected from 1931 to about 1990.[6]

That little from the Maritime English atlas data was published did not hamper Alexander's teaching and supervision, however, as he could give his own students and graduate students access to his materials and, above all, train them to be state of the art. In a way, Alexander's major achievement is in the education of his graduate students, among whom Murray Wanamaker and Walter Avis stand out. Wanamaker would use his knowledge in dialect geog-raphy in his dissertation on the dialect of King's County, NS (Wanamaker 1965). Avis would do so more immediately when, in 1949/50, while still in Kingston, he distributed a dialect questionnaire at Queen's, the first of its kind in Canada, starting a tradition that would not just rescue the written questionnaire method from oblivion but also teach us over the next six decades a lot, if not most, of what we know about Canadian English (Dollinger 2015a: 87–129).

While Avis' questionnaire data would be used in the mid-1950s for three important publications in what is now the *Canadian Journal of Linguistics*, it is reasonable to assume that some of his term papers for Alexander's courses were based on it as well. Avis would at that point cut his teeth in historical linguistics and become a well-rounded linguist, versatile in both the historical and present-day modelling of language and variation.

Excellence Made in Ann Arbor

For his Ph.D. dissertation, Wally and Faith went from Kingston to Ann Arbor, Michigan, as would Murray Wanamaker a few years later. Ann Arbor simply was *the* place to be for dialectologists, historical linguists, and sociolinguists of the 1950s and early 1960s, and a heaven for any linguist of English. It was the time and place in which the intelligentsia of both the Old World and New World met, and, for a while, it must have been the most stimulating venue, outperforming the more prestigious universities in the field on both the East and West Coast. Among others, more than one refugee from Hitler's Nazi terror – Austrian, German, and Eastern European scholars of Jewish ancestry, and political dissenters – found their way to Ann Arbor.

Ann Arbor's programme in English linguistics had a number of most eminent scholars to boast of: Charles C. Fries (1887–1967), internationally renowned descriptive and corpus linguist pioneer; Sherman M. Kuhn (1907–91), long-term Editor of the *Middle English Dictionary* (now *Middle English Companion*); and Hans Kurath (1891–1992), Austrian émigré to the USA in 1907 at the age of 16 and naturalized American by 1912, who convinced the Modern Language Association that a linguistic atlas of English in North America was a good idea as early as 1926, with fieldwork commencing in 1931. Kurath was also the initial force behind the *Middle English Dictionary*. There was Albert H. Marckwardt, dialectologist and historical linguist, who experimented with written questionnaires and theorized, among other things, about a linguistic colonial lag. Did Avis get infected with the workaholic bug in Ann Arbor? He must have had the bug earlier, because his Queen's MA thesis showed all the trappings of it.

Not only the right and the best people were present in Avis' own programme (English linguistics). There were, equally importantly, also the right people in the sister departments. Romance and Classical linguistics had Ernst Pulgram (1915–2005), who had escaped the Nazis in Vienna just hours before he, being of Jewish heritage, would have been taken into custody by the Vienna Gestapo (the Nazi secret police) and deported to a concentration camp, most probably to his death. The warning to leave Austria, just a week before his scheduled doctoral defence at Vienna University and the evening before his planned imprisonment, came from a personal friend of his who was a Nazi working for the Gestapo. This Nazi friend did him a great service and showed how bizarre 1930s Vienna must have been, but also that some acts of kindness were present even in this most brutal and inhumane of regimes. As a result, Pulgram survived, but had to start over with his Ph.D. when in Michigan, where he studied under the GI Bill. (In between, he had gone to Europe as a US solider, fighting to liberate his former home.)[7]

There were still more big names at Ann Arbor. There was Upper-Austrian Herbert Penzl (1910–95), who was one of the greats in German, English, and, by strange coincidence, Afghan linguistics. Penzl studied under renowned English historical linguist Karl Luick at Vienna University and went on to a career in the USA, around the time of the Berlin Olympics in 1936 – originally with a recommendation from fellow Viennese Sigmund Freud. This led him, via Brown University in Rhode Island and work on the New England part of the *Linguistic Atlas*, to Michigan, where he taught from 1950 to 1963, when Avis was there. At that point, Penzl moved on to Berkeley, but "he basked in the glow of Michigan's unchallenged productive atmosphere for current linguistic research", reportedly saying that "Michigan seemed like heaven to me", as the obituary quotes the man (Emenau *et al.* 1995: 146).

In this "heaven" was also Kenneth Lee Pike (1912–2000), another towering figure, who, with the Christian stance he's often been criticized for, "studied well over a hundred indigenous languages in the field" and founded and ran for many years the Summer Institute of Linguistics (SIL) (Headland 2004: 288). After graduating from Michigan under Fries and examiner Leonard Bloomfield, the great American structuralist, Pike continued to work there for almost six decades.

The Midwest was simply the place to be for dialectology, historical linguistics, and sociolinguistics. If that armada of expertise in Ann Arbor was not enough, Fred Cassidy was nearby in Madison, Wisconsin, whetting his appetite on what was to become the *Dictionary of American Regional English* (*DARE*) by 1965. *DARE* can be considered the best historical dictionary for its unequalled detail and wonderful treatment of regional (and, to a degree, social) variation. The talent pool in the middle of the US plains was truly remarkable, so much so that Avis got the best of the best in nearly everything he did. McDavid, who would succeed Kurath as *Linguistic Atlas* director, spent a year in Ann Arbor to finish off his "retraining" as a linguist, as he called it. (His Ph.D. was in Milton studies.) Wally Avis was there, then in his role as teaching assistant, and he taught McDavid (1981: 119) a great deal.

For his Ph.D. dissertation, however, Avis took a different tack than one might expect. Probably listening to his advisor Hans Kurath, Avis did *not* embark on a topic of Canadian English at the time, sticking instead with the New England mid-back vowels for which data already existed from the atlas. Kurath may have had good reason to discourage the Canadian topic that was closer to Avis' heart. We may speculate that, with a Ph.D. in a Canadian topic, Avis would have seemed much less attractive for the American, British, and, by way of the colonial inferiority complex, even the Canadian markets at the time. But we may indeed wonder what might have happened had Avis carried out a study of similar detail on a Canadian topic. Be that as it may, the effect was that Avis did not do an awful lot with his Ph.D. dissertation (Avis 1955b), apart from publishing a few years later an updated, concise version as Avis (1961). This meant that, straight out of grad school, Avis had to reinvent himself as a Canadian linguist and was unable to use the thesis as a spring-board, which cost him valuable time. As he did not have that many years left, listening to his advisor may have cut short the number of Canadian projects Avis was able to finish; his record remains impressive, regardless.

Two Workaholics: Lovell and Avis

From the archival record, we are in the position to reconstruct some of the exchanges between these two pioneers of Canadian English. Their letters are our little flies on the walls of these long-gone scholars. We know, for instance, that, even before Avis took over from Lovell as Chief Editor in 1960, he was involved in the dictionary and would have played a major role in it regardless. So, for instance, on 30 March 1955, less than a year after the idea of Canadian dictionaries was first vented at the founding meeting of the Canadian Linguis-tic Association, and two years prior to any significant support, Avis wrote to Lovell about sorting and alphabetizing some slips:

I've been working at alphabetizing several boxes of slips – a most boring chore. By the way, you might see if you can get the cartons in which 48 boxes of Jell-O are packed; they are dandy for filing about 3,000 4 x 6 slips. (Avis to Lovell, 30 March 1955, University of Victoria Archives, 90–66)

There are practical tips on which cartons work better for the 4- x 6-inch slips that were the "technology" behind dictionaries till about the year 2000. We do not know to which slips Avis is referring – perhaps part of Lovell's collection – but they seem to have been dealing with thousands of slips at that point already.

Lovell and Avis were getting ready to present the material in the orderly fashion required for such projects as early as 1954/55. We know from Avis' later letters that Lovell, always pressed for time, with no funding of any sort, was not the most tidy record keeper, so it is not a coincidence that Avis gives tips on organization above. At that point, however, Lovell was already a sick man. Avis was still healthy, but Lovell definitely not so. Lovell had been working in the Chicago offices of Mitford Mathews' team for the *Dictionary of Americanisms* since 1951 and, after suffering a serious setback to his health in 1953, Lovell was forced to avoid the long commute from Willow Springs, IL, to downtown Chicago and to work from home. That Lovell certainly, much like Avis, was a workaholic can be gleaned from his 3 January 1954 letter to Avis. Replying to Avis' letter, Lovell wrote:

When your [Avis'] letter came yesterday nothing would do but that I must answer it at once, so I sat down and did about 2 pages, taking up each subject in detail. But I taxed my strength too much, and am feeling bum again today. So I'll have to wait a month or so hence, until I can complete the letter. (Lovell to Avis, 3 Jan. 1954, University of Victoria Archives, 90–66)

It seems that Lovell replied to lexical queries from Avis, whom he would have first met at the inaugural meeting of the CLA in Manitoba later in 1954 (usually around late May). By answering to specific queries in a fact-checking manner, Lovell must have exploited his weakened body more than he had anticipated.

The two became friends, the one at RMC and soon-to-be a Ph.D. holder from Ann Arbor, while the other had in terms of formal education nothing but a high school degree and the respect of both Mencken and Mathews. On 30 March 1955, the two men performed in their letter the ritual of switching to a first-name basis. Avis, as the more senior in the academic hierarchy, offered what in French would be *tu* and in German *du* but in English is just a plain "first-name basis", which meant something in the day (unlike today in Canada, where most strangers are addressed with first names alone):

Dear Wally:
Ok – if it makes you happy, "Wally" and "Charlie" it is! (Lovell to Avis, 30 March 1955, University of Victoria Archives, 90–66)

From then on until Lovell's death, Wally and Charlie would pan out the best route towards *DCHP-1*, and we can only wonder what role Lovell, formally appointed Chief Editor in 1958 by W. J. Gage Ltd, would have bestowed on Avis in that project.

To give you a better idea of the kind of "obsessed" workaholics they were, here is Lovell's depiction of him working – mind you, not two years after his heart attack – on the material he cared for so much:

Dear Wallie [sic!]:
Have been working 12 hours or so a day, 7 days a week, on DCE [*Dictionary of Canadian English*] research, for 3 straight weeks. The absence of my family has given me such an excellent opportunity for work that I can't pass it up. (Lovell to Avis, 9 April 1955, University of Victoria Archives, 90–66)

Even the very healthy, fit, and young researcher would feel the toll of working 84-plus hours a week over three weeks without any noticeable break. Clearly, this was not a good thing for someone who was recuperating from a heart condition. We can only speculate how the off-on of sitting down without end and then going for mountain hikes, which he would occasionally still do, would have affected Lovell's health.

It is also useful to put the activity of these two men in relation to what was going on in the CLA at the time – the one body that would offer a venue for all those with an interest in Canadian English. Chomskyan linguistics was not yet around the corner and neither was Labovian variationism, so it seems that there would have been interest from a wide range of scholars.

As in most – if not all – societies, the work in the CLA was done by but a few hands. It is fair to say, if the correspondence in the mid-1960s can be trusted, that without Avis there would probably be no CLA today, as it would have folded around 1963–64, which was reported as its worst year. Today, the CLA is very different in character and a forum for, mostly, generative linguistics – linguistics of the Chomskyan kind that is, in its abstractness, a far cry from Avis' work.[8]

Avis the Dictionary Editor

Wally came to dictionary editing by chance, not design: trained as a historical linguist and dialect geographer (language in geographical and social space), editing *DCHP-1* and its sister dictionaries was a task that needed to be done, not one that he would have chosen, had Lovell lived. I don't think, actually, there is much debate as to whether Avis would have become a dictionary editor under other circumstances; he would have contributed to the dictionary, that much is for sure, but he would not have taken the helm. Who would voluntarily do that? Yet Avis did.

In Avis' case, he had already made a name for himself in cutting-edge cross-border research and he had a lot of opportunities lined up for himself. The choice was all his, and yet he rescued the project that seemed dead in its tracks with Lovell's passing. As Raven I. McDavid put it, after Avis wrote his initial papers in the 1950s on the dialect geography of Canadian English (written while doing his Ph.D. thesis on the mid-back vowels in the Eastern USA), he took on the role of observer and benevolent commentator, rather than researcher, in the field of dialect geography proper. The reader may speculate why we have Canadian English dictionaries today, but no Canadian English linguistic atlas.

After Lovell's unexpected death in March 1960, the entire dictionary programme's future was at stake: beyond the flagship historical dictionary, *DCHP-1*, the Gage publishing house wanted a three-tiered graded dictionary series for schools – a very bold idea for a country that had only comparatively recently begun to consider itself a nation in its own right. Dictionaries of Canadian English were only one type of dictionary that the new nation would require. The Canadian Linguistic Association's newly founded lexicographical committee was left with a crisis in its biggest language, English. Here is how Scargill, in his capacity as Chair of that committee, described the committee for the preface of *DCHP-1*:

At the founding meeting of the Canadian Linguistic Association, held at the University of Manitoba in 1954, some discussion was given to the possibility of preparing dictionaries of Canadian English; but it was not until 1957 that the Association established a Lexicographical Committee to begin promoting and co-ordinating lexicographical work in Canada. The membership of the original committee was as follows: M. H. Scargill (Chairman); H. Alexander; W. S. Avis; W. H. Brodie; P. Daviault; R. J. Gregg; C. J. Lovell; J. E. Robbins; G. M. Story; J. P. Vinay; H. R. Wilson. Since 1957, separate committees have been established to deal with French-Canadian and Ukrainian lexicography and with dialect studies. (Scargill 1967)

The all-male committee, in line with our findings in Chapter 2 about the missing matrilineage, was composed of a who's who in Canadian linguistics; besides Scargill, Henry Alexander was present as the most senior linguist at the time.

Who, though, were the other people on the committee? Avis, as one of the young Ph.D. holders in linguistics, was hailing from the undisputed centre of English linguistics in the 1940s and 1950s. He was trained exceptionally well. W. H. "Steve" Brodie was the first supervisor of broadcast language. As "Brodie embodied the corporate CBC language attitude" (McGovern 1989: 10), he was an influential man, setting the CBC pronunciation norms that were broadcast coast to coast. There was Pierre Daviault, President of the Royal Society of Canada in the 1950s and instrumental in setting up professional translation services in Canada. Robert J. Gregg, hailing from Northern Ireland with a Ph.D. in linguistics, would eventually make the University of British Columbia his academic home and managed to produce innovative work in Canadian English well into the 1980s, and, above all, in Ulster Scots, on which he is to this day an authority.[9]

Lovell is, since Chapter 2, no stranger to us. Other members of the lexicographical committee were equally of high standing. There was also J. E. Robbins, director of the Division of Education Statistics with Statistics Canada, who was completing *Encyclopedia Canadiana* at the time; George M. Story from Newfoundland, who'd go on to become the initiator behind the *Dictionary of Newfoundland English*; Jean-Paul Vinay, the Montreal-based lexicographer of French who moved to the University of Victoria; and, finally, H. Rex Wilson, who worked at the University of Western Ontario and was later Executive Secretary of the American Dialect Society. Wilson's (1958) Ph.D. thesis on the dialect of Lunenburg County, NS, is an early scientific dialect study.

That Avis achieved so much in his relatively short career becomes especially clear in comparison to the very talented pool of University of Michigan graduates, his peers:

of the graduate students attending Michigan at that time, Wally's career stands out. Most had as good training; most had better opportunities for research at their institutions; most had as understanding and supportive families. Yet none achieved as much. (McDavid 1981: 123)

As of the mid-1950s, there were a lot of options for Avis. At the time, anyone with a Ph.D. in basically any field had a good range of choices, and it is a safe bet that the task of dictionary editor was not one he would have chosen. However, as the need arose in the wake of Lovell's death, Avis took charge. It's the kind of service whose likelihood decreases as the sense of entitlement in the student population increases. It's just a hunch, but there is a sentiment that the World War II generation somehow grew up doing what was required. In 1957–58, what was then called the University of Alberta, Calgary, and what would later morph into the University of Calgary, became the first home of *DCHP-1*, and while materials arrived from its various contributors, the editorial work, in Scargill's words prior to 1963, "proceeded very slowly" (1967). It "was obvious that arrangements would have to be made to free one of our colleagues from his [*sic*] normal academic work so that he [*sic*] could devote at least a full year to dictionary editing" (*ibid.*). Who raised his hand? Avis.

Supported by a Canada Council (now SSHRC) Senior Fellowship, Avis was eventually able to spend the full academic year of 1963–64 at the Lexicographical Centre in Calgary and worked his b*tt off:

By the summer of 1964, as a result of [Avis'] hard work, it was thought possible to advance the publication date of the dictionary from 1970 to 1967. (Scargill 1967)

This assessment suggests that Scargill, who was located in both Calgary and Victoria, preferred not to carry the big editorial load himself; this task was left to Avis, who visited the collection twice, first in Calgary for a full year, and once more, in the summer of 1965, in Victoria. For the rest of the time, Avis corresponded with the Lexicographical Centre, where it was assistant Joan Hall, as we have already seen in Chapter 2, who enabled Avis to do the job.

The question of how much actual editing work Scargill did needs to be asked; it seems that, in any case, Scargill preferred to coordinate and plan and lobby for the project. In the context of the *OED*, perhaps the most famous lobbyist was Frederick J. Furnivall, and this role for *DCHP-1*, if my reading of the files is correct, would fall fair and square to Scargill. From Scargill's preface to *DCHP-1*, we also know that from 1964 onwards Douglas Leechman, who had retired to Victoria, was an official research associate at the Centre and worked from that point towards the publication of the dictionary in 1967. Furthermore, in the summer of 1966, Chuck Crate, whom J. K. Chambers quite aptly considers the "mystery man" (pers. correspondence) among the Big Six, joined the Centre for work on site.

The correspondence between Mr Avis and Ms Hall testifies to the cumber-some method of shipping quotation slips back and forth, sending queries in the mail, and keeping copies of what was sent. When a package of thousands of unique quotation slips was once delayed by a few weeks, everybody got very nervous. Luckily, Canada Post saved the day when the package resurfaced unscathed after a little while. Some of the lighter parts of the correspondence we have seen already in Chapter 2. From these texts, we also get a glimpse of the awkward nature of work in the pre-digital age, in a country as vast as Canada, with the main proponents located thousands of miles apart from one another and no feasible way to replicate or make back-up copies of the all-important "slips".

We know, in the context of the *Oxford English Dictionary*, of Murray's hunt for quotation slips that had been given out by his predecessor Frederick James Furnivall to "sub editors" years and decades earlier.[10] In *DCHP-1*, the location of the slips was mostly known, but the logistics of so many cooks dealing with the same broth was the problem: Lovell, Crate, Avis, Leechman, all keeping files of their own, with Scargill and Drysdale either learning to extract and collect quotations, or already beginning their own files.

Everything had to be carried back and forth physically – not just slips but also people. For instance, on 14 September 1964, Avis writes to Joan Hall[11] about their tire blowout some 200 km before Kingston on the way back from Calgary, which greatly inconvenienced Avis and his wife, who were travelling with their 3-year-old son John. This accident must have happened just before the dictionary materials were moved from Calgary to Victoria.

We will hear in the next chapter about the "slips", which are paper filing cards that used to be required for any dictionary that aimed to describe and document a variety. When we were working on the second edition, *DCHP-2*, some fifty years after the original team worked on the first, we did so in a digital context: at www.dchp.ca/dchp2, you can access this representative of the first born-digital generation of historical dictionaries. For *DCHP-2*, my associate editor(s) and I, student editors, student researchers, volunteers, IT programmers, and proofreaders worked remotely on one and the same copy. While this was difficult enough, it pales in comparison with what the editors of *DCHP-1* – which we digitized at www.dchp.ca/dchp1 – had to go through.

Postage was a big thing, an enormous expense. While cheap in the day, it added up: stationery, envelopes, carbon sheets, morning and evening deliver-ies. *DCHP-2* was very different from *DCHP-1* in that regard. When I did get a real, physical letter in the *DCHP-2* editing process, as opposed to an email, it was from Bonnie Lovell, who had read about *DCHP-2* in some news coverage and, bibliophile that she is, wanted to say hello in style rather than with an email. Our editing process, while not without its profound challenges, was a great deal more convenient (and faster!) than half a century earlier. So much so that it is hard for me to imagine how Avis pulled it off. But pull it off he did!

The next chapter will be the most detailed one in respect to the actual making of a dictionary in the mid twentieth century: its "technology", technique, methodology, process, and, of great relevance in all such projects but often overlooked, logistics and funding – including budgeting for postage! As it all boils down to having the right slips in the right place at the right time in the right quantity to be handled by the right editor who has acquired the right background knowledge, preferably all with the right (and complete) bibliographical information, the next chapter will revolve around the "slip". Before we go there, though, let us address *DCHP-1*'s reading programme and Avis' slowly failing health. As it turns out, Avis managed to do the legwork behind *DCHP-1* in record time despite considerable health problems.

Doing the Legwork

Who collected the slips, handled them, retyped them, sorted them, and made sure that they, as unique resources, were in the right place with the right person at the right time? There is very good evidence in the archival files that – apart from Lovell, who brought in the original collection and thus the lion's share – Avis, Crate, and Leechman were responsible for the bulk of data collection and the editing work on *DCHP-1* in the years 1963–67. In 1967, the focus shifted from collecting to editing, though collecting never stopped. The cut-off date seems to have been 1966, as the youngest quotations are from that year. While Avis, Crate, and Leechman brought in the additional material on top of the Lovell collection, this statement of fact is not intended to diminish the important roles of Drysdale on the publishing end in Toronto, and Scargill, who ran the show as director of the Lexicographical Centre in Victoria. To employ hockey[12] terminology, if Drysdale was the head coach, Scargill was the president who argued with the league (the funding agencies, the university administration, and the press landscape) and took charge of the PR aspect and did all other higher-level tasks that the star players of the team – the Wayne Gretzkys, Sidney Crosbys, and Gordie Howes – did not have time for or did not want to do. Scargill created the team, while Drysdale ran the operation and made sure the right lines were out on the ice (i.e., Avis had the resources he needed). Avis, with the *C* for "captain" on his imaginary jersey, ran the show and orchestrated his left winger (Leechman) and blue liner (Crate), who all grew with the challenge.

Lexicography, like hockey perhaps, is a special skill that you become better and faster at if you have the right talents. These four men – Avis, Crate, Leechman, and Lovell – surely had the patience, tenacity, attention to detail, and, in the last instance, passion, to see through the data-collecting, editing, tracking-down of evidence, compiling of the long bibliographical list, and proofreading. They shared the necessary qualities, of which Murray, Craigie,

Burchfield, Simpson, or Wilhelm and Jakob Grimm, among others, had so much. To anyone using Canadian English, they should be remembered as the people who, essentially, created Canadian English – with Scargill's and Drysdale's important help. True, the usage patterns and the meanings are profoundly Canadian and no one but the Canadian collective may lay claim to them: they were created by the invisible Canadian hand that is behind all social developments in this country. But the patterns' discovery and documentation and, to use Einar Haugen's term, their codification in dictionaries is the accomplishment of the Big Six alone. All of us scholars who came later and are working on Canadian English, in whatever aspect, owe a debt of gratitude to them.

At the end of the first term of his stay in Calgary, Avis wrote an interim report on the progress of the dictionary, just before Christmas 1963, emphasizing the

generous and extensive assistance being afforded me by the University of Alberta, Calgary. I have been provided with spacious and well-equipped quarters, as well as with a full-time assistant and such part-time help as is necessary to keep reasonably up to date with the filing. Without such co-operation, I would have little chance of getting control of this outsize undertaking. (Avis in Calgary, interim report, 15 Dec. 1963, University of Victoria Archives, 90–66)

This note is interesting, as it means that Avis did get help in the form of one full-time assistant, from his sabbatical's host university, which, it is to be assumed, was arranged by Scargill who had been at Calgary for a while and who often took care of the bigger constraints, facilitating the work being done. While Scargill was in Calgary, the linguistics programme was also expanded and, with his moving to the University of Victoria in the fall of 1964, there was an opportunity for more than a good share of hires. There is a chance that the Calgary assistant was also Joan Hall, as at no point is any mention made of her being trained at the University of Victoria.[13]

On the topic of changing employers, Avis writes to Jean-Paul Vinay, Professor of Linguistics in Montreal, shortly before the latter's relocation to the University of Victoria, revealing aspirations that scholars usually keep close to their chests:

At Calgary, some provision is being made to advance linguistics, the first step being to bring Hunter Smeaton here, and the second, so far unsuccessful, an attempt to bring me out here [to Calgary] permanently. (Avis to Vinay, 15 Oct. 1963, University of Victoria Archives, 90–66)

If Avis had had hopes of transferring from RMC Kingston to Calgary, the hopes were at least temporarily quashed. In the end, however, even postpublication, Avis, the undisputed expert in Canadian English, would stay in Kingston with a teaching and administrative load that was anything but ideal for a researcher like him. Today, the annual RMC Walter S. Avis Lecture remembers this giant of a scholar in his home academic setting. The connection between RMC and Avis is a little bit like Stephen Hawking having worked at Victoria's Camosun College – a very fine institution but not the best place for the top theoretician on the evolution of the universe.

Help from the Public

At the outset of research on this book, it appeared that *DCHP-1* did not obtain substantial volunteer help. That is certainly the impression I've had all along until I found contradictory evidence in the archives. Compared to the public support harnessed by the *OED*, *DCHP-1* volunteer work may seem small but it was not insignificant. It is indeed easy to fall short in a comparison with the one project in English language and linguistics, the *OED*, that set the bar for PR and outreach so incredibly high. Before Murray even joined the project officially in 1879, 1.5 million quotation slips had been collected since 1857, mostly by volunteers of the Philological Society. In 1957, when, after a hiatus of a generation (and a World War), work on further supplements to the *OED* began again in earnest with the appointment of New Zealander Robert Burchfield as Chief Editor (once more, outsider alert), the successful engagement of public volunteer readers was once more stressed. As Burchfield wrote at the time, "it is quite clear that production of the Supplement will only be possible if we can persuade a great many more people to start hunting for quotations" (Burchfield, 18 July 1957, quoted in Gilliver 2016: 454).

The *DCHP-1* reading programme was the brainchild of Scargill. He would later go on to coordinate the national *Survey of Canadian English* (Scargill and Warkentyne 1972) in the fall of 1971, and it seems he cut his teeth on what appears to have been a 1957–59 programme, eliciting help from the public for *DCHP-1* and its sister dictionaries. The goal was "to have a substantial field of citation slips assembled by April, 1959". The call is not nearly as nicely printed or as targeted as Burchfield's appeals to the public, which started around the same time and listed terms that needed antedatings and documentation. Scargill's scheme was more general. Figure 12 shows Scargill's instructions, which are followed by a second page, listing "good sources" and detailing the format of the quotation slips with instructions.

It is difficult to estimate precisely how much help with the quotations, the heavy front-end work in (historical) lexicography, was available to *DCHP-1*, short of documenting and counting the readers' names and submissions in the 102,000 quotation slips that comprise its backbone but are not the complete collection of quotations that were used. It seems, however, that what is there is made up, first and foremost, of the quotations by Lovell (about 50 per cent),

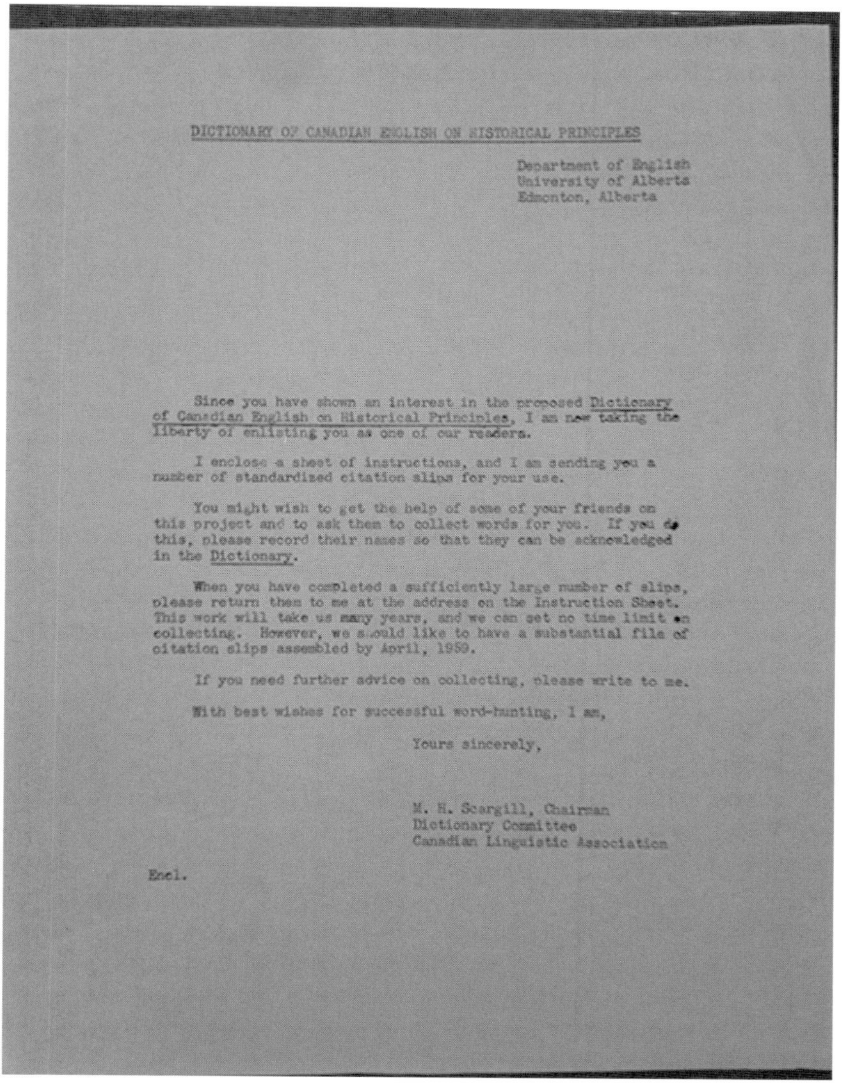

DICTIONARY OF CANADIAN ENGLISH ON HISTORICAL PRINCIPLES

Department of English
University of Alberta
Edmonton, Alberta

Since you have shown an interest in the proposed Dictionary
of Canadian English on Historical Principles, I am now taking the
liberty of enlisting you as one of our readers.

I enclose a sheet of instructions, and I am sending you a
number of standardized citation slips for your use.

You might wish to get the help of some of your friends on
this project and to ask them to collect words for you. If you do
this, please record their names so that they can be acknowledged
in the Dictionary.

When you have completed a sufficiently large number of slips,
please return them to me at the address on the Instruction Sheet.
This work will take us many years, and we can set no time limit on
collecting. However, we should like to have a substantial file of
citation slips assembled by April, 1959.

If you need further advice on collecting, please write to me.

With best wishes for successful word-hunting, I am,

Yours sincerely,

M. H. Scargill, Chairman
Dictionary Committee
Canadian Linguistic Association

Encl.

Figure 12 Info. sheet for the reading programme (Scargill, late 1950s)
(University of Victoria Archives, 90–66, Box 3; photo: S. Dollinger)

Avis, Crate, and to a lesser degree by Leechman — so, four of the Big Six, but there is good evidence that substantial parts of the collection are missing.

There have been outside submissions, however. The table on the word *Stickeen* in Chapter 4 lists, for instance, thirteen quotations, three of which are by unidentified contributors, which would be submissions by volunteers. There are other indicators, too. Lovell, for instance, refers to slips provided by John Lyman on nautical terms in *M* in a letter to Avis dated 30 January 1960, and a request to be sent more. A volunteer called Patricia S. Barry offered material on the Canadian Arctic, which included an "8-page list of catchwords and special constructions" that she collected in the Western Arctic (letter to Avis, dated 22 April 1962). A certain Grace S. Lewis, from Yarmouth, NS, sent in at least four letters with information on Maritimes English but not in the quotation slip format that Scargill would have preferred. In addition, Ms Lewis informs *DCHP-1* that J. E. Goudey had recently worked on *cat spruce*, *canoe*, *moccasin*, *fly beer*, and possibly *for grass* but we do not know in which form or at whose behest, if anyone's. This is very precise information indeed, from volunteers who are not listed in *DCHP-1*.

While the final verdict remains to be made, it is a safe bet to say that outside and volunteer help for *DCHP-1* was not unimportant. If three of thirteen *Stickeen* slips are from non-Big Sixers, an estimate of the number of outside quotations might come in at a quarter of the total, though that rate seems too high. Perhaps 5 per cent came from the public? It would be somewhere around there – not much more, in any case. For this question, further study (and counting) would be required to calculate a more accurate figure and to identify individual volunteer readers for *DCHP-1*. In the case of the *OED*, very interesting stories were unearthed, including that of mid-nineteenth-century grammar–school Professor Hartwich Richard Helwich from Oberdöbling in Vienna's bourgeois 19th district. Helwich extracted the entire Middle English *Cursor Mundi* and contributed no fewer than 50,000 quotations. Or the infamous murderer and madman, W. C. Minor, who was written into widespread fame in Simon Winchester's *The Professor and the Madman*. Minor shared a philological bond with Murray more than anyone else, perhaps, making a mind-blowing contribution to the *OED* and the English language from his prison cell. For the most part, however, volunteers remained, like Helwich, the unsung heroes of *OED*.

Who, we may wonder, were the Helwichs and Minors among the *DCHP-1* volunteer readers? This question remains yet to be explored.

The Ailing Chief Editor

We said earlier that Lovell and Avis, both driven by what they saw as something that needed to be done, probably worked themselves to their deaths.

There is solid evidence for this interpretation in the extant letters. We know from Drysdale's (1980) text that Avis had been living with a heart condition for upwards of a dozen years, which means during the time he was working on *DCHP-1*.

Then, in a letter dated 20 April 1965, Avis writes to Joan Hall the following telling lines, indicating earlier medical problems for the then 45-year-old:

Sorry for the delay. Have been in hospital for about two weeks but am much better now. Hope all is going well. I am, as ever, up to my neck in work.

Sick in the hospital but "as ever" up to his "neck in work". This sounds, from today's perspective, like the perfect recipe for a heart attack. It is one thing that Avis called the packages of quotation slips "bundles of joy" (Avis, added on 20 January 1965 to a letter by Hall, dated 11 January 1965), but it's quite another when the person cannot stop, as if they are addicted to the task and thus neglecting their health. So, just eight days after informing Hall about this hospital stay and having confessed to being swamped with work, he writes for yet more work:

You had better send me "R"; I expect to be through "P" before mid-May and I should be able to get a lot of the "R" done before I reach Victoria. WSA (Avis to Hall, 28 Apr. 1965, University of Victoria Archives, 90–66)

Avis was to spend the summer of 1965 in Victoria to edit more efficiently. While there, he would attend a conference on lexicography with Scargill, Leechman, and others, on which occasion Leechman would be giving a paper on the origins of *hootch*, which refers to *home brew* and, in a second meaning, by extension, to any alcoholic drink (see www.dchp.ca/dchp2/Entries/view/ hootch for the legacy entry from *DCHP-1*).

It is remarkable that, instead of taking the summer off to relax from his duties at RMC and to recuperate from his hospitalization, which today would almost certainly include making changes to his daily routines, Avis plunged right into a most intensive work period in Calgary, feeling the full brunt of the project whose fortunes rested so much on his shoulders. There was no word of rehabilitation stays or rest and recuperation to recover from the heart attack, however. He had to prove to the publisher, the Canada Council, and his colleagues and peers that such a dictionary could be produced. That's not good for anyone's health, generally speaking, and an aspect that is difficult to grasp for anyone who plays second fiddle in any project or is an associate or assistant of some sort. When the latter go home, the chief editor keeps working or at least thinking about the problems that lie ahead.

Figure 13 The "Quotation File" Room at Oxford University Press, Walton St. The *DCHP-1* collection was several magnitudes smaller. (Photo: S. Dollinger, 2013)

4   The "Technology": Slips, Slips, and More Slips

Busy as a bee and happy as a —— lexicographer?
Douglas Leechman to Wally Avis, 22 May 1964

PS: Thanks for the coupons; and please forgive this "Avis-Type" answer.
(Wally Avis to Joan Hall, 20 Jan. 1965, replying to her typed letter from 11 Jan. by adding handwritten comments in the margins; University of Victoria Archives, 90–66, Box 4 File 2)

Writing a dictionary requires hard, painstaking, and detailed work over prolonged periods of time. Dictionary work has traditionally started with *A* and, unless one was beyond *S* in English dictionary making – the letter with the most entries in that language – the odds were stacked against any particular project seeing the light of day. It is perhaps no overstatement to surmise that more dictionaries have landed on the junk heap of unfinished work than on bookshelves. In typical lexicographical understatement, this process, which is infinitely harder than writing "normal" books, is usually and in false modesty called "editing". This nomenclature has its origin in the idea that language is "out there" and therefore, unlike a book's idea that came from its author, *not* the idea of the lexicographer. While this might sound reasonable, the interpretation overlooks one crucial fact: no one out there "writes" a dictionary for you and, besides, how many ideas in the world are actually truly original ones that no one has thought about before? Very few, if you think of it. So let's call dictionary editors what they actually are: dictionary writers.

Dictionaries Are Written, Not Edited

A simple analogy will make this point clear. In the same sense as language is out there, Einstein's relativity theory is out there, too. No one, however, would for a minute think to say that Einstein did not write, but merely edited, the paper in which he predicted it. You get the idea: calling a dictionary "edited" puts it on the same level as editing other people's original ideas, which, while this is also very hard work and intellectually very challenging if done right, grossly understates the complexities of dictionary making.

So what is entailed in making a dictionary? While embarking on *DCHP-2*, I was made fun of by more than one of my friends (then in their late 20s or early 30s). One of them joked that one day I woke up with the idea in my mind, "Today, I'll write a dictionary." My old friend Jack Tse, himself an engineer and urban planner (so *very* down to earth), even presented me with a button showing a young Noah Webster with a speech bubble containing the above line. It's just the kind of ridicule one has to laugh with and I didn't mind – quite the contrary, I welcomed it. But, in reality, no one wakes up one morning with the wacky idea of writing a dictionary.

Why not? Because writing dictionaries is indeed a very strange activity, especially if one does so, as virtually all dictionary writers to this day do, in the nonsensical alphabetical order. Dictionaries are a very strange text type and genre. You can compare a dictionary editor (better: dictionary writer) with a musician who, rather than writing their own songs, meticulously studies some oeuvre – let's say all the 208 songs by The Beatles. The musician takes the songs apart, cadence by cadence and verse by verse, and then embarks on explaining in book form, line by line, why the Beatles were so good and what made them special. That would be strange, right?

But that's quite precisely the work that is entailed in writing a dictionary. The 1941 screwball comedy *Ball of Fire*, written by Viennese émigré Billy Wilder, makes that point very well. Gary Cooper, the middle-aged, handsome scholar – a generation or two younger than the rest of his colleagues – is enthralled by Barbara Stanwyck's character of a 1940s jazz singer. Having been socialized in his ivory tower of learning, Cooper's character is nonetheless magically attracted to that femme fatale and fails to see she is entangled with the Mafia. Bad boys and girls are oh-so-attractive. While others are fighting for their lives, Cooper's lexicographical character tries to document the slang he hears. The movie shows a clash of worlds: the stale academic world and a jazzed-up world of the femme fatale whose boyfriend is a Mafioso and who knows the coolest slang but won't share it when asked.[1] It is this tension that the movie thrives on: the life-endangering brush with the mob, and the professor's utterly abstract, and socially void and sterile, attempts to improve his entry on *slang*. In the process, of course, the femme fatale shows him, more by happenstance than by design, that there is more to life than books.

Dictionaries are even a bit of a strange animal to some of the people who should know quite a bit about them. They are, for lack of a better word, very different from any other kind of book. Take book publishers, for instance, which are the companies that take your manuscript and turn it into a beautiful printed book. Even some very experienced publishing houses, some of them having been around for decades or even centuries, have little or no experience in publishing newly written dictionaries. Sidney Landau, who was in the

American dictionary-writing business for almost the entire second half of the last century, has clear words about this little-known fact:

Usually the publisher is ignorant as to what's involved in preparing a dictionary, and the lexicographer is quite irresponsibly optimistic.... [A dictionary] is usually written simultaneously by a great many people who must be trained and supervised and persuaded to follow a set of consistent rules. . . . It's an awful job getting *any* dictionary written, even a bad one. (Landau 2001: 347–48)

So dictionary writing and publishing is a gamble, and there is a long record of projects being abandoned even after decades of work on them, without much to show for it. Bad dictionaries, as Landau writes, may still be a lot of work, but – and this is the sad news – they may even pay off financially more than good ones, which is probably a good reason why bad dictionaries are quite numerous on the market. Good marketing and PR are often used to camouflage defects – usually successfully so, because who actually *reads* dictionaries? Even worse, sometimes good dictionaries do *not* pay off commercially, usually for all the wrong reasons. And sometimes, bad dictionaries are extraordinarily successful, just because no one has bothered to take a closer look. Why not? Because it's not just odd to write dictionaries, it's also odd to review them competently – it's so much easier to *trust* them. But, overall, even in the cut-throat world of dictionary publishing (see the section on the Great Canadian Dictionary War in Chapter 7), quality has a decent chance of winning the day. That is as good as the news on dictionary publishing gets. So, you see, it's a bit of a loaded game from the start, with the odds stacked against anyone with the wacky idea of writing a dictionary.

What Is a "Quotation Slip"?

Today, any dictionary that is worth its salt must start with a database of neatly organized bits of language: the quotation file (which is usually *citation file* in the American lexicographical tradition). The more bits of language there are in the quotation database, the merrier. Back in the day – as late as about the year 2000, to the surprise of the tech-savvy reader – quotation files were generally in *paper format*. I repeat: on PAPER. This has only to a small degree to do with the non-avant-garde tech behaviour of lexicographers (refer to the screwball comedy *Ball of Fire* from before) and much more so with the problem of integrating older paper quotation files with newer quotations in digital formats. The legacy data on paper have made the adoption of digital modes in the dictionary world so much harder.

So what is a "quotation slip" – sometimes called *citation slip*, or just *citation* (US) or *quotation* (UK), with Canada somewhere in the middle using both? We will settle on *quotation slip* or simply *quotation* or *slip*. It's usually a 4- by

6-inch piece of paper that contains one instantiation, one example, of a given word in authentic context, snipped from real-language use (such as a newspaper or a transcribed audio recording). Traditionally, quotations have been limited to the sentence (or clause) that the word in question – the "catchword" – appears in, but today more and more context is included in the hope that the data can be used for other linguistic purposes as well, such as historical syntax.

In *DCHP-2*, we usually included the entire paragraph in which the catchword occurred, plus the preceding and succeeding paragraphs, for the quotation database (the "Bank of Canadian English"). When we needed a quotation, we "clipped" the long quotations to the length that would work with the dictionary context. Traditionally, in non-digital contexts – which were all that there was until the 1990s – the catchword was presented in the sentence (sometimes just the clause) and occasionally, only if crucially needed, another sentence or two. But the more one copied out, the longer it took, and that time was then missing from somewhere else.

Slips are overly important; they are the *sine qua non* of lexicography. John Simpson, who retired as Chief Editor of the *OED* in the fall of 2013 after twenty years at the helm of the biggest dictionary operation on earth, knows a

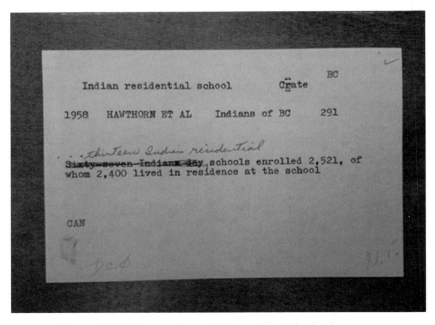

Figure 14 A 1958 quotation on *Indian residential school*.
The only one on file for that headword, with corrections by hand
(University of Victoria Archives 90–66, Box 18; photo: S. Dollinger, 2017)

thing or two about slips. Simpson recalls his first day on the *OED* staff in August 1976, when he was writing out example sentences on to "index cards called", as he would "soon learn, 'slips'" (Simpson 2016: 30).

Slips can be handwritten, typed out, or cut-and-pasted text from newspapers, books, fliers – you name it – on to the 4 x 6 slips. Figure 14 shows one such slip, extracted by Charles Crate on the headword (catchword) *Indian residential school*, which was a euphemism for a system of forceful and violent assimilation of Canada's Indigenous children and youth into mainstream white culture (so, a euphemism for cultural genocide).

The top left in Figure 14 shows the catchword, which often has a good chance of becoming a headword in the dictionary. In this case, the headword became *residential school*, though *Indian residential school* is also listed in *DCHP-1* with one quotation, but not the one shown here; this quotation remains unpublished. The quote in the picture is taken from the 1958 revised report of a 1955 University of British Columbia anthropological research project led by H. B. Hawthorn (see Hawthorn, Belshaw, and Jamieson 1958). The full context reads:

Sixty-seven Indian day schools, located on reserves, enrolled 3,118 children, and thirteen Indian residential schools enrolled 2,521, of whom 2,400 lived in residence at the school. Another 118 children lived at the residential schools and attended junior or senior high schools. Three hospital schools taught 166. The Indian Affairs Branch records show fifty-four children attending various institutions offering higher than a specialized or vocational education. The increasing achievement of the schools shows in the increased number in all higher grades. (Hawthorn, Belshaw, and Jamieson 1958: 291)

While the basic message is sad – the "achievement" doubtful and meagre by any standard, facts to which we shall turn in the decolonization chapter (Chapter 8)[2] – the larger context also shows how a lexicographical error was made in quotation extraction, which was later caught and corrected. In Figure 14, the subject of the first sentence, "Sixty-seven Indian day schools" was originally continued with the verb phrase of the second sentence "enrolled 2,521, of whom 2,400 lived in residence at the school"; the error can be attributed to skipping a line in the original layout.

In the image, we also see the reader's name (Charles Crate), the publication year (1958), author(s) (Hawthorn, Belshaw, and Jamieson), short title (Indians of BC), and page number (291). We can see the word *CAN* for a suggested Canadianism, which is not found in the Dictionary of Canadianisms (denoted in pencil as "DC 0"), probably referring to their work-in-progress headword list of what was then called "DC" – the *DCHP-1* they were compiling, or perhaps the *Intermediate Dictionary*, which was published in 1963. The term *BC* is shown for a BC regionalism, which turned out to be, with the knowledge of hindsight, not correctly labelled, since the gruesome institution called *residential school* was a national idea – and a very bad one. As can be seen, this slip is very neatly typed up, with the correction inserted by hand.

Many thousands to many millions of such slips provide the data that dictionaries are built from. You can see that it would take a while to collect such information, which is often the biggest deterrent to the prospective dictionary writer. On top of all this, there is a lot of information in any quotation database that is *not* used. In the *OED*, of about 5 million slips that were collected until the 1989 second edition, perhaps some 1.5 million were used. For *DCHP-1*, there were, by my count, probably around 130,000 quotation slips, of which 102,000 are located in the University of Victoria Archives today, while only 30,000 were printed and used in *DCHP-1*. So, one can see, *DCHP* is a tiny project compared to the *OED* (yet the ratio of collected to printed quotations is roughly the same).

In addition, there is a host of information in the *DCHP-1* file that was excluded "after much deliberation", as we know from Avis' introduction to *DCHP-1*. Figure 15 shows four such slips on *Stickeen*, a northern BC First Nation, which belong to a category of slips that were excluded quite late in the game on the principle that all First Nations and aboriginal names would be withheld entirely, presumably to save them for a more focussed publication; that publication unfortunately never appeared. There was so much material held back in the legacy file that another edition, a *DCHP-3*, is warranted on account of that material alone.

We can see, on the top left, the catchword under which the slip would be filed in alphabetical order, followed by the bibliographical detail, including the page number. On the top right we can see the name of the reader: two quotations by Lovell and one each by Avis and Crate.

The slips show various forms or spellings, including *Stickine*, and some word compounds, e.g. *Stickeen Territory*. There are in total thirteen quotations for that catchword in the legacy file, which are transcribed in Table 3. They range from 1859 right up to the publication period – in this case, 1964.

As you can see, the majority of quotations were typed out (* and no mark), which indicates a great deal of effort by the editorial team and, most likely, Joan Hall and, as far as we can reconstruct, one or two unknown Calgary assistants. As we speculated earlier, one of these was possibly also Joan Hall. We also know that Charles Crates' students from Alert Bay Elementary were "encouraged" to help with the typing, possibly for class credit. Most of them, if not all, were First Nations students, which, as we will see in Chapter 8, may represent a more subtle, undetected way of colonial imposition: Indigenous youth were used to type up material for a dictionary of the colonial language, Canadian English, when it would have served themselves and their culture so much more if they had worked on their own Indigenous languages.

These slips are the bricks and mortar from which the best and most suitable ones are selected for the construction of the dictionary text; it's a slow, bottom-up process that is difficult to coordinate. You can see in quotations 5 and 7 that Lovell extracted the same quotation twice, which shows the duplication

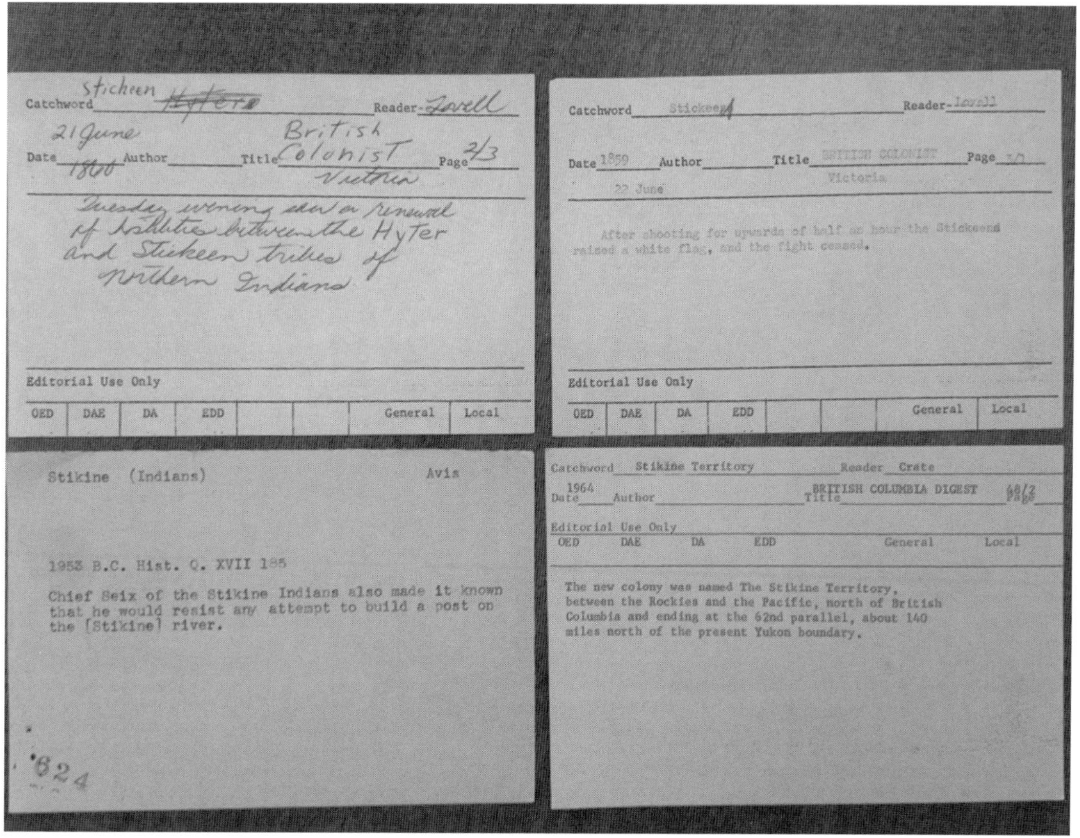

Figure 15 Quotation slips for *Stickeen* from *DCHP-1*
(University of Victoria Archives, 91–41, Box 8; photo: S. Dollinger, 2017)

Table 3 *The quotations for* Stickeen *in DCHP-1 legacy file (University of Victoria Archives, 91–41, Box 8)*

	Catchword	Date	Quotation	Reader	Codes
1.	Stickeens	1859	After shooting for upwards of half an hour the Stickeens raised a white flag, and the fight ceased.	Lovell	
2.	Stickeens*	1859	A large crowd rushed towards Victoria Bridge, and from there witnessed the fight bewteen [*sic*] the Songish Indians, on the west side of the Harbour, and the Stickeens on the eastern side.	N/A	44
3.	Stickeen	1859	An Indian woman, a Stickeen, was stabbed on Victoria bridge [*sic*], on Wednesday afternoon, by two Cowitchen Indians.	Lovell	
4.	Stickeen+	1860	The Stickeens and Tongas tribes have allied against the Hyders [*sic*] and fighting commenced at daylight on Sunday morning, and continued until noon of the same day.	Lovell	
5.	Stickeen+	1860	Tuesday evening saw a renewal of hostilities between the Hyter [*sic*] and Stickeen tribes of northern Indians.	Lovell	
6.	Stickeen+	1860	The Langley Indians caught two of the Stickeen tribe above Langley on Sunday last, and killed one.	Lovell	
7.	Stickeen+	1860	Tuesday evening saw a renewal of hostilities between the Hyter and Stickeen tribes of northern Indians.	Lovell	
8.	Stickeen Indian*	1880	This custom obtains also among the Tshinsians and Stickeen Indians.	N/A	# code illeg. (8_?)
9.	Stickeentribe*	1880	Among the Indians of the Stickine tribe, near the Alaska boundary, the obsequies have in some instances assumed a more serious aspect.	N/A	37
10.	Stikan (Indian), Stick (Indian), voyageur	1910	. . . a strayed Stikan from the coast stood side by side with a Stick from Lake LeBarge, and beyond, a half-dozen French-Canadian voyageurs, grouped by themselves.	Crate	(Yukon) USA
11.	Stickeen, Stickeen Territories	1914	The Stickeen Territories as separate from the Colony of British Columbia had but a short existence. In July 1863, an Act was passed by	Crate	(BC) CAN

Table 3 *(cont.)*

	Catchword	Date	Quotation	Reader	Codes
			the Imperial parliament whereby the greater part of Stickeen was included within the boundaries of the colony		
12.	Stikine (Indians)*	1953	Chief Seix of the Stikine Indians also made it known that he would resist any attempt to build a post on the [Stikine] river.	Avis	624
13.	Stikine Territory	1964	The new colony was named The Stikine Territory, between the Rockies and the Pacific, north of British Columbia and ending at the 62nd parallel, about 140 miles north of the present Yukon boundary	Crate	

Table 3 lists the catchwords, which are not uniform. The readers, who are listed on the right, generally used the forms from their particular contexts and, only if they knew for certain, a more standardized form. The diacritics next to the catchwords mean the following:

* = the quotation was not entered on a printed template card but some other paper
\+ = the note was handwritten
no mark = the quotation was typed on a printed template card (such as in Figure 15)
[the text is reproduced verbatim]

that inevitably occurs in even the best-managed of projects, slowing the process down further. Once you have the material, you start with the data and then seek to identify different meanings. To use another metaphor, dictionary writing is a bit like beginning university essay writing: there is so much you could say, but you can't say it unless you have documentation for it. And, as everyone who has tried to find proof for a given statement knows, locating sources post hoc is among the most tedious and most labour-intensive of work, which includes many false leads and "wasted" time.

Paddy Drysdale, the last surviving member of the *DCHP-1* team and formally "editor at large", informs me that he was generally not involved with the data collection, and that he was not an "editor at large", but more, in his words, an "editor of last resort". But he illustrates well the one occasion when he did get to try his hand at meaning differentiation, which is another way of trying to see the (semantic) forest for the (quotation slip) trees. Here's how Paddy put it:

one Friday I received from Kingston a package containing all the citation slips for *muskeg*. Wally had tried to break the uses of the words into discrete meanings but had given up and so asked me to try. I spent much of the weekend sorting the slips and came up with an answer. He then jiggled my results a bit and otherwise accepted them. (Paddy Drysdale: pers. correspondence, April 2018)

Stickeen is just one example in the First Nation band name file, and not the most complete one – not even close. This distinction might go to *Ojibway*, which comprises fifty-nine slips with compounds, such as *Ojibway Indian*. The five dozen or so quotations are a historical testament to how a western colonizing civilization was obsessed with the written medium and "moulded" terms and names which had been passed down in an elaborate, well-protected and revered oral tradition into the written medium. It is clear that the colonizers neither understood nor appreciated the oral tradition and these problems and conflicts are reflected in the wide range of spellings, as if the band names resisted the colonizers' attempt to make them fit their moulds.

The earliest of the quotations for *Ojibwa* is from 1793, and employs the spelling *Ibawa* for *Ojibwa*. The quotation as such confirms the typical late eighteenth-century colonial attitudes of superiority towards the aboriginal peoples:

Upon the departure of the Ibawa man, the Otawa Indian came often to my house and boasted of great feats that he had performed, particularly of his having killed three English like me, and said he would think nothing of killing me and my brother also. (Acc.#94–41, Box 8, from D. Ramsey, 1973. *Campbell Travel's*, p. 152)

It is important to note that many of the quotations related to First Nations peoples cast them in an unfavourable light, such as the one above or the top left (handwritten) quotation for *Stickeen*. So, by leaving these out, the editors – knowingly or not – kept a lot of disparaging language use in relation to the Indigenous population under wraps, simply because the colonial attitudes of much of Canada's history overrode the more positive sentiments of Indigenous–non-Indigenous relations. We address the colonial baggage of *DCHP-1* in Chapter 8, where we also explore pathways to decolonizing *DCHP-2* – then, now, and in possible future editions.

There are also more specialized slips in the file. For bigger terms, such as *Ojibway*, Avis wrote "overview slips", such as this one, which prefaces the alphabetically ordered sequence:

Ojibwa, n. or Ojibway, an Indian belonging to several organized bands of the Algonquian linguistic stock, living north of the Great Lakes in Ontario. Also Ojibbeway etc.

Besides another overview slip for *Ojibwa* (the language), there is another such overview for "Ojibwa, also attributive". So you see how the editor is trying to pre-sort it, all while the data keep coming in. The linguistic variation is difficult to handle though. For example, the spelling variants for *Ojibway*, which today is being replaced itself by *Anishnabe* (the preferred self-denominator, rather than the externally assigned *Ojibway*), are documented in the following spellings:

Ojibwa, Ojibway, Ojibeway, Ojibbeway, Ojibbewas, Ojibbewa, Ojibeway, Ojibbreways, Ojibbeways, Ojibbeway band, Ojibewa, Chippawa Indians, Ibawa, Otchibway Indians, Outchipwais, Chippewa bands, ojibway, Chippewa

Avis' preferred form was, judging from his three overview slips, *Ojibwa*, which he uses indiscriminately. This, of course, was long before the change to *Anishnabe* happened, which is now the preferred label for self- and external identification for many members.

While most of the evidence in the files for *Ojibway* – as for most terms, actually – dates from the eighteenth and nineteenth centuries, or what scholars call the Late Modern English period, there are also profoundly older attestations that form part of early Canadian English. A case in point are the quotations for *Mohawk*, the oldest of which date from 1694 and 1697 from the *Kelsey Papers* (the quotations were extracted from a 1929 edition):

To day about noon ye french came to ye woods Edge & fired some guns at us & so we went away we [*sic*] have a discription [*sic*] y^t they have brought mohocks (*Kelsey Papers*, 1694, quoted in Doughty and Martin 1929: 41)

This evidence exhibits features typical of Early Modern English, the English of Shakespeare's period, such as its shortenings of articles and pronouns *the* (y^e) and *that* (y^t). For the Eastern USA, we have studies on Early Modern English, e.g. on the Salem witchcraft trials,[3] but nothing of the sort has yet been attempted for Canada, beyond two monographs for eighteenth- and nineteenth-century Ontario English.[4] In this context, the inclusion of Early Modern evidence in *DCHP-1* is quite sensational: the Big Six were half a century ahead of the curve.

Occam's Razor: the Case of *Canuck*

While the specifics of interpretation and sense-making in historical linguistics are not the focus of this book,[5] we should say a little bit about how linguists make sense of all the many quotations and arrive at consistent, plausible, and sometimes outright-unbelievable-yet-empirically-supported etymologies – or histories – of words. Who, for instance, would have thought that *Canuck* 'Canadian', perhaps one of the most endearing terms in Canada today, has the same root as German *Kanake* (meaning '[bloody] foreigner') or French *canaque* ('South Sea dweller')?

Once the data are collected – which is arguably the most thankless and most tedious part of the job of historical dictionary writing – it's all about interpreting them. And here it is not just enough to go by whatever data one has, as the data are always incomplete and spotty, no matter how hard you have tried and how many resources you've thrown at data collecting. It is also necessary to know a lot about language history, cultural, social, and political history, and to have seen many different walks of life – in short, to be an expert in things human. How do people tick? How did they tick 1,000 years ago? That is the kind of information that will get you etymologies that have the best chance of being right and standing the test of time (and bringing to light more puzzle pieces).

As is often the case, though, you'll end up with more than one plausible word history. In these cases, a principle called Occam's razor comes in handy. It was popularized in western culture by the medieval monk William of Ockham and got canonized in the Latinized spelling of the place name: Occam. We referred to Occam's razor in Chapter 1; it's now time to explain it. The principle states that if two explanations offer the attested outcome, *the one which rests on fewer presuppositions is to be preferred*. In the case of *Canuck*, the question concerned competing etymologies of whether the word form arrived in Canada via the West – that is, British Columbia – or via the East – that is, the New England whaling fleets – and then spread to the provinces of Quebec, Nova Scotia, Ontario, and New Brunswick.

Canuck, as you need to know, comes from the Hawaiian word *kanaka*, which simply means 'man, person' in that language. This explains why it is found in other former colonial languages (French, German German) or unsuccessful colonial languages (Austrian German). The full answer, which is offered in *DCHP-2* (s.v. "Canuck"), cannot be repeated for reasons of space, but suffice it to say that the more likely scenario is through the whaling ships, which routinely stopped in Hawaii (then called the Sandwich Islands) to take on provisions and cheap labour – men who referred to themselves as *kanakas*. Via that connection, the term travelled to the eastern shores of North America, where it made its way to nearby Quebec. In those overtly racist days, it did not go unnoticed that Hawaiian *kanakas* and Quebec francophones often had darker skin colour,[6] so the transfer of the term to refer to French Canadians was widespread in the nineteenth century, so much so that in Quebec even today some speakers still perceive the originally negative connotations of the term as a term of abuse for francophones. In the early days, the word was sometimes spelled as *Kanuck*, with a *K*, which appears to reconfirm the connection with *kanaka*.

While in the USA, the term kept its derogatory undertones for a long, long time, by 1849 we have the first fictional anglophone Canadian refer to himself, in New Brunswick, as "a Canuck, a Canadian". A scenario that would see *Canuck* arrive in New Brunswick via Western Canada as the primary route would need a few more presuppositions – such as, to be overly bizarre, Martians transferring the term from the West Coast to Eastern Canada, where the term was most widely used. Occam's razor is a good principle to abide by. For full details on *Canuck*, including a more elaborate transmission route, see www.dchp.ca/dchp2/Entries/view/Canuck.

The Summer of 1958

We mentioned above that dictionaries are very, very strange books. So strange that even most publishers don't realize it. Dictionaries are, in any case, very front-heavy projects in terms of time and financial investment. As a result, many projects have failed, which is the biggest reason why dictionary projects have a difficult time obtaining research funding, having acquired a sort of "bottomless pit" reputation. Lovell, in a snippet of a letter early on in the project, even before he was appointed Editor-in-Chief in 1958, writes about precisely that problem:

I don't feel that I can wait 20 or 30 years for somebody to help me with collecting material for a dictionary of the style of the DAE [*Dictionary of American English*]. Time is of the essence, as our legal friends say. The Canadian dictionary will not have the benefit of materials collected for earlier dictionaries, as did the DAE and DA [*Dictionary of Americanisms*], which had sizeable hand-me-downs from the OED. What do you think of the idea of a work of 400 or 500 pages, on the order of my sampling, dealing with the core typically Canadian terms, somewhat more thoroughly than DAE or DA coverage? (Lovell to Avis/Scargill, *c*. 1957)

This scaled-back dictionary, which would have been about half the size of what *DCHP-1* turned out to be, was expected to be completed within two years of work, based on Lovell's collection alone. Planning originally did not include Gage but McClelland & Stewart, the Toronto publisher that would play a major role in Canadian literature shortly after, publishing Margaret Atwood, Pierre Burton, Leonard Cohen, Peter Gzowski, Margaret Laurence, and Farley Mowat, to name only a few. Lovell specifies his plans:

Two years of Guggenheim-financed research would take care of the research; with that out of the way, McClelland & Stewart might see their way to financing a year of editing. (Lovell to Avis/Scargill, *c*. 1957)

But it was not McClelland & Stewart that would take care of this project. W. J. Gage Ltd stepped up to the plate in 1958, and the Congress of the Humanities and Social Sciences in Edmonton that year – in combination with the CLA summer school in Edmonton starting just ten days later – turned out to be the decisive moment.

"Congress", as it is called today, is one of the biggest meetings of human-ities and social sciences researchers in the world, yet it is a Canadian affair. In 1958, the meeting – which today is the meeting point for some seventy associated societies across the country – became the backdrop for talks between Wilf Wees (Dr W. R. Wees, the Vice President of Publishing at Gage and the man behind *DCHP-1*'s foreword) and the dictionary committee of the Canadian Linguistic Association, whose members we got to know earlier, with Scargill as chairperson.

Drysdale remembers that Wees wanted to publish school dictionaries, while the CLA wanted historical dictionaries – *DCHP-1* – of terms "special" to Canada, followed by a general historical dictionary of Canadian English, including all terms of the English language in Canada – an *OED* from an entirely Canadian angle: the history of *aardvark* in Canada and so forth, all the

way to *zydeco*, documented by Canadian sources. This comprehensive historical dictionary was never seriously embarked on, though Scargill collected
some 20,000 quotations for it with his reading programme. In good Canadian
fashion, the compromise was that the CLA would do both kinds of dictionaries
for Gage. As Drysdale put it: "Wees, I understood later, drove a hard bargain,
but it was agreed that members of the committee would work on both projects,
while Gage would finance the whole undertaking" (Paddy Drysdale: pers.
communication, 2 April 2018).

Shortly after Congress, the CLA would hold its 1958 Summer Institute in
Edmonton, which included as teachers some of the top linguists of the day, and
the young Paddy Drysdale, who was asked to teach an introductory course.
There it was: Paddy had been granted access to the upper echelons of Canadian
linguistics. For a reason not entirely clear to me, Paddy went down a somewhat
different route after 1959, resigning his tenure-track position at Memorial
University in Newfoundland. I know that Paddy was impressed by the meticu-
lous, all-in nature of Avis, so one interpretation would be that Paddy chose to
have a little life beyond his job, which, as he's now 90 and all fiery and
kicking, seems to have been a very good choice. Paddy recalls the decisive
summer of 1958 in the following way:

I was at those CLA meetings [in Edmonton at Congress 1958] but knew nothing of the
above negotiations until I returned to Edmonton after a ten-day break to teach an
Introductory Linguistics course at summer school. This was a heady experience. I was
teaching an overflow class of Scargill's course, and other members of the faculty
included Wally Avis, Jean-Paul Vinay, Bill Mackie, and Martin Joos. I gradually heard
about the negotiations with Gage, and one day Harry Scargill came into my office
holding a letter and complaining that now Gage wanted him to find someone who could
co-ordinate all the dictionary work from within Gage's office. Almost on a whim I said
I might be interested. The result was that on my way back to St John's I broke my
journey in Toronto, met Wilf Wees, his editor-in-chief, and the production manager, and
was offered the job and given a week to make up my mind. I then joined Gage in the
summer of 1959 and I stayed till 1982. (Drysdale, pers. correspondence, 2 April 2018)

It is a safe bet that Gage didn't know what they were up for and neither did
Paddy. Who knows the problems of dictionaries before the fact? No one who
hasn't done it.

The problems start immediately. Landau writes in his textbook introduction
to dictionary making about the problems of budgeting for a dictionary and,
worse, a historical dictionary. The basic unit is the "editor week", the work an
editor is able to perform in a week, an average week, sustained over long
periods. The typical scope for an English dictionary is given by Landau, who
does the math for us. The scope

means that it would take 20 editors working 52 weeks a year (with no vacations or
illness, and of course no turnover) almost twelve years (12,432 [editor weeks] divided

by 20 = 621.6 weeks divided by 52 = 11.95 [years]). If the editors averaged $[60],000 per year, the editorial costs would be $[1.2 million] per year or about $[14.4 million] overall. One turns pale, sits, asks for a glass of water. "Well," one says, after a time of limp reflection, "maybe they can work a little faster." (Landau 2001: 350)

And if one gives in to the thought of "working a little faster", one has in all likelihood another "dictionary zombie" on one's hands: not dead yet, but a dictionary that will never be born. On the contrary, any such calculations as the ones above need to be prodded by a factor of 1.5 or 2 – vacations and other problems (many of them unforeseeable) would need to be budgeted for, so the idea of "working a little faster" is exposed for what it is – outright ridiculous and nothing short of irresponsible. Others have summarized the problems of dictionary making more generally, blaming the "frail human condition".

Collecting Data: Sisyphus or Icarus?

Assembling a quotation database is well and good and a requirement for any dictionary. But how does one know what to look for in that process? Quotation collection is the trickiest, most labour-intensive part, and the part that is most prone to error – costly error, because if one reads a book and focusses on the "wrong" words for whatever reason, one will have to go back to re-read and re-excerpt that book. Conversely, if a project does not meticulously keep track of what has been read and excerpted and by whom, chances are that some books are read more than once, in some cases time and time again, which happened for the *OED* but also for *DCHP-1*. Such error is almost inevitable for any bigger dictionary. If there is a lot to be done, the opportunity is ripe for error and unnecessary duplication.

For *DCHP-1*, we have some of Lovell's "documentation sheets". In the context of the *OED*, Simon Winchester referred to sheets that offer what is basically an index to each book as a special feature by the "madman", the convicted murderer W. C. Minor, who, as you recall, supported the *OED* with thousands of its most valuable quotations and antedates from his prison cell. In fact, Minor's "curious working methods" (Gilliver 2016: 201) are perhaps more effective than the wording suggests and the most detailed way of getting at the data. Time-consuming, but highly effective nonetheless: while reading a book or other text, one notes down "special" words alphabetically on a single sheet of paper, with the page number on which they occur. So, in a Canadian dictionary, *A-frame* 'type of house' would be at the very top of the sheet, *jolly jumper* 'baby's restraint' in the middle, and *zombie* 'WWII soldier' at the end. In the context of the *OED*, this method allowed Minor to respond to Murray's queries for specific quotation gaps in the *OED* from his files. These files Minor had collated while sitting in his cell, and they very often contained precisely the answers to the most difficult queries that Murray needed help with.

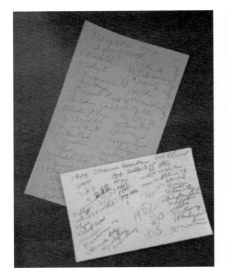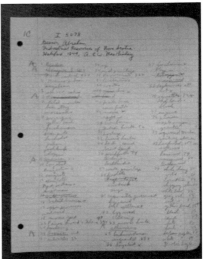

Figure 16 Documentation sheets by Lovell (University of
Victoria Archives)
(Photos: S. Dollinger)

Figure 16 shows one of Lovell's documentation sheets on the right, which
looks very much like it applies the indexing principle that Minor had used half
a century earlier. The smaller sheets on the left show the more ad-hoc
"scribblings" of page numbers of interesting words.

Speaking of interesting or "special" words, what precisely does that mean?
What is it that one would document? Lovell published, from the beginning in
the 1950s, his assessments of "fruitful" literature for Canadian purposes
(C. Lovell 1955b, 1956): some sources bore out the expectations, others did
not. While such literary recommendations are helpful in the process, focus on
certain types of genres – for instance, Canadian farming almanacs from the
1830s – would still give us no indication of what precisely to look for. In the
case of *DCHP* as an "exclusive" dictionary – i.e., a dictionary whose interest is
merely in things that are Canadian by some measure and excluding everything
else – the question of knowing what to look for is an especially difficult task,
impossible of solution: one can only after the fact, post hoc after a long phase
of tests, conclude with any certainty whether a given term or meaning is
Canadian. A verdict of "non-Canadian" would inevitably mean that one has
to disregard all quotations for a given term that is proven as not Canadian for
DCHP. A frustrating task, for sure, but there is no way around it. In that sense,
the *OED* had, believe it or not, on some level an easier goal: by simply

adopting, within reasonable limits, "all" terms of English, everything was fair game and nothing was useless per se. On the other hand, they, *de facto*, were forced to include anything and everything (which, of course, they didn't, but they got admirably close).

I believe this is one reason why we know a lot about the public reading programme of the *OED*, its appeals and calls for help, and not so much about the *DCHP-1* reading programme, as the desired content could be more efficiently related to the interested reader: *everything* is relevant. In the case of *DCHP-1*, any reader would have required substantial training to get a "feeling", a "*Sprachgefühl*", for what might be a good use of time and what not, which would have reduced the number of potential readers by a magnitude.

If we compound this structural difficulty in the study of "-isms" – Americanisms, Canadianisms, Englishisms – with the generally chaotic ways of the scholarly genius, we are faced with a profound logistical challenge of getting one's hands on the "slips". In the case of *DCHP-1*, we have good testimony that a lot of extra miles went nowhere. Such extra work was often owed to Lovell's unexpected death, as in the following assessment by Avis, who was picking up the pieces at the beginning of his sabbatical year in Calgary and who bemoaned the lack of a bibliography for Lovell's material:

Charlie's failure to prepare a list of books read, with the result that some books have been read by three, and a great many by two people. . . . I have no solution for this problem since I do not have enough time to go through the files to determine which words are already over-cited. (Avis to Crate, 15 Oct. 1963)

To give you a better idea of the magnitude of the problem, let me quote a few more lines from the correspondence in 1964, when editing had begun and while data collection continued full throttle. Joan Hall, the Lexicographical Centre's assistant, informed Avis in September 1964 of Leechman's reading programme:

Dr. Leechman has read *Beaver* issue 1923–1927, 1928–1934, March 1937–March 1941, and March 1944–December 1946 in addition to a couple of books. You can imagine the number of cites resulting! (Hall to Avis, 21 Sept. 1964)

Avis replies: "I can indeed!"

So, sixteen years' worth of journals and two or three book editions would explain why *Beaver* attestations are quite frequent in *DCHP-1*. A little earlier, Avis had written to Leechman on a particular year of magazine issues that triggered "useable cites" and while the material turned out not to be very promising, it still triggered some fifty slips that had to be "typed up". This meant that Avis marked up the magazine copy or copied it out by hand on a scribble sheet, such as the ones on the left in Figure 16 (the same method was still applied in *DCHP-2*):

I am in a volume of the Canadian Illustrated News, 1869–70 and there are half a hundred useable cites I must get typed up. The source was, however, disappointing; much too literate and too afraid of alarming British readers (?) to use native words and expressions to any extent. (Avis in letter from Calgary to Leechman, 12 May 1964)

You can imagine, if a bad source triggers fifty slips, how many a good source would yield in any given year! A Sisyphean task: once you think you've covered an area, you're bound to find other material you missed. Meanwhile, the sorting and "readying" of slips went on and old shoeboxes played an important role. Around that time, Avis replies to Hall:

Have now half a shoebox of readied clips for <u>M</u>, up to <u>May apple</u>; slow going. The bundles of *Beaver* cites you sent will slow me down somewhat, alas; but that's the way it goes, I guess. WSA

[Note added by hand:] Joan, The 4x6 pads are under separate cover – the parcel weighed too much! A.

Avis is referring to the *Beaver* quotes that Leechman had excerpted. That the weight of the slip shipment to Victoria would interfere with sending all in one shipment is another indicator of the "bulkiness", the literal "heavy load" of the work. One can think of the Greek legend of Icarus: reaching for the stars on his flight, Icarus got too close to the sun, which caused the wax that kept his wings in place to melt, and Icarus plunged and drowned in the sea. Likewise, many lexicographers die trying to capture *all* of the language: *OED*'s Murray, *DARE*'s Cassidy, and the Grimm Brothers, working on their *Deutsches Wörterbuch*, to name just a few.

But let us assume for now that the nitty-gritty of daily data collection was taken care of in one way or another: how does one actually write a dictionary from these "scraps" of language? This we will address next.

A Plan for a Dictionary: Lists, Lists, Lists

It all starts with lists: many lists, more lists, and still more lists. I mentioned the catchword collection and documentation sheets in the previous sections, which are but two lists. Then there is the all-important "headword list", or lexeme list. This list contains all the words that should be listed in the dictionary and are therefore actually researched. For *DCHP-2*, the new edition, the original headword list started with *AA* for *Adult Accompaniment* and ended with *zombie*, which is a military slang term for a World War II conscript for home defence (rather than for overseas service).

For *DCHP-1*, they had an "Old File" for what they thought at some point they'd include; a "Delayed File" that they were lagging behind on and which Avis was supposed to work on in the summer of 1965 and thereafter (for there is *always* more than you can handle); and a "New Entry File", with terms they caught on the go, possibly after they had edited that particular section in the alphabet. In addition to these, Avis had from Gage's *The Beginning*

Dictionary – a Grade-5 dictionary – a "general word list" of English words, *A*–*Z*, and a "Canadian word list" of terms that would qualify as Canadian (see below on how to tell Canadian words from others). Avis would have used these lists to get a head start for *DCHP-1*. In addition, they had smaller linguistic surveys – one by a certain Christine Bonhomme and the other by Calgary linguist Smeaton. But with all these lists, how do you go about the writing?

We are lucky enough to have Avis' notes from the fall of 1963. In these, he lays out three stages for the writing of the dictionary. This little plan is telling and shows that even Avis was not quite sure what he was up against. Keep in mind that, at that point, he had only worked on the Canadianization of an existing dictionary – Gage's *The Beginning Dictionary*, which was published in 1962 – but not on a novel kind of dictionary for which he had to build the headword list from scratch. Avis' three stages look deceptively simple:

Stage 1: putting files and bibliography in order
Stage 2: separating the general file from the Canadian file – a word list. Cross-checking with dictionaries "to determine whether or not they come within the definition of 'Canadian terms'".
Stage 3: "double-checking the appropriateness of the terms selected, refining the definitions, and where necessary, establishing the etymologies, pronunciations, and usage labels."
"Once this stage is complete, the manuscript should be ready for setting up in galley proof." (quoting and paraphrasing Avis, interim report, 15 Dec. 1963)

Avis expected Stage 2 to be completed by the end of the summer of 1964, which was just six to eight months after writing this memo. This suggests that Avis had already, by Christmas 1963, devised the plan to aim for publication in the centennial year – therefore long before he had completed his sabbatical year in Calgary. In fact, Drysdale independently confirms a 1967 publication date from the outset, and he adds that he was even sent by his employer to an Ottawa meeting on centennial projects, long before 1967. This is very different from Scargill's wording in the preface of *DCHP-1* that presented the publication date as being pushed forward from 1970 to 1967 as an unexpected result of Avis' year's work in Calgary. Drysdale reasons that, perhaps, Scargill was more sceptical about an initial 1967 deadline.

What is striking in Avis' plan is that Stage 3 is so overly large compared to the other ones. While Stages 1 and 2 appear to be tasks of months, Stage 3 is really the "writing" of the dictionary with all the leaps and bounds, detours and revisions that come with it. The fact that that stage is not specified at all and reads more like an idea than a plan shows that Avis was really not very clear himself about this stage at that time.

But there were unanticipated problems in Stages 1 and 2 as well. The bibliography would be another list, but it was one with considerable challenges. If five people are sending in quotations, the chances are great that some – perhaps many – page numbers, publishing locations, or titles would be missing. Add in five volunteers, and the bibliography would be so much more chaotic already. The retrieval of any of these missing bibliographical details would be very time-consuming, the kind of work that no one wants to spend time and money on, not even lexicographers. It's a bit like certain repair jobs are not the faves of the handy(wo)men: fixing water leaks in tiled bathrooms and the like. Unsurprisingly perhaps, Lovell complains bitterly about some volunteer readers in a letter to Avis:

Dear Wally: February 1, 1958
    Thanks for the notes from [name 1] and [name 2]. Such material is of no use to me; why can't they learn that what we are interested in is not "just words," but documentation of their time and place of use?
    One reason why dictionaries take so many years to complete is because of the time wasted upon tracking down matters of this sort. (Lovell to Avis, 1 Feb. 1958)

But that was not all in terms of problems with the bibliography. Driven by the goal of saving time, Crate resorted to a coding system, rather than copying out the full bibliographical details. What in theory sounds like a good time-saving shortcut caused Avis some of his biggest headaches. Crate had assumed that the Lexicographical Centre would be in a position to hire more than one typist and that a code such as "1947/E89/" – a source published in 1947, from locator "E89" – could be used to save time. "E89" would then serve as the index to a list with the full bibliographical detail, to be completed by the typist.

    That list, however, never materialized. Instead, the system was organized in sections of 100 books each. That the system was a bit odd can best be gleaned from Joan Hall's neutrally worded letter to Charles Crate, from September 1964:

There are four sections in this bibliography [that you provided us with] labelled A, B, C, D. What are these sections for – i.e. what purpose do they serve? (Hall to Crate, 14 Sept. 1964, University of Victoria Archives, 90–66, Box 4 File 3)

The letters stood for individual book stacks in Crate's study: Stack A was the first hundred, Stack B the second hundred books, and so forth. So A5 would be the fifth book in the first stack (it is not known whether from the top or the bottom). What sounds good in principle is practically a librarian's nightmare.

    Crate devised this scheme to avoid an entirely different nightmare of his own, as he writes in a letter dated 3 January 1961 to Scargill: "The occasional book I have marked will run as high as 1,000 quotable quotes, and a date & code system will enable me to catch up in my typing" (University of Victoria Archives, 90–66, Box 4 File 4). Scargill did not seem to have caught the fundamental problem of "codes" in collaborative work: they often result, in the end, in more harm than good. Avis, who had to make sense of these codes as the "last man to get the slips", wrote after the publication of the *DCHP-1* that "fortunately", he "caught this monumental folly before the system had progressed beyond E, but I still had thousands of cryptic slips on my hands" (Avis 1969: 2). Indeed he had, with more than three years of collecting by Crate after sharing his "code plans" with Scargill.

Shipping Slips across the Continent

Having the slips is one thing, but as Avis' post-publication account tells us, having them in clean-enough format is another. When arriving in Calgary in 1963, Avis "had been assured that mountains awaited my attention". "I had not been misinformed", he writes, "for there was a mountain of material, unsorted, unchecked, unfiled, and unnerving" (Avis 1969: 1). Even after publication, some materials in the most substantial Lovell collection remained untapped, for, in 1969, Avis wrote that:

Even now there are boxes of marked newspaper and bundles of paper-scraps which someday must be converted into citations [slips]. Mr. Lovell, you see, devoted nearly all of his time to amassing citations and very little of it to keeping an orderly shop. (Avis 1969: 1)

This, to be fair, should be expected of those working in their free time – unpaid, one might add. Especially since the paid lexicographical worker often does not keep an orderly shop either, as in all Sisyphean tasks, leaving one with the unnerving feeling that one is always lagging behind, no matter how hard one is working.

Once the slips were put in reasonable order, they had to be shipped to the right place and the right people at the right time. Naturally, there was quite a bit of "traffic" between the Lexicographical Centre in Calgary – and, later, Victoria – and Kingston (Avis), Alert Bay and, later, Quesnel (Crate), Oak Bay near Victoria (Leechman), and Scarborough, Toronto (Drysdale at Gage). For a few years, Canada Post will have turned a good profit from the heavy boxes of unique materials being shipped back and forth, and the many cards and letters. As Hall in Victoria writes to Avis in Kingston:

The box of M's arrived here on January 4th or 5th. I then sent the box containing the first bunch of P's to you on January 6 by Canadian National Express. This box will arrive on or around January 14. (Hall to Avis, 11 Jan. 1965)

At the other end, Avis was at times anxious about the safety of the all-important slips when they criss-crossed the country. He implores Hall to offer acknowledgements of packages received:

Please drop me a card whenever you get a box, for I worry about the delivery. (Avis to Hall, 7 Jan. 1965)

At the same time, Crate was sending in slips from then-very-isolated Alert Bay, BC. Crate, in his letters to Avis, "included with his notes quite a number of citation slips", which Avis would check and then send along, as necessary, to Hall in Victoria "to go in with the old file or the unedited file, that is, beyond N" (Avis to Hall, 14 Sept. 1964).

At the same time, Leechman read for slips as well and performed copy-editing or proofreading tasks on drafts of the manuscript, which underwent a number of changes and at least one re-start. But Avis, either in Kingston, in 1963–64 in Calgary, or in the summer of 1965 in Victoria, would always be the bottleneck and switchboard, like all good chief editors are. All of this was happening in a day and age when long-distance phone calls were outrageously, if not prohibitively, expensive, postal mail quite cheap, and mail delivery the make or break of this project. As Hall reminds Avis:

So perhaps you had better let me know about 10 days in advance when you want another box – 3 days for the letter, and 7 days for the box. (Joan Hall to Avis, 11 Jan. 1965)

The mentioned boxes are shoeboxes with about 3,000 quotations slips in each of them. In order to get them where you needed them, you, as the sender or receiver of a box, had better think on your toes, factoring in the delivery times, the strong suits and weaknesses of your posties, whether out in the behemoth corporation called Canada Post or in your university's postal department. That *DCHP-1* was finished is as much owed to the impressive performance, reliability, and affordability of Canada Post as to the skill of the *DCHP-1* team. Three cheers for Canada Post!

Manuscript Writing *à trois*

In the writing process, a number of moving targets emerged: an unfinished headword list, an unfinished quotation slip file, an unfinished bibliography, sections of an unfinished manuscript at multiple stages – first draft, copy-edits, proofing – and an unfinished and ever-growing additions file for things that were discovered after a particular section of the manuscript was written. Unfinished is the word.

That a manuscript was indeed in the making in the fall of 1964, we know from a letter by Joan Hall to Charles Crate. Avis had left a couple of months earlier from Calgary to Kingston, and Hall had just started up the operations under Scargill's direction at the University of Victoria. Hall writes:

We are working on a tentative manuscript now. It is really quite exciting to see the first page of the manuscript typed up. However, I imagine that it will be redone many times before it goes to the publisher. (Hall to Crate, 21 Oct. 1964)

At the same time as a manuscript was being composed, we see revision cycles taking shape. It seems that Avis, after editing a draft section, sent it on to both Leechman and Crate, who went through it with their own corrections. Hall informs Avis in January of 1965 that:

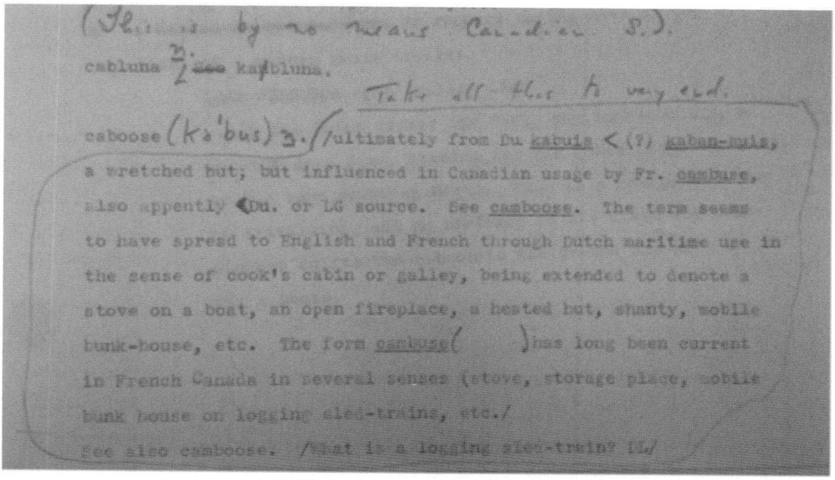

Figure 17 Leechman fonds (above, BC Archives MS-1290, Box 47 File 1); the final version in www.dchp.ca/dchp1 (below)

Dr. Leechman has now finished the manuscript up to canot allège. **Good.** (Joan Hall to Avis, 11 Jan. 1965; "Avis-Type" answer in bold)

Crate reports of his revision progress to Hall that spring:

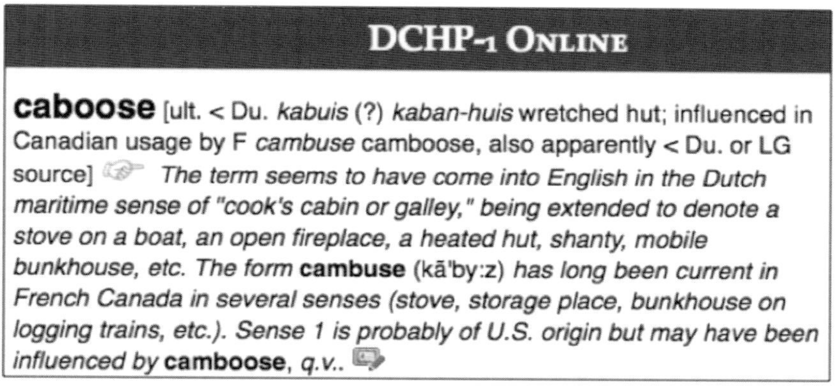

I have received two more "installments" of the dictionary and have been going over them. I have a quarrel with some of the definitions and will send Avis these or perhaps forward them to Victoria for perusal and re-forwarding. (Crate to Leechman, MS-1290, Box 3 File 17, 6 March 1965)

So it seems that at least three sets of eyes saw the text before it was sent to Drysdale in Toronto, where it underwent another round of checking, at least for the copy-editing and proofreading part, but there is evidence of more substantial checking of isolated items.

In the Leechman fonds at the BC Archives in Victoria, we find part of a *DCHP-1* manuscript, which consists of *C* and *M–Q*.[7] As *canot allège* is in *C*, which was acknowledged by Avis, it would be likely that Leechman started in *A* and might well have copy-edited the entire manuscript.

Figure 17 shows an example of Leechman's "going through the manuscript", followed by the final version (from the verbatim version of *DCHP-1* at www.dchp.ca/dchp1). It can be seen that Leechman's corrected manuscript is very close to the published version (with only the IPA special characters missing, which were not provided for "normal" words that would not present a problem to the fluent speaker of Canadian English).

The most important difference between the manuscript and the final version is the addition of the last sentence with the assessment that Sense 1 is of US origin. There was not a lot that Leechman added, in this example or more generally, which speaks to the quality of Avis' editing. The addition, at the top in a different hand, signed "S", suggests that the comment is actually Scargill's.

That Patrick Drysdale's role was more than the usual publishing role becomes evident in correspondence from the spring of 1967. At that point, as the first parts of the dictionary were being typeset, Drysdale successfully argued for the inclusion of the word *canoe*, which was originally omitted. Very late in the game, on 1 April 1967, Drysdale wrote to Scargill that he "realized that we had to cover the word [canoe] in some way". While possibly not being Canadian in origin, *canoe* "we could hardly omit" "when we claim to include words illustrative of 'distinctively Canadian history, life, and culture'". Drysdale delivers an entry for *canoe* that "was put together by me and revised and added to by Wally just in time to go to the typesetter with the corrected galley proofs for the first part of 'C'".[8] That Drysdale is listed as an editor seems like a logical decision, given his involvement.

In all of this, though, Avis, Leechman, and Crate, alongside Hall, appear to be the main agents. What is surprising is that Scargill is not referred to much at this stage of heavy work, Drysdale's letter on *canoe* above representing one of the few instances of Scargill's involvement; his apparent edit in Figure 17 came as a surprise. So the assumption would be correct that Scargill enabled this project and acted as director, with a much lesser role in the active editing of *DCHP-1*. The fact that the *Intermediate Dictionary*, for which Scargill was the main point person,[9] was published in 1963 would be another reason for his lesser hands-on role in *DCHP-1*. The *Intermediate* was the second dictionary in the series of three graded school dictionaries. Scargill had, in some ways, paid his dues and had kept up his end of the bargain.

Reading for Slips and Glory

The information on the backgrounds of the Big Six is uneven. The biographical notes in *DCHP-1* are a kind of benchmark, a biographical ground zero, for each of them. Most distinct in terms of what we can construct of their lives is Leechman, as a retired anthropologist of international standing. For instance, we have substantial material in the BC Archives for him. For Crate, by contrast, it is infinitely harder to obtain – well, anything really. As far as Crate's early years in Ontario are concerned, there is uncertainty as to what he did. For Leechman, we are offered information on a silver platter down to the very minutiae of daily routines, including daily planners, while for Crate the situation is opaque.

At some point between 9 January and 21 February 1965, Crate met Leechman and his wife in Victoria. The men were both dealing with similar problems while reading for *DCHP-1*. Both of them lived on Vancouver Island, yet even in that regard the two men could not be more different. While Leechman lived in Oak Bay on the southern tip, overlooking Ross Bay, in what is the most affluent neighbourhood on the island, Crate lived a few hundred kilometres away in Alert Bay, close to the island's northern tip. Half of the 470 kilometres that separated the two towns would need to be driven on dirt roads at the time, in addition to a short ferry trip from Port McNeill to the island of Alert Bay, which was a near-frontier community at the time. These dirt roads with their potholes allowed speeds of no more than 20 km/h, rather than the 120 km/h one drives on the modern highway that was built in the late 1970s. While, by Canadian standards, Crate and Leechman lived in relative proximity, it was still a costly two-day trip for Crate to come to Victoria. Scargill and Hall were, of course, in Saanich, BC, on the grounds of the University of Victoria campus and its older transitory locations nearby, so merely a 10-minute drive from Leechman's home.

On 2 March of that year, Crate expressed his hopes to be staying in Victoria for six weeks in the summer of 1965, as his "wife and youngest daughter plan to fly to England for a six-weeks trip this summer". Crate was

considering taking [his] Summer University courses in Victoria instead of U.B.C. and bringing [his] older girl over to keep house for [him]. If this transpires, [he'd] be available to work with [Leechman] on the dictionary. (2 March 1965, BC Archives MS-1290, Box 3 File 17)

Crate did indeed spend these six weeks in the summer of 1965 at the Centre, as well as some time in the summer of 1966.[10] While Avis was working during his year in Calgary on *DCHP-1*, he exchanged information with Douglas Leechman, who had just moved to Victoria. Leechman was working on files there and Crate on some other files in Alert Bay, BC.

You may be familiar with Samuel Johnson's tongue-in-cheek, self-deprecating definition of *lexicographer* in his 1755 dictionary as "a harmless drudge". I think it is fair to say that Leechman would fail to see the humour in Johnson's *bon mot*. Leechman, who was new to the dictionary-editing job, wrote to his own surprise the following lines to Avis, the experienced editor:

I find I am neglecting practically everything else on my desk for this job [working on *DCHP-1*], and, like you, am enjoying it immensely. (Leechman to Avis, 6 May 1964 on quotation extraction and query solving. BC Archives MS-1290, Box 4/2)

This does, indeed, not sound like drudgery at all – more like all-engrossing activity, at the peril of other jobs that needed to get done. Sure, there is a good deal of drudgery, too. But Leechman's engrossment reminds me of the, indeed, caring mom who confessed, years after the fact, that she feared she temporarily neglected her children because Dan Brown's *The Da Vinci Code* was such a page turner that she was unable to tear herself away from it.

We are lucky enough to know something about the progress in these years from bits and pieces in the letters that relate to the creation of a manuscript that would be typed up by Ms Hall. When, on 12 May 1964, Avis reports that he had edited "A till Fo-", and on 14 July he offers the estimate "to be getting up to the end of L before I leave for Kingston" by mid-August, we can gauge how fast he was working. And fast he was indeed. Much faster, actually, than the editing process of *DCHP-2* would be half a century later: editing 5¾ letters, or almost 3,500 words (*A* to *Fo-*), in some eight months is indeed staggering. The work of the three months from mid-May to mid-Aug, from *Fr-* to *L* or 2,250 words, is reminiscent of a speed-writing record.[11] This speed also explains, without seriously criticizing the work, the detail in *DCHP-1* that is sometimes missing. It's logical: what was not in the files was just not there, and there was little time to chase down difficult cases in what we may call the *paper age*. There was no feasible way to find missing information at that point in the game, without the digital sources that would allow for relatively quick ante-datings half a century later.

There are also interesting, long-forgotten details that the archival record reveals. Avis, drafting single-handedly, expressed his hope that Leechman might take over from him when Avis would have to attend to his RMC duties again. Avis writes that:

Things will slow down as far as this office is concerned after 15 Aug. and I'll have only my spare time for the job during the coming winter. I'm hoping to be able to pass on some of the editorial work to you, when we get set up in Victoria. Pity you can't get down here for even a day, just to get the BIG PICTURE. All the best. Sincerely [no signature] (Avis to Leechman, 14 July 1964)

Such a hand-over, however, from Avis to Leechman never happened. The Leechmans – Douglas and his wife, Ruth – did in the end visit the Avises, Wally and Faith, in Calgary, as we know from Ruth Leechman's day planner. From 10 to 13 August 1964, the Leechmans spent a couple of days in Calgary with the Avises.

While Avis shouldered the lion's share of the editing, he was not alone with the task – far from it. There was Drysdale in Toronto, who corresponded with him on a few items and ensured that the publisher was on board. More significantly, there was Leechman, who did the (copy) editing and similar tasks, and Crate, who kept sending in materials and checked the manuscript as well. As Joan Hall reports, at the beginning of the spring of 1965:

Dr. Leechman was in this morning and is coming along very well with the Bibliography. Mr. Crate is sending a lot of cites in again. (Joan Hall to Avis, with mark-up by Avis dated 22 March 1965)

Through the archival record, we can reconstruct how the work on *DCHP-1* progressed. Ruth Leechman's daily planners from the years 1963–65 are extant (BC Archives MS-1290, Box 16 Files 1–3), and from that record we know the most detailed and random things about the making of *DCHP-1*, details that are awaiting further exploration. For instance, around a period of some weeks when Leechman is reported by his wife to have worked on the dictionary – e.g., "Douglas in a.m. to Archives" (23 March) or "to U.[niversity] in am" (30 March) – on Sunday, 28 March 1965, Ruth Leechman writes

Douglas still working
  on the bibliography
  for Dictionary
  Cloudy but sunny (Ruth Leechman's planner, 1965)

There are other indicators of linguistic connections in Ruth's diary. Other bits include, on 12 May 1964, "Douglas to Archives in a.m. & found first use of the word 'District' in B.C."; on 20 May 1964, "Douglas in study all day. Did Bendix laundry in p.m. Rain & wind. Chris"; and on 28 July 1964, "Douglas was working in study every day & sometimes in the evening on Dictionary." From her diary we also know details of the Leechmans' visit to the Avises from 10 to 13 August 1964 in Calgary:

At Royal Wayne Motel. Douglas & I for cocktails at Faith's and Wally's then to dinner – guests of Dr. Scargill at The Highlander in Angus Room. (Ruth Leechman's diary, 10 Aug. 1964)

This was "Family Fun", as Ruth put it, for $159 airfare for Douglas and Ruth Leechman from Victoria via Vancouver to Calgary – $1,300 in 2018.[12] This was probably a bit of an extravaganza, with being "guest of" having the air of colonial times. On 10 October that year, a Saturday, the entry "Scargills 7 o'c 4019 White Rock St. to meet Dr & Mrs Malcolm Taylor" indicates a well-connected, personally befriended group of individuals and their wives, if not families. Saturday, 14 November 1964, reveals "U. of V 2 p.m. Gym. at Gordon Head. Installation of Dr. Gordon Taylor as First Pres. of University & Opening of McPherson Library. Shopped in Bay for food in a.m. [. . .] Nice day but cold." Today, a lot of the key materials for *DCHP-1* are located in the McPherson Library that the Leechmans helped to open officially in style.

Tracking Down *Beaver Stone* to 1696

In a previous section we learned about *DCHP-1*'s reading programme in comparison to the *OED*'s. The reading programme now offers interesting data on how quotations were collected, as in the case study of the documentation of *beaver stone*, which is one of the oldest terms in *DCHP-1*. *Beaver stone* refers to the animal's scent sacs, sometimes called *beaver castors*, which were in Early Modern times believed to have medicinal powers. This example shows the principle behind editing but also reveals some of the effects of that 1967 "centennial rush" on *DCHP-1* (more on that in Chapter 5).

The top half of Figure 18 shows the final *DCHP-1* entry for *beaver stone*, with the oldest attestation from Henry Kelsey dated 1696 and taken from Doughty and Martin's (1929) edition.[13] The term and sentence were found on

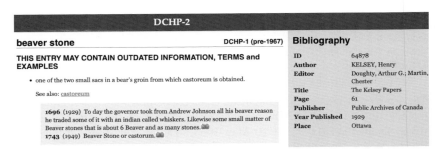

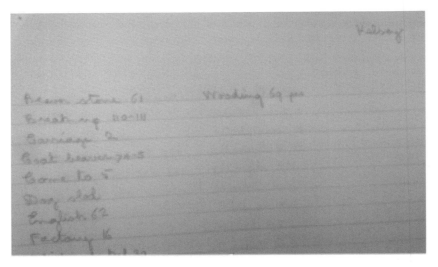

Figure 18 *DCHP-1* entry for *beaver stone* (above); *beaver stone* on Leechman's "documentation list" (below)
(BC Archives MS-1290, Box 47 File 3; photo: S. Dollinger)

page 61 of the *The Kelsey Papers* (see the "Bibliography" box at the top right). The lower half of Figure 18 shows the index sheet for this quotation, which came from Leechman's reading programme. On the top right "Kelsey" stipulates the source for Leechman and the first line on the left, "beaver stone 61", indicates the page number. With this information, Leechman or Avis or one of their helpers was in the position to locate the quotation when needed and copy it to a quotation slip. Then, in comparison with the other slips, Avis would enter it as evidence to the documentary quotation paragraph during the editing progress.

So much for the process of dictionary making. It is interesting to note that the *DCHP-1* files do *not* hold any quotation slips for *beaver stone*, however – not a single one. There are three for *beaver castor*, from 1920 (Leechman), 1921 (Crate), and 1929 (Crate), which makes one wonder how this entry came about. Did Leechman have his own quotation file, separate from the University of Victoria files? If so, is it missing in the Leechman fonds at the BC Archives? Or did Leechman send slips to Avis for checking-up, which did not find their way back from Kingston to Victoria for some reason? Were they even lost in the mail? Or were they just filed out of alphabetical order, like the slip for *black spruce* that was found within the quotations for *beer parlour*?

Perhaps such snags can be attributed to the 1967 rush. But there is more: rush produces errors. The editorial team was aware of inconsistencies, as a year or two after publication they worked on assessing error rates, presumably in preparation for the revision. One such mistake is seen in the 1696 quotation for *beaver stone*. The source of the quotation, the 1929 edition of *The Kelsey Papers*, indeed shows on page 61 the quotation from *DCHP-1*, which appears without the slashes, while the spelling corrections are a much more serious error. Here is the original edited version:

to day the governer took / from Andrew Johnson all his / beaver by reason he traded some / of it with an indian called whiskers / Likewise some small matter of / Beaver stones that is about 6 / Beaver and as many stones one indian / & one English man went to yᵉ fourteens / / [59] (Doughty & Martin 1929: 61)

We see some grave mistakes in comparison – mistakes that do not affect the catchword but the character of the quotation, such as the original *governer*, which is re-spelled *governor* in *DCHP-1*, or the deletion of the preposition *by*, which makes clear that this particular quotation was not cross-checked. This leads me to surmise that Leechman did more parts on his own in the actual editing processes than assumed. Other features are preserved, however, such as the lower case *indian* and the singular *Beaver* after the numeral 6.

Leechman appears to be the most underestimated scholar among the Big Six when it comes to the recognition of his role. He had published in *American Speech* on Chinook Jargon as early as 1926 and had corresponded with Mencken in 1940 at a time when Avis had not even thought about doing linguistics.

Leechman is not just in this respect full of surprises. In the "Memo" pages at the end of Ruth Leechman's 1965 planner was one more. The note read "Eric Partridge birthday Feb. 6th, 72 years in 1966". There it was, the connection with Eric Partridge, one of the most astute linguists and lexicographers of his day. There were more surprises like this about Leechman beside his wife's regular weather reports. For those who may remember or wish to check: on 30 December 1965, Ruth reported "Blizzard in afternoon. Snow, rain & wind", and "1 Jan 1965" [that is, 1966], she writes "Snow flakes as large as big feathers". Both events seem like a rare thing these days for Oak Bay, BC.

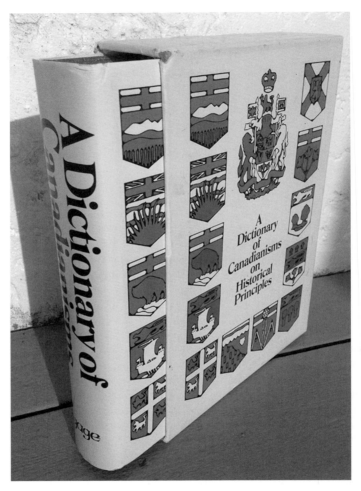

Figure 19 Presentation copy of *DCHP-1* with slip case
(Originally owned by Patrick Drysdale; photo: S. Dollinger, 2018)

5   1967 – Excitement and Hype

Everyone here is very satisfied with progress now. We all are holding our breath just hoping that we'll be done in '67.
(Joan Hall to W. S. Avis, 11 Jan. 1965)

That's a long time to hold your breath. I fully expect [this] to be a posthumous work for W.S. Avis.
(W. S. Avis' reply to Joan Hall, 20 Jan. 1965; University of Victoria Archives, 90–66, Box 4 File 2)

In early November 1967, *DCHP-1* was finally delivered to bookstores and sellers, with some advance copies being sent out to the press for review. Drysdale recalls an October release but cannot support it other than from memory (pers. correspondence, 26 May 2018). In any case, the book came out late for the Christmas shopping season. If we take Lovell's initial petition at the founding meeting of the Canadian Linguistic Association in 1954 as the starting point, it was a mere thirteen years from start to finish. This math, however, disregards Lovell's fifteen years of data collection as something that would just happen overnight. Half a century later, *DCHP-2* would require twelve years from 2005, when some people first speculated about a revision, to its 2017 publication at www.dchp.ca/dchp2. In the context of historical dictionaries, a dozen years or so is not long – not long at all. Such projects' time frames are usually counted in multiple dozens of years or half-centuries, though they often, if not always, tend to be bigger and more ambitious in scope than *DCHP-1*.

Dictionary-project Delays in Five Countries

The best example is perhaps the historical dictionary of German by the Grimm Brothers, the *Deutsches Wörterbuch* (*German Word Book*), the "ur" historical dictionary. Started some time in the early 1830s, the *Deutsches Wörterbuch* was begun in 1838, long before anyone even thought about an *Oxford English Dictionary*. The *Deutsches Wörterbuch*, however, would not be finished until 1961.

The *Oxford English Dictionary*, which was initially conceived as *The New English Dictionary* when it was associated with the London Philological

Society, took from 1857, when Reverend Trench delivered his scathing speech on the deficiencies of all English dictionaries, to 1933, when the supplement to the main sequence was published – so, 76 years. The four supplements of the *OED* under Burchfield's direction took from 1957, his hiring, to 1986 – 29 years. The current third edition of the *OED* was anticipated first in 1993 as an e-product online (Simpson 2016: 284), has published fully revised parts since the year 2000, and will take another generation or so to be completed – about 45 years.

Funny as this may sound, there are even more extreme cases in historical lexicography. A telling example is from Norway. The *Norsk Ordbok* (*Norwegian Dictionary*)[1] took from 1930 to 2016 – or 86 years – to complete. But perhaps the crown for the longest-lasting historical-dictionary project that was finished must go to the Dutch *Woordenboek der Nederlandsche Taal* (*Dictionary of the Dutch Language*),[2] which took from 1851 to 1998, and thus an unrivalled 147 years. By comparison, the US *Dictionary of American Regional English* (*DARE*), which is the best dictionary of English in terms of geographical and, to a certain degree, social dimensions, was downright fast with work lasting from 1960 to 2013 – a "mere" 53 years.

So why does this all take so long – so long that half a century is fast, one and a half centuries is slow, and an average project length is roughly the western life expectancy (the *OED*'s 76 years)? In other words, why are dictionaries considered in funding agency circles nothing less than "bottomless pits"? Sidney I. Landau, who completed more dictionaries than perhaps anyone else, has the perfect answer.

Dictionaries take so long not because they are done by perfectionists but because there is so much to be done. In fact, dictionary editors are far from perfectionist. They become expert in judicious compromise, weighing the cost in time against the possible benefit of an improved definition [or similar] before undertaking any new research effort. (Landau 2001: 349)

These words from Landau's insightful textbook show the financial constraints of any dictionary operation. If a dictionary gets finished, it is first and foremost thanks to manoeuvring the project successfully for many years through all funding, legal, and logistical challenges. This was no different for *DCHP-1*. Like any other English dictionary since 1604 (which is usually taken as the start of the English discipline), *DCHP-1* did not start from scratch but had related historical dictionaries to consider. Besides the *OED*, there was Craigie and Hulbert's *Dictionary of American English*, which was published in four volumes from 1938 to 1944, then Mathews' *Dictionary of Americanisms on Historical Principles*, on which Lovell perfected his skills and, while working on it, saw a major deficiency in North American lexicography and a mistreatment of Canadian English that he resolved to correct.

When *DCHP-1* was published, it was met by favourable critique. It probably helped that Avis and associates played their cards right and got the
blessings of some of their predecessors. We know about the correspondence
between Avis and Mathews in 1961–62 and that *DCHP-1* met with Mathews'
general approval. Besides Avis, Scargill, and Leechman also corresponded
with Mathews: they were well connected. Before we look at *DCHP-1*'s
reception, both in the public's and the expert's eyes, we need to address one
more question, a question that we sneakily kept out of the previous chapter:
what is a Canadianism, anyway?

What's a Canadianism?

Any dictionary of Canadian English is confronted with the additional challenge that it must, unlike British or American dictionaries, show for each and
every item why a given meaning is considered Canadian or not. In Britain and
the USA, such assessment is usually forgone, as the politically and socially
more powerful nations are generally assigned the social licence to codify their
variety as if it developed in isolation from all other varieties. Such behaviour
and shortcutting is sociolinguistically incorrect but this is an impossible case to
make against socially powerful entities. This fact makes dictionaries from
non-dominant varieties of a language by definition generally better in terms of
delimitation than those of the dominant varieties. We can also say that every
good Canadian dictionary (or Australian, New Zealand, Irish, Welsh English –
you name it) is by definition a cross-linguistic one: when you study a term,
say, *gong show*, in Canadian English, you can only tell if it is Canadian in any
way by researching all related varieties, such as American and British English
at least – preferably *all* other English varieties, too. (And *gong show* is
Canadian by virtue of frequency, though we didn't know that before publishing of *DCHP-2*.) Simplifying somewhat, where British and American lexicographers do one kind of search, Canadian lexicographers do at least three
such searches.

Let's take a simple example with the word *hood*, as in the *hood* of a car. In
Britain, folks say *bonnet*. As in, "Open the car's bonnet and let me check your
windscreen-washer fluid." In the USA, folks would more likely say *hood*, *the
car's hood*, and *windshield-washer liquid*. So, we can say, as British and
American dictionary makers have routinely done, that *hood* is American and
bonnet is British. Now that's not quite correct, is it? It's not utterly wrong
either, but it blanks out the fact that *hood* is also Canadian and *bonnet* also
Australian, New Zealand, and South African. So, the question would be: where
do you draw the limits? It's in the interest of all lexicographers – because, as
Landau wrote, "there is so much to do" – to minimize the work involved where
you can. American colleagues can draw the lines much more narrowly than

Canadians, because their country is – and this is the short explanation – bigger. Had the British-Canadians managed to hold on to the western half of North America, we might now speak of Canadian English in a dominant sense, and the Americans would be trying to get the word in that *hood*, for instance, was *also American*. A funny thought, isn't it?

The crucial problem for the Canadian lexicographer is, then, how to tell a Canadian word (Avis' "Canadian list") from a non-Canadian word (Avis' "general list"). In *DCHP-2*, we developed a six-tier typology of different kinds of Canadianisms, plus a class of "Non-Canadian" terms, which are those that were thought to have been Canadian but turned out not to be. That we still operate in *DCHP-2* with Avis' 1960s definition is a testament to Avis' – and ultimately Lovell's – ingenuity. We merely built on and expanded it in a more finely meshed pattern than our predecessors were able to, harnessing the achievements of the IT revolution and fifty years of sociolinguistic insight. Avis defined a Canadianism much more precisely than the current definitions of Americanism, which might surprise some readers:

> Since our approach to our material is clearly quite different from that of lexicographers in the United States, we have chosen to define *Canadianism* less exclusively than they have defined *Americanism*. A Canadianism, then, is a word, expression, or meaning which is native to Canada or which is distinctively characteristic of Canadian usage though not necessarily exclusive to Canada; *Winnipeg couch* falls into the first category, *chesterfield* ("sofa") into the second. (Avis 1967: xiii)

After stressing the different nature of Canadian English lexicography, as we discussed in detail above, Avis expressly states that it is not just "origin" in Canada that counts – which is in *DCHP-2* Type 1 (see Table 4) – but words, meanings, and expressions that are "distinctively characteristic of Canadian usage". That definition was hypermodern, as it foreshadowed the approach that the discipline of linguistic pragmatics would, a dozen years later, only begin to propagate. *DCHP-1* fared well with that definition, which *DCHP-2* merely operationalized.

"Canadianisms": a Six-tiered Typology

Each new term or meaning in *DCHP-2* is classified as one of six types of Canadianism, or is labelled "Non-Canadian". All six types are rooted in Avis' precise definition from 1967 and are defined and illustrated in Table 4, with the seventh type tacked on to complete the picture:

Certain cases, e.g., *pencil crayon*, can be assigned more than one of the six categories – in this case, either a preservation (Type 2) or a Canadianism by virtue of frequency (Type 5) – though there is generally a type that is more dominant or important. The prominent choice is selected, while the other option(s) are discussed in the "word story". For *pencil crayon*, for instance,

Table 4 *The six types of Canadianisms in* DCHP-2, *plus one non-Canadianism*

- **Type 1 – Origin:** when a form is created in what is now Canada (and with it its meaning), e.g. *garburator* 'in-sink organic waste disposal', *humidex* 'subjective heat index depending on humidity', *loonie* '1-dollar coin', *toonie* '2-dollar coin', and *T4 slip* 'employed earnings tax form'.
- **Type 2 – Preservation:** when a form or meaning that once was widespread in many Englishes is now preserved in Canadian English, e.g. *government wharf* 'wharf funded by the government', and *pencil crayon* 'colouring pencil', which were forms that were common in other varieties of English. The latter, *pencil crayon*, is used most frequently in Canada, as is *parkade* 'parking garage', which was first used in the USA.
- **Type 3 – Semantic Change:** terms that have undergone semantic change in Canadian English, e.g. *toque* 'beanie, woolen hat', which earlier referred to other kinds of hats; *Canuck* 'Canadian', which was formerly a racist term of abuse derived from Hawaiian *kanaka* 'Hawaiian, dark-skinned person' that was brought via whaling ships to Canada and the USA. In the former country it quickly underwent amelioration to today's term of prestige.
- **Type 4 – Culturally Significant:** these are terms or meanings that have been enshrined in the Canadian psyche, e.g. *universal healthcare, gun legislation*, and most hockey terms, e.g. *goalie mask, wraparound* 'hockey move trying to score from behind the net', *Zamboni* 'ice-resurfacing machine', and the like, terms that are widely considered 'Canadian', including discourse marker *eh*.
- **Type 5 – Frequency:** terms or meanings that are Canadian by virtue of discourse frequency, e.g. *cube van* 'moving truck', *to table something* 'bring forward, rather than to postpone [as in US English]', as in *to table legislation*; and *washroom* 'public bathroom, toilet'.
- **Type 6 – Memorial:** these terms or meanings are the flip side of cultural salience. Whereas the latter is something Canadians take 'pride' in, *Memorial* terms refer to negative entities in Canada's history, e.g. *residential school* 'schools that abused aboriginal people, schools for cultural genocide'; ethnic terms of abuse, e.g. *chink* 'Chinese', *wop* 'Italian'; or now inappropriate terms, e.g. *Eskimo* 'Inuit people', *iron chink* 'fish-gutting machine, named for the predominant role of Chinese labourers in gutting fish before the machine's invention'. In other words, terms or meanings that were once widespread and form part of Canada's negative legacy today.
- **Non-Canadianisms:** in addition to these six types, the category of 'Non-Canadianism' is for terms that have been labelled 'Canadian' in other sources, but for which no proof of their Canadian status was found, such as *ASA, clawback*, or *sunset clause*.

(Dollinger 2015b: 3–6)

Preservation makes more sense in the Canadian context, as the neighbouring USA no longer uses the term to any comparable degree.

The "Centennial Dictionaries"

Hunting down meanings that were "distinctively characteristic" of the way Canadians use English, the Big Six and their publisher reasonably might have expected great resonance and attention in the Canadian centennial year. It was, after all, the period of nationalism of the Canadian-liberal type, which became popular and a mainstream movement during Trudeau the Elder's first tenure as prime minister. Some years earlier, in 1959, a quote in the business correspondence of Dr Leechman drives home this point and shows that it was not an overnight feeling that was pulled out of the hat in late 1966 or so in the lead-up to the centennial. One is reminded of Edgar W. Schneider's (2007) Stage IV, endo-normative stabilization, which we know from Chapter 1:

Things will break in a big way for you any day now. People are becoming more aware of being Canadian all the time and your work should be in demand. (G. Joy Tranter, Editor of *The Canadian Red Cross Junior*, 4 May 1959, to Douglas Leechman, BC Archives MS-1290, Box 3 File 16)

Break big they would within a decade. Scholars refer to this time as "a seismic shift in English Canadians' sense of themselves and their nation in the Trudeau era" (Wright 2008: 111), in the 1960s and early 1970s.

A slam dunk, to use basketball terminology, was expected not just for *DCHP-1* but for the entire dictionary series called Dictionary of Canadian English, of which *DCHP-1* was merely one part, yet arguably the most important one, as all other dictionaries benefitted from its quotation file. *The Beginning Dictionary*, a dictionary for Grades 3–5, was published in 1962 under Avis' leadership. *The Intermediate Dictionary*, for Grades 6–9, was headed by Scargill and published in 1963. Robert J. Gregg, dialectologist and soon-to-be head of UBC Linguistics, took charge of *The Senior Dictionary*, originally for Grades 10–13, which would soon become the bestselling and most widely used dictionary of English in Canada from 1983 to 1998. This rise of *The Senior* happened, as Figure 20 shows, against the long-standing dominance and hegemony of American and British dictionaries. In 1983, *The Senior* was renamed the *Gage Canadian Dictionary* after considerable expansion and revision – as such, it became the key dictionary in the codification of Canadian English. It is fair to say that the success of the *Gage Canadian* in the 1980s, long before the *Canadian Oxford Dictionary* was even envisaged, is the most impressive success story of linguistic autonomy in the history of the country.[3]

In one of his last papers, Robert J. Gregg offers a clear rationale for the Gage series:

The raison d'être for these dictionaries is very simple. Before they were published, British or American dictionaries were the only ones available in Canada. The situation naturally caused difficulties for Canadians. (Gregg 1993: 35)

Breaking Foreign Dominance

It took the *Gage Canadian Dictionary* fifteen years to break the dominance of American and British dictionaries (of American and British English) on the

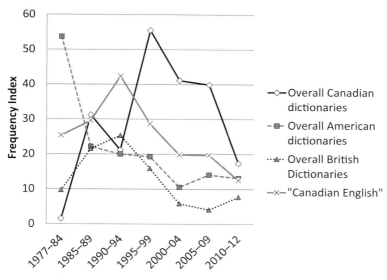

Figure 20 Overall mentions in the Canadian press of US, CDN, and UK titles

Canadian market. Figures 20 and 21 quantify the mentions of the respective dictionary names in 300+ Canadian newspapers and visualize a development that is otherwise difficult to assess. The rationale used here is that newspaper mentions directly correlate with market share or frequency of use – the more mentions, the more often that dictionary is used.

The Frequency Index is a normalized measure that allows us to compare the number of mentions across the periods. When seen in Figure 20, which respectively lumps together all major Canadian, American, and British dictionaries on the Canadian market, American dictionaries were the ones most often referred to in the Canadian press in the first period, 1977–84, followed by British dictionaries, with Canadian titles only in third and last position. They were negligible in that period. It is due to the *Gage Canadian* that Canadian dictionaries became most popular in 1985–89, a position they would not surrender until 2010–12. We can see in Figure 21 ("Major dictionaries' mentions") that, as of 1990–94, the *Gage Canadian* was the most-often-cited dictionary until the pre-publication PR of the *Canadian Oxford Dictionary* set in around 1995/96.

Those who wonder what happened from 2005 to 2009 and what is behind the steep drop of Canadian dictionary names are reminded that the *Canadian Oxford Dictionary (COD)* was shut down in that period – to be precise, at the end of October 2008. At the time, my colleagues and I lamented the loss, as we

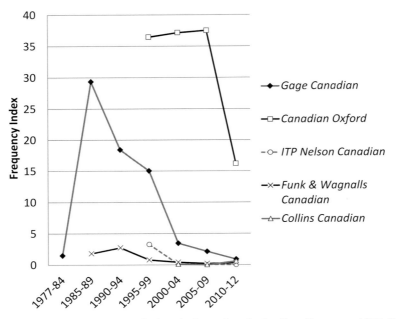

Figure 21 Major dictionaries' mentions in the Canadian press, 1977–2012

did not believe Oxford University Press' (OUP's) assurances that the diction-ary would be "revised from Britain". A decade on, we are still left with the old 2004 edition.

Figure 20 also shows the use of the term *Canadian English* over the years. The success of the *COD* was so overwhelming that it pushed aside the Gage dictionaries in all but their elementary and high-school markets. It seems, however, as if the PR geniuses at Oxford did not lastingly plant the idea of Canadian English into the minds of its speakers and that the notion scarcely went beyond the word level. Once the dictionary was moved to the UK, the staff at Oxford University Press Canada around editor Katherine Barber were laid off, the dictionary was left to drift off into oblivion, and with it – with no one left standing beside the *COD* (with Gage focussing on non-language reference markets by that time) – Canadian English was effectively cut loose.

How did that come about? Let's take a look at the Canadian dictionaries alone, as shown in Figure 21, listing five major titles in the same period as above, 1977 to 2012.

We can see that the *Canadian Oxford*, even long before publication in 1998, apparently "siphoned off" PR from the *Gage Canadian* and generally knew how to attract the interest of the press. This effect is much owed to Katherine

Barber's relentless outreach work, a real strong suit of "Canada's Word Lady". (Find her on Twitter under that handle.) However, when the *COD* was shut down at the end of 2008, a void was created, since that title had effectively destroyed the reputations of the *Gage Canadian* (1997) and the *ITP Nelson* (1997), which negatively affected not just Canadian dictionaries but the perception of Canadian English as a whole. When the last dust of what I call the Great Canadian Dictionary War of the late 1990s had settled, we saw no winner and only a long list of losers that, by 2008, was completed with the *Canadian Oxford Dictionary*. Since 2004, *COD*'s last edition, Canadian English has been left without a full-size up-to-date general dictionary (*DCHP-2* is a specialized one) for the first time since 1967.

We can say that the centennial was a remarkable point in Canada's history, despite the post-hoc academic criticism and blanket charges of nationalism that now occasionally surface. There was something in the making that was, if not outright positive, apparently necessary for large segments of the population. Sociolinguistically, for the first time, four up-to-date dictionaries – from a school dictionary for Grades 3–5 to a scholarly historical dictionary – were available. This point, November 1967, has been the high point of Canadian lexicography to date. This high point included the school dictionaries that Edmonton Professor and Oxford scholar John Considine rightly called "the work of good scholars" (Considine 2003: 257). Paradoxically, Considine's assessment was rare among the choir of voices that, for mostly non-linguistic reasons, preferred the *Canadian Oxford Dictionary* as of 1998.

What we will see in later chapters is that it is not always the best work that wins the day. It's a bit like the late 1970s format battle over the VCR (video cassette recorder) market: with VHS, Betamax, and Video2000 systems, three systems were available globally as of early 1980. The fact that the latter two were technically superior to VHS did not help them gain any foothold, and VHS walked away victorious. The reasons for the dominance of Oxford in the Canadian dictionary market as of late 1998 or so were to a considerable degree, as will be shown later, what in New Zealand is called "colonial cringe":[4] everything that is from the UK must be so much better.

But this apparent step back – in Schneider's model, from endo-normative stabilization back to some kind of exo-normative rule – did not happen for another three decades. In November 1967, there was a moment in linguistic history when Canadians seemed to forget about any colonial inferiority complexes of their own, when four types of dictionaries were ready for the buying: made in Canada, by Canadians, for Canadians, tailor-made in four "suits". And bought these dictionaries were. It was the first year of "linguistic home rule", if you will.

Publishing in the Centennial Year

It is understandable that the centennial celebrations and the goal to make *DCHP-1* a centennial contribution created considerable excitement and momentum. As a result, there were simple omissions that are clearly owed to the cutting of corners as the deadline was looming. They are, by and large, no biggies and are limited to offering, for instance, *Stanley Cup* with 1958 and 1962 quotations only, but not one from 1893, when, as the definition states too, the cup was first awarded. (Though it wouldn't be ready for presentation until much later; Lord Stanley had to be reminded a few times to send the promised dough, moolah, bucks. A gentleman may be slow but keep his word he must.)

The publisher knew the importance of the deadline and also saved time where possible. Paddy Drysdale, who had coordinated the school dictionaries from Toronto, made the executive decision not to send out final proofs of *DCHP-1* to the editors in order to meet the 1967 publication deadline. His rationale is understandable:

I was not going to send out copies of the page proofs. I can let you have a copy for interest and reference, but I agreed with Wally and Harry that there was neither need nor time for the editors to read page proofs. I am having the corrections carefully checked against the marked galleys, and the page breaks, guide words, and folios are being checked. In addition, I am having a reader go through them to guard against lacunae, broken type, and other mechanical errors. (Drysdale to Leechman, 17 May 1967)

That it was a race against time becomes clear by how quickly *DCHP-1* was turned around. In January 1965, it was all but unclear when the book would be ready, as the epigraph at the beginning of this chapter shows. Then, just one and a half years later, the finished manuscript for *A–Z* plus the substantive bibliography had been sent to the publisher for typesetting:

The entire MSS is now at Gage's; Paddy took it back with him yesterday. Nevertheless, antedatings etc. (in very limited numbers) should be sent to me for clearing. (Avis to Hall, 8 Oct. 1966)

We know that, from at least January 1967, possibly earlier, to about May 1967, Avis had been checking a first set of proofs:

I'm glad to hear you are now making progress through the letters. It will be a long job, but I hope you find it gets quicker – or at least no slower – as you go on. (Drysdale to Avis, 10 Jan. 1967)

While reading proofs, the team would still bring up major questions of revision and addition, as the following correspondence from Drysdale (in Scarborough at Gage's office at 1500 Birchmount Road) to Avis in Kingston shows:

The word in question [*ballicater*] was on a list of some 50 items that George Story & I drew up to test for vocabulary distribution, & he would probably know more. When we come to using consultants to check specialized material, it might well be worth submitting Nfld. items to Story. He has his own files, & he had access to Kirwin's findings on pronunciation. (Drysdale to Avis, 10 Jan. 1967)

It is clear that another couple of years would have allowed the Big Six to get a lot of the detail on Newfoundland in, whose lack was later criticized (see Story & Kirwin 1971) in what is the most important critique of *DCHP-1* until Görlach (1990). We will make the point below that precisely this kind of substantial critique – perhaps delivered in a more constructive manner – was generally what was missing in the initial period following publication. But first, it's worth taking a look at the praise for *DCHP-1*, some of which was nothing less than exuberant.

Public and Peer Reception

In academic circles, review is crucial – for critique's sake, for improvement, correction, and the eventual acceptance of an idea until someone might find fault with it for some other reason later on. While peer review, blind or not, doesn't guarantee that the findings and claims are correct, it usually increases the likelihood of them being so. In any case, peer review asserts acceptance (if passed). In publishing circles, likewise, reputation is everything: a book with a good "rep", regardless of its actual quality, will sell. And sales are important, especially so in the dictionary world. In this competitive setting, the letters from what were nominally Gage Publishing's competitors were buoyantly positive. Jess Stein from Random House Inc. in New York, for instance, wrote about wasting an entire work day reading *DCHP-1*, praising it as "first-rate, a real landmark in English lexicography".[5]

Mr Stein was not alone. Sidney Landau, who would later publish his successful textbook on lexicography in 1984 (from whose second edition from 2001 we have seen some wise quotes at the outset of Chapter 4), perhaps even tops the previous praise. Writing to Wally Avis, Mr Landau states:

As I told Mr Houghton [of Longmans], now that we have it I cannot imagine how we managed to get along for so long without it. It is the best thing to happen in lexicography since Mathews' Dictionary of Americanisms. (Sidney I. Landau to Walter Avis, 29 Nov. 1967)[6]

Back then, Landau was Editor-in-Chief of Funk & Wagnalls dictionaries – so, the competition. In any case, it is a good thing for any publishing project to get the competitors to appreciate the work. And attention it did get. The University of Toronto Press, the biggest academic press in Canada back then, would publish historical dictionaries as of the 1980s. Back in 1967, however, the Press' Director, Marsh Jeanneret, wrote the following to Dr Wilf Wees, Vice-President of Publishing at Gage:

I am more than delighted to have the copy of your Dictionary of Canadianisms, and I now feel that the Centennial year has been well worthwhile. This is a superb piece of work from every standpoint – production as well as editorial . . . My repeated congratulations on a magnificent production. I have never been so envious. (Drysdale, quoting M. Jeanneret to W. R. Wees, in a letter to Scargill, Avis, Crate, and Leechman, 12 Dec. 1967)[7]

DCHP-1 was, in its heyday, something like the "envy" of the publishing industry, who were not too blinded by competition and so freely acknowledged the competitor's success.

Besides the publishing peers, the academics and language professionals are the other important groups that need to be convinced. Both were likewise positive, though not all of the academic reviewers were at "arm's length", which means that they were in a kind of close association, professional or personal, with the makers of the product. Raven I. McDavid, a long-time friend of Avis, for instance, wrote that, since every editor is responsible "for any shortcomings, so must Avis receive the major credit for the production of so good a dictionary in so short a time" (McDavid 1967: 56), which are glowing words from any academic reviewer, a group that generally tends to be on the hypercritical, perhaps even nitpicking side (a common side-effect of the profession).

To be fair, while McDavid was among the reviewers closest to Avis, he also wrote one of the most insightful reviews, including a real point of critique. Mitford M. Mathews was probably the one person who was in the best position to critique DCHP-1 for what it was worth. He called it "a work of unusual interest and value" and, in the typical somewhat stiff-upper-lip praise that academics usually prefer, "a valuable contribution to American historical lexicography" (Mathews 1969: 90–91). What is striking in his review is that it is written as a kind of staccato-style collection of background information and history and not so much as a close reading and scrutiny of DCHP-1 as such. It reads as if Matthews was highlighting his connections with the project, which were only indirect via Lovell. His review, however, can be read as the best form of compliment among senior academics, "claiming" projects in which no active role had been played.

What is noticeable in both these high-profile reviews is that Mathews utterly dispenses with a word-by-word, entry-by-entry critique in any way: there is almost no kind of critical information. McDavid does offer some antedatings and shows some omissions, above all in the paragraph below:

There are naturally some gaps. Chowder, likely of Canadian French origin, does not appear. For Nova Scotia I miss Lunenburg dory and L. Dutch; for New Brunswick, skedaddler and Skedaddlers Ridge. But anyone acquainted with the construction of historical dictionaries can forgive such omissions, especially since the editors promise further editions as well as a more extensive *Dictionary of Canadian English on Historical Principles*. (McDavid 1967: 57)

These five terms represent the harshest critique of *DCHP-1* until and including 1970 – so, during the period immediately following publication when reviews have the most impact. The critique is arguably not harsh at all, especially since it is toned down right away based on promises – neither of which would materialize, but no one would have known that in 1967. No revision would see the light of day until 2017 (and the 2017 edition, *DCHP-2*, is much more of an update than a revision of *DCHP-1* content), and no fully fledged historical dictionary of English in Canada has ever appeared (and probably never will, as the window of opportunity for such a project has disappeared).

This "big" historical dictionary would document not just terms and meanings that are characteristic of Canadian English but any English word used in Canada. So, for instance, while *child* or *desk* are used in many places, when were they first used in Canada? In other words, it would be an *OED*-type of "book of everything" but with evidence solely drawn from what is now Canada. The big historical dictionary was originally planned in addition to the Gage series and *DCHP-1* (which was envisaged as merely the stepping stone towards the big "Canadian *OED* based solely on Canadian evidence") and Scargill reports he had collected 20,000 quotations for it (*Time Magazine*, 17 Nov. 1967: 18). I think it is safe to say that today the ship for such a book has sailed; such content would today be better picked up in a new dictionary of the English Language Complex (which includes all varieties of English globally, from Nigerian Pidgin English to Indian English to Finnish Lingua Franca English to Prince Charles' and Barrack Obama's English) or within the *OED* – to a small degree, the latter has already begun to do this.

Academic praise was offered from other philologies, which attests to *DCHP-1*'s reach. Eastern European, German, and French reviews were very positive. G. B. Poceptsov, writing in Ukrainian in a Kiev-published journal, speaks of *DCHP-1* in the highest tones: "The publishing of this dictionary is an important event in English lexicography." It "illustrates the lexical-semantical distinctiveness of the Canadian variety of the English language" (G. B. Poceptsov, as translated from the Ukrainian by Gage Ltd).[8] A French scholar writes that *DCHP-1* will take its place alongside the *OED* and the *Dictionary of Americanisms*, which is very high praise indeed.[9] Closer to home, in the *Saskatchewan Bulletin*, *DCHP-1* is elevated to "official" status, which in reality it has never had, as the Canadian government does not micro-manage dictionary use. *DCHP-1* was therefore incorrectly claimed to be "the official reference of the Canadian Government".[10]

Like the academic and publishing peer reviews, the public reactions to
DCHP-1, led by language professionals, were overwhelmingly positive.
So much so that it seems fair to say that, in 1968, *DCHP-1* was well on its
way to becoming a Canadian household name. The news reporters at the
Toronto Telegram were "much impressed by this work"[11] and would consult
DCHP-1 in the newsroom, a function it had not been intended for and for
which *The Senior Dictionary* would have been more suitable. Other writers
apparently went *much* further in their praise. Norman Dresser (1968) in
Manitoba is perhaps the most exuberant of them all, declaring *DCHP-1* to
be "Perhaps the most significant contribution to Canadian letters in the past
300 years."[12]

Superlatives were easy to come by in the early post-publication days. There
was also a great feeling of achievement among all those involved. Paddy
Drysdale still speaks about *DCHP-1* with a great deal of pride, and rightly
so. "There was nothing to compare it with", he told me in March 2017 when
I visited him and his wife, Olwen, in their Oxfordshire home. Paddy is not
alone. Gage Love, the president of *DCHP-1*'s publisher W. J. Gage Ltd,
considered *DCHP-1* "his greatest legacy by far, and one of his proudest
achievements".[13]

These quotes allow us to glean the cultural importance of the work for those
who were around in the centennial year. Mavor Moore (1967), in what must
have been the first review, in the November issue of famous Canadian monthly
magazine *Saturday Night*, considered *DCHP-1* as bearing "lively and scholarly
witness to that most elusive of Centennial projects, the Canadian identity".
While Moore offers some critique, his text is more general in addressing the
method (no oral quotations) and bias of *all* historical dictionaries at the time,
not just *DCHP-1*. Above all, however, Moore's tone-setting review is ripe
with praise:

I can think of no more fitting Centennial project for a nation only now beginning to see
itself as something other than a loose collection of societies – but let us hope we do not
have to wait another century before we get a real dictionary of Canadianisms. (Moore
1967: 54–55)

That "real", presumably all-words-of-English-documented-in-Canada, dictionary was Scargill's pipe dream, as we know today.

It is not easy to reconstruct precisely when *DCHP-1* was published. We
know that on 3 Oct. 1967, a first "form", which is a batch of 16 pages on one
sheet that would then be bent, folded, and cut on the sides, went to the printers
(a method basically used since Gutenberg's days). Drysdale wrote on that day:

Publication is now in hand, and the first form should actually go on the press today.
Provided that there are no crises, it looks as though we should have books in good time
for our November 15th publication date. (Drysdale to Leechman, 3 Oct. 1967)

Since Mavor Moore managed to publish the first review in the November issue of *Saturday Night*, which was the key landmark publication in Canada's popular magazine market, some advance copies, perhaps unbound, must have gone out. Given that we would allow at least a couple of days for perusal of the book and the writing of a short review, with November issues usually appearing in late October, it is safe to assume that at least some sets of full print sheets of the entire book were ready around 20 October.

That this first print run may have been very small may be gleaned from another message to Leechman, more than three weeks later, when Leechman had still not received his contractual copies of *DCHP-1*: "you will very soon have copies of the book itself" (Drysdale to Leechman, 26 Oct. 1967). There is reason to hypothesize that *DCHP-1* did not hit the bookstores, considering the supply chains, before mid-November 1967, which is late for the Christmas business.

Praise would not remain limited to *Saturday Night* magazine. Other cities' magazines were quick to chime in. *Vancouver Life* described *DCHP-1* simply but powerfully with a Chinook Jargon word, *skookum* – 'big, great, strong' – effectively the superlative of West Coast praise: "This is a skookum book."[14] In the 1960s, the word would still have been known to many West Coasters. *Weekend Magazine* was also not shy, using one of the more nationalist headings with "We speak Canadian",[15] which headlined a licensed pre-print of *DCHP-1* content and paraphrased some twenty-eight words from *DCHP-1*.

The Business Case

In dictionary making, the business case plays a somewhat different role than in publications that are less labour-intensive. While the *OED* has never made any money as such (and never will), it has been maintained all these decades as a cross-financed prestige project. After initial quibbles till about 1897, when the *OED*'s dedication to Queen Victoria was accepted by Her Majesty,[16] it was finally accepted that this prestige project would not add to Oxford University Press' coffers directly but would feed into their commercially viable desk dictionaries and subscriptions – which benefit from the *OED* in indirect ways – in addition to increasing the Oxford brand's prestige factor.

As for the business case, the *OED* is a bit like the vintage Ferrari that is parked on the car dealership's lot and that you may drive though you'd never be able to afford it. Instead, you hope that you can buy at least the Golf GTI with or without the Ferrari-red hubcaps and trims, and not the littler and cheaper Polo version.

In the case of *DCHP-1* and the non-existent Canadian lexicographical tradition at that point, prestige would not have gone a very long way in the

1960s, despite Gage Ltd having had a century-long publication history in Canada. Structurally, the historical dictionary – like the *OED* in the case of Oxford dictionaries – fed into the "smaller" Gage dictionaries. So the business case was important, of course, especially since Gage Ltd did lay out money from the late 1950s onwards that they would need to recoup to a degree.

So it must have felt soothing for Wilf Wees, then Gage's Vice-President of Publishing, and Gage Love, President of W. J. Gage Ltd., to hear good news concerning the sales after publication. When Drysdale was delivering first assessments during the following one and a half years after publication of *DCHP-1*, Gage Ltd "brass" must have known that the dozen-year investment on their part would pay off:

Sales of the dictionary are proceeding steadily. The reviews we had in the professional library journals have resulted in a great many orders for single copies from public and academic libraries all over Canada and the United States. (Drysdale to Leechman, 3 July 1968, BC Archives MS-1290, Box 4 File 13)

That trend had been going for a few months at least, starting with the November publication of *DCHP-1*, as we know from a December letter:

Orders for the Dictionary of Canadianisms are coming in quite steadily, and the book seems to be arousing a good deal of interest, as indeed it should. (Drysdale to Scargill, 12 Dec. 1967, University of Victoria Archives, 90–66, Box 4)

There is, however, always a difference between the qualitative assessment and the sales figures. "Steadily" is a relative term and says nothing about the sales figures. How well did *DCHP-1* sell? Only with this information can we gauge the business case, so it's worth taking a closer look at the accounting end of the project.

Top Secret: *DCHP-1* Sales

How many copies of *DCHP-1* were sold? We are in the rare position to get more than a glance at the actual sales figures. The Leechman collection and its benefactor's zeal as an archivist afford us a very exact view of what is otherwise one of the best-kept trade secrets: actual sales figures. The data in Table 5 are owed to Leechman's complete royalty statements for the years 1967–77.

The total of some 6,800 copies sold in a decade is a very good indicator of how much money was made. At the hefty price of $25 – almost $200 in 2019 dollars – and with the usual bookseller's discount of 40 per cent, Gage Ltd would have earned $15 a piece, which would yield over the decade some $105,000 in earnings from *DCHP-1* alone. While some copyright fees for

Table 5 *Sales figures for* DCHP-1, *1967–1977*

Royalties Statement Period	DCHP-1 Sales
31 Dec. 1967	1,255
31 Dec. 1968	1,213
31 Dec. 1969	3,213 (13-month period)
31 Dec. 1970	326
30 Apr. 1973	102 (only four months)
15 May 1974	236
30 Apr. 1976	321
30 Apr. 1977	152
TOTAL 1967–77	**6,818**

reprints – e.g., $250 for excerpts in the *Weekend Magazine* – would slightly increase this figure, the earnings would overall be somewhat lower, because as of 1975 Gage offered, in addition to the $25 encased deluxe edition, a trade version for "just" $19.95 (see Figure 22).

Income of about $100,000 in a decade, or $725,000 in 2019 dollars may sound like a good business case, but it doesn't consider the outlay. Starting in the late 1950s with some $2,000 to Scargill's Lexicographical Centre, the advances went on to include fees for consultants – with Crate being the most regular one, receiving some $250 bimonthly for a time towards the collection of quotations – and, of course, payments for staff time, in addition to Drysdale.

A benchmark for the success of the pricey *DCHP-1* can be offered by Leechman's own textbook, the 1956 *Native Tribes of Canada*. Ten years after it first appeared, Leechman's textbook still sold 2,267 copies that year and, though at the much lower price of $5.45, almost twice as many copies as *DCHP-1*. The year 1968, which should have been *DCHP-1*'s strongest year, sold a few copies *less* than the couple of months in 1967 in which *DCHP-1* had been available – not the signs of a runaway bestseller. In 1968, *DCHP-1* again did not fare better than the textbook: *Native Tribes* sold 1,772 copies, *DCHP-1* 1,213 copies. It must have been a bit sobering for the Gage marketing department when they looked at the figures to see that the decade-old *Native Tribes*, which did not require any research outlay by the publisher, was a greater success in copies sold than the brand new *DCHP-1*.

With these benchmarks, which publisher would embark on a dictionary project that may not even be finished, like so many others before? Only a publisher like Gage, who made it a labour of love while trying to maintain a reasonable business case.

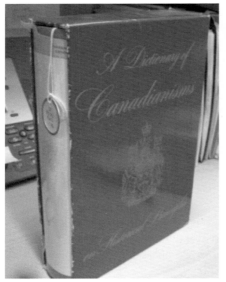
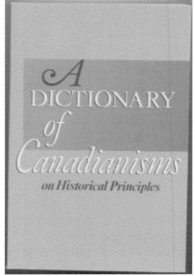

Figure 22 A 1970s edition of *DCHP-1* (left) and the 1991 reprint (right)
The hardcover comes with a new, less expensive slip-cover design (see
Figure 19 for a comparison).
(Photo: Chelsea Shriver, used by permission)
The 1991 reprint, paperback edition. (No hardback was produced.) See the
footnote for ordering a paperback copy[17]
(Photo: S. Dollinger)

The decision to package *DCHP-1* as a deluxe version was not taken lightly,
however. As late as May 1967, Drysdale reports to Leechman that "We are
trying to arrive at a format that would make the book commercially feasible to
us" (Drysdale to Leechman, 5 May 1967, BC Archives MS-1290, Box 4
File 12). This indicates that Gage Ltd was well aware of the issue surrounding
dictionary sales. In stark contrast to Leechman's textbook (any textbook usually), which does not require any noticeable expenses, *DCHP-1* did not come for
free. In order to boost sales, Gage went to considerable lengths to market the
book to as wide an audience as possible. There were special pre-order forms, as
shown in Figure 23, with lavish fonts and elegantly spelled-out years.

In addition to these marketing and PR expenses, there must have been
significant postal fees. As Drysdale writes, 60,000 information-and-order
fliers, similar in design to the dedication stationery in Figure 23, were mailed
(Drysdale to Leechman, 26 Oct. 1967). Even at the standard 6-cent postage at
the time, this alone would be $3,600, or about 4 per cent of the earnings of the

Figure 23 *DCHP-1* PR material; *DCHP-1* billed as a Gage centennial project
(Photo: S. Dollinger)

full print run in a decade! Add to this a full-page ad and reply card in the
November issue of *Saturday Night*, the staff hours and the like to prepare all
this, and you can see, with almost 7,000 copies sold in a decade, *DCHP-1* was
probably barely breaking even.

What Was Missing

Despite the joy and welcoming words during the "hype" of *DCHP-1*, at
least two things have generally been given short shrift. First, beyond all
Canadiana-focussed celebration, *DCHP-1* contributed to the study of World
Englishes at a time when that academic field did not exist; it was barely
emerging by 1967. Second, the reviewing process was somewhat atypical –
the resounding praise for *DCHP-1* was not matched with competent and
detailed critique by the field of experts.

From the World Englishes angle, *DCHP-1* was – jointly with Cassidy and
Le Page's *Dictionary of Jamaican English*, published that same year – the first
scholarly historical dictionary of a non-dominant variety of English – i.e., of
neither British nor American English – that would have an immediate impact
on English linguistics.[18] This is important, since a focus on non-dominant
varieties triggers a shift of perspective and enriches the views of varieties of
English and standard English in important ways. All of a sudden, there was not
just a British and American standard but also a Canadian standard, and one
could point to the completed four-part Gage Dictionary of Canadian English
series to prove it.

Today, the situation is a little different, also because Canadian English has been without a full-size up-to-date English dictionary since 2004. But those who are in the know still appreciate the important role of *DCHP-1* as the "flagship" dictionary – the "Canadian *OED*", if you will. This praise extends to more recently practising lexicographers, such as Katherine Barber (2010: 142), who considers *DCHP-1* a "truly wonderful work of scholarship". I often think McDavid delivers the best *bon mot* about *DCHP-1*:

> There is glory enough in this dictionary [*DCHP-1*] for all who participated, even as we recognize Wally's drive as what got the work ready for the centennial of Confederation. . . . The work is a model, to which Wally attached no proprietary claim, only a wish that it be used, and revised accurately as often as practicable. (McDavid 1981: 124)

With enough glory to go around, it is easy to forget about the book's shortcomings, which, of course, exist, as in any other work under the sun.

The atypical review record for *DCHP-1* is a puzzling case today, which is best explained by another large-scale project. The biggest punishment of any academic project is not to be heavily critiqued but to be ignored – *not* mentioned, *not* discussed, *not* reviewed. This is what happened, by and large, to the *Survey of Canadian English* (*SCE*) (Scargill and Warkentyne 1972), in some part because of the newly arrived variationist sociolinguist approach. Practitioners of this approach considered, not completely unjustifiably, the survey's idea of "region" as too vague, lumping respondents from different places in the same category because of their province alone. While the critique is valid, what has not been considered appropriately is that the adoption – indeed, pioneering application – of novel delivery and processing methods limited the choices. All results, for instance, were coded for IBM paper-punch-card software, which was being used to process the data very quickly: less than a year from sending out some 30,000 sheets and receiving more than 16,000 in return, the results were published! The early punch-card computer had its limitations, as it did not allow for a number of things that were easy to handle just ten years later. So, in short, the *SCE* was sidelined for many wrong reasons. It is, to this day, a valuable source of linguistic variation and a kind of benchmark for the early 1970s that would be unavailable otherwise.

With *DCHP-1*, the case was suboptimal in other ways. It surely, as you have seen, was not ignored; it was, I would argue, simply praised *too much* – so much so that very few dared to highlight its shortcomings. Story and Kirwin's (1971) review is remarkable in this context in that their critique is worth its salt, honouring the work and its editors by critiquing it from a principled and detailed account. The provocative title, "National dictionaries and regional homework", is perhaps unfortunate wording, but the critique is sound. And yet, Story and Kirwin also acknowledge that:

The book has been widely reviewed in both the United States and Canada, and it has been warmly praised as a pioneer attempt to record the English vocabulary of the Canadian Dominion. That praise is well deserved. (Story and Kirwin 1971: 19)

They then deliver the most detailed review from any angle – in their case, that of the Newfoundland and Labrador vocabulary – a kind of critique that is the *sine qua non* of scholarly activity. They go on to

Consider how certain fundamental problems have been handled by the editors, and then to examine the degree of precision with which the **Dictionary of Canadianisms** treats the regional vocabulary and meanings most familiar to us – those of Newfoundland and Labrador. (Story and Kirwin 1971: 19)

Ballicater is one case in point, first mentioned by Drysdale to Avis in a letter from January 1967, as discussed earlier. The review points out that the Newfoundland files at Memorial University list thirty-four spelling variants, while *DCHP-1* lists "only" nine. It is relatively clear that Avis did not get in touch with Kirwin, as recommended by Drysdale, on that item, hence the clear and somewhat heavy-handed critique.

I can confidently say so, because in *DCHP-2* we are still dealing with the same problem of how to treat any linguistically highly distinct region within Canada in a national dictionary; Newfoundland is the "nightmare scenario" because it is so wonderfully diverse (Dollinger 2015c). This is an area that is lacking an easy solution. And who can blame Avis for not getting in touch with another scholar a couple of months before he would have had to send off the manuscript, knowing that it would require him to go back and redo many parts, not just one word here and there? Avis did not dare to open this Pandora's box. He probably felt that that ship had sailed and was thinking ahead to the announced revisions. While critique such as Story and Kirwin's is central to academia, many academics have a hard time taking it. But not Avis, who acknowledges, neutrally, that Story and Kirwin consider *DCHP-1*'s treatment of Newfoundland as "inadequate" (Avis and Kinloch 1978: 127).

At times, authors think strategically of how reviewers may be enticed to be pleased. In the archival files we can find some testament to the editors' awareness of the public reviewing process. Crate writes the following lines to Avis in April 1966, expressing his concern with the early parts of the alphabet that are generally tackled first and that are subject to an evolving editorial practice:

I have been very concerned about the first parts of the DC, esp. the "C"s, as I expect the reviewers will want to be first out with their reviews when we publish, and it is in this section they will do their nit-picking, if given opportunity. It is unfortunately true that most of the professional reviewers are out to find fault with anything Canadian – and I refer to Canadian reviewers. (Crate to Avis, 20 April 1966)

For Crate, it was the letter *C*; Avis himself was more worried about *A* and *B*.[19] In any case, it is almost always the first letters in dictionaries starting with *A* that are not as good as the later ones; this is the case in *DCHP-1*, in *DARE*, *OED*, or any other big research dictionary.

The "New" File: Revision Materials

In at least two locations, in Victoria and in Kingston (Avis), the collection of materials for *DCHP-1* went on post-publication. The Kingston materials are found in the Strathy Language Unit (and in *DCHP-2*'s Bank of Canadian English quotations database), while the "New" file in Victoria has not been digitized. The Victoria New file is compact, with about 5,000 quotations, but includes quotations from *c.* 1967 to 1970 from some treasures that are difficult to come by digitally at present – local journals, magazines, and simple fliers and posters, the latter of which may be irretrievable by other means today.

With the benefit of hindsight, one wonders if the post-publication material in Victoria and in Kingston could not have been put to better use for *DCHP-1* in at least one respect. Much of this material is lying dormant in some archival boxes, spread out over the Canadian archival landscape. In Victoria, for instance, there are fourteen quotations from between 1968 and 1970 on *hippy*, *hippies*, and *hippie bums*. One of the slips is marked "slang" in pencil, probably by Avis. Another of these quotations, from the magazine *Saturday Night*, January 1969, page 26, column 3, reads: "For these reasons I find more hope for change in the hippies and their generation than in any royal commission" (codes on slip are "fr" and "AM"). Other words like this are *hooker*, *horny*, *hung-up*, *hype*, *hyped*, and *hyper*, and one gets the idea that what is documented here is an untapped little treasure of late 1960s / early 1970s slang and lingo. It offers something that in *DCHP-2* we were also unable to deliver to the degree that we would have liked. Surely, this calls for a third edition, *DCHP-3*. Who's up for it? Please do get in touch.[20]

The real achievement of the Big Six can only be seen in hindsight and, as Paddy Drysdale indicated to me, it indeed seems true that there were very few who were in the position to review the work competently and critically. Mathews, certainly, was not at his best in his review, and McDavid, as a close friend of Avis, did what he could but naturally had to fall short of an arm's-length review. Many, however, who might have written a review did not, which has to a considerable degree to do with the direction that linguistics was taking at that point in time. On the one hand, you had the early Chomskyans, for whom dictionaries were just simple lists, and on the other hand were the early sociolinguists, who would rather study one word in all its social aspects than write or review a whole book with thousands of them, with no entry being up to the new scratch. Neither of them really understood the relevance of dictionaries, let alone historical dictionaries.

It was not until 1990 when a proper arm's-length review appeared that went beyond critique from one regional angle. This review was undertaken by a scholar of World Englishes in the context of dictionaries of "transplanted Englishes" – what we now call *postcolonial Englishes*. Like in the nineteenth century when German-speaking scholars led the field, it was a German scholar who – finally – put *DCHP-1* into its proper international context. The reason for this is that, in the Old World, old academic traditions are not discarded as quickly as in the New, which, in cases such as this, serves as an advantage. In the review, Canada takes a disproportional share and, while the assumption that the distinctly Canadian English vocabulary is "not large" (Görlach 1990: 1483) should be disputed,[21] Manfred Görlach's overview – from North American to Caribbean and African Englishes – shows very nicely that "the lexicography of Canadian English was almost non-existent before W. S. Avis" (Görlach 1990: 1484), and ultimately, as we know, Charles J. Lovell and the other Big Six members, plus Robert J. Gregg as the man behind *The Senior* and the *Gage Canadian Dictionary*. It is perhaps in the overview and know-ledge of scholars of World Englishes that the achievement of the Big Six comes to the fore for the first time and is appreciated for what it is worth to the fullest extent. Isn't that funny? From abroad, you apparently have a better chance to appreciate fully what the Big Six did for Canadian English.

Figure 24 Paddy and Olwen Drysdale in their home in Oxfordshire,
March 2017
(Photo: S. Dollinger)

6   Riding the Wave of Success

No hist.[ory] of Can. Eng. [is] yet written
Few would attempt it at present
(Douglas Leechman, manuscript notes, mid-1960s; BC Archives MS-1290,
Box 47 File 3)

The new wave of national pride continued into the 1970s. Cautiously so, because we're Canadian, but nonetheless. The Big Six were "made men" by the late 1960s, as invitations to speak started to flow. Some of them, having caught the lexicographical bug, went on to other dictionary projects. Most noteworthy is Douglas Leechman in this regard, as he became a paid long-term reader for Burchfield's *Supplement to the OED*. Avis, likewise, kept collecting quotations for the revision of *DCHP-1* and left a mountain of them. There were others, such as Henry Warkentyne, a linguistics professor at the University of Victoria in Scargill's department, who collected quotation slips and gave extra credit – 5 per cent – for students who produced them in the early 1980s (Margery Fee: pers. communication). Drysdale, still working for Gage, was by then in the fortunate position of marketing an excellent dictionary series, consisting of four titles by 1967 and five by 1973, to an audience that was quite eager to buy and use them for a while. Only of Crate do we know, once more, little.

Generally, the 1970s can be characterized as a period of consolidation, of reaping the rewards of the hard work of the 1950s and 1960s. But, characteristically, that decade did not see the frequent updates of the existing editions that were promised; *The Senior Dictionary* was updated in 1979 for the first time, while no new material was added to *DCHP-1*. Even the 1973 abridged version of *DCHP-1*, entitled *A Concise Dictionary of Canadianisms on Historical Principles*, did not include new information, which would have been relatively easy to provide: add *eh*, include *homo milk*, research *garburator*. The first substantial revision of any title in the Dictionary of Canadian English series, however, was 1983's *The Senior Dictionary*, which was then re-branded as the *Gage Canadian Dictionary*. There were also 1973 and 1979 editions, making the current 1997 edition the fifth. It is no easy task to identify a particular dictionary title with its real content, as publishers do all in their

143

power to conceal interrelationships between editions and products in the hopes of some marketing advantage. After all, who wants to buy a revised dictionary, or perhaps just a reprinted dictionary, when one with a new name and copyright date would make it appear completely new?

Return on Investment

As the 1970s rolled in, the decade's profound social changes did not fail to leave their mark on the dictionary market. While the Gage school dictionaries must have seen steep trajectories and good growth in that decade, we have reason to suggest that interest in *DCHP-1* started to wane. The idea of producing an abridgement with the 1973 *Concise DCHP-1*, for a fifth of the price of the unabridged work, is probably a reflection of the belief that interest would not be sustained with a second, revised edition.

With a price tag of $25 for *DCHP-1* and just $4.95 for the *Concise DCHP-1*, the respective sales figures can be interpreted. Consider this: in 2019 dollars, who would buy a $200 book when they could have a $40 abridged book for a Christmas present, personal reading, as a supply for school libraries in multiple copies? Drysdale was in charge of all editorial issues but, paradoxically, not at all regarding the business end of things – which amounted to an "unwritten rule" at Gage's (Drysdale: pers. correspondence, 2 April 2018). Correspondence in which Drysdale was merely relaying marketing rationale to Leechman seems to confirm this interpretation. Drysdale writes in the fall of 1968:

We have been trying for some time to find a way of introducing The Senior Dictionary and A Dictionary of Canadianisms [*DCHP-1*] to a wider audience than we can normally reach. Quite shortly, Maclean's are going to try a sample mailing to see whether direct-mail sales of the two dictionaries are likely to be profitable. (Drysdale to Leechman, 29 Oct. 1968, BC Archives MS-1290, Box 4 File 13)

There were high hopes for *DCHP-1* to introduce regular updates for historical dictionaries, though these hopes would not materialize. Avis wished "that energy and resources will permit a revised edition for there is much to add and much to reconsider" (Avis 1969: 5) in a December 1969 speech. It seems in light of such reasoning that the financial base would not have sustained frequent updates, as a revised edition would render earlier print stock obsolete.

While material was collected throughout the 1970s by Avis in Kingston and by the Lexicographical Centre in Victoria, as well as some individuals, by the late 1970s a lot of the enthusiasm had vanished. When Scargill (1977) used the data from *DCHP-1* to write a cultural narrative as evidence for Canadian identity, the resulting book, *A Short History of Canadian English*, not only disappointed from a scholarly viewpoint – McDavid (1980: 47) even attested instances of "professional irresponsibility" in it – but also had little public impact, which can only partly be attributed to the small local Victoria publishing house that Scargill had chosen.

Boom and Bust

Avis' 1979 death was the last nail in the coffin of a revision project by the original Big Six. While Scargill was still around and Warkentyne kept encouraging his students to collect quotations, which would go into the files of the Lexicographical Centre, in 1990 the Centre's files would be mothballed in the University of Victoria Archives. Out with the old, in with the new. The 1980s had seen with corpus linguistics yet another school of linguistic thought become dominant, which snubbed, like other schools before, the previous methods (in our case, the quotation file). The methodology of corpus linguistics was not new; it had been known in principle for half a century, but only affordable home computing made it accessible to many at that time. It was a harbinger of what was to come with digitally connected networks and the internet, as of 1992 in principle and a couple of years later in practice. All these changes resulted in a full-blown shock to the long-established routines of pen-and-paper lexicographers and their 4 x 6 "slips".

As a result, *DCHP-1* was quickly forgotten after 1990, not just in the public eye but also in the scholarly one: a search for "Dictionary of Canadianisms" in the *Globe and Mail* returns a mere 11 since 1977. Sales figures for the 1980s and 1990s were negligible, while 1,000 or more copies of a newly printed paperback edition lay in a warehouse as of 1991 with, soon after, no sales catalogue listing;[1] by the turn of the millennium, *DCHP-1* was a non-entity. Scargill, the hero of the first pages in Chapter 1, died in 1997; just recently, Paddy Drysdale says of Scargill, the enabler, that *DCHP-1* "probably would not have happened without him" (pers. correspondence, 2 April 2018). Robert J. Gregg, who had worked in the Gage school dictionary team and had shouldered the main responsibilities for *The Senior Dictionary*, died in 1998. Warkentyne, who worked at the University of Victoria, died in 1997, keeling over while playing golf at the age of 71.[2] Clearly, a factor in *DCHP-1* being forgotten is that so many scholars of Canadian English died relatively young and have, for some reason, not had the longevity of their colleagues: Bill Labov, for instance, the founder of the variationist sociolinguistic paradigm, turned 90 in December 2017 and is still going strong. At the Salt Lake City American Dialect Society meeting in January 2018, as respondent on the panel on the Canadian and California Vowel Shifts, Labov laid out the bigger issues for all. Imagine what we would have got on Canadian English had Avis lived to see his ninetieth birthday in 2009, or Lovell in 1997?

Marketing efforts for the Gage dictionaries, however, continued throughout the 1970s. Some of them were on a large scale – the biggest one perhaps a dictionary brochure, shown in Figure 25, which was sent out to all English departments in Canadian universities and colleges. This brochure showcases cleverly the theme of the "Word Bird" and the four-dictionary series, from the elementary-school dictionary to the scholarly historical dictionary. The angle of the PR is clear: "Gage is the word for Canadian dictionaries" reads the front page of the expensively and nicely produced multiple-colour brochure. It is illustrated with a sample entry from each of the four dictionaries for *able*, *about*, and *riding*, while *The Senior* fits only *able* and *riding*, and the *DCHP-1* box has room only for *riding*, illustrating how the increasing information requires more space. The sales figures show that for *DCHP-1* this 1975/76 measure had little effect, but, as Figure 21 in the previous chapter shows in the line for the *Gage Canadian*, the desk and school dictionaries took off and put – seen in Figure 20 – Canadian dictionaries on the map at the expense of American and British titles in an act of "endo-normative stabilization": from then on, for a while, Canadian linguistic standards were set exclusively in Canada, based on Canadian norms.[3]

The *Concise DCHP-1*: a Business Move

The late 1960s also saw new economical realities in Canada's publishing industry. With revenue losses amounting to about 30 per cent due to imported textbooks from the USA and Britain between 1967 and 1969, W. J. Gage Ltd President Gage Love saw himself forced to sell 80 per cent of his company. There is information in the files that the sale was to "Scott, Foresman", a US company (BC Archives MS-1290, Box 4 File 13), though staff only knew of Canadian entrepreneur Ron Besse, who was believed to be the sole purchaser and, on completion of the sale, became president of the company (Drysdale: pers. correspondence, 2 April and 28 May 2018). In any case, what was referred to as the "New Canadian Publishing Company" was now no longer W. J. Gage but "Gage Educational Publishing Limited" (MS-1290, Box 4 File 13, 28 Sept. 1970). Gage Love had only informal assurances that the strong Canadian programme would be continued. No more than six years later, however, "much to Mr. Love's delight" (Ray 2003: R9), another Canadian company bought the company back.

On the business front, sales were obviously important but it may well be that they would have played a greater role for any other owner than the philan-thropical Mr Love, who gave so much of his personal money away that his accountant is said to have exhorted him to curb his charity spending (Ray 2003: R9). By the late 1970s, the complete *DCHP-1* was finally available in a somewhat less expensive edition – though, at $19.95 rather than $25, it still cost the equivalent of $90 in 2019 money. In January 1976, Drysdale informed the rest of the editorial team about this product diversification:

Figure 25 Promotional flier for Gage's Dictionary of Canadian English series "The Word Bird Says", sent to English departments countrywide, mid-1970s

We had long been concerned about the high price that had to be paid by any purchaser of the complete dictionary. Now that our trade division is established and building up very good sales to bookstores and libraries across the country, it seemed time to do some price cutting and to provide different packages for different markets. Accordingly, we now have three different "items":

> text edition, acetate wrapper (as before) $15.00
> trade edition, with new jacket, $19.95
> de luxe edition, with new jacket and slip case $25.00

for the moment, we are not going to offer the middle item ($19.95)

Not ready for the Christmas market because of "delays over the making of the box". (Drysdale to Scargill, Avis, Crate, and Leechman, 20 Jan. 1976)

It appears that the $15 text edition was withdrawn, unless one counts the 1991 reprint (see Figure 22) as such, which was unconnected to the mid-1970s packaging proposal. As the sales figures for 1977 in the previous chapter reveal, the re-packaging had no positive effect. On the contrary, sales in 1977 were less than half of those in 1976. It appears that the re-packaging came too late and, by leaving out the $15 version, with a discount not large enough.

But a cheaper *DCHP-1* was not the only publisher-driven innovation in the 1970s. Earlier in the decade, plans for a cheap abridged edition at a normal textbook price-level were deliberated. Plans for this *Concise DCHP-1*, with about a third of the content of the mother dictionary, were finalized between February and April 1972, with very fast production later that year:

It is hoped that in this way we will achieve a volume of sales that has not proved possible for the original Dictionary of Canadianisms, and also that we will lead people to the use and purchase of the parent volume. (24 April 1972, Drysdale to Leechman)

The *Concise* went on sale by December 1972 for a very affordable $3.95, which is about $25 in 2019 dollars. Early reviews were positive and included calls such as that the *Concise DCHP-1* "should be placed in every resource centre. Pupils should be encouraged to buy their own for reference",[4] and Gage's commitment to invest in marketing is documented in Richard Lee's letter to Douglas Leechman. Lee was the head of the editorial department, putting forth policy and monitoring performance, but was not involved in any editorial tasks. Lee stated that the *Concise*

will be promoted vigorously to secondary schools and colleges during the next few months and to bookstores and the general public next fall in the hopes that many will find their way under the 1973 Christmas tree. (Richard H. Lee of Gage to Leechman, 20 Feb. 1973)

We are again in the fortunate position to have royalty statements for the first four years of the *Concise* (see Table 6).

The figures show that the *Concise* did garner some Christmas 1973 sales, with perhaps 2,000 copies sold in the second half of 1973, but was perhaps not the

Table 6 *Sales figures for* Concise DCHP-1, *1973–1977*

Royalties Statement Period	*Concise DCHP-1* Sales
30 Apr. 1973	473 (only 5 months)
15 May 1974	2,211
30 Apr. 1976	654
30 Apr. 1977	249
TOTAL 1973–77	**3,587**

bestseller all had hoped for: just about 3,600 copies were sold in four and a half years, a benchmark that almost certainly remained below expectations. It is therefore doubtful that universities and senior high schools acquired the *Concise* for their classroom teaching in large numbers. Some did, as we know from anecdotes, but the expectations that Drysdale had sketched in 1972 were higher:

> The main aim in preparing this abridgement has been the provision of a book of a size and price that will make it feasible for use as a course text in universities and senior high schools and for purchase by individual students. (Drysdale to Leechman, 24 Apr. 1972)

In a word, by the late 1970s the success of *DCHP-1*, then in a $25 and a $20 edition, and the *Concise DCHP-1*, at about $4, had run its course: the more affordable edition of the complete *DCHP-1* probably came too late and was not discounted enough, while the abridgement didn't cost much but did not deliver any new content. For instance, *eh*, for which good evidence about its status as a Canadianism had existed since at least 1970, was again not listed in the *Concise* (for a summary of *eh* in about 5,000 words and 11 meanings, see www.dchp.ca/dchp2; for an early history of *eh*, which goes back to Shakespeare's time, see Dollinger 2018).

Given the prominence of that term and the yearning of the media for as little as just one high-profile word, one can only wonder whether the inclusion of *eh* would have made a difference.[5] After all, Orkin's humorous 1973 *Canajun, Eh?* went on to sell more than 100,000 copies. His book gave rise to a Canadian "word book" market that is not uninteresting. Word book authors have taken on what professional linguists did not do and therefore deserve our respect – e.g., the many books by Bill Casselman (1995, 1999, 2002, 2004, 2006), or the one-offs by Thay (2004) or Telfer (2009), to name just some of the more recent ones. The name of Telfer's book is, however, unfortunate, creating confusion with the historical *Dictionary of Canadianisms* that is the topic of the present book. We must not forget Katherine Barber's (2007) book, which I reviewed by a high standard (see Dollinger 2008b).

The writing was on the wall for *DCHP-1* as the 1970s were closing down. Just two years later, in December 1979, with Wally Avis' death at the age of 60, the main driver behind the project was gone. The next summer, Leechman passed away on 10 July 1980 at age 89. With two main movers gone – two who really did a lot of the legwork – and the sales figures in the cellar, it seems quite logical in hindsight – almost inevitable – that *DCHP-1* would fall into oblivion throughout the 1980s. The 1991 edition, spurred by Oxford University Press' announcement that they were to enter the Canadian market – this time for real – was primarily a legal move (OUP's "small" early 1960s Canadian dictionary folded, as Katherine Barber can confirm by hearsay: 13 April 2018 via Twitter). In any case, the opening of OUP's reference unit in Don Mills, Ontario, in 1992 promised to stir up the Canadian market, and a stir up it was.

What Didn't Get Finished

The early 1980s were a troublesome time for Canadian lexicography, and Canadian English more generally. In Murray Wanamaker's wise words from the obituary of his long-time friend Wally Avis, "One of the problems of research in Canadian English is that so little of it has been made public" (Wanamaker 1981: 89) – and we are not talking about the missing revision of *DCHP-1*. The extent of the tragedy can only be gauged via archival research and was surprising even to the cognizant, who had known full well that a lot of the material had been stashed away in some drawer or filing cabinet, inaccessible in principle and, at some point, often thrown out because of the ignorance or unwillingness of succeeding generations. Examples are indeed many: there is Henry Alexander's unpublished, unanalyzed work for *The Linguistic Atlas of the US and Canada*; there is Ian Pringle and Enoch Padolsky's work in the Ottawa Valley (see Padolsky and Pringle 1981),[6] which is now, hopefully, in boxes in some archives and not in the recycling bin; there is Murray Kinloch's work, which, hopefully, is still somewhere at the University of New Brunswick.

There are much more shocking cases, which can also be written off as a colossal waste of taxpayers' dollars. In the next example, for instance, one wrong judgement at the end of a decade-long project sent it not to the publisher but to the dustbin. At the University of Victoria Archives, one finds a second edition of the bilingual *Canadian Dictionary* in a computer printout file on endless paper. The *Bilingual*, whose first edition was published in 1962, made the express point of working from Canadian English to Canadian French and vice versa. Both editions were Paul Vinay's project and, when the second edition was about 95 per cent finished, it was abandoned. The project folded in 1980 and, from a letter that is found in the archives, for an unexpected yet also a very Canadian reason – a reason that demonstrates how deeply the English–French conflict must have run at the height of the referendum crisis in 1980.

Here are the facts: three days after Vinay, whose health had been failing, handed over the completion of the *Bilingual* to his long-term (anglophone) colleagues of many years at the University of Victoria, he withdrew his agreement that put them in charge, out of the blue, and had the custodianship transferred to the Ottawa translation bureau, where francophone lexicographers were supposed to complete the dictionary by 1983.[7] This deadline, however, was not met. What is noteworthy is that this sudden change of mind happened three weeks before the 1980 Quebec referendum on secession from Canada. It seems plausible to speculate that the referendum played a role in the demise of the project – after all, the *Bilingual* was a francophone project whose updating was hosted in the West, where French has had little influence. In the heightened anglophone/francophone setting, one can easily see that such a move would not have been to the liking of many separatist/sovereignist Quebeckers. For Scargill, the change was that the *Bilingual* should be completed in Ottawa by a "Francophone team".[8] It appears that, in hindsight, the second edition of the *Bilingual* was *de facto* killed in the name of separatism, or perhaps sovereignty (see www.dchp.ca/dchp2 for the difference).

Another example of unpublished work is Avis' monograph on Canadian English. We know of it in principle, but not how far along he got with it. But there is more. In the Leechman fonds, another complete typescript for a book can be found, a book with the working title *Canadian English: A Romance of Canadian Words*. It is the kind of popular word book that presents, in accessible yet precise language, selected words and meanings from *DCHP-1*: for example, *aboiteau, acre, advances* (see *DCHP-1 Online*), all explained and illustrated on one page each.

For *aboiteau*, a Maritime word, this meant that the technical and somewhat terse definition in *DCHP-1* of

n. a dike (def. 1) or dam equipped with a gate which functions as a valve releasing flood water from behind but preventing sea water from entering at high tide.

was replaced with the following more reader-friendly, coffee-book type of phrasing that would have been a boon to have and would have played its part in establishing the notion of Canadian English more lastingly beyond the 1967 hype.

ABOITEAU
Everybody along the shores of the Bay of Fundy knows what an aboiteau is, but nobody, it seems, knows how it got its name. In this part of the world and others where similar conditions obtain, dykes are built along the salt-hay meadows to keep the sea out. At intervals along these dykes are sluices fitted with an aboiteau, which is a gate provided with a clack-valve which opens in one direction only. If the level of the water rises on the inland side, the hinged clack-valve opens to let it out, thus draining the meadow, but when the tide rises and presses against the valve, it closes, thus keeping the salt water out. Similar devices, some of them very large, are well known in the Old World, especially in Holland. Some say aboiteau is a form of boite a l'eau, or water-box. Others want the derivation to be a boie l'eau, that is: at bay the water, or a rig to keep the water at bay as dogs keep a deer at bay. Whatever the true origin may be, people may still be heard asking, "Where's Fred?" "Oh, he's gone down to the 'bito after ducks." (Douglas Leechman, typescript, BC Archives MS-1290, Box 47 File 3)

This word story tells a good deal more than the entry in *DCHP-1*, if only by filling in the gaps that are usually left by shorthand abbreviations in historical dictionaries. It was precisely these gaps that we tried to fill in *DCHP-2* with "Word Stories" for each meaning, but it is now clear that Leechman beat us to the idea by a few decades – once more, as so often in Canadian English, in *unpublished* work.

Moonlighting for the *OED*: Leechman 1968–1978

As it turns out, Leechman, the academically educated anthropologist, had been in touch with a number of linguistic greats since the 1920s. There is correspondence from 1940 with Mencken, in which the latter expresses his surprise about the word *bugger*, as it "never occurred to anyone here [in Baltimore] that the word could be obscene".[9] Mencken would use Leechman's "most interesting and valuable notes" for the "next time the chance offers itself to revise my book", by which he meant *The American Language*, the book whose 1919 edition helped establish the notion of a Standard American English. "That", Mencken continues, "may be only too soon! The last time the job came near finishing me" – which would have been the fourth edition from 1936. You can see that the linguists and word nerds, like the good writers and literati, are prone to making puns – like Lovell and Avis in the earlier chapters.

Leechman had had more than one occasional brush with linguistic questions. He published, for instance, an early note and commentary on Chinook Jargon, the contact and trade language of the Canadian West Coast and US Pacific Northwest. He published his text in 1926 in *American Speech*, when the journal was in its second year. What is interesting is that Leechman appears to have been one of the few linguists to have actually spoken Chinook Jargon, a variety that he documented by writing down, in 1910, Chinook songs from the BC Interior. By then, Leechman suggests, the language was already quickly receding.

It is perhaps no wonder that, with this linguistic background and experience, Leechman would continue the lexicographical–linguistic work he enjoyed so much (see the opening quote of Chapter 4). Having caught the "lexicographical bug" with *DCHP-1*, Leechman contacted Robert Burchfield, the Chief Editor of the *OED*, after completion of *DCHP-1*. Burchfield had been working on the revival of that big project since 1957 and was working towards a new supplement. Once more, the *OED* had asked the public for help, and Leechman, now with lexicographic laurels to his name, got in touch with the Editor-in-Chief.

Originally, Burchfield had expressed the hope that Leechman might contribute his reading services on a voluntary basis, a hope that was quickly disappointed. Burchfield, on his end, responded to Leechman's first bigger sample of slips for the *OED*, not without some slight criticism about the cost:

We are grateful to you for your letter of 24th September [1968] and for the quotations aeroplane spruce – woodlift that came separately. I am glad that you are finding the work interesting. The material looks fine, and the time factor is acceptable on our side though we would hope that the ratio of slips to time spent would not tend to drop any lower than it is in this sample. You may like to know that some readers have achieved a rate of ten slips per hour, but it is impossible to generalize about the merits of various kinds of reading as so much depends on the type of source. (Burchfield to Leechman, 30 Sept. 1968)

At 44 hours of reading in the months of August and September of 1968, Leechman earned, at $4/hr, a total of $176 for part-time work, which is almost $1,300 in 2019 money, a really nice sum. As of May 1975, the rate was raised to $6/hr, which would not have happened for a mediocre reader. Consistent with Burchfield's mandate for the new *OED* supplement, he steered Leechman towards twentieth-century terms.

Leechman became a regular consultant-reader for Oxford University Press, as cheques for between 40 and 100 hours every two months are found from 1968 onwards until November 1977. On 23 March 1971, Burchfield writes to Leechman:

Very many thanks for your excellent comments (and quotations) and crease and Creditiste which reached us yesterday from our New York office. They are most helpful. (Burchfield to Leechman, 23 March 1971)

Receipts of bundles of slips of 580, 730, and 800 slips were acknowledged roughly every other month, which, over the years, must have led to some 25,000 slips by Leechman for the *OED* at a cost of *c.* $800–$3,000 per year (the latter for 1975) – not an insignificant sum.

Clearly, Burchfield's initial request to Leechman, to "read some issues of Canadian newspapers, if these are accessible to you, in the period since 1900, taking out quotations for specifically Canadian terms" (Burchfield to Leechman, 23 May 1968), was not granted *pro bono*. Burchfield's request, "I wonder if you are offering to do this reading on a voluntary basis" (11 June 1968), cost Oxford University Press an annual average of $1,500 over ten years, or $87,000 in today's money.

It seems clear that Leechman's services were needed and it says it all that the *OED* and Oxford University Press paid for them, especially since Leechman would not have been the only paid contributor. Leechman's engagement led to his "receiving a presentation copy of Volume II of the Supplement when it is published on 4 November this year" (Burchfield to Leechman, 8 Oct. 1976). At the same time, the cost factor would eventually put an end to Leechman's long stint with the *OED*, a stint whose end more or less, as we know in hindsight, coincided with Leechman's failing health. Burchfield writes in early 1976:

The choices open to me are all distasteful. One of the areas which can be curtailed is outside reading since we are now past the half-way mark in the Supplement, and it is possible that we shall need to abandon the systematic reading of Canadian sources that you have been carrying out so impressively for a number of years. (Burchfield to Leechman, 13 Jan. 1976)

The payments, however, kept coming regardless, as Leechman's work continued until 11 July 1978, when Burchfield, then "pressing on with Volume III" of his four-volume supplement, was "sorry to hear that you [Leechman] are still in the hands of the doctors and clearly much incommoded". Like with so many other dictionary makers, it was the failing human condition that put an end to Leechman's contribution. He was the prime Canadian reader for *Supplements I, II*, and *III*, and would probably have played that role in the final *Supplement IV* as well.[10]

We may wonder what would have happened if Leechman had not redirected his efforts to the *OED*. If he had contributed his 25,000 quotation slips to the *DCHP* files instead, would we have seen a *DCHP-2* or at least a *DCHP-1.1* by the Big Six? It is possible, but we will never know for sure. Leechman, in any case, is the most profound connection between the *DCHP* and *OED* to date.

The Missing Revision of *DCHP-1*

The archival record is ruthless. McDavid wrote so confidently in his review of *DCHP-1* that "revisions" (note the plural) would be regularly forthcoming. In that light, his statement reflects badly on the "maturity" of the field in Canada:

> The assurance of such revisions is unprecedented in historical dictionaries, and one more bit of evidence of the maturity of Canadian conducted lexicography. (McDavid 1967: 57)

Unprecedented it would remain, as the field would turn out not to be so mature, after all. Good intentions were in place and even some of the preparatory legwork was being done, however: the Avis update collection; the Leechman collection;[11] Avis' list of some 2,000 hockey terms, neatly typed up with first attestation dates for each, that he composed post-publication throughout the 1970s; even the "raunchy" terms that Avis kept collecting in his last years.[12]

When Avis died in December 1979, all hope for a revised *DCHP-1* by the original team, the Big Six, was quashed. At the time of his passing, Avis was very much in his intellectual prime. Linguists in the day were exuberantly positive in regard to Avis' legacy. Avis believed, in the words of someone who knew him well, "as true scholars must, in the obligation to provide the next generation of builders with the materials for something better" (McDavid 1981: 125). The customary thinking in "schools of thought" and the fight for the "supremacy" of one grad school at the expense of others were directly opposed to this nobler and more productive approach of scholarly sharing and collaboration. Avis is directly credited as adding great momentum to the field:

> The increased research in Canadian English since the Second World War is as much a tribute to Avis as the work south of the border since 1919 is a tribute to Mencken. (McDavid 1981: 125)

Such words are praise in the highest terms indeed and is more than any professional can hope for. Paul Vinay, the man behind the *Bilingual* dictionary from 1962 and the folded second edition after years of work, shared an admiration for Avis in Canada's second official language:

le nom de W. S. Avis est indissolublement lié – avec celui de mon collègue et ami H. M. Scargill – à l'expansion des études de linguistique canadienne, domaine Anglais.

[the name of W. S. Avis is indelibly connected – together with that of my colleague and friend H. M. Scargill – with the expansion of studies in Canadian linguistics, English domain. (transl. SD)] (Vinay 1981: 150)

Murray Kinloch, a linguist from the University of New Brunswick, also paid tribute to Avis' lifetime work, saying that

It is no belittlement of the work of C. J. Lovell or of others of his associates to say that it was Avis who put Canadian English on the map. (Kinloch 1980: 108)

A central point is raised by the above statement: that each one of the Big Six played their parts, with Lovell and Avis taking the lead and neither diminishing the contributions of the other.

DCHP-1 was a labour of love to some degree, a "philo-logical one" in both the literal sense – lover of language – and representing a particular approach, a stance, towards language. As much as the social-science approach to language has contributed to language study, it has unfortunately also taken away from it via a neglect, and perhaps belittlement, of the historical-philological approach that is rooted in a profound knowledge of texts and their historical-social contexts.[13] Kinloch goes on to elaborate on the issue of creation and/or invention versus discovering or revealing a variety:

I don't say he [Avis] invented it [Canadian English]; like Australia, it was there all the time. But his writings, perhaps more than those of anyone else, helped to gain recognition for its existence and its importance. (Kinloch 1980: 108)

I encourage the reader to see the title of this book in the same light. With Avis' death, an era in Canadian linguistics ended. With Scargill publishing little in the 1980s and the field taking off in other directions, Avis must be considered as the best philological linguist of Canadian English, perhaps, in Canada. Why, then, we may ask, was no one in the next generation of Canadian linguists *interested* in taking up Avis' legacy? Surely, academia has room for a plurality of approaches, so why did it not pan out that way?

Such expertise did not go unnoticed in the wider context. After having dedicated much of his time in the 1950s and 1960s to the Canadian Linguistic Association and to roles within the American Dialect Society, Avis was poised to become president of that august international association in late December

1981. "Had events taken their expected course", Kinloch writes (1980: 108), "he would have been Vice-President of the ADS in 1980, and the President thereafter".

Good scholars are like good wine: they take a long time to fully "ripen" and "develop". When Avis was at his peak, he was axed down, two weeks before embarking on the route to the presidency of the ADS. Unfinished projects of his there were many: his monograph on Canadian English and the "revisions for the Dictionary of Canadian English series" (Vincent, Parker, and Bonny-castle 1978: viii), to name two big ones. Why was nothing carried on? It is as if throughout the 1980s the linguistic "fashions" were pointing in other direc-tions so that peers and newcomers did not feel enticed to take up Avis' projects. We shall look at this "non-philological turn" in linguistics next.

New Chomskyan and Labovian "Schools"

Besides the initial success of the "old guard", of which the Big Six are representative, the 1970s saw an unprecedented diversification of linguistic approaches that were often turned into paradigm-setting "schools", which were in fierce competition with one another. One change can be seen in the journal that Avis helped found, the *Journal of the Canadian Linguistic Asso-ciation*, which as of 1961 was renamed the *Canadian Journal of Linguistics*. The renaming was one thing; it also heralded a profound change in focus that made the journal, over time, into an outlet of formal linguistics in the Chomskyan paradigm. Some colleagues call this approach *theoretical linguistics*, but I won't use such a general name for a particular approach, as it implies that all other approaches are non-theoretical. This is, of course, utter nonsense.

The 1970s was also the time when "linguistics" was often confined to such formal approaches. This loss of diversity reflected changes in linguistics depart-ments across North America, departments which would for a time hire formal linguists almost exclusively. Formal linguistics is an interesting field; formalists are interested in very abstract ways of doing linguistics. At the time, formalists were the cat's meow, it seemed: out with the old, in with the new; they were replacing retiring colleagues across North America. Those who were replaced had generally done more concrete things of a philological-historical nature, such as writing dictionaries or working on phonetic rules, amongst other things.

The retiring linguists often used to work in structural, dialectological, or historical paradigms that were complementary to one another, and had had, often as a result of World War II, significant linguistic experiences abroad. For instance, knowledge of Chinese started that way for M. A. K. Halliday – the founder of Systemic Functional Linguistics – as did Burmese for Raven I. McDavid; Avis' exposure to varieties of English and other languages, such as French, Italian, and German, in addition to Eastern European languages, was a result of his fighting the Nazis.

So, in the late 1960s and 1970s, when linguistics departments in their own right were founded across North America, they often took a very different approach from the linguistics that was being taught in the modern language departments. We have this dichotomy at the University of British Columbia: for instance, UBC Linguistics was founded in 1967. UBC's English Linguistics programme is older, with a 1963 start date as a programme within what used to be the English department and is now, appropriately renamed, the Department of English Language and Literatures.

With Chomskyan linguistics being the "older newcomer", formalists had a leg up and took over large parts of the field before too long. For the record: I appreciate formal linguistics in its very grand layout and how it skilfully establishes common ground between, say, Bavarian German (e.g., Thoma 2016), Blackfoot, Coastal Salishan, Dene, and Yeruba. Some of its prime practitioners are my colleagues and friends at UBC (e.g., Wiltschko 2014; Matthewson 2008; Matthewson, Guntly, and Rochemont 2018) and elsewhere.

The problem with formal linguistics at the time was a more general one and one that could have happened to any school. It was that "linguistics" came to be interpreted as just one particular approach that was practised by particular proponents and, more often than not, in the 1970s these were formal linguists. This went so far that non-formal linguists were no longer deemed to be linguists. The idea that you cannot be a linguist unless you work in a department "of Linguistics", which was occasionally heard from senior BA and lower-year graduate students, is a very pronounced expression of the core problem.

A new school that took a different approach – in many ways diametrically opposed to formal linguistics – was variationist sociolinguistics, as founded by William Labov's important work in 1963 and 1966. Coming to academia later in life at about 40, and after holding a job in industrial chemistry, Bill Labov has proven once more that it is often the atypical biography that produces the brightest ideas. By 1972, the variationists, who elevated the quantitative approach in language to new heights, had their own conference series. In Canada, an early proponent of this type of sociolinguistics is J. K. Chambers, who has been working at the University of Toronto since 1970. Initially working as a formal linguist, Jack (as he is called) soon took a different tack and has made important contributions to the study of Canadian English throughout his long career.[14]

Montreal, Canada, happened to be an early variationist centre, with Gillian Sankoff and Henrietta Cedergren and others working in the new quantitative paradigm. It would become nothing less than the second most important place for the variationists in North America, after Labov's Columbia

University days in New York and later his University of Pennsylvania home base in Philadelphia. Then there was Peter Trudgill, a Ph.D. student in England, who, as early as 1972, published in major journals on the new quantitative approach. He and Labov would become good buddies, excellent scholars, and great mentors to dozens of students over the decades.

Tagliamonte (2016b) does an excellent job relaying these details in linguists' self-reported anecdotes of events in the early years. Soon students of Labov's would come to Canada and continue Labov's legacy in direct lineage. Shana Poplack was the first one; she started at the University of Ottawa in 1980. About the same time, Sandra Clarke, who had worked on the Montagnais Indigenous language in a formal paradigm, turned to variationist work in St John's, Newfoundland (1982).[15] Clarke was building on the local dialectological tradition that was influenced by Harold Paddock (e.g., 1981) – who was taught by Drysdale at Memorial – and applied the new Labovian methods. Like Chambers, Clarke read Labov's books and got inspired without any personal ties. Also around that time, T. K. (Terry) Pratt on Prince Edward Island would turn to dialectological research, though not in relation to the quantitative variationist paradigm. So there was a lot of action in Canada in those days when it comes to linguistic variation and change.

The direct Labovian lineage was first continued in Canada by Poplack. Chambers considers Labov as "the fountainhead" of his variationist thinking, reading the "beat-up copy" of Labov's (1972) *Sociolinguistic Patterns* that Peter Trudgill lent to him in Reading in 1976/77.[16] Eventually, Poplack would have her own students and by the 1990s some of them would – two "generations" removed from Labov – found their own research groups; Sali Tagliamonte is perhaps the most prolific of them. James Walker and Gerard Van Herk, studying at the University of Ottawa in the 1990s, are also prolific and well-established variationists. Charles Boberg came directly from Philadelphia, albeit a bit later, in the mid-1990s (so he is, to keep with the analogy, a younger "academic sibling" to Poplack – and an "uncle" to Tagliamonte, if we push the analogy to the somewhat absurd extreme). Gerard Van Herk is another Poplack student from the 1990s, who is now working in Newfoundland, in Sandra Clarke's department.

It is funny that the family analogy is actively used by Labovians, which proves a sense of "pride" about the "genetic" relationships in that field. Once a year, the "big family" meets at the get-together called NWAV – the conference of New Ways of Analyzing Variation. Not that the "New" in the title should be taken all too seriously; there are often meetings when all that is new is the data, but in some years there is real innovation. If you are allowed to partake in the meeting, which is difficult (with a submission success rate of 1 in 4 or lower),[17] you can see all the family dynamics that you could imagine, like in a real big family. It is – and this is no secret – a bit of a cliquey affair and you need to meet certain benchmarks to be really taken seriously. That lesson I had to learn the hard way, like other European-trained colleagues who confided in me. NWAV does good work, fantastic work, in their small part of the field. But it's much less open if you come to it from a grad school that doesn't have a long track record in a very particular way of doing variation.

What both variationist and formal approaches had in common is that they, every so often, would position themselves in opposition to what came before, at least as their fields were gaining more momentum – if not expressly so, then in attitude. While one can see the contrast between traditional dialectologists, sociolinguists (such as Avis), and formal linguistics, the point is much harder to see in relation to variationist sociolinguistics, which, in reality, is a development of a subarea of what had come before, although with methodological innovations. Labov himself has made that point clear time and again, from his early co-authored paper (Weinreich, Labov, and Herzog 1968) to the *Atlas of North American English* (Labov, Ash, and Boberg 2006), which puts the variationist paradigm in direct lineage with the *Linguistic Atlas* tradition. Labov has, in the last decade or so, turned more and more into a historical linguist (e.g., Labov 2008 is a key text in that regard), and the field follows with a greater appreciation of historical ways of thinking than hitherto.

But academia is, in this respect, like competition in business: if the structuralists (selling VHS recorders) are pushed back by the dialectologists (with their DVDs), then the formalists (Blu-ray) and variationists (Netflix) offer different "packages" and points of view on the same activity (in the analogy: movie screening). It should not be so, but it happens all too often because people are people – even academics are. For the "Netflix" viewers – the variationists – Sali Tagliamonte has written a fine book on the early history, and often quirky development, of the method (Tagliamonte 2016b). While the fields of psycholinguistics and experimental linguistics each take a different approach and have a history of their own, it is in these areas where the University of Alberta in Edmonton has played a major role in Canada.

In the interest of full disclosure, I myself come from a field that has – I think, quite incorrectly – been considered as old-fashioned: historical linguistics. My historical linguistics teachers' (Schendl, Ritt) teachers (Koziol, Pinsker) were trained by the Vienna philologist and *Anglist* Karl Luick. *Anglist* is best translated as 'linguist of the English language with philological expertise'. I have learned the variationist methods on my own and with colleagues, by trial and error, but not in affiliation with any particular school. In my approaches, I often include a philological element, which I can describe as an intimate knowledge of the texts I'm dealing with – a *Sprachgefühl*, 'feeling for a particular language' – and that requires you to learn the language before you study it. The latter step has not been very fashionable as of late.

While I have also worked with present-day material, which is the focus of the variationists, I like the trajectories that only an implicitly historical approach can afford.

Linguistics on the Move

academic camps/silos

Given this background information, it should not surprise that the field of linguistics was moving on in the 1980s, leaving dictionary making and linguistic atlases behind, for the most part. Very few things symbolize this shift better than the list of contributors to a 1986 book from Queen's University's Strathy Language Unit, edited by its then-director, W. C. Lougheed. The Strathy had been established in 1981 by an endowment of Canadian businessman J. R. Strathy to "establish ... a unit for the continuing study of standard Canadian usage".[18] The volume's list of contributors includes nineteen speakers from the conference. About ten speakers were academics, but the main point is that Chambers and Pratt were the only two members of a new generation of academics that would establish themselves, with Chambers being the only one in the variationist camp.

How is it possible, we might ask, that just one Canadian variationist would be at what might have – and should have – become the all-important meeting for the standardization of Canadian English? After all, the conference and volume were entitled *In Search of the Standard in Canadian English*, surely a topic of linguistic interest. But here is where the reader is easily mistaken. At that point in time, the standard had ceased to be a topic of linguistic interest and had become a topic that was only interesting in negation: linguists were interested in non-standard language, while the public at large would have liked to know more about the standard. Professional linguistics would go to great lengths to avoid discussing and researching the standard.

There are a number of reasons for this change, a change that has only in recent years been reversed on a grander scheme (the work of the mostly L2-speaking European English linguists had a great deal to do with this – see, e.g., Tieken-Boon van Ostade 2010). By contrast, the variationists, much like the dialectologists, set out to show that non-standard language, "dialect", was just as systematic and regular as standard language. As H. G. Widdowson shared with his grad seminars in Vienna, academics are, above all, one thing: people. And just as other people do, academics associate in groups that compete with other groups in what it is that they do or aspire to do, and there is in principle nothing wrong with that as long as basic measures of respect are maintained. On the contrary: healthy competition encourages us to do our best. But sometimes fields are abandoned for all the wrong reasons. It is clear by now that the downplaying of the notion of "standard language", its abandonment by professional linguists for much of the latter part of the twentieth

century, has not served us well. It is the one thing that the public thinks –
indeed, assumes – that linguists are dealing with and it is, justifiably so, one
part of what it is that people do with language. So why not study the standard?

   With academic linguistics moving away from dictionary making and linguistic atlas production, the field of dictionaries was left to commercial
publishers. While, at the beginning of the nineteenth century, for instance,
commercial publishers existed and produced good dictionaries (e.g., Merriam-
Webster), there were always the academic projects, or those, such as the
Gage series, that were firmly rooted in academia, with one commercial publisher (W. J. Gage Ltd) taking care of the business and feasibility end. Until the
late 1990s or so, such academic / private enterprise partnerships seemed to
work quite well. But the development of free dictionary content on the
internet – free dictionaries on the web that offered "good enough" solutions
for most users – changed user behaviour and therefore undercut the cash flow
that has driven commercial dictionary publishing for 250 years. As a result,
Gage, which had transmuted into Nelson Ltd by 2003, withdrew from
language reference publishing entirely.

Figure 26 Canada–USA border at Stansted, QC (Canada) and Stansted, Vermont (USA)

This remarkable photo visualizes the arbitrariness of political boundaries, with, as Chambers (2009b) highlighted, the international boundary running right *through* the house with the slim chimney. Yet over time, such human-made lines produce linguistic cross-border differences.
(Photo: J. K. Chambers, 2009, used by kind permission)

7   A Global Village and a National Dictionary War

> I know well and was sometimes witness to the painstaking industry and dedicated talent that went into that labour of love [the *DCHP-1* by Avis *et al.*], and I feel one cannot mention this new dictionary of Canadianisms [the *Canadian Oxford Dictionary*, 1st edn 1998] without acknowledging what must be the enormous debt owed to its predecessors. . . . I assume that editor Katherine Barber has fully acknowledged her indebtedness to the stage-setters: Avis, Scargill, Lovell, Drysdale, et al.
>
> (Joan Finnigan MacKenzie, letter to the editor)[1]

The early 1980s was an interesting period in the expansion of the study of English and the formation of yet another field of English Studies, the field of World Englishes. A key paper in that study was published in 1985 by Braj Kachru (1932–2016), the Illinois-based scholar who, a few years later, was to enter a debate with one of the most renowned British linguists, Sir Randolph Quirk (1920–2017). Quirk initiated the Survey of English Usage at University College London in the late 1950s, and this survey became the empirical basis for the most detailed *A Comprehensive Grammar of the English Language* (Quirk et al., 1985). This grammar of English offered, for the first time, description based entirely on naturally occurring and attested language. It was a quantum leap in the field. The term *English language* was, however, limited to British English of an educated type, but both Survey and *Grammar* were a real achievement.

Into that period of success, Kachru introduced some legitimate doubts. He would describe in his 1985 paper what has come to be known as the Circle Model of English. It was a first attempt to make sense of the varieties of English that had been developing around the globe but had been ignored by mainstream linguistics. While Kachru's model is not perfect, it was new and has since remained psychologically appealing, to a degree that it has clearly proven its usefulness. Here is where Kachru, the newcomer from the "colonies", if you will, and Quirk, the knighted English grammarian (knighted in 1985 as a result of his achievements for the English language), disagreed – and vehemently so.

Kachru argued that Outer Circle countries such as India (his native Kashmir) and the Philippines had developed their own standards, standards which were better suited for their speakers' uses than any external (foreign) British standard. Quirk was not ready to restrict the role of British English to Britain alone. One needs to keep in mind that English as a Second Language (ESL) has been an important economic factor for Britain; Kachru's point would have threatened such hegemony and thus an important economic branch in the UK. Accepting Kachru's logic necessarily means that Standard British English would be limited to domestic British affairs only. Quirk even went so far as to argue, quite against the descriptive principles that he had advocated all his life, that British English would be the best kind of English for international communication. The Quirk–Kachru debate was about the inclusion of the Outer Circle, made up of the countries in which English played an institutionalized role.

World Englishes and English as a Lingua Franca

Kachru was one of the first to put into a theoretical framework the fact that after World War II the English language had been expanding its use in unprecedented ways. Besides the Outer Circle, Kachru recognized an Inner Circle – the UK and the former colonies where English was generally taught as an L1 (Ireland, the USA, Canada, Australia, New Zealand – with South Africa being a more difficult case). The model was completed with the Expanding Circle, which is comprised of all those countries in which English had no institutional ties and has been taught as a foreign language, i.e., countries in central Europe and, more recently, Russia, China, and South America.

A generation after the Quirk–Kachru debate, which happened in 1990–91, we are no longer dealing with the "rehabilitation" of Outer Circle Englishes alone, which is pretty much accomplished in linguistic circles. Instead, we are dealing with the increasing importance of the Expanding Circle Englishes today. The concept of English as a Lingua Franca, as discussed in Chapter 1, takes as its base the communicative behaviour of (sufficiently proficient) non-native speakers of English, which are globally six times as numerous as native speakers. There is a substantial population of speakers of English who use the language on a daily basis, comfortably so and effectively, but who did not learn English as a first language and have made it "fit" their purposes and contexts. These speakers use varieties of what we call *English as a Lingua Franca*: they "own" the language in their own way and in their own form.

It is in this context of a radically changing ecosystem of English varieties globally that, in the 1980s, Canadian English was being repositioned, almost by an "invisible hand", without the doing of scholars or Canadianists. Would Canadian English serve as a teaching model? There had been very few ESL textbooks based on that variety. (It turns out that this is still the case today, while Australia has managed to establish their variety as a model in the Southern Pacific regions since then.) The world was changing, culminating in the economic collapse of the Soviet Union at the end of the 1980s and the unification of what used to be two spheres of political influence. In that seismic shift in world politics and that ensuing fresh and hopeful wind of change (just as in the 1991 Scorpions hit single), the Cold War was over surprisingly quickly. At least for a decade or so, that wind of change kept a-blowin', but very little of the optimism from then is left today. Before the geopolitical earthquake of November 1989, however, sociolinguists had been applying the new variationist methods to Canadian English for the first time, bringing up questions that no one had asked before (see Cheshire 1991 for a period document and accompanying edited collection).

Cry Wolf: the "Americanization" of Canadian English

With the old movers and shakers largely gone, new voices were coming to the fore. J. K. Chambers, for instance, applied new variationist methods to Canadian English. Chambers had spent a sabbatical in 1976–77 in Reading, UK, which was at that time a hotbed for first-class linguists. David Crystal was there (this was before he resigned his academic post in protest at the Thatcher austerity measures,[2] to move on to write some of the best language books in the world, to all our benefit); Peter Trudgill, who was the first to apply the Labovian paradigm in Europe and the UK, had been hired in Reading. Chambers dovetailed with the avant-garde and brought these methods back to Canada, rather than importing them directly from Labov's Philadelphian home base.

With the expansion and reorganization of linguistics that had begun a decade earlier, more fundamental questions were increasingly being asked. Philosophers have thought long and hard about what is needed to explain a phenomenon. In the world of knowledge creation, few are more renowned than Sir Karl Popper (1902–94), the Austrian-Jewish emigrant who was chased away by the Nazi brute. Austria's loss was New Zealand's gain, as Popper would be instrumental in intellectually enriching his World War II home base, Christchurch University in New Zealand.

Another philosophical Viennese émigré, Ludwig Wittgenstein (1889–1951), is often seen as the antithesis to Popper, and there is something to be said for such views.[3] Both were outstanding, though in knowledge theory Popper is the gold standard.[4] To put the problem very simply, when does one see the forest and when just a few trees, and how can one tell the difference? A question of that sort was dealt with in Canadian English, just as the young variationists were gathering critical mass and the old ones were either gone (Avis, Lovell), not partaking in these discussions (Scargill), or not taken as seriously as they should have been (Gregg).

So when the first generation of Canadian Labovians started out at the beginning of the 1980s to deal with Canadian English in their way, it looked from their perspective as if the variety was sentenced to doom: North American integration was pushing ahead in what soon turned out to be pre-NAFTA negotiations; Canadian nationalism, however "soft" it may have been, was declining compared to the 1967 centennial hype, and the economic and cultural power of the USA was steadily increasing. On the face of it, this was not good news for the Canadian mouse next to the American elephant, to paraphrase Trudeau the Elder's famous comparison of Canada and the USA.

In that environment, the sociolinguists, working in one part of "the language forest", were starting to find data that looked a lot like Americanization to them. Part of the problem was that in these early days they only studied the Canadian trees and did not have the time or resources to look more closely at the American side to compare the results. The verdict that Canadian English was "Americanizing" came as early as 1980.[5] By the 1990s, some went all out in their claims of Americanization. Howard Woods (1993: 174), for instance, asserted the following: "It appears that English Canadians will have to (and may want to) define their identity by means other than language." Such sentiment was widespread and it is quite easy to find equivalent statements in the public discourse at the time. The mirroring of public discourses in scholarly debate shows how researchers may be influenced, unless they are aware of possible biases *and* actively take measures to check them. It was only through Boberg's comparative studies (2000, 2005, 2008) that we were first in the position to prove that these voices had been "crying wolf" – false alarm – throughout the 1990s.

Figure 27 The Canada–USA border along "0 Avenue"
near Vancouver, BC. Surrey, BC (left), and Blaine, WA (right)
(Photo: S. Dollinger, 2011)

Like the line on the road in Figure 26 that forms the international border in Stansted, Quebec, the border marker on what used to be called the longest unguarded land border in the world, with Canada on the left and the USA on the right in Figure 27, has measurable attitudinal, perceptual, and linguistic consequences.

Lamenting the Similarity of American and Canadian English

Avis is reported as having told a story about Canada–US differences, which was first documented in one of his 1950s articles. In the story, a Canadian asks a salesperson in a US department store in upstate New York or Michigan for *chesterfields*, only to find herself, after following directions, at the cigarette counter. While the Canadian wanted to buy a couch, the American clerk interpreted her request as the cigarette brand with a capital *C*. In 1996, journalist Howard Richler picks up that story in a *Toronto Star* article entitled "Questions of survival and Canadian language", which illustrates well the sentiment at the time – as did NAFTA, or the unsuccessful expansion of the Canadian Football League (CFL) to the US market in the mid-1990s. In other words, the stars did not shine brightly for things Canadian. In analogy to Avis' example, Richler writes:

> I suspect, however, that if our countryman were shopping in 1996, his vocabulary would correspond to a much greater extent to American usage. Let's face it. With the exception of language usage in the Maritime provinces and Newfoundland, what sometimes has been called Canadian English is not overly distinct. Considering the constant bombardment by American English, it is remarkable that Canada has any remaining national speech characteristics. (Richler 1996: L7)

It is this defeatist, negative, and in the end probably colonial "Let's face it" that is one of the biggest problems in Canadian English: it characterizes the voice of the sceptics, who are sometimes being heard and given greater credence than Canadianists, who, "let's face it", must be biased simply by virtue of defending Canadian things. There is a segment in the population, not unlike in Austria or other "smaller" countries, that is defeatist: hey, we are not the superpower, so why do we even bother? It's people's right to be negative, but it is the duty of everyone else to show that there is another way, a Canadian way. The most extreme case of the let's-face-it pessimists is a paper by the then literature master's student Jan Lilles, published in the year 2000. Lilles wrote without any data or analysis on Canadian English. Instead Lilles, as a speaker of Canadian English, certified that there was no such thing – "let's face it".

    It would be unfair to attest to variationists such a wilful attitude, but it may be surmised that a discipline that is characterized to an overwhelming degree by an ahistorical perspective is more exposed to misinterpretations concerning a particular moment in time compared to any discipline that takes the longer time frame more seriously. It's just easier to see leaps and bounds in the latter perspective. In addition, a discipline that would *not* be married to one kind of method (a quantitative one) and that would *not* treat data, at times, in isolation in a way that can be considered as somewhat naïvely positivist, would also be better equipped against wrong conclusions. The fact remains, however, that a number of studies of early 1980s data suggested that Americanization had come over Canadian English.[6] On another level, we might – and perhaps should – simply say that these errors were the growing pains of a new school and approach.

With the benefit of hindsight, even then the linguistic picture was more varied. The biggest disadvantage of thinking in methodological paradigms, schools, and lab groups, more generally, is that practitioners of one group, one sociolinguistics lab, are often unaware of work directly relevant to them from other approaches. This is particularly dangerous when this other research would contradict or correct one's own interpretation. There *always* were smart people with other interpretations around, even in the 1980s when almost all variationists cried wolf about Americanization. People like Tom McArthur (e.g., 1989) and Margery Fee (e.g., 1991) – the latter my long-term Associate Editor on the *DCHP-2* and one of the *grandes dames* in Canadian Studies – had already taken a different tack on the autonomy of Canadian English, and on Canadian English in general. Margery Fee recounts these early days in the mid-1980s the following way:

[Henry Warkentyne at the University of Victoria] thought that there might be a job coming up for which I could apply [in the Strathy Language Unit at Queen's]. When it did, George Logan, the Head of English at Queen's, wrote me saying that I was a "long shot," but that they might get back to me. Of course, and rightly, they were looking for a linguist, but their usage guide project (see Fee and McAlpine 1997, 2007) was in an area where few linguists at the time cared to go, trained as they almost all were in formal (Chomskyan) linguistics. Most regarded dialectology as outmoded and guides to usage as analogous to etiquette books. In my defence, I had taken more than one course in Canadian English. (Fee 2011)

We see again, this time in Margery's words, that there was no real interest by professional Canadian linguists in doing linguistics that the general Canadian public would directly and immediately benefit from. Not that the public might not necessarily care about formal linguistics – which is great, too – but they do care a great deal about linguistic usage. In any case, if you dealt with that kind of stuff in Canada at the time, word had it (and I know so, because I still heard the same when I came to UBC many years later) that you couldn't possibly be a serious linguist or a linguist that anyone would want to associate with. This is tough stuff to work on for the young academic who needs to enter academic circles. Only tough cookies like Margery, with some luck, would be able to stomach that. The dice were surely loaded against folks like her for many decades, and the headwind was always strong.

Today it is more widely acknowledged that the evidence for American influence is by no means clear-cut, and is more complex than we were made to believe then. Above all, some cases of apparent transfer from American English have proven upon closer scrutiny to be subject to more than simple "Americanization" claims. Take, for instance, Boberg's work on "foreign a", which is the vowel spelled <a> in original loan words from other languages that were adopted by English, such as *pasta*, *Iraq*, or *drama*. While Boberg found an increase in typical American "ah" pronunciation – so, *drama* pronounced as "drahma" with the "ah" sound in *father*, which pushed back in frequency the traditional Canadian foreign <a> as in *bad* – the change was not on account of adopting American forms, though it *looked* as if it were. Reality is much more complex, and here the reason for the increase is that expressing a linguistic change of not saying *drama* with the <a> as in *bad* but rather as "drahma" signalled supposed learnedness, sophistication, and worldliness in Canada and the USA alike. It generally did *not* signal Americanness, however. If Canadians had had another choice to signal learnedness on such items in non-American ways, most of them would have done so. As Boberg put it:

Canadians do not want to sound like Americans, so that when a variant is marked [+American] rather than, say, [+young] or [+trendy] it will not be readily transferred. (Boberg 2000: 23)

More complex identity constructions such as the one behind the foreign <a> example have turned out to be the norm, so that features that "look" American at first glance usually turn out to signal social meanings of another sort, as with yod (Clarke 2006).

Yod-dropping concerns words such as *student*, *news*, *tune*, or *duke*, which can be pronounced with yod – so, "styu-dent" – or without – "stoo-dent". Until recently, the retention of yod has been seen as a marker of Canadian English by both the public and linguists alike. As many commentators have argued, the yod-ful variants are vehicles for Canadians to assert their Canadianness in opposition to variants that are considered American. In 1970, Mark Orkin (1970: 124) summarized this attitude: "When a particular pronunciation is clearly identifiable as American, the majority of Canadians tend to shun it without hesitation."

But what is American, really? The identification of what is American and what is not is far from trivial. Three large-scale sociolinguistic studies in Canada report on yod-dropping in three Canadian cities: in Ottawa (Woods 1999 [1979]), Vancouver (Gregg 2004), and St John's, Newfoundland (Clarke 1993b). Putting these studies in relation to one another, Clarke (2006: 234) says that the variant with yod – so, "styu-dent", "nyuze", etc. – "is not the formal target for all groups", which means that simplifying statements such as Orkin's above from 1970 no longer apply. The variable yod has undergone what sociolinguists call a "change in indexicality", showing that the variants – with or without yod – "have come to symbolize different social values for different segments of the Canadian population". It is what Schneider's Dynamic Model, which we know from Chapter 1, predicts for Phase V: Diversification.

The situation with yod is complex and, in addition, depends a lot on the situational context. This means that if someone wants to signal [+scholarly learning], one is more likely to say "styu-dent" than "stoo-dent", while if one wishes to appear closer to common folks, one would probably use "stoo-dent" in Canada. In one study, a law student in his 20s from Saskatchewan showed precisely this behaviour in a chameleon-like linguistic manner.[7]

Linguistic Autonomy (vs Heteronomy)

The Canada–USA border has off and on been called an arbitrary and imaginary line. And while both are true in some ways, the line is very real in many ways. We know today that a political border usually, if not always, changes speaker focus and has real linguistic and cognitive effects. Speakers on one side of the border will orient themselves towards their country's prestige forms and, if available, norm-providing institutions, while speakers on the other side of the border will do the same for their country. Along the Czech and Slovak border, for instance, very similar if not identical dialects have been spoken for centuries; they were found in a unified Czechoslovakia. At that point, both regions were orienting themselves towards the elites in Prague for their linguistic standard: they converged towards the Prague standard.

Since the early 1990s' peaceful separation (the Velvet Revolution), Czechoslovakia has ceased to exist, as it was divided into a Czech Republic and a Slovak Republic. The separation happened somewhat unintentionally and not in a very motivated manner, owing to an administrative oddity that came into effect by default, as no other agreement was reached by 1 January 1993. However "accidental", the peaceful separation has resulted in real change since then. Since that time, only the Czechs are continuing to orient themselves towards Prague for their linguistic models, while the Slovaks have started to look towards Bratislava, their new capital. As a result, what used to be the same language is now diverging into two different national varieties.

This change is particularly obvious in adjacent border regions in the two countries. Before 1993, the Slovak border dialects were aligned to – what sociolinguists call "heteronomous to" – the Prague standard of the Czechoslovakian language. From 1993 on, the same Slovak dialects along the border have been autonomous from Standard Czechoslovakian – which was renamed Czech – and heteronomous to, aligned to, Standard Slovak, which had not been created by then. There is a profound cognitive dimension to the 1993 separation on many, if not all, levels of social encounter. On the linguistic level, it means that the Slovaks consider themselves now, by and large, as speaking Slovak, while the Czechs consider themselves as speaking Czech, but no longer (for the most part) as speaking Czechoslovakian. Both can understand one another. (So it's like Canadian and American English in that respect.)

The same basic effects can be witnessed along the Canadian–US border, the German–Dutch border, the Luxembourg–German border, the Austrian–German border, and the Flemish/Belgian–Netherlands border, and many others. One might predict: any political border. Political borders do have linguistic and cognitive effects. The example shows the arbitrariness of our labels. What on the one hand we call a language (Dutch vs German), we call on the other hand a national variety of the same language (German German vs Austrian German) for what is the same process of codification (setting norms) and abstraction (we move away from the language on the ground to something "constructed"). In that sense, all standard languages are constructed, hence this book is called *Creating Canadian English*, as it deals with the social developments of the variety – its social licensing, if you will.

Border effects in Canada have long been subject to speculation. While Avis' papers from 1954–56 showed a great deal about Ontario, it was not clear at all how other regions would fare. Only since around 2005 to 2010 have we received more substantial data, data which take a continental North American approach that is capable of revealing the linguistic realities of the often so belittled Canada–US border. Here is Boberg's summary of a detailed study of some fifty everyday vocabulary items, such as *parkade / parking garage*, *cottage/cabin/chalet*, or *garburator / disposal / garbage disposal* and the like:

Perhaps the most remarkable fact to emerge from [the data is that], whatever the relative importance of lexical differences between each Canadian region and the adjacent region of the United States, Canada's regions have more in common with each other than any of them has with the United States. (Boberg 2010: 188)

Such data put an end to the choir of Americanization, but, for about two decades, throughout the 1980s and well into the 1990s, the talk of the town was on the alleged Americanization of Canadian English. When I came to Canada in 1999–2000 to study for a year in Toronto, such voices sounded, from my Austrian German experience, strange, but I was in no position to object. In addition, there was louder talk about the "homogeneity" in Canadian English, which variationists considered to be more "real" or "relevant". This idea – the "sameness" of Canadian English, regardless of where one is – requires a closer look.

Linguistic Homogeneity (vs Heterogeneity)

The idea of linguistic homogeneity (linguistic similarity) and heterogeneity (linguistic differences) between one and another or more regional and social loci has played an important role in theoretical work on Canadian English. The notion has a long pedigree, at least going back to a 1951 paper by University of Toronto English Literature scholar F. E. L. Priestley. Homogeneity has figured quite prominently in the discussion of linguistic features in some colonial settings, which, in contrast to Old World settlements, are often found to be less linguistically diverse in any language (this fact may be considered a sociolinguistic universal). Canadian linguistic homogeneity, it has been argued, has its roots in the westwards movement from Ontario, when Ontarian speech patterns were planted in the western towns and cities. It has since been maintained, the story goes, via the manifold connections between Canadians from coast to coast. Already, around 1950, homogeneity had been called "the most surprising thing about the English currently spoken in Canada" (Priestley 1968 [1951]: 75). Homogenization as such is a fairly general concept; to make it meaningful, one requires, just as with questions of autonomy, a comparison of at least two data sets. And this generally did not happen. The Canadian data were there, but the American were often "imagined", which led to the comparison of real Canadian data with American impressions, anecdotes, or stereotypes, with a few exceptions – e.g., Zeller (1993), Chambers (1994).

Homogenization is, moreover, not a stand-alone phenomenon. If it is occurring, it is co-occurring with other phenomena. Generally, not all linguistic levels of description (phonetics, syntax, vocabulary, etc.) partake in a concerted move in one direction. It's often a hodgepodge and a tug-of-war in many directions, with sometimes one winning, sometimes the other. In addition, homogenization may occur on various levels. There is homogenization on the national level – with or without Newfoundland, the most linguistically distinct province. "Mainland Canadian" linguists (e.g., Chambers 2012) do not always agree with "island" linguists (e.g., Clarke 2012) on what is going on. Gerard Van Herk, who was trained on the mainland and has been working in Newfoundland for a few years now, put the situation very nicely. Picking up the theme of the idea of the *Groundhog Day* Loop, which is the repetition of the same topics about Canadian English in the media over and over again with no progress, he writes:

Now, these Groundhog Day Loops, for both Canadian and Newfoundland Englishes, aren't a matter of the media getting it wrong, or even imposing an agenda on what they report. Journalists are, for the most part, pretty smart people.... And there's the first problem. Language is the stuff of journalism. You use it to show how good you are. As a result, media people have a blind spot when it comes to covering language as a story. For them, there are three kinds of language: right, wrong, and colourful. (Van Herk 2011)

This mindset of right (black), wrong (white), and – at best – some grey ("colourful") language does not help in the study of, and reporting on, language.

On top of the national level are other levels of potential homogenization, such as a level that crosses the border – so, Canadian English and American English may become more similar. Then, overlaid on top of the homogenizing tendencies are many, many heterogenizing tendencies, working actively against the homogenizing ones. It's all a bit like a *teeter-totter* 'see-saw': if it gets too boring up high, you lean forward to go down again, and vice versa. As Van Herk puts it, for his adopted province:

The funny thing, of course, is that NE [Newfoundland English] is not "gone" at all! In rural areas, traditional features like verbal s- marking (*I goes, you knows*) and inter-dental stopping (*dat ting* for *that thing*) are still extremely healthy. In urban areas, they seem to be making a comeback among youth after a generation of decline. In both rural and urban areas, non-standard features that aren't part of local identity discourse never declined in the first place – things like *I seen it* for *I saw it* and associative *and them* (*Jim and them are coming*). And even if there is a decline in the overall rate of use of some non-standard features, that doesn't mean that NE as a variety is in decline. Features come and go, or grow and shrink, in every language variety. Nobody thinks African American English is disappearing because its speakers no longer have [certain pre-World War II features]. (Van Herk 2011)

What Gerard Van Herk makes very clear for Newfoundland English applies as a general principle to mainland Canadian English and any other variety, really: it's all complex and there are at least fifty shades of linguistic grey.

In Search of the Standard in Canadian English

In a way, even before the 1985 conference organized by the Strathy on the "standard in Canadian English" had begun, it was clear that the topic would *not* stir the heart of many a Canadian *linguist*. It is fair to say that the 1986 paper by Chambers that he does not consider as one of his important ones (pers. correspondence, 2009) deals, more so than any other paper, with a part of language use that is central – perhaps most central – to many Cana-dians: what the standard, written more so than spoken, really is. I like that paper for this very reason: it is one of the few papers by a contemporary sociolinguist on questions that interest, I'd guess, 99 per cent of the Canadian *population*.[8]

The quest for a Canadian standard has a stunningly long pedigree in Canadian English, given the quarrels as of late. In 1920, an unknown author eloquently speculated about the future formation of a new standard in Canada that would – as he put it, axiom-like – neither be the standard of London nor the one of New York (Anon. 1920). This prophet-like voice was talking about educated usage and suspected that the Canadians would develop, as they became a country in their own right, a standard of their own. In 1937, Henry Alexander – Avis' teacher at Queen's and whom George Story from New-foundland called "that fine scholar" and "pioneer in dialectology of the Maritime Provinces"[9] – produced a revised and Canadianized version of an American dictionary published in 1927 by Holt, Rinehart. Copies of this

Winston Simplified Dictionary: For Home, School and Office (Brown and Alexander 1937), which was produced for the Canadian market, are hard to come by today. It was Canadianized by Henry Alexander without changing the print plates of the 1927 American original. This had the effect that no head-words were added or deleted, with only spelling adapted to present the dominant Canadian use.[10] In any case, it is remarkable that, even before World War II, Canada had *any* dictionary of its own.

At the 1985 Kingston conference discussed earlier, George Story, editor of the *Dictionary of Newfoundland English* and one of the most incisive review-ers of *DCHP-1*, acknowledged Avis' role as the leader in Canadian English:

the most signal Canadian contribution to lexicography, and one with a marked Kingston stamp through the work of W.S. Avis has of course been the series of graded school and university dictionaries of W.J. Gage Limited, with the historical *Dictionary of Cana-dianisms* (1967) as the national linchpin. (Story 1986: 43)

Having the role of "national linchpin" assigned to *DCHP-1* by Story, who had just earlier in the decade completed his regional and historical *Dictionary of Newfoundland English*, would have been much to Avis' liking. In terms of moving forwards, however, Story had very little to say, other than that any dictionary should be "resolutely *descriptive*"; he must have known that he was preaching to the converted.

T. K. (Terry) Pratt, perhaps the youngest academic at that conference, took the lectern and stated that he had heard, by that point in the conference, eight times "a muted call for something fresh in Canadian lexicography" (Pratt 1986: 55). But what would that fresh start be? The Australian *Macquarie Dictionary* had been published a few years earlier in 1981 by Pam Peters and others, taking an English English dictionary as its base and turning it into "an aggressively Australian dictionary", in the words of its editor. Story, quoting this phrase, had just claimed that a "more improbable epithet for an equivalent Canadian work it would be hard to imagine" (Story 1986: 52).

How so? Because Canadians don't aggressively pursue any cause? Hardly. Certainly, Story would not want to have done so. Pratt, in his response to Story, is then much more explicit than the more senior Story and acts as a kind of loudspeaker:

I would like to make explicit what I believe is implicit here [in the conference contributions]: Canada needs a dictionary of its own: an authoritative, one-volume, fat, general, desk dictionary, that, as well as giving the full measure of standard English and North American English, would also contain standard and regional Canadian words, spellings, pronunciations, usages, subtleties of definition and outlook; a diction-ary to judge between the American and British varieties of English; and at the same time a fully commercial dictionary to compete with Webster's and Oxford for a profitable share of the market. (Pratt 1986: 56)

The call would be answered on a number of levels, but not fully until 1997 (then, twice) with the latest edition of the *Gage Canadian Dictionary* (though still "only" a Grade 12 dictionary) and, more importantly, the *ITP Nelson Canadian Dictionary of the English Language*. The latter was a commercial flop, for all the wrong reasons, while the former continued to be a success in the school market.

In 1998, the *Canadian Oxford Dictionary*, a real latecomer to the field, would trigger what I termed the "Great Canadian Dictionary War", in allusion to the American dictionary war between Webster and Worcester dictionaries in the 1860s. One might add the little-known fact that there had been talk about Oxford entering the Canadian dictionary market three decades before they did. We know so, because Robert J. Gregg wrote about it in 1962:

we are awaiting a Canadian English dictionary from the Oxford University Press; the first volume of Gage's *Dictionary of Canadian English* [*The Beginning Dictionary*] has just appeared. (Gregg 1962: 68)

Gregg is not just anyone. If I were to add one member to the Big Six and make them the Magnificent Seven, as it were, it would need to be Gregg. Gregg's word counts for something.

When Oxford did finally enter the Canadian English reference market, it was in retrospect a bit like a bull in a china shop, as I will explain below. While this characterization is certainly somewhat unfair, it is not totally devoid of historical fact. Ten years on, in 2008, Canada will have gone from three up-to-date desk dictionaries that were being maintained on a regular basis to zero such dictionaries – nada, zilch, rien, nix! This is what can happen in a rapidly changing world, where no academic institution feels the need to monitor current language use – unlike in other languages (e.g., the Meertens Instituut in The Netherlands for Dutch, the Institut für Deutsche Sprache in Germany – at least for German German — and I won't even begin to talk about the Académie française, because their approach to French has been a bit, well, not of the descriptive kind we'd need). True, there is the Strathy Language Unit. But to compare it with the other departments in terms of funding would be like comparing a shiny road-racing bicycle to the Formula 1 racing team of the Scuderia Ferrari.

What is Standard Canadian English?

You will have noticed that I am a bit critical of variationist practices. To be clear, the approach is extremely valuable but would benefit from taking other approaches more seriously, especially qualitative ones. In my opinion, one of the biggest successes of this first phase of variationist sociolinguistics in the 1980s for the study of Canadian English was the clarity that it brought to how

Standard Canadian English (StCanE) can be defined. (This may look like an odd thing, as variationists typically are *not* interested in standard language – not at all.)

The most clear-cut definition of StCanE comes from Chambers (1998: 252), who describes the "standard accent" as "urban, middle-class English as spoken by people who have been urban, middle-class, anglophone Canadians for two generations or more". By extension, we apply this definition not just to accent – i.e., sounds of the language – but to all other linguistic levels, and expand it from monolingual English speakers (anglophone) to the multilingual speaker, so that we define StCanE as the following:

Standard Canadian English is spoken by those who live in urban Canada, in a middle-class job (or one of their parents holds such employment), who are second generation or later (born and raised in Canada) and speak English as (one of their) dominant language(s).

If this definition is taken literally, StCanE is indeed spoken by a large section of the population, but it is not the variety of the majority: based on the 2006 census, only about one third (36 per cent) of the Canadian population would be speakers of StCanE (Dollinger 2011a: 5). This means necessarily that any claims to national homogeneity only apply to that share of the population. And here is the point: rather than modelling it as a case of a homogenization in Canadian English, one could and perhaps should look at homogenization as the effect of standardization and codification of the variety. This might be the better explanation and would offer a more nuanced model than a purely diffusion-based model (spread of features from east to west) that is ultimately too narrow.

There is one more aspect we need to discuss: while 36 per cent may not sound like much, it makes StCanE a widely spoken variety in comparison to other standard varieties of English (e.g., Received Pronunciation in Britain – think Prince Charles – is used natively by only 3–5 per cent; Trudgill and Hannah 2002: 9). It remains to be seen to what extent more socially diverse data – including non-middle-class speakers – would alter the picture of Canadian English homogeneity. Standard Canadian English is a useful concept, as it makes clear that 90 per cent of what we know about Canadian English deals with this variety, which is overlaid with heterogenizing tendencies.

The standard language is also what is found in desk dictionaries. Unlike the sociolinguistic definition offered here, however, lexicographers have usually had more fuzzy criteria for what defines the standard. As we turn back to dictionaries, these methodological aspects will play a more minor role, as they have in public discussions about dictionaries and standards. It's time to focus on a much more prominent aspect and development: the Great Canadian Dictionary War.

The Great Canadian Dictionary War

My first brush with the Canadian Dictionary War happened in 2002 and illustrated its very real effects. At the time, I did not know what had happened. Only years later would I be able to contextualize it. With the benefit of more years of hindsight, I'm now calling it, in keeping with a Canadian tradition, the Great Canadian Dictionary War. It sure was great and is as relevant for Canadian English as the great "Canadian Railroad Trilogy" is for Canadian music (it should, really, have been named "The Great Canadian Railroad Triology"), *The Great Canadian Baking Show* for hobby pastry chefs, or the Great Canadian Oil Change for motorists.

As a first-year student in the English Ph.D. programme in Vienna, I was trying to get to grips with my selected topic of historical Canadian English, which was a *tabula rasa* in historical linguistics at the time. In December 2002, I travelled to Toronto to collect source materials on the development of Canadian English. It was then that Jack Chambers was kind enough to let me browse his library and freely copy from it, while he was marking student papers. Both in Jack's library and in the Archives of Ontario, I hit pay dirt. In study breaks, I spent my time looking up information on *DCHP-1*. This involved phoning people, because there was no time to lose now that I was so close to the source. The phone chats were a welcome break from hour-long reading sessions.

With Jack's help, I got in touch with Debbie Sawczak, a linguistics graduate from the University of Toronto, who was then working for Gage Ltd. When I called Debbie and inquired about the quotation files and materials for *DCHP-1*, she said that she'd be happy to help and that this "will be no problem". It was linguistic collegiality at its best. Because the field is so small, there is this kind of "sisterly–brotherly love" at the best of times. When Debbie got back to me a few days later, she said that she was very sorry, but that she couldn't comment on the materials anymore, on "order from above". That was strange indeed. Her 180 was one of the consequences of the Great Canadian Dictionary War that had gripped the field for much of the 1990s and, in the end, has crippled the Canadian English language reference market since.

So what was the Great Canadian Dictionary War about? It was, in essence, a war between publishers for market share in the compact Canadian language reference market. Gage Ltd was the market leader in Canada and must be, as we have seen in the previous chapters, credited for bringing Canadian-made dictionaries to the forefront and for helping create the variety in the minds of its speakers. This does not mean that all Canadians used these resources. While many did, there certainly was still room to grow, especially among the older, non-school-age population, as most of these still stuck with their older American *Webster's* or British *Oxford* titles – i.e., their foreign products. But a publishing war was not the only problem in the Canadian language reference market at the time; there was another, much more drastic and wide-sweeping change coming upon it. In hindsight, it was like the perfect storm.

T-shirt-wearing Corpus Linguists and Bow-tied Lexicographers

In the 1980s, John Sinclair at the University of Birmingham produced, under the COBUILD-Collins brand, the first dictionaries of English that were fully based on corpus linguistic principles. By the time the new *ITP Nelson Canadian Dictionary* was being planned, which was in the early 1990s (David Friend recalls coming to the project, which was then in full swing, in 1995, with publication in 1997), lexicographers knew that an electronic corpus was needed to produce a dictionary that the public would accept.

What is corpus linguistics? A corpus is a balanced, structured, and representative collection of texts (written and/or spoken) that can be queried by computer. By studying uses of words that were actually written or uttered in actual communicative situations, grammarians, such as Randolph Quirk and his team, discovered new patterns. In 1990s Canada, it was up to the lexicographers to raise their game in the way the grammarians had shown them (a key publication was Quirk *et al.*'s 1985 reference grammar). The concordance (keywords-in-context, or KWIC, list) in Figure 28 shows the last ten quotations for *cool* from a total of 1,663 in the *Strathy Corpus of Canadian English*, the best-known corpus resource for Canadian English (compiled by the Strathy Language Unit).

In its essence, the difference between a corpus-based dictionary and a quotation-file-based dictionary is a matter of data selection and quantity. Whereas, previously, editors had to deal with dozens of quotation slips for a given word, as we've seen in Chapter 4, corpora offer thousands of attestations, such as the 1,663 instances of *cool* in the (by today's standards, small) 50-million-word *Strathy Corpus*.

With the advent of corpora, the traditional method of lexicography focussing on quotation collection was not fully replaced but augmented by the corpus. This is because large corpora for a particular variety often did not exist, so that resource construction was a major part of any project. In line with its mandate, corpus building was thus also the foremost task of the Strathy

1654	2006	SPOK	CanRadioTVComm	A	B	C	--- Laughter / Rires ! MR. -CRERAR: More practical but not as cool. ! COMMISSIONER-LANGFORD: --- this great curiousity. And yet, the disconnect
1655	2007	SPOK	CanRadioTVComm	A	B	C	of classmates or co-workers to be a user, to be hip, to be cool. For AIR-FM, the process of getting the content and context of this story
1656	2007	SPOK	CanRadioTVComm	A	B	C	, it could be showcasing young students. We have all got kids. How cool would it be to hear about your own kids on the radio? We have
1657	2007	SPOK	CanRadioTVComm	A	B	C	hear a lot of stories about how radio has a chance to dictate what is cool to students, and the general consensus is that they are doing a bad job
1658	2007	SPOK	CanRadioTVComm	A	B	C	at before and give them an opportunity to dictate to radio what they think is cool. Thank you. ! MR. -MICKELSON: Thanks very much, Dave.
1659	2007	SPOK	CanRadioTVComm	A	B	C	but just as a mother who wants their child to know that there are really cool people that you want to be like out there that are expressing their art and
1660	2008	SPOK	CanRadioTVComm	A	B	C	3M of course, McCormick's are expanding their operations. And one of the cool companies that's opening up nationwide is called The Original Cakerie, which makes cakes
1661	2008	SPOK	CanRadioTVComm	A	B	C	emerging band. A station nicknamed The DUKE has no choice other than to be cool. Our presentation style will reflect this. Our features will underscore this style.
1662	2008	SPOK	CanRadioTVComm	A	B	C	, hosted by Blackburn Farm Broadcaster Andrew Campbell, is a lifestyle program, a cool show for young students and professionals in agricultural sciences, as well as residents who
1663	2008	SPOK	CanRadioTVComm	A	B	C	Hot 103 FM in sales, and then General Manager and Sales Manager for 99.1 Cool FM in Winnipeg. Most recently Brian was the director of local sales for the

Figure 28 *Cool* in the *Strathy Corpus of Canadian English* (1985–2011) (retrieved from http://corpus2.byu.edu/can)

Language Unit in the 1980s. Margery Fee's 2011 guest column tells the strange tales of those days when "machine-readable" text was very hard to come by and basically limited to newspapers, which were the first to switch to digital systems, allowing their tapping for linguistic purposes. The *Guide to Canadian English Usage* (Fee and McAlpine 2011), which is the grammar of Canadian English, is based on the *Strathy Corpus* and sets a real Canadian corpus-linguistic and World-Englishes benchmark. The *Guide* was first published in 1997, fifteen years after the Strathy Unit was founded, which gives you an idea of the front-heavy labour of corpus-linguistic projects.

Work with text corpora as such was not new, as they had been in general use in linguistics since the 1920s. Antecedents go back to the 1800s, of which William Dwight Whitney's (1884) study on the Sanskrit tense–aspect system, written by *the* most important founder of language study in North America, is just one early example. Of greatest influence was the work on corpus-based learner dictionaries by Michael West, Harold E. Palmer, and A. S. Hornby, who conducted frequency analyzes with manual counts by pen on paper out of Japan in the 1930s. One of the people who consulted at Hornby's Tokyo institute was Edward Thorndike, and with him the approach came to North America. Note also that the innovative *Thorndike–Barnhart School Dictionaries*, based on this revolutionary idea of corpus-informed lexicography, became the starting point for the three school dictionaries in the Dictionary of Canadian English series. They were excellent dictionaries, but the uninformed merely saw them as "American", which can be a serious handicap in the Canadian context.

The first electronic corpus, however, was a quantum leap, and it came about in the form of the *Brown Corpus of American English*. The *Brown Corpus* was compiled by W. Nelson Francis and Henry Kučera at Brown University, Rhode Island, from 1963 to 1964. It was a 1-million-word corpus and was used heavily until well into the 1980s. After hesitation throughout the 1980s, the Canadian and American publishing industries were finally confronted with the need to adopt corpora, at least in more prevalent supporting roles, as the older method was no longer viable on its own. Sidney Landau, who had been there before and was still there after corpora had changed the dictionary industry, put the problem the following way:

Unless the publishing industry had also changed to make computerized composition the norm, the acquisition of large electronic corpora would have been immeasurably difficult. People have been interested in corpora for a long time, but they hadn't had the means to create them without employing an army of workers copying texts by hand. (Landau 2001: 285)

The link between the mode of composition (writing and typesetting of the book) and the methodology used to write it (paper file or electronic corpus) has been the principal reason why lexicographic publishers were very slow to embrace the new corpus technology. Landau identifies this very clearly as the over-riding reason for hesitation to up one's game. With a switch to digital printing techniques, corpus linguistics would be easily managed, but such a technological–methodological move would also mean the layoff of many players in the lexicographical industry, starting with the printers. Writing in 2001, Landau was referring to the USA, but the same was true for the Canadian market, the UK, and the global dictionary market in most other languages as well:

The changes have taken longer than predicted because composition houses saw, correctly, that moving to electronic composition would put many of them out of business. Those that remained were forced to lay off most of their compositors and hire programmers and others familiar with electronic files. (Landau 2001: 285)

This massive change in dictionary publishing, which was related to the change from analogue typesetting in printing to desktop publishing, was the context in which the Great Canadian Dictionary War unfolded. It was the time when the philological – perhaps multilingual (one of the original meanings of the word *linguist*) – linguist, who had read many of the texts that were put in the dictionary, was being replaced with – stereotypically – young, T-shirt wearing, fast-food-munching, video-game-playing programmers. It was the change from the bow-tie wearer (a staple in English lexicography for much of the twentieth century) to the T-shirt-wearing computer geek.

By the early 1990s, Oxford University Press apparently felt that it was time to offer something specifically for the Canadian market. The Oxford dictionary operation was, after the re-issue of the *OED* and its release on CD-ROM, ready to open up new markets for their desk dictionaries. So, rather than continuing to sell the British dictionaries unchanged in Canada – which they had done before Canadian Confederation and all the time since, during which time the Gage Canadian titles had become available – the Press finally deemed the time ripe for Canadianized dictionaries of their own. The Gage series must have hurt them too long in their (Canadian) pockets, so they decided to make an investment, more than thirty years after Gage created that market single-handedly.

Oxford had been focussing on selling contemporary dictionaries, such as the *Concise Oxford Dictionary* or the *Pocket Oxford Dictionary*. While they were trying in that way to recoup some of the investment that the *OED* demanded, they were also figuring out what to do with the historical *OED* in the long run, and the computer had to play a key role in all of that, though no one really knew how to go about it (Simpson 2016: 130). John Simpson would eventually lead the transfer to the online medium and start the complete revision – the third edition – which was begun in the year 2000 and will surely take another twenty years before it's done.

To give you a sense of what the avant-garde in digital lexicography was in the 1980s – right when the *OED* produced their CD-ROM version – it will be helpful to look at a trendsetter and trailblazer in lexicography at the time: the sometimes-curmudgeonly, towering, brilliant, and "scholarly entrepreneurial" Laurence "Larry" Urdang (1927–2008), who did what no other dictionary publishing house managed to do. This is how Urdang is reported to have done it:

Seeing the potential for [the] then-new personal computer, in 1981 Larry purchased a battery of PCs for LUI [his company's] staff and freelance editors to compile and encode dictionary data directly to disk. . . . Compiled and typographically coded entries on 5½ inch floppy discs were sent in to the LUI offices, where in-house staff printed out, copyedited, and corrected the encoded data and sorted it as need be. In the pre-hard-drive early years, data was sent on floppy discs to a compositor for automatic typesetting. (Abate 2008: 5)

Here comes the punchline: LUI, Lawrence Urdang Inc., was a private business that did the work and *sold* it to Oxford, Random House, Simon & Schuster, Longman, and Nelson, among others. Like the successful TV shows, such as *Oprah*, produced on their own to then be sold to the networks, Urdang was so good that he could pull that off in dictionary making. He was early out of the starting box: 1981 was the year that IBM went to market with what became known as the PC, so Urdang lost no time. The reader can imagine why Urdang, a true innovator and trailblazer, felt he was better off going with his own company, rather than trying to change the game from within.

When in 1992 Oxford University Press finally opened up a reference unit in Don Mills in northern Toronto, it used the new corpus technology, by then running the data on hard, not floppy, disks. Oxford University Press hired a team of five lexicographers under the leadership of Katherine Barber with the goal to produce something that would grab market share from Gage Ltd. This was not just any competitor entering the fray. Oxford is a big name in the dictionary market – many would say *the* name as far as English is concerned. The prestige the name carries goes a long, long way, regardless of the quality of the work as such. News coverage started almost immediately with the office's opening, years before anything would be finished, and a lot of pre-publication PR was offered by the fact alone that Oxford was here now.[11] On the one hand, Oxford University Press entering the Canadian market was a compliment to the reality of Canadian English and its acceptance as a mon-etizable entity by foreign publishers. On the other hand, it could be seen as an attack on linguistic (publishing) authority. Overall, though, Canadians seemed rather pleased that Oxford would finally enter the game.

Gage reference staff knew that there would be trouble ahead in any case with such a formidable competitor. So they took measures to protect their more than forty-year investment by re-issuing *DCHP-1* in a somewhat bizarre move. While *DCHP-1* sold alright in the early 1970s, as we have seen, towards the end the sales were dropping rapidly, and in the 1980s they must have been nil

(David Friend: pers. conversation, 2006). The re-issue of a paperback version in 1991, just before the Oxford University Press office would open, is interesting in this context. The paperback *DCHP-1* is a reprint of the 1967 version, yet it had to be re-set and is thus not 100 per cent identical – only 99.99 per cent, or so. There was no editorial change or update in any way, just a very negligible number of print errors. It shows that Gage was willing to take money in hand to re-issue a book that was no longer selling for more or less strategic reasons. Why?

Plagiarizing Lexicographers Always Go Scot-free

In order to understand Gage's reasoning, you need to know the history of English lexicography. In 1604, Andrew Cawdrey compiled what is generally considered the first English dictionary. It was slim and very different from what a dictionary is to us today, as it only included some one and a half thousand "hard" words. "Hard" words literally meant difficult words. So don't look up *child* or *room* or *family* in Cawdrey; you won't find them. In those days, English was being put to more and more uses, as Latin and French, the traditional languages of learning and prestige, were being pushed back. This meant that English had to be put into shape, which could be done either by using foreign words and adapting them ("hard words") – such as *autodidact* or *homogalact* – or by native means of word-formation – so, in the above two cases, *self-taught* and *foster brother*. While *autodidact* survived, *homogalact*, which is an authentic Early Modern English example, died out and was replaced by *foster brother*. For the Early Modern English user, however, both *autodidact* and *homogalact* would be "hard words", both equally opaque to native speakers without university learning, so that dictionaries such as Cawdrey's were becoming a necessity. The reader who is interested in this exciting time of change in English is referred to Considine (2008).

And here is the scoop: from Cawdrey on, every dictionary writer copied – in some cases, wholesale – from previous works. It seems likely that the 1991 reprint was meant to show Oxford University Press some teeth. The message must have been, with a new copyright from 1991, "We're watching you! Do not copy us. If you must, alter your wording really thoroughly!" You can see that even the first skirmishes were not very nice and not cheap. (How much does a re-setting and full print run cost when sales were "nil"?)

Oxford University Press and the soon-to-be chief editor of what was going to be the *Canadian Oxford Dictionary* (*COD*), Katherine Barber, entered the scene in 1992. This was paradoxically a time when the market was comparatively well served, with the *Gage Canadian* (1990, fourth edition); the very hefty 1988 (and more influential 1989 reprint) *Funk & Wagnalls Canadian*

College Dictionary; and the *Winston* dictionary that had transmuted into the 1990 *The Penguin Canadian Dictionary* (edited by Thomas M. Paikeday). In that setting, Barber and her team adapted, between 1992 and 1998 – which was not reported – the 1990 edition of the British *Concise Oxford Dictionary* to Canadian standards. The adaptation angle has been virtually unknown and the belief has been stubbornly sticking around that the *Canadian Oxford* was created from scratch. As anybody in the industry knows, however, no dictionary is created from scratch, not since Cawdrey some four centuries back. In any case, in 1998 it hit the market with a big "boom", and Oxford University Press had another bestseller on the books, this time in Canada. So far, so good. Gage Ltd was, of course, not amused, as more Oxford sales meant fewer sales of their own products. But this scenario, while true in principle, does not even come close to what really happened in and around 1996–99, when the dictionary war was at its height.

Backtracking a little, 1997 was an important year in Canadian lexicography. In that year, Jack Chambers embarked on a task quite atypical for a variationist, with the result that it gave us a baseline on Canadian English lexicography by a disinterested, knowledgeable non-lexicographer – a neutral judge, so to speak. Chambers undertook to review the two newly published dictionaries: the 1997 revision – and thus fifth edition – of the *Gage Canadian Dictionary*, to this day its latest update;[12] and the 1997 *ITP Nelson Canadian Dictionary of the English Language*, which was a new product, built as much from scratch as any dictionary these days – i.e., all "new" dictionaries start from some sort of pre-existing dictionary. Anything else would be plain nonsense, economically unfeasible, and a reinvention of the wheel.

Don't Judge a Book by its Cover

Covers are not good indicators of quality. But neither are publishers, despite the firm belief by some that the most prestigious publishers necessarily produce the best books. Sometimes this is the case, but other times it is not. In order to make sense of the plethora of books, outlets, or programmes, it is easier to go by prestige. What holds for publishers also holds for universities. Who knows, for instance, that one of the foremost authorities of global Englishes works at a small – indeed, tiny – Belgian university (Jan Blommaert), when we can turn to someone at Oxford, Harvard, or Stanford for expertise? You may not get the most qualified person, but you'll get someone who knows something and you can always say that your source is from "enter name of prestigious school". As even experts are not immune to the lure of prestige, with a prestigious name you have a lot on your side regardless of how much that person really knows about a given subject.

In late 1996, two books were rushed with a 1997 copyright into the fall market. Sheerly by title alone, the *Gage Canadian* would win any marketing competition over the overly long and awkward *ITP Nelson* title.[13] Both dictionaries were published in anticipation of Oxford entering the market, and both works were years in the making. The *ITP Nelson* especially had a big price tag, which indicates the chance for good work. It has been rumoured that the making of that dictionary cost $1 million at the time (David Friend: pers. conversation, 2007).

We are in the lucky position of having Chambers' long, comparative review of both dictionaries, as he spent a good deal of time test-driving these dictionaries. Here is what he thought of them:

For Canadian content, G [*Gage Canadian*] is clearer about spelling preferences but N [*Nelson's ITP*] probably has clearer definitions. I was pleased to find how different the two dictionaries are from each other. They present a real choice, and by no means an easy one. The choice is all the harder because these two are not alone. For years I have used (and endorsed) *Funk & Wagnalls Canadian College Dictionary* in the Canadianized edition published by Fitzhenry & Whiteside (reprinted 1989). I wonder if either of these will supplant that one on my shelves. A little more than a year from now, Oxford Canada will weigh in with its inaugural *Oxford Canadian Dictionary* (for which I serve as an editorial adviser). I wonder what it can possibly offer that these two have overlooked. (Chambers 1997: n.p.)

The last line, which is also the last line of the review as a whole, is remarkable, since it confers a level of quality upon both the *Gage Canadian* and the *ITP Nelson*, a level that would, about a year and a half later, no longer be considered possible in the light of the Oxford publication that eclipsed the other two. The review is so important because it came early and is detailed and high in quality. After such a review, one wonders how it was possible that the *ITP Nelson* became a complete failure and the new *Gage Canadian* did not manage to garner market share in the general population, outside of the high-school dictionary market in which it was the leader. Praise for the *ITP* was not a singular event, as this quotation makes clear: "If the Nelson is the Holt Renfrew of dictionaries, the Gage is the Canadian Tire" (Garnett 1996). (Holt Renfrew is a high-price quality clothing store.) The *Gage Canadian*'s comparison with the solid, beloved, carrying-everything Canadian Tire stores that are not over-the-top was also a misrepresentation of its value. So, what were these dictionaries really about?

Counting Canadianisms: the *Gage*, *Oxford*, and *ITP Nelson*

The counting of dictionary entries is an area that publishers have often tweaked and twisted in efforts to gain an advantage over their competitors. Landau refers to it as "the delicate subject of what is meant by saying that a dictionary has [x number of] entries". He continues:

The current practice is clouded by deliberately confusing nomenclature used by many dictionary publishers, eager to tout their books as bigger than their competitors'. (Landau 2001: 109)

The practice has not improved since – quite the contrary. As with database entries, whose true number is often shrouded in the smokescreens of the PR departments (you'll never find out how many movies your national Netflix service holds), counting Canadianisms is as unpopular a task. With the help of then-undergraduate student and co-Editor of *DCHP-2* Alexandra (Sasha) Gaylie, I was in the position to feel the pulse of the big three Canadian desk dictionaries.[14] Since then, graduate student Skylet Yu (2018) has scrutinized the 2010, 2011, and 2016 editions of the *Collins Canadian Dictionary*.

Data on the Canadian content of all of these dictionaries is meagre and difficult to come by. The most easily accessible information – overall counts of Canadianisms found on the dust jackets – is often all there is. This information is simultaneously subjected to all the PR spin imaginable. On the dust jacket of *COD*'s second edition in 2004 – henceforth *COD-2* – we are informed that the "Canadian Oxford Dictionary sets the standard for dictionaries in Canada, providing the most reliable information on English as it is used in Canada" – an overstatement. *COD-2* claims "2,200 uniquely Canadian words and senses".[15] For the fifth edition of the *Gage Canadian Dictionary* – henceforth *Gage-5* – we are left without a figure for Canadianisms, but are told on the back cover that "13 000 new entries – 30% more content" were added. The front flap (note, not on the cover proper) speaks of "THE AUTHORITATIVE DICTIONARY OF CANADIAN ENGLISH" – we are told that "OVER 450 000 COPIES SOLD IN PREVIOUS EDITIONS": closer to the facts, but still PR. The back flap quotes Professor Sandra Clarke attesting that *Gage-5* "unlike most of its competitors, has a thoroughly Canadian grounding, and is not a superficially Canadianized version of an American product" – clearly an attempt to pre-empt anti-American bias. The Canadian Style Guide by the Department of the Secretary of State of Canada is also quoted: "The spelling authority recommended by this manual is the Gage Canadian Dictionary, since it reflects the usage of the majority of federal government departments and agencies more closely than do the Webster's or Oxford dictionaries." Later printings of *COD-2* add, on the front cover under the title, "Official Dictionary of THE CANADIAN PRESS and THE GLOBE AND MAIL". This all reads a bit like: "Take that, *Gage-5*!" This "exchange" has all the trappings of the Great Canadian Dictionary War. Price-wise, the *Gage* cost $29.95, while the *COD-2* cost $59.95.

So what do the dictionaries really contain? All counts for the dictionaries had to be done manually, with pen and paper, as no – or only inadequate – digital versions are available. Table 7 shows the counts of terms and meanings

Table 7 *Count of "Canadianisms" in three Canadian desk dictionaries*

	Gage-5	COD-2	*ITP Nelson*		Gage-5	COD-2	*ITP Nelson*
"Cdn."	1,638	2,211	1,443	"Cdn."	1,638	2,211	1,443
–				Canadian content not overtly marked	74	1	550
TOTAL	1,638	2,211	1,443	**TOTAL**	**1,712**	**2,212**	**1,993**

that are overtly labelled "Cdn.". *COD-2* is the leader only at first glance. On the left, *COD-2* lists 2,211 such terms and thus about a third more than *Gage-5* and even more than that of *ITP Nelson* – e.g., from *Gage-5*, *Revenue Canada* 'the Canadian tax authority', and from *ITP Nelson*, *Albertan clipper* 'a NE wind, originating in Alberta', are *not* labelled "Cdn.". The right half shows a more sophisticated analysis and includes Canadian terms that are only found in Canada and are introduced by "(in Canada)" or the like but are not labelled Canadian as such. A different picture emerges, with *ITP Nelson* closing the gap to *COD-2* on account of a more cautious labelling practice alone.

If one considers that *COD-2* is the revised version of the 1998 dictionary and added about 250 Canadian terms (from the dust jacket), it is clear that *ITP Nelson* included at least as many Canadian terms as *COD-1*.

The counts for the overt "Cdn." label in *Gage-5* and *ITP Nelson* are lower because their editors' goal was not to win some sort of counting contest, as it were. In the case of *COD*, one is sceptical. *COD-2* data reveal what the critical reader of the *Canadian Oxford* would have noticed all along: that *COD* marked many things Canadian – even things that clearly aren't. The terms in Table 8, from *A* to *Z*, illustrate the extent of the problem. Of these twenty terms, only *single point* and, historically speaking, *zombie* would be Canadianisms in any meaningful way: the other eighteen would be either too narrow and specialized (*reversing falls*, *wreckhouse winds*), pronouncedly historical (*Orkneyman*), or not Canadian according to any of *DCHP-2*'s six types, e.g., *intersession, minor league*.

Not shown in Table 8 are the numerous Canadian institutions, prizes, military ranks, and abbreviations that are labelled "Cdn." in *COD-2*, which serve as particularly good examples of how the Canadianism count was inflated. Among them are 142 abbreviations that are labelled "Cdn." in *COD-2*. While not technically wrong, such encyclopaedic content should not be used to promote the dictionary as "more Canadian" or "better" than *Gage-5* or *ITP Nelson* – or *Funk & Wagnalls*' 1989 edition for that matter – as most of these abbreviations

Table 8 *Select items marked "Cdn." in* COD-2 *(2004)*

arse	*esp. Brit & Cdn (Nfld),* 'variation of ass'
Beaver Club	'*hist.* 18th c. social club in Montreal'
coffee cream	'cream with 10% (or 18%) fat content'
ecogift	'land given to the government for environmental protection'
farmer's sausage	'type of raw pork sausage'
gold	'an especially good seat in a hockey arena etc.'
house league	'internal league of organization, school'
intersession	'a short university term, usu. in May and June'
landing	'*Forestry,* an area where logs are piled before being loaded for transportation'
minor	'amateur team sport level for children, *minor hockey, minor soccer*'
nose	'the northeast portion of the Grand Banks of Newfoundland'
Orkneyman	noun (pl. -men) *hist.* 'a native or inhabitant of the Orkney Islands working in the N American fur trade, esp. with the Hudson's Bay Company'
principal	'a lawyer who supervises an articling student'
reversing falls	'a set of rapids on a tidal river, the flow of which reverses regularly'
single point	'*Cdn Football,* a single point scored when the receiving team fails to run a kick out of the end zone'
tent ring	'a ring of stones for holding down a tent etc., indicating a past campsite'
UFFI	'urea formaldehyde foam insulation'
VAdm	'Vice Admiral, a naval officer ranking below admiral and above rear admiral'
wreckhouse winds	'extremely strong winds which blow across Cape Ray from the Long Range Mountains in Newfoundland'
zombie	WWII slang: 'a conscript, orig. for national defence as opposed to overseas service'

are overly narrow and specific: *MB* 'Medal of Bravery', *WRCNS*, and the like. Especially for an internet-age dictionary, such a high degree of encyclopaedic entries seems excessive – Table 9 lists twenty examples.

Of the twenty terms, only the four in boldface are in any considerable and *general* use. Surely, *DM* (Deputy Minister) is important if you work in government and *MS* (Master Seaman) if you're in the military. The question is, which terms should be listed in a general desk dictionary vs a governmental structural diagram or a list of military ranks given to recruits? The terms in that list include some that are useful to some people but also include historical terms (*WRCNS*), military abbreviations of little to no use outside of the Canadian Forces (*VAdm, SLt, Maj. Gen., LCdr.*), and others that seem quite banal, e.g., *Conc.* and *Counc.* Once more: poof! No fewer than thirty-four terms, or almost 2 per cent of *COD-2*'s overall Canadianism count, are shown as subject to inflationary counting which thus suggests they were added to increase the token count.

Table 9 *Twenty (of 142) abbreviations marked "Cdn."*
in COD-2

ADM	Assistant Deputy Minister
BIA	Business Improvement Association
CGIT	(in the United Church) Canadian Girls in Training
C	Commons – for House of Commons
Conc.	concession
Counc.	councillor
DM	Deputy Minister
EI	**employment insurance**
FAC	Firearms Acquisition Certificate
FN	**First Nation**
GN	Government of Nunavut
LCdr.	Lieutenant Commander
Maj. Gen.	Major General
MB	Medal of Bravery
MS	Master Seamen
RCMP	**(not marked abbr.)**
ROC	**Rest of Canada**
SLt	Sub Lieutenant
VAdm	Vice Admiral
WRCNS	*hist.* Women's Royal Canadian Naval Service

While putting such terms in a desk dictionary is questionable in the internet age, in the late 1990s it was more justifiable to do so – but still doubtful. The real problem emerges when such terms are included in token counts to gain a competitive advantage over other, potentially better-made dictionaries. Treating, for example, *Conc.* on a par with *parkade* not only hides the work that went into establishing that *parkade* indeed is a Canadianism – here of Type 5 (highly frequent in Canada)[16] – but ultimately looks a bit embarrassing, as if Canadian English had no "better", more pervasive terms than military structure or the like that are, in Avis' words, "distinctively characteristic of Canadian usage" (Avis 1967: xiii).

Another problem is the inclusion of regional terms in dictionaries for nationwide use. By regionalisms, we mean such vocabulary items as are only used in particular parts of Canada. This, on the face of it, is a strong suit of *COD-2*, with 697 regional terms, while *Gage-5* lists "only" 201. A closer look reveals problems once more. For instance, 40 per cent of *COD-2*'s 697 terms are regional Newfoundland terms, which begs the question how many regional, non-standard terms should be included in a dictionary that for the most part is supposed to document Standard Canadian English.

The verdict is solid that *COD-2* inflates its Canadianism count beyond what had been customary in the Canadian reference publishing market till then. *COD-2* was, I would argue, measured on a different, higher-scoring scale, while in terms of quality it is no better than the other two. It was just, a priori, perceived by key stake holders to be better than the other dictionaries. It failed, however, on the revenue-making scale in a rapidly changing market. What was unfortunate is that *COD-1* and *COD-2* contributed disproportionally to the failures of the other two dictionaries, and one may speculate that, without Oxford University Press' entry into Canada, we might still have an up-to-date dictionary today. This may seem like a somewhat harsh critique, but considering the facts and the remnants of colonial sentiment, plus a yearning for a fully accepted dictionary, I think it is an inevitable conclusion.

It appears that from the start the dice were loaded against *Gage-5* and *ITP Nelson*, more so than they may have realized. What their publishers could not know was that the Canadian public would hold, in a leftover from a colonial reflex perhaps, the American origin of the *Gage* and *ITP Nelson* dictionaries against them. Both of these dictionaries had purchased licences for American reference works – Thorndike–Barnhart school dictionaries by the former, and *American Heritage College Dictionary* in the latter case – as the starting points of their editorial work. This is good practice. The problem of lexicography as a discipline now largely decoupled from academia comes to light, as even the professional linguists did not know that no dictionary is started from scratch and thus must secure a good dictionary base - which all three did:

N [*ITP Nelson*] and G [*Gage Canadian*] are both based on American dictionaries. The American bases exert an ineradicable influence on these Canadian versions. N is a newcomer, based on *The American Heritage High School Dictionary* (Houghton Mifflin). G has the advantage of having been Canadianizing its base dictionary for thirty years, to the point where its American source is no longer acknowledged. (Chambers 1997: n.p.)

The "ineradicable influence" is, of course, nonsense. The *Gage Canadian* has had five editions and thirty years to purge any remaining traces, and the *ITP Nelson* was gone over with a fine-toothed comb for many years, turning over every single entry, as an ITP editor confirmed.

We can interpret this statement above as ignorance, a colonial reflex, or anti-American sentiment, because the *Canadian Oxford* has also had its foreign base, which was the eighth edition of the (British) *Concise Oxford Dictionary*. The prime difference was, with Oxford owning copyright to the *Concise*, there was no obligation to list that base in the book, though academic transparency would have mandated it. The *ITP Nelson* and *Gage Canadian* did not have that luxury: their licence agreements obviously stipulated public acknowledgement, at least initially. This was the most important reason for the trade-book market failures of both the *Gage-5* and *ITP Nelson*.

We are left with the well-worn phrase: don't judge a book by its cover. Cover claims, dust jackets, copyright attributions, or publisher's claims are all subject to spin. Not to be fooled, however, is an awful lot to ask of anybody who just wants to get the best dictionary. If language professionals and experts fall for the spin, how can you expect general readers to cut through all that smoke?

No Winners, All Losers

By October 2008, Oxford University Press Canada announced the closure of its lexicographical offices and laid off the remaining four lexicographers, including Katherine Barber, the Chief Editor behind two editions of the *Canadian Oxford Dictionary*. Earlier that year in January, I had hired my first eight student workers to hunt for quotations digitally for *DCHP-2*, the project that would offer a scholarly but accessible historical dictionary for free at www.dchp.ca/dchp2 by March 2017. Until about mid-2010, though, we were in no position to speak to Canadian English from our own data: we were building our resource, from *A* to *Z*. While Oxford University Press was closing shop, we had barely gotten off the ground, spending two years on preparatory work from 2006, and were trying to raise the funds we needed. The first stages were hard: of the $225,000 applied for, we received just 16 per cent. I remember well the phone call from the principal investigator of that grant, Laurel Brinton, as I was not eligible for such funding at the time: Laurel was, to use the Queen's phrase, "not amused". With that seed money, we established the Canadian English Lab. While it took a little longer to get out of the starting gate, *DCHP-2* was produced more efficiently than if we had raised the whole amount upfront. In hindsight, it was a smart move by SSHRC to give just enough not to totally discourage us.

The Dictionary Society of North America, having heard the news of Oxford giving up Canadian English after having monopolized it, asked me in the fall of 2008 to comment on this event. This is what I wrote then:

While *CanOx* [*COD*] was based on an electronic citations database (a first for Canadian English lexicography), in approach and scope it did little different from other Canadian dictionaries (*e.g.*, *Gage Canadian*, *ITP Nelson Dictionary*). Spurred by the PR savvy of its editor-in-chief, the *CanOx* sold more than 200,000 copies. In paper *only*. . . . The decision of OUP has shown that commercial publishers are no longer willing or able to support even highly successful products. If reference dictionaries, such as *Merriam-Webster* or *American Heritage*, are available online and free of charge, Canadians, especially the younger generations, will use those resources rather than buying a paper copy of a Canadian reference tool. (Dollinger 2008c: 1; 3)

I called the article "The canary in a coalmine", after the miners' trick of bringing a bird down into the mine with them, which would, in case of toxic air, succumb much earlier than the workers and thus alert them to get out. The *Canadian Oxford*, I argued then, was an early warning sign of what happens when a country outsources, by accident or by design, one's crucial resources, including language reference. These resources will be, if the business case warrants it, left in the lurch, and a few more lexicographers would need to look for new employment. It's not personal; it's business. That's why the business end must necessarily be decoupled from the editorial end.[17] There still is no equivalent alternative to these outdated Canadian reference sources today, while the 2016 *Collins Canadian Dictionary*, much smaller in size, is the sole sign of life.

Why Not Google Canadian Terms?

I am sometimes asked which up-to-date Canadian resources exist, and I say there aren't any that are younger than fifteen or twenty years old, big *and* worth their salt. When asked what Canadian writers usually do, I answer that, like the rest of the world, they google words, using dictionary.com, vocabulary.com, merriam-webster.com, oxforddictionaries.com, ahdictionary.com, or any of the other commercial sites that are listed first in web searches.

This sorry state of affairs reminds me a bit of the period when MP3 players became available and were cheap and easy to use. As a result, music ceased to be listened to on audio systems and was played more on one's mobile devices; as a result of this convenience, the (sound) quality suffered, but the convenience factor trumped the loss of quality. It's exactly the same with googling your words. If Canadians are happy with this, fine. That's okay. But I think, as I show in the last chapter, that Canadians would prefer better tools: tools that are built by Canadians, based on Canadian sources, and just for Canadians and all those who'd like to learn about Canadian English. That is, if such tools are offered in a convenient manner, preferably for free or at least with a decent free option. And here, the industry has failed them to date.

In future work, the focus needs to be taken off Canadianism counts – we have seen in the Great Canadian Dictionary War how this PR battle backfired. A small field such as Canadian English would require that all those who are editorially responsible for reference works – and hopefully there will be healthy competition – collaborate on a shared project, to a degree at least. If there is competition, it would need to be rooted in respect (which the Dictionary Society of North America is admiringly modelling, with all kinds of publishing houses exchanging ideas with academics in a congenially relaxed atmosphere of mutual respect). As a benchmark: *DCHP-2* features 1,002 new terms and 1,348 meanings, though this is just the tip of the iceberg of what can be discovered about the lexis of Canadian English. The point is that the more you look, the more you'll find. Canadians use the language on an everyday basis and therefore, as speakers, they only notice the most obvious things: *toque* – oh, it's *hat* elsewhere; *garburator*, oh, is a *waste disposal*; *parkade* – oh, others may understand it but would probably use *parking garage*. In the latter example, it's already not so easy to discern what's used where.

I sometimes hear people suggesting that there are supposedly "not very many" Canadianisms. While the basic sentiment is understandable and at times a sign of true internationalism – after all, we can talk to the Americans, Brits, and beyond without too much hassle – this statement is mistaken as it confounds lexical information about words with strategic information on how to interpret language in context. When someone says *disposal* and turns on the electric switch, you can hear the *garburator* working, so in this example the lexis is not a problem of communication. Like most language use, such negotiated understanding is the result of the situational context, the shared knowledge about how the world works, and humans' uncanny ability to guess correctly. *DCHP-2* has offered 1,348 new reasons to dismiss the idea that the Canadian English lexis is small or insignificant. Those residing in Canada can check what they hear against www.dchp.ca/dchp2. If you live elsewhere, similarly pay attention to your language for the next two days and you'll inevitably notice people saying things you'll think you'd never heard them say before. That's because you've routinely been focussing on the message, not on the vehicle of its delivery.

Even if the number of lexical Canadianisms were indeed small, it is not as important as it is made out to be. Why not? For identity purposes, discourse frequency is far more important than the size of the lexical inventory that is different from other locations, nations, and speakers and used for such purposes: only a handful of terms, *when used frequently*, may act as powerful linguistic identifiers. For example, *washroom* and *parkade* may just be two TYPES of lexical items, but there are millions of occurrences (or TOKENS) of them around the country daily.

While the frequencies (tokens) always trump simplistic counts of distinct words and meanings (types), there is a whole range of words and word combinations that look ordinary but turn out to be distinctly Canadian, one way or another. A few of these are words such as *all-candidates meeting*, *cube van* 'moving truck', *to lob (a question)*, *puck board* 'type of hard plastic material', *take up* #9 'go over / review the answers to a test, etc.', or *wingy* 'crazy'.

Who knew that all of the above are Canadianisms, tried-tested-and-true Canadianisms, and most of them fairly recent ones? Whenever one detects a potential Canadianism, it is about falsifying it, about shooting down the idea that it might be Canadian. Only when we fail to falsify our hunch after trying really hard can the linguist feel certain about a particular Canadianism. In all 1,348 cases from *DCHP-2*, only the systematic, scientific study of language

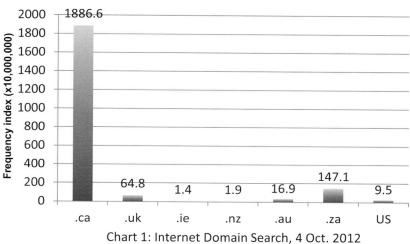

Chart 1: Internet Domain Search, 4 Oct. 2012

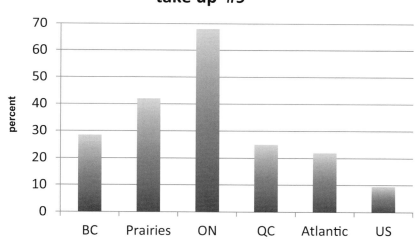

Figure 29 *Puck board* (since 1996) and *take up* #9 'go over correct answers'
(www.dchp.ca/dchp2)

was able to reveal the characteristics of the fact that Canadians, while internationally oriented, talk much more often to other Canadians.

To stress this point, Figure 29 depicts the *DCHP-2* data for *puck board* and
take up #9.

In *puck board*, we can see, through internet frequency searches – normalized searches to allow for cross-comparison across the various internet top-level domains – that the .ca domain is almost 1,900 index points, much higher than the second-placed South Africa (.za) with not even 150 index points, and the UK with just about 65 points. *Puck board* was, therefore, deemed a Canadianism by virtue of frequency. Other cases are more complex, and one of them is *take up* #9.

Take up #9 and "Dictionary Genealogy"

Take up #9 is a socially complex variable that is tied to regional diffusion and transmission. In Figure 29 at the bottom we see the responses from 316 questionnaire respondents who were asked to paraphrase the sentence, "The math teacher took up the test this morning." Only those that clearly paraphrased the sentence as the teacher going over the test answers as a class, one by one, pointing out what the class did right and what wrong, were counted. This narrow semantic analysis revealed the Ontarian origin of this meaning (70% from that province passed the strict paraphrasing test), a meaning that has been spreading along the east–west axis to other Canadian regions. In a second sample of some 100 Ontarians, more than 90% correctly paraphrased this variable (see Dollinger 2015a: 101). The recognition rate in the USA of under 10% is statistically very different from *all* Canadian regions, which were

Table 10 *Comparison of entries for* take up *(Concise Oxford Dictionary, 8th edn, and* Canadian Oxford Dictionary, *1st edn)*

Concise Oxford Dictionary (Eighth edn)	*Canadian Oxford Dictionary* (First edn)
take up 1 become interested or engaged in (a pursuit). **2** adopt as a protégé. **3** occupy (time or space). **4** begin (residence etc.). **5** resume after an interruption. **6** interrupt or question (a speaker). **7** accept (an offer etc.). **8** shorten (a garment). **9** lift up. **10** absorb (*sponges take up water*). **11** take (a person) into a vehicle. **12** pursue (a matter etc.) further. **take a person up on** accept (a person's offer etc.). **take up with** begin to associate with.	**take up 1** become interested or engaged in (an interest, pursuit, hobby, etc.). **2** adopt as a protégé. **3** occupy (time or space). **4** begin (residence etc.). **5** resume after an interruption. **6** join in (a song, chorus, etc.). **7** accept (an offer etc.). **8** shorten (a garment). **9** go over the correct answers to (homework, an assignment, a test, etc.). **10** lift up. **11** absorb (*sponges take up water*). **12** take (a person) into a vehicle. **13** pursue (a matter etc.) further. **14** interrupt or question (a speaker). **take a person up on** accept (a person's offer etc.). **take up the gauntlet** accept a challenge. **take up with** begin to associate with.

[handwritten annotation: "every dictionary should have a source page."]

between 22% and 50%. Even Atlantic Canada, at just 22%, was significantly different from the USA. This is an Ontarian meaning that has been exported, with teachers from that province moving elsewhere in Canada and taking their local ways of speaking with them (see www.dchp.ca/dchp2/Entries/view/take %252520up).

Why is this meaning called #9? Because the *Canadian Oxford Dictionary* can be credited as first including this meaning, listing it as meaning #9. Table 10 is a visual comparison of how one dictionary copies from another one. On the left, we see the 1992 *Concise Oxford Dictionary*, which is the base of the Canadian editions, and on the right, the 1998 adapted version for the *Canadian Oxford Dictionary*. We see that, in a largely identical entry – the insertions are underlined – meaning #9 has been inserted in the Canadian edition.

What is odd in Table 10 is that meaning #9 was inserted by *COD* but was *not* labelled as Canadian. Surely, *take up the gauntlet* or 'join in a song', which were also added, are not Canadian. But *take up* #9 is, so why was it not marked as such? Here we have a prime example of what happens to speakers of Canadian English habitually, to which language professionals are not immune. Did the Canadian dictionary editors really miss the chance to label a bona fide Canadianism, or Ontarianism, in a dictionary that labelled everything and anything Canadian that they possibly could, as we've seen above? An over-sight can be almost certainly ruled out, as *take up* #9 appears identical in both the 1998 and the 2004 editions.

The most likely explanation is that the editors themselves did not know that *take up* #9 was Canadian. Here's why: five of the *COD*'s six lexicographers grew up in areas (Ontario and NE Manitoba) where meaning #9 is habitually used and very strong. They appear to have failed, in the absence of profound comparative data, to recognize the Canadian dimension of this meaning because almost all of them used it by default (see Dollinger 2015a: 99–104).

It is for this reason, the difficulty of detecting Canadian features, that Canadians deserve the best possible Canadian language resources. Canadian English is just too complex to be documented from abroad with freelance writers, however good and open and up-to-date these freelancers might be. Canadians also deserve reference books that are decolonized in the more historical meaning of the term, on top of the now pressing Indigenous decol-onization we'll be discussing in the next chapter.

Figure 30 Tl-chess (Discovery and Chatham Islands) at low and high tide. At low tide the land bridge is visible in the middle, while at high tide the water of the Salish Sea can be discerned.

First Nations knowledge runs deep. So deep, that even local marine expert and tour operator Brian Glennon, who knows these waters like no other, told me that he'd never seen a land bridge between Chatham and Discovery. Being the nice guy that he is, Brian checked the tidal maps to confirm that, at super low tides, you can wade across "the gap", as it's called, from Chatham to Discovery. Brian can be reached at www.oakbaytours.com.

(Photos: S. Dollinger, 11 and 10 August 2018)

colonial artifact

8   Decolonizing *DCHP-1* and *DCHP-2*

Some effects of colonialism, as seen through the eyes of a well-meaning Westerner:
"Of fourteen kids I have, I figure 9 are in the special class, through emotional disturbances of one kind or another, three are normal and shouldn't be in a special class and two are brain-damaged (and probably insane)."

(Charles Crate on his class in Alert Bay, BC, to Joan Hall, 9 Jan. 1966)

Na'tsa'maht!
(Lekwungen [and Coast Salishan] rallying cry to "pull together"; used in canoeing, to collectively overcome difficulties to succeed (also the name of The Gathering Place sacred house, designed by Lekwungen Elder Butch Dick, at Camosun College)

From 16 to 22 September 2013, the Truth and Reconciliation Commission of Canada stopped in Vancouver for its British Columbia event. A big part of the event was to hear testimony from First Nations, Inuit, and Métis (FNIM) survivors about individual and institutionalized abuse, colonialism, discrimination, and racism. Knowing history in the abstract is one thing, listening to survivors telling their stories an entirely different matter. How is it possible, one must ask, that small children, some as young as 4 or 5, were forcefully separated from their parents, families, and Indigenous Nations and brought to institutions euphemistically called "residential schools"?

How is it possible that these children, yanked out of their social and familial networks, were forbidden, by corporal punishment, to speak their languages? Their languages, the singularly most important vessels of their cultures, were literally beaten out of them: one Indigenous word, one beating. Children were relocated hundreds, if not thousands, of miles from their homes. What would this do to one's connection to oneself, to one's people? Things happened at these residential schools in the name of somebody's god. The schools offered at best a sprinkling of formal education but also, much worse, physical, psychological, and sexual abuse. What society lets that happen in the name of "civilization"?

Such measures are only possible by the demonization of Indigenous cultures, and colonization was the vehicle to do it. The travesty and injustice of the mindset that was so widespread in the day, and is still with us to a greater or lesser degree, can perhaps best be seen in the great lengths that an entire society went to in order to prevent First Nations, Indigenous, Inuit, and Métis children from succeeding. It was not always as bad as during the height of the residential schools, which lasted from the 1880s until 1996 (!). While in the early 1800s intermarriage was common among Hudson Bay people and FNIM members, and with it a certain form of respect, such relations were considered, a generation or two later, as threatening to white society.

A key turning point towards the worse seems to have been the withdrawal of the Hudson's Bay Company (HBC) as a major landholder. When "land controlled by the Hudson's Bay Company was transferred to Canada and as white settlement reinforced racist attitudes in the new nation" (Fee 2015: 127), we see perhaps the ugliest part of Canada's history take shape. When the Government of Canada took over, it all got particularly bad. It is important to keep in mind that the escalation was *state-controlled*, in the name of the people.

There was a perceived Indigenous "threat" to white society, a threat of the "other" that Victorian gentlemen did not want to accept. We were light years away from a multi-faceted society that allowed for a wide range of identities and lifestyles. Pauline E. Johnson (1862–1909) is a case in point as the daughter of a Mohawk medical doctor and an English woman. Knowing both worlds, Johnson considered herself first a Mohawk and then a Canadian. From 1892 to 1909, she was famous as a performer – in both buckskin dress and English evening gown, or vice versa – and a poet, with her work being published in London. Margery Fee describes the threat that exuded from people like Pauline to the white establishment and its hierarchy of "races", which was presented as the "natural" order of things:

She [Pauline E. Johnson] and other accomplished Indigenous people of the day demonstrated that Indigenous people could succeed – even excel – by the standards of white society. Their success, in fact, threatened the primary rationalization for Canadian colonization, which was that Indigenous people lacked civilization and required white educators, missionaries, and Indian agents to help them achieve it. (Fee 2015: 121)

In the eye of the colonizer, such developments had to be stopped. As the forced assimilation of FNIM people was more and more institutionalized starting around 1900, we need to ask ourselves what role universities and scholars have played in this shameful and cruel programme. *DCHP*, as an academic project and like any other institution and individual, must face this scrutiny for biases against FNIMs.

Unwillingness and Refusal

There were some who advised me of the colonial issue a few years back, such as MA student Katrina Lo, who had worked in the Canadian English Lab on data collection for *DCHP-2*. At that point, I was not ready to hear her out. Instead, I was trying to insist that 1960s folks needed to be judged by 1960s standards, not the ones of the 2010s. Fortunately, Margery was able to take up the topic (see Katrina's MA thesis about decolonizing *DCHP-1* [Lo 2012]). What follows is my attempt to situate *DCHP-1* in its sociohistorical context in relation to the blight of colonialism.

One does not need to look hard to spot the effects of colonialism in *DCHP-1*. As a project of the 1950s and early 1960s, it is bound to fall short of today's expectations. So much is certain. In that way, *DCHP-1* is as colonial as such projects were at the time. In which ways, however, might *DCHP-1* fall short of reasonable expectations from the background of its historical period? Where does it stand by today's standards? The legacy dictionary from 1967 can be accessed free of charge at www.dchp.ca/dchp1 so that everyone can test *DCHP-1*.[1] *DCHP-1* documents words, meanings, and expressions, and as a historical dictionary includes, of course, a lot of outdated and at times outright offensive terms. Since such terms need to be listed unless one wishes to "bury" some part of history, it would be the task of the dictionary editors to distance themselves appropriately from them, either by including labels such as "derogatory" or "offensive", or with a definition that reflects the current sentiments and the editors' stance. In *DCHP-1*, labels perform that function for the most part. For instance, in the entry *peasouper* 'French Canadian', the labels "Slang, Derog." are used, which is a minimum of distancing by today's standards. However, in *half-blood* or *half-breed*, which is defined as 'a person of mixed Indian and white ancestry', no labels are found. To a Martian getting hold of *DCHP-1* in an attempt to learn the language, *half-blood* would be in the same category as *parkade*, *landed immigrant*, or *Mountie* 'police officer of the Royal Canadian Mounted Police'. Clearly, we have a problem.

Knowledge Gaps: the *Canadian Press Stylebook*

What is more often seen in recent years is that non-Indigenous people are trying to improve the treatment of Indigenous matters symbolically, though they don't always know how to go about it. The eighteenth edition of the *Canadian Press Stylebook: A Guide for Writers and Editors* is a case in point.

The many errors in a short section of less than a third of a page, offering advice on Inuit matters in writing, are telling:

- The suffix for "Labradorimiut" is spelled incorrectly as "muit" instead of "miut."
- "Nunavummiut" is spelled with an "i" instead of a "u."
- "Inuvialuit" is spelled incorrectly on second reference as "Inuvialiut."
- [It] incorrectly states that the word "Inuvialuit" represents a "region." In fact, the word "Inuvialuit" represents the name of a people, the Inuit who live in the six communities of the Inuvialuit Settlement Region.
- The term "Inuvialiummuit," which [the *Canadian Press Stylebook*] assigns to Inu-vialuit, should be spelled as "Inuvialungmiut" or "Inuvialummiut," or not used at all, since "Inuvialuit" already denotes a people and the suffix "miut" means "people of," making it redundant. (Brown 2017)

This is difficult stuff if one does not deal much with Inuit matters, but in that case it would be a good idea to outsource the writing of these sections to people who do know.[2] Given tight deadlines and the difficulty of reaching those in the know at short notice via the usual journalistic means is a problem, but no excuse.

Other than interpreting this as a simple oversight, as having failed to include a final community-based round of proofing, it could also be read as a further manifestation of colonial attitudes, which are notoriously difficult to get rid of. The present author is not immune to this kind of error, as an early version of Chapter 1 "made do" without reference to the First Nations languages, which are now central to that chapter. When a colleague pointed it out, I was speechless. It's true that the book is on Canadian English, but these days there can be no more books on Canadian English that don't acknowledge the embedding of the colonial language in the multitude of First Nations linguistic diversity.

Since we are dealing with cultures – cultures that most Canadians have heard little or nothing about – one needs to tread carefully on any level; for instance, one cannot assume that "western" ways of communication will be appropriate or even successful. An email to the info line of the Friendship Centre will not get the job done. Why not? Because in many Indigenous cultures email does not play the role it does in western business circles or in journalistic circles. It's a learning curve by trial and error, and one needs to bring time and a willingness to admit mistakes, such as my (horrible) mistake of "forgetting" the First Nations in Chapter 1.

The section in the *CP Stylebook* was well meant but reveals a basic problem: the continuing unfamiliarity of most Canadians with Indigenous cultures, which is the real problem behind the error and another effect of colonialism. With Indigenous cultures being vilified and discredited from Day 1, public debate seems to have reached a point where the pervasive problems of systematic, long-lasting ignorance, domination, and sidelining can finally start to be addressed. I will attempt to do so for *DCHP-1*, with a peek towards *DCHP-2*, though the latter task requires an "arm's length" from the project, which is why that part is very brief.

Example 1: from *Eskimo* to *Inuit*

Reading *DCHP-1* today raises more than a few eyebrows. Simple searches for Indigenous terms and historical terms reveal the part of the book that is least flattering. On one level, *DCHP-1* – and by implication *DCHP-2* for taking over its legacy data – must be considered a colonial narrative. This applies, despite our best efforts, to a certain degree also for the new content in *DCHP-2*. There is a lot of outdated terminology in *DCHP-1*, such as *Eskimo*, which is defined (meaning 1) as "a member of a large group of North American aborigines inhabiting the Arctic and northern coastal areas from Greenland to Siberia. Also spelled *Esquimau (pl. -aux)*." The definition as such is nearly acceptable, but it is clear that the inclusion of the term alone, not marked at all, will irritate the present-day reader. *DCHP-2* distinguishes the legacy entries from *DCHP-1* visibly by setting them on yellow background and adding disclaimers on the top right in bold, as shown in Figure 31.

The disclaimer, "**THIS ENTRY MAY CONTAIN OUTDATED INFOR-MATION, TERMS and EXAMPLES**", is added in addition to the date stamp of "*DCHP-1* (pre-1967)". It is not perfect, but it should ensure that the legacy entries are put in their historical context and not confused with *DCHP-2* update entries.

DCHP-2

Eskimo † [< Algonk., probably through Cdn F *Esquimau* with spelling influenced by Danish *Eskimo*; cf. Cree *askimowew* he eats it raw; Ojibwa *askkimē* raw-flesh eater]   **DCHP-1 (pre-1967)**

THIS ENTRY MAY CONTAIN OUTDATED INFORMATION, TERMS and EXAMPLES

• See also: Husky Inuit

    ☞ *Although several other etymologies have been advanced (see quotes below), the evidence unquestionably supports the Algonkian source. The remarkably large number of variant spellings in early writings of the Labrador-Hudson's Bay region suggest constant reinforcing from contact of the English traders with the Crees.*

    ☞ Since the 1970's, the more appropriate term in Canada to describe Aboriginal peoples of the Arctic is Inuit (see *Inuit*, meaning 1).

Figure 31 Legacy entry in *DCHP-2* on yellow background with disclaimer (new entries on white, non-Canadianisms on red background, colours shown on website)

Some might wonder why we included the old entries at all. This is an important question to ask. The answer is simple: we included old entries because we did not have the means to revise the legacy terms, not even the culturally sensitive ones, of which *DCHP-1* contains many. Like the *OED* revision, such work would require many years and funding that is more than all the funding we obtained for *DCHP-2*. The marking of older terms as "obsolete" and "derogatory" or "(extremely) offensive" is one thing, the adaptation of definitions and the new selection of examples another. While in *DCHP-2* we researched the use of *Aboriginal*, the new development and most recent switch to *Indigenous* was just beginning to take off as we were winding down the operation in 2015–16.

Example 2: 137 Headwords with *Indian*

The second example deals with a term that many Canadians tend to avoid today – *Indian* – replacing it with *First Nation*. The term *Indian*, while colonial in nature, has acquired a number of meanings, of which the definitions in the Indian Act alone – the piece of legislation from 1876, revised in 1951 – offer a few different senses. Only now has discussion ensued regarding the total abolition of the Act, though the legal ramifications of that step would need to be checked. The problem here is that a number of Indigenous rights are tied to the Act, which is a tricky issue, since the Indian Act has been used to keep the number of status Indians, those who are eligible for federal benefits, at a minimum – so much so that the rules were designed to shrink the eligible pool of status Indians, via marriage and the like. The Indian Act is the colonizers' dictating of who does and does not count as a member of Indigenous communities, which is one of the big problems. With such complex legal and social histories in Canada, it should be no surprise that no fewer than 137 entries in *DCHP-1* include the term *Indian*. All of them would need to be revised.

Does the inclusion of the compound terms with *Indian* alone make *DCHP-1* colonial? It would be an odd thing not to have such terms in the book, as they are part of the Canadian heritage, though no one is proud of them; they are to a great extent Type 6 – Memorial terms, if you remember from Chapter 5. That alone would not make the book colonial; the verdict would depend on how the terms are presented.

How, though, should *DCHP-1* be assessed? The editors were children of their time and, given that that time was fundamentally blind to the plight of the Indigenous population, the level of awareness was very low. So anything that is better in *DCHP-1* than the average way of dealing with Indigenous matters should be, I think, counted on the positive side. But there are problems. The entry for the term *good Indian*, which is defined and glossed as a "peaceful Indian", repeats long-held stereotypes: an *Indian* is not peaceful by definition, only a *good Indian* is. Clearly, we have a problem! Combined with the historical evidence – e.g., the 1791 quotation in Figure 32 – the light cast on the matter is not favourable at all.

What is utterly missing here is contextualization – contextualization that would have been accomplished in the form of a fist note (which is a depicted hand with finger pointing) and with labels that categorize the term as "derogatory", "offensive", "colonial language use", or the like. Worse, perhaps, the 1966 quotation promotes the practice of cultural assimilation as being "good". Such entries expose the blind spots of *DCHP-1* to the fullest. Such errors reveal the "default" position, which is the colonial subtext, and illustrate colonialism as a "cultural practice" that permeated every aspect of human life in Canada, including academia. It will take some time to undo that damage.

Please also note that the use of racist quotations as documentary evidence is not colonial by definition, as they are authentic examples of language use. The shorthand style of traditional lexicography and the perennial space constraints did not make it easy to include this information, but other examples – such as the two fist notes in Figure 31 – show that space was dedicated to more elaboration when considered necessary. We must therefore conclude that the example of *good Indian* was not deemed worthy of comment: it was just "how things were". A similar case can be made about *go Indian* (Figure 33), which is listed in *DCHP-1* with just one quotation, from 1934, which is especially damning and, without explanation, downright unacceptable, even by 1960s standards.

DCHP-1 ONLINE

good Indian ▣

- an Indian friendly to the whites; a peaceful Indian.

See also: bad Indian white Indian

> **1791** It is true the Master of Life has sent me here to those Indians whose hearts are full of poisoned blood, and as they mean to change my climate, I shall go with courage to a better trading ground, where I shall find good Indians. ▣
>
> **1860** Peguis was always a good Indian--the best that was ever known in the colony. ▣
>
> **1926** At this juncture William McKay, a Hudson's Bay man . . . rode amongst the still excited crowd and brought up to the shack Indian after Indian whom McKay vouched for as "good Indians" and to whom bags of flour and sides of bacon were dished out by Crozier's orders. ▣
>
> **1966** They were good Indians . . . and . . . they had adjusted to the white man's rigid laws remarkably well. . . . ▣
>
> **1967** But at least Charlie Wenjack died an Indian--not a slavish, obsequious, pandering, "good" Indian. ▣

Figure 32 Entry for *good Indian (DCHP-1 Online)*

DCHP-1 ONLINE

go Indian 🖭

- of white men, adopt the ways of the Indian.

> **1934** The Indians, though nominally Christians, were utter savages at heart, and close contact with primitive life and passions, and the almost complete absence of moral sense amongst those with whom I was so closely associated had a disquieting effect. Only the strictest self-discipline could prevent one "going Indian," with all that it implies. 🔳

Figure 33 Entry for *go Indian (DCHP-1 Online)*

Such bias is perhaps one of the least-analyzed parts in *DCHP-1*, though one would need to assess these cases more fully and completely to gauge the extent of this kind of colonialism.

Is there anything that can be said in favour of the editors? While the damning presentation of the entry in Figure 33 cannot be excused, another perspective is that, by including 137 compounds with *Indian*, *DCHP-1* put Indigenous issues in the spotlight, which is more than most 1960s publications can claim. Combine that with the many terms of Indigenous origin that are documented in *DCHP-1* and you have quite an advanced dictionary for the time.

Example 3: *Residential School*

The *DCHP-1* team were at the time also among the most knowledgeable settler scholars as far as First Nations issues were concerned. They clearly were not the average Canadian, but much more advanced in their thinking about Indigenous–settler relations. And yet the entry for *residential school*, shown in Figure 34, makes these institutions out to have been aimed at assisting Indigenous people: "a boarding school ... to accommodate students, especially Indians and Eskimos", to make it easier for them to go to school as they study "at a considerable distance from their homes". The 1954 and 1965 quotations in this figure below reveal that these institutions were often the first schools in a given area and, as a rule, worse than "schools for whites". That a lower academic standard is not ideal is clear, but, seen in the context of Charles Crate's description from Alert Bay, it is a euphemism for the facts. The 1965 quotation is downright misleading and the framing of the entry as an act of benevolence is problematic, revealing bias and ignorance. The defence that the Big Six might have is that, at that point in time, few had cared enough to find out what was really going on in the residential schools.

Figure 34 Entry for *residential school* (*DCHP-1 Online*)

In the quotation file for *DCHP-1*, Box 20 contains the alphabetical order from *rat* to *timberline* – in total some 7,000 slips in just that one archival box of 11 x 14 x 11 inches. It is surprising that this box contains only one quotation for *residential school*, from Hawthorn, Belshaw, and Jamieson (1958):

I didn't choose him. I came home from residential school and my mother said, "there is a man with a good house, you will marry him."

This quotation is not found in the corresponding *DCHP-1* entry, where instead we see the two quotations in Figure 34. Box 16 includes an update file of about 1,500 cards. This update lists five quotations from 1967 to 1969 for *residential school*, thus concerning the post-publication period. Three quotations are from Avis and two from "DS", apparently one of the volunteer readers. All of these quotations are more critical than the three dating from prior to publication.

It seems that around 1967 a change towards residential schools was noticeable in the public eye. If that was indeed the case, the editors would be somewhat vindicated for their naïve definition of *residential school*, as knowledge about the systematic abuse had not been available in mainstream sources. It is possible that "white Canada" did not want or care to know. The clearest of these post-publication quotations is from the *Globe Magazine*, 28 October 1967 (p. 9, column 1). The excerpt, taken by Avis, reads:

Some attended residential schools, where as recently as 15 years ago the white authority-figures inflicted cruel and humiliating punishments on boys and girls for such offenses as speaking their own language, getting letters from sweethearts or trying to run away.

Another quotation, by "DS", from Ian Adams in *Maclean's* magazine from February 1967 (p. 30, column 3), which would (almost) have been too late to be included in *DCHP-1*, also suggests something is wrong with these institutions, as "It's not unusual that Indian children run away from the residential schools they are sent to." As we have seen earlier, Avis and the other editors tinkered till the spring with the entries and added, at Drysdale's behest, an entry for *canoe* as late as April and May 1967, so these quotations might have been added, in theory.

There are more problems. The entry's "See also" links are a real can of worms. One link is to *hostel*, which is labelled as "Northern Canadian" use. Meaning 2 (def. 2) is defined as

a boarding school operated or subsidized by the federal government to accommodate students, especially Indians and Eskimos, attending classes at a considerable distance from their homes. (*DCHP-1*, s.v. "hostel" (2); www.dchp.ca/DCHP-1/entries/view/hostel)

If there was any doubt regarding the misinformation about residential schools in *DCHP-1*, then the above definition exposes the misrepresentation of an institution for cultural genocide, funded by Canadian taxpayers, as a boarding school. Meaning 1 in *hostel* is no better:

a residential boarding house for Eskimos or Indians attending school away from home. (*DCHP-1*, s.v. "hostel" (1); www.dchp.ca/DCHP-1/entries/view/hostel)

Someone coming to the issue of residential schools with no advance knowledge might wonder whether the problem is really as bad as I make it out to be. To dispel any doubts, the clash between the above definitions and reality is best illustrated through the voices of residential-school survivors.

Elaine Durocher is a residential-school survivor who has given testimony at the national Truth and Reconciliation Commission's hearings. She testified that she did not get an education at her residential school in Kamsack, Saskatchewan. Instead, she "learned the tools for a life on the fringes of society in the sex trade" (TRC Final Report 2015: 120), as the commission's final report summarizes her testimony. Reading Elaine's statement in her own words is most horrifying. Who does such things to children – or to any human, for that matter? This is what residential schools were really about:

They were there to discipline you, teach you, beat you, rape you, molest you, but I never got an education. I knew how to run. I knew how to manipulate. Once I knew that I could get money for touching, and this may sound bad, but once I knew that I could touch a man's penis for candy, that set the pace for when I was a teenager, and I could pull tricks as a prostitute. That, that's what the residential school taught me. It taught me how to lie, how to manipulate, how to exchange sexual favours for cash, meals, whatever, whatever the case may be. (Elaine Durocher, TRC Final Report 2015: 120)

This sad and outrageous reality is a far cry from the harmless "boarding school" definitions. I think it's fair to say that the Big Six didn't know. They didn't know because colonial society did not want to know; there were no written reports on this. Could Crate have known, who was teaching in communities with a very high First Nations population? Possibly, but it's hard to tell. Given the new quotations that were collected since 1967, however, it stands to reason that the editors would have devised a different definition and treatment of the term, had they had this information a couple of years earlier.

Subtler Issues: *Treaty Indian*

Beyond the examples discussed so far, there are many more subtle issues pertaining to the colonial legacy in *DCHP-1* – issues that may cast *DCHP-1* in a doubtful light in terms of reconciliation. The entry for *treaty Indian* seems clear and straightforward. It is defined as "an Indian who is in receipt of treaty money or who adheres to a treaty (def. 1a)" and lists four quotations, from 1881 to 1965:

1881 The best wheat that has been brought to mill this season was raised at White Fish Lake by **treaty Indian**s.

1923 The dogs brought in by the **treaty Indian**s were in a terrible condition–the extreme of emaciation in many harrowing instances.

1957 Being a Canadian **treaty Indian** I am not eligible to vote but, if I could, I'd be proud to vote Conservative.

1965 Paul Mocassin [is] a **treaty Indian** from the Cochin Reserve. (Quotations for *treaty Indian* in *DCHP-1 Online*)

In the *DCHP-1* file, we find sixteen quotations, none of which appears in the *DCHP-1* entry, which begs the question of where the quotations that were selected came from. It is clear by now that, in contrast to what I surmised in 2006 when I visited the *DCHP-1* collection for the first time, not all *DCHP-1*

Table 11 *Quotations by year from* DCHP-1 *quotation file for* treaty Indian

assess whether quotations that are(were) chosen are biased..

Year	number of quotations
1885	1
1887	1
1889	1
1949	1
1954	2
1955	2
1958	1
1960	1
1961	2
1963	3
1964	1

data are in Victoria. This means that the 102,000 quotation slips – by my estimate – are not the complete collection, though it is uncertain where the remaining materials are.

For some reason, we only have in the file the "extra" quotations that were deemed not as good as the printed ones. Quotation selection is, of course, a key process in historical lexicography, and in lexicography in general: from the riches, one gets to select only a handful of quotations for the entry, originally due to space constraints and now in the digital medium more to editorial or "aesthetic" constraints. The fact of limited space has been referred to, and lamented, by every lexicographer who was working in the paper age (that is, until very recently), including Avis in his introduction to *DCHP-1*. Usually, the earliest quotation is listed in a definition – here in *treaty Indian* from 1881 in *DCHP-1* (1885 is the earliest in the archival file). This quotation is the one quotation that must be selected. The choice of the 1923 quotation stands out, however, as it implies that the dogs were badly treated by the treaty Indians. Could this be a sign of subtle bias against First Nations? Table 11 lists by year the quotations for *treaty Indian* that are found in the archival file.

The quotations that stand behind Table 11 come from Lovell, Avis, Leechman, and Crate, and one from a volunteer reader named "B. G. Chandler". In addition to finding a first quotation earlier than 1885 (an "antedate" to 1885, as it is called), Avis supplied a more recent example – from 1965 – than in the file (1964). One can see in the table a noticeable gap between 1889 and 1949. Being the good lexicographer that Avis was, he went looking for an attestation in the middle, so as not to leave six decades without proof of the term's use. It appears that the quotation Avis apparently found in the period between 1889 and 1949 (ideally somewhat in the middle) is the one that presents the FNIMs members in a negative light. It seems like an innocent coincidence. The 1957 quotation, on FNIMs being forbidden to vote, can be seen as supporting the FNIM cause. I think the examples illustrate well that both colonial "stains" intermingled with some early "decolonization" steps can be found in *DCHP-1*.

A picture emerges from this study that renders the blanket charge of colonialism at the level of quotation selection as doubtful. It is also clear that the sensitivities among the team were not so advanced as to add an explanation to the 1923 quotation or to look for another one, which would have been difficult to next-to-impossible in the pre-digital age. One can see an overhang of quotations from the mid-1950s to publication date, with eleven unused ones. Avis and his team must have been busy, writing the entry for *treaty Indian*, filling the emerging gaps in the quotation record that they probably did not expect to have. The many 1950s quotations were, in effect, not very useful. They didn't hurt, but they also didn't make the historical dictionary much better.

What could have been shown, or what one would definitely want to show now, are quotations that foreground the discriminatory practices that made the FNIMs' lives worse – for instance, laws that cause people to lose their treaty status, which are in the archival files:

1961 On her mother's marriage to a non-Indian Denise was enfranchised, but on her own marriage to John, she became a treaty Indian again. (*DCHP-1* file)

Why were none of those quotations selected, one wonders? Or, for instance, historical documentation that the right to vote came very late for FNIMs in Ontario:

1955 About 1,200 Treaty Indians in the district will be eligible to vote for the first time. (*DCHP-1* file)

There was also a situation that could have been used to highlight systemic injustice. As Indigenous people were still forbidden to vote provincially in Alberta in 1964, they feared repercussions, the tit-for-tat they'd been used to from various settler governments, which is most telling from the following two quotations:

1964 Alberta's 2,000 treaty Indians want a written guarantee from the provincial government that their lands and treaty rights will not be affected if they accept the right to vote.
1964 Treaty Indians cannot vote in provincial elections but they can vote in both municipal and federal elections. (University of Victoria Archives, *DCHP-1* file, s.v. "treaty Indian")

This is how *DCHP-1*, ultimately, exhibits a subtle colonial narrative in every entry: it buries quotations such as these four in the quotation file that no one has seen.

A lack of sensibility with regard to these issues is evident. There is a different narrative that was not told. By not publishing quotations such as the one from 1954 on "Mike [who] was arrested" on the charge of "selling liquor to a treaty Indian", the reader will not know about the legislative corset of the day. We also don't read another 1954 quotation that at first glance appears to be positive, yet reveals in a simple sentence that the general expectation was not equity towards Canada's First Nations:

1954 Educational facilities identical with those provided for other children have been instituted at Pelican Narrows in northern Saskatchewan for the children of treaty Indians. (University of Victoria Archives, *DCHP-1* file, s.v. "treaty Indian")

The newsworthiness of the item as such makes it clear that the societal expectation was not one of equal treatment. When such treatment occurred, against all odds, it was celebrated as an achievement of "civilization". There is a subtle brutality in these quotations that did not make the cut in *DCHP-1*. Their exclusion is perhaps the biggest – because a subtle – shortcoming: the story that is *not* told from the file – the story that could have been told but wasn't.

These examples should illustrate that a general revision of *DCHP-1* content in a completely revised edition, a *DCHP-3*, is a gigantic task. A task that requires that legacy data and legacy entries are gone through (all 10,000 of them with a yellow background in *DCHP-2*) line by line with a fine-toothed comb, including the quotation selection. Such an enterprise is bound to reveal many new meanings and thus change the structure of many *DCHP-1* entries to a degree as well. Surely, editorially, *DCHP-3* would be a bigger task than the work from 2006 to 2017 on *DCHP-2*, which included all the digitization, software programming, and data collection phases.

One Big Sixer in Alert Bay

We said earlier that, among the Big Six, Charles B. Crate is a bit of a "mystery man".[3] Not a linguist by training, not in any scholarly communities like Leechman, Crate did some of the heavy lifting for *DCHP-1*. Unfortunately, a full identity check of the Charles "Chuck" Brandel Crate who worked on *DCHP-1* in relation to a man of similar age and identical name, who went by the name of Charles Brandel (Crate) or Charles Brandel-Crate, was not possible. The reason for comparing photos or birthdates is that the latter man was a co-leader of a Canadian fascist political party, the Canadian Union of Fascists (CUF), in mid-1930s Toronto. The reason we know of the fascist is through a Google search. This is probably only an artefact of big data, though the small chance of a very dark connection of *DCHP-1* to Nazi Canada cannot, unfortunately, be categorically ruled out. From present knowledge, however, such a connection is unlikely, if not unimaginable, with what we know from *DCHP-1*'s Crate.

In the interest of full disclosure, I decided after much deliberation to report this finding. I do not wish to inflict any harm on Crate's extended family, but as this information is so easily attainable by googling Crate's name, I would be remiss not to report on it and try to contextualize it. The repercussions for *DCHP-1* would be substantial if we were talking about one and the same person (which, I think, is not the case).

What's this all about? The Charles Crate of the *DCHP-1* was born on 26 January 1915 in Weston, Ontario (the location and birth year we know from his bio pic in *DCHP-1*). The precise birthdate was confirmed in the Archives of Ontario register. *DCHP-1*'s Crate's birth record carries the number 901423.[4] The fascist is listed on Wikipedia as born in 1916, which would clear *DCHP-1* Crate.

The details of the other Crate are grim. The fascist Crate was a (co-)leader of the CUF, which praised Hitler, admired Mussolini,[5] and blamed, in its magazine *The Thunderbolt*, "all of society's problems" on the Jews (McBride 1997: 57). If one of the Big Six had moved in such circles earlier in his life, we would likely only speak of the Big Five and a black sheep, or we would nominate Robert J. Gregg as a member of the new Big Six. Despite considerable effort, however, I was unable to clarify in the last instance whether *DCHP-1*'s Charles (Brandel) Crate and the 1930s Ontarian Charles Brandel, Brandel Charles, Charles Brandel (Crate), or Charles Brandel-Crate – these are the names I found used for the fascist – are one and the same person or not. One source offers "Charles Brandel (alias Crate)" (Principe 1999: 160). The death records in both Ontario and BC, where *DCHP-1* Crate used to live, are of no help yet: they are kept under wraps for some 120 years after a person's birth. I simply do not know for certain. The fact that there is a Saskatchewan painter with the name of Charles Brandel Crate makes me believe that there are more Canadians with this name than it seems.

The timelines would in theory allow for both Crates to be one and the same person. It is theoretically conceivable that someone at the age of 19 or 20 would be associated with a fascist group and would shortly after realize that he had hung out with the wrong crowd and reinvent himself in the West. He would not have been the only one to start over again in this part of the continent – think of Lovell, who left behind his foster home's neglect and misery that way. If Crate reinvented himself in the West, there is no proof whatsoever for this interpretation. There is nothing in the *DCHP-1* correspond-ence or any other material that would implicate Crate as a former fascist – quite the contrary. Paddy Drysdale, who knew and corresponded with Crate in his function as Gage's editor, said the following:

I very much doubt that Crate was a fascist. He might have been a socialist, even a communist. He was very much a union man and concerned for downtrodden or exploited workers as he was, as you say, for his students. (Paddy Drysdale: pers. correspondence, 2 Apr. 2018)

Before getting Paddy's feedback, I had already been somewhat confident that the *DCHP-1* Charles Crate is *not* the fascist Charles Crate. Paddy's words now make me believe that the Google age has dredged up something that has nothing to do with our Crate. It would not be the first time that big data profiling gets the wrong person, nor will it be the last.

The final exoneration of Crate from that terrible suspicion is something that will be difficult to carry out, for the time being. I need to, and can, assume at this point that Crate is the victim of an unfortunate similarity of names. His letters, for instance, show a real concern for his First Nations students and are perhaps, together with Drysdale's characterization of the man, the best indica-tor that Crate's mindset was not the one of a fascist.

Let's now focus on what we know about Chuck Crate for certain. Crate took an active interest in all things Northern and Western Canadian. Educated at "York Memorial Collegiate and at the University of British Columbia and the

University of Victoria", as we know from *DCHP-1*'s front matter, he was a radio and newspaper journalist in Yellowknife and worked for the miners' union in that city. He was politically active, was "twice elected Councillor of the Municipal District of Yellowknife", and in 1957 was a candidate for the 1954 Northwest Territories Council – what would be the equivalent of a provincial parliament. For that election, Crate appears to have come in fourth with a respectable 13.7 per cent of the popular vote.[6] As Drysdale reports, "Crate remained a mystery man" throughout their work engagement. He remembers Crate

as being a prickly person with a chip on his shoulder as a result of his rough childhood and the feeling that he was excluded from levels of society where his brain and talents would be recognized. (Drysdale: pers. correspondence, 2 April 2018)

Through Crate's letters, we are in the position to gain some insights into Crate the man and into his attitudes towards FNIM people. It is, overall, a caring picture that emerges, a picture of concern and willingness to help to alleviate the plight of the Alert Bay First Nations members and, later, the Quesnel school students he was teaching. At the same time, colonial threads emerge and it is clear that, while Crate was hoping to help the children, he was not specifically trained to do so. He did what he could and thought best.

Crate took a teaching job in the fall of 1964 in Alert Bay, a small community on an island in the Strait of Georgia, not far off the northeastern coast of Vancouver Island, within sight of Port McNeill. Writing from Alert Bay on 4 October 1964 to Joan Hall, the Lexicographical Centre's admin assistant, Crate says that he was teaching from "Grade 7 to Grade 12" in classes that are not large, "with one exception". Crate's comments show the general level of awareness – or lack thereof – concerning Indigenous culture in 1960s Canada, as he writes the following lines about his new job at Alert Bay Secondary School:

I teach mainly Social Studies, but also typing, English, Health, Guidance, Civics, Reading. The most difficult Class to teach is my Home Room Occupationals. They are a group of High School Age who, because of low IQ, delinquancy [*sic*] or very poor background, are unable to handle Matriculation. I found, however, that four of them were smart enough to handle Matric. and so for their own good passed them on to other classes. However, their absence makes it harder to teach the others. Some of the little Indian lads from up the coast are, I think, basically quite intelligent but have been raised in Indian villages where next to nothing is known of the outside world. They have no idea of who is the Queen, either of the Premiers, or what a city is like. They register low on the IQ tests, because their English vocabulary is so limited that they cannot recognize the problems. I am going to use moving pictures and film strips as far as possible to help these. With the genuinely low IQs, repetition and drill, with good humour and patience has the most effect. (Crate to Hall, 4 Oct. 1964)

It is clear that Crate is presented with an impossible task that would entail nothing less than solving the contradictions and deprivations of colonialism. In that regard, his comments are not intended to be demeaning, though some of them sound so. He points out that the low scores in IQ tests are the result of the students' ESL background, and thus an effect of the colonial situation. This assessment and recognition are refreshing to read. With it, Crate goes some distance towards the eventual realization that such tests should not be used on non-western (or possibly non-anglophone) cultures because of their implicit biases, if they should be used at all. He seems to be positive about helping even what he calls "the genuinely low IQs", whether his assessment of them is justified or not.

Joan Hall, sitting in the Lexicographical Centre at the University of Victoria, is obviously shaken by the misfortune of Crate's Indigenous students. She replies to Crate:

Is there anything I can do to help the situation [with the children]? Would magazines, pictures, etc. be of any use? If you think of anything that is available in Victoria, or Vancouver which I can send to you, please let me know. (Hall to Crate, 6 Oct. 1964)

She closes her letter, "And please don't forget to tell me if there is anyway [*sic*] I can help the children."

The reader of these letters senses a genuine concern and willingness to help, even to give some money and some of her time to make a bit of a difference. Crate's response to Hall's offer delivers some insight into the cultural clashes in expectations, even for an experienced frontiersman such as Crate:

Many thanks for your offer to send pictures, etc. I have been getting a good deal of material of use and I subscribe to quite a few magazines. However, one thing I'm short of and that is [*sic*] pictures relating to British History. If you run across any, they would certainly be appreciated. It is most difficult to relate British History to a native child who has reached teen-age without knowing even that we have a British Queen. (Crate to Hall, 18 Oct. 1964)

That British history and a photo of the Queen were considered a pressing desideratum for Indigenous students seems like a topic worthy of discussion. It is clear that the expectation of assimilation was prevalent in those days. Even the early anthropologists who are today praised by some FNIMs,[7] such as Harry Hawthorn, the lead author of Hawthorn, Belshaw, and Jamieson (1958), did not in general question assimilation. *DCHP-2* defines assimilation as:

the policy and practice of encouraging or forcing Aboriginal people to integrate into mainstream Canadian society. (*DCHP-2*, s.v. "assimilation", www.dchp.ca/dchp2/Entries/view/assimilation)

One must see the context of British history teaching in Alert Bay in that light. For Crate, who did not stay long in Alert Bay – just about a year – and who later taught at Quesnel High School in the BC interior's Cariboo region, where Indigenous students would mix with non-Indigenous students, we can attest that he is put in a situation that was impossible to solve. He was the one who saw the problems of colonialism first hand, and it speaks for him that he recognized some of the cultural biases that the West exerted upon the Indigenous students. At the same time, of course, Crate was probably not fully aware of his own cultural biases, but he was much more aware than the average Canadian.

A Benchmark: Attitudes in the 1960s

It is difficult to judge a historical project appropriately. If one takes an absolute approach, one would say that the faults of the past are inexcusable. For the victims of neglect and abuse, this is certainly the only legitimate perspective. For the historian, however, it is not a possible line of thought. Rather than gauging the past by today's standards, it is necessary to reconstruct the past's standards and then measure individual behaviour against that standard and in comparison to future developments.

If we take a famous textbook, more scholarly than Leechman's own 1956 *Native Tribes of Canada* (which is almost devoid of source documentation), we see what the benchmarks may have been. In doing so, we will get a better sense of the extent of colonial bias in *DCHP-1*. Diamond Jenness' book *The Indians of Canada*, first published in 1932 by the University of Toronto Press, had appeared in seven editions by 1977, the latter of which I quote from below. It has been reprinted several times since, the last time in 2015, and remains available at the bargain price of $25 in the Kindle edition – a cash cow, this book. It is touted as remaining "the most comprehensive work" on Canada's First Nations[8] and was republished time and again by the Minister of Supply and Services Canada, with the Government Catalogue Number NM93–65/1977. This book comes as close as any to an officially adopted text in Canada, and stands perhaps for the default attitudes towards FNIMs throughout the latter half of the twentieth century. Here is a passage from it that we may take as the typical attitude towards Indigenous cultures, characterizing the settlers as sophisticated:

Let us consider, for a moment, some of the advantages the colonists possessed. They imported with them the seeds of various grains and vegetables, such as wheat, oats, rye, barley, potatoes, and turnips, and they possessed the knowledge of their cultivation. They knew how to irrigate and to fertilize the land, how to rotate their crops. They brought steel axes and saws to clear the ground, ploughs and oxen to break up the soil, scythes to cut the grain, and vehicles to gather the harvest. Cows, sheep, goats, and poultry provided them both meat and clothing. The newcomers could anchor themselves to any fertile plot of ground, certain that with reasonable industry they could wrest from its few square rods sufficient food to keep starvation from their doors. They could erect substantial buildings of brick or stone, since the same soil that provided their

Figure 35 Public mural in Victoria, BC, Pembroke Street
(Photo: S. Dollinger, 2018)

sustenance would provide sustenance also for their children's children; and they could concentrate their homes as a single community, facing the river that linked them during the summer with the motherland. (Jenness 1977: 28–29)

About the Indigenous population, all that is said is this:

> The Indians lacked every one of these things.
>
> (Jenness 1977: 29)

This is a scathing misunderstanding of Indigenous culture, a culture that had everything they needed and wanted and, in contrast to the colonizers, a culture that was living in a sustainable manner. In comparison to that context and that gross misrepresentation of the economic situation of the Indigenous populations, the colonial attitudes found in *DCHP-1* appear relatively minor; they are present, for sure, in some cases quite unacceptably so, as we highlighted with the examples above, but minor compared to this statement from one of Canada's most decorated anthropologists, Diamond Jenness, who was also a very vocal proponent of assimilation of all Indians into the Canadian mainstream.[9] Such assimilation would have promoted the final decline of FNIM culture in the "Sixties Scoop", which was the last big push and concerted effort by the Canadian government to eradicate Indigenous culture. This was in the 1960s, the time of *DCHP-1*'s making, not the 1860s (see www.dchp.ca/dchp2, s.v. "Sixties Scoop").

Despite his mindset of obvious western superiority, Jenness continues to have a good standing in the Canadian public, having a peninsula in the Canadian Arctic named after him (Diamond Jenness Peninsula) and, quite recently in 2004, a Mars rock that was examined by the rover *Opportunity*.[10] In that regard, *DCHP-1* appears to be quite a bit more advanced, on account of making Indigenous terms front and centre of the book.

Jenness' attitudes should act as a warning: how can a man, who is still considered as one of the greatest Canadian anthropologists, have represented entire civilizations in such an utterly negative light? Figure 35 shows a public mural in Victoria, BC, depicting the aspects of knowledge, competence, and stewardship of the planet that anthropologist Jenness seems to have missed completely.

What's Next for *DCHP-2*, If Anything?

While *DCHP-1* exhibits the basic colonial trappings of projects at the time, on another level *DCHP-1* was itself a product of an anti-colonial attitude as far as British and American culture are concerned. Because the people of Canada did not want to be dancing to another's (foreign, colonial, British) tune, they started to write their own music. From that perspective – and only from that one – *DCHP-1* is anti-colonial. In that process, however, it reasserted the whole range of colonial attitudes towards the First Nations, Métis, and Inuit populations, though less than what we have seen elsewhere (e.g., Jenness' assessment). It is obvious, however, that the inclusion of Indigenous people and scholars was what was missing.

This inclusion did not happen in *DCHP-1* and *DCHP-2*. Like *DCHP-1*, *DCHP-2* did not have any Indigenous scholars on the editorial board, though *DCHP-2* was more diverse, culturally as well as in gender, so that *DCHP-2* may be seen as a step in the right direction. At least, I hope so. We did get valuable insight into Indigenous issues through some of our Indigenous colleagues, who gave their time to read drafts and ensured that some zingers were edited out, and, in the process, set us straight on one blind spot or another that I and my students had. What was missed in that process was then usually caught by Margery Fee, who has been working on Indigenous issues for a long time. I remember a draft for an entry that we had forgotten, on the infamous Oka incident, and I remember how Margery corrected, very gracefully, my misconceptions of the use of force against the First Nations as an isolated event in the second half of the twentieth century. My ignorance was glaring, as force is today still used on a daily basis against Canada's FNIM population.

It is clear that, for a *DCHP-3*, one would need profound Indigenous involvement, ideally an Indigenous chief editor. It may also well be, however, that this project is just considered to be "beyond rescue" and that Indigenous scholars will devise their own projects from scratch – e.g., a historical dictionary of Indigenous terms or the like – or that the sum of around half a million dollars that one would likely need to revise the legacy entries will be better spent on language revitalization efforts. That latter point, I think, is a most pressing one for many FNIM languages that have only a very few native speakers left, while some languages are "sleeping", waiting to be revived.

As I am writing these lines in May 2018, the Canadian government is behind closed doors preparing their Indigenous Languages Act, which is a direct result of the recommendations set forth in the Truth and Reconciliation Commission Report we mentioned above (TRC Final Report 2015). While we know little about its content, one thing is certain: if done right, the Indigenous Languages Act would need to expand the two official languages of Canada (English and French) by bestowing official status on the sixty or more Indigenous languages, from Lekwungen to Cree to Bungee (a Métis language), Michif (another Métis language), and the varieties of Inuktitut. The Act will be announced in 2019. Unless we have sixty-two or so official languages in Canada by then, the Act is bound to be a failure. It's because you can't pick and choose some languages (e.g., Cree, with tens of thousands of native speakers) over others (e.g., Lekwungen, with no native speakers left today). We will see how the Canadian government fares.[11]

In the hopes of a good new languages act, *DCHP-2* can be improved in many ways. I'd be most happy to hand over and explain the systems we built for anyone qualified to take on *DCHP-3*, and then to step back, because such a dictionary you can only do once in a lifetime, and "my" edition was the second one. A third edition would probably include a complete revision, if not of the entire legacy data, then of all Indigenous terms – which are many. By the time work on a *DCHP-3* is in progress, all Indigenous languages of Canada will hopefully be supported as official languages of Canada.

Figure 36 *Yay* or *yeah* spelled the Canadian way with "*eh*"[1]
(Photo: S. Dollinger)

9   Is There Really a Canadian English?

> The worker in the vineyard [of linguistic variation] is sometimes frustrated by
> the very complexity of the evidence, but the irritations are more than balanced
> by the utterly thrilling discoveries one makes and by the pleasure that comes
> with deepening one's knowledge of [hu]man[kind]'s most precious
> possession – [their] language[s].
>
> (Walter S. Avis 1966: 30)

As the previous chapters have shown, the discussion about Canadian English
is old, older than most people realize. Yet, as the provocative title of this final
chapter indicates, there are doubters. The discussion about Canadian English
has also had, off and on, an international dimension and angle to it. It's a bit
like Canada's creation in the slow cooker compared to the US' "Big Bang" on
4 July 1776. The Canadian "broth" was so slow to gestate that you can't even
date the decade, let alone the year, when Canada really gained independence
from Britain: no tea party, no midnight ride, no Battle of Saratoga, no Independence Day. Maybe an Independence Century – that would be the twentieth? Or do we count the nineteenth for the creation of the Dominion? Like
other things Canadian, it is complicated, and maybe it is precisely this complexity that comes closer to people's realities than other creation stories.

Even the international angle on Canadian English is older than one might
think. In the late 1950s, the world's most renowned daily newspaper published
a detailed report to Canadian English. On Sunday, 29 November 1959, readers
of *The New York Times* were able to discover details about "a 'new' language",
Canadian English (see Figure 37). It was reported in a fairly detailed article,
some of which is shown in the image, that "Canadians are becoming aware that
they speak and write English in a distinctive way."

That was six decades ago. Now, the problem is that, if the quoted lines were
published in November 2019, they might *still* be considered as newsworthy as
they were then. That's a slow-cooker project if we've ever seen one! The
details would be different in 2019, a different conference or another event as
the trigger, but the basic message would be one and the same: surprise or
"coming about".

A 'NEW' LANGUAGE: CANADIAN ENGLISH

Its Particular Flavour Being Caught by Scholars and Put Into Dictionaries

---

Special to the New York Times.

TORONTO.   Nov. 28 – Canadians are becoming aware that they speak and write English in a distinctive way.

They are discovering what some go so far to call the Canadian language – a unique conglomeration of spelling, pronunciation and vocabulary.

Figure 37 Headline from *The New York Times*, 29 Nov. 1959: 148

What's going on? How long can Canadian English really be "coming about"? How long can this phase take? Fellow Austrian Edgar Schneider is the man who thought perhaps longest and hardest about such questions, and he has come to the conclusion that no predictions on the length of stages towards the creation of new varieties can be made (Schneider 2007): we can only predict the sequence of these stages. As with many things Canadian, for instance, such as becoming one's own country, the answer is: longer than in most cases. Canadian statehood was reached sometime between 1867 and 1982 and was thus a long, drawn-out process. The acceptance of Standard Canadian English as an entity in its own right seems to be an equally drawn-out process. Sixty years in the making – and still counting – it relates to questions of identity and, as the research shows, it's never a good idea to leave speakers in the lurch or to deny them the necessary expression of their identities.

Relating to Canadian English, there have been a number of strange developments, lack of developments, and arrested developments that need to be pointed out. Above all, Canadian English *as such* is not taught in most high schools (this is *not* a critique of the teachers); it is barely taught at universities in Canada (this *is* a critique of the university teachers). Every summer, usually in the lead-up to Canada Day on 1 July, I get phone calls from another generation of Canadian rookie journalists, younger than the year before, journalists who "discover" Canadian English anew, with stories that promise to be filling the summer hole in news reporting. While I happily talk with anyone, journalist or not, on Canadian English, my anecdote suggests the extent of a much bigger problem. This is the problem that I called the "*Groundhog Day* Loop" of Canadian English (Dollinger 2011b) when I first noticed it. The *Groundhog Day* Loop is a loop that allows reporting on Canadian English in only one of two cases: either through the "newness" factor, or through the weirdness factor. Let's deal with them in turn.

The "*Groundhog Day* Loop" of Canadian English

In the 1993 movie *Groundhog Day*, Bill Murray stars as a mean news reporter curmudgeon from the big city who is sent on what to him seems like an unattractive assignment in the hinterland of Pennsylvania. His task is to report on the annual end-of-winter ritual and fun event involving the groundhog Punxsutawney Phil and his shadow on 2 February, Groundhog Day. It is said that if the groundhog sees his shadow (and returns to the lair), one must expect six more weeks of winter; if not, we're lucky that year and spring is just around the corner. As Murray's ill-tempered character treats everyone badly, some higher force that is not known or mentioned apparently decides that Murray's character must be taught a lesson and sends him, time and time again, back to 6 a.m. to re-live every step of this 2 February until he changes his attitude and starts being nice to the people he meets. So, in a mixture of Ghosts of Christmas Past and plain old kismet, an important life lesson is learned.

As *Groundhog Day* makes clear, it's all about attitude – in our linguistic case, linguistic attitude. Linguistic attitude is the keyword when it comes to Canadian English – or any variety, really, which has been stuck in some sort of *Groundhog Day* Loop of the linguistic type. The following headlines from news coverage about Canadian English over the past sixty years illustrate the point:

- 1957, *Edmonton Journal*: "A Canadian Language?"
- 1958, *Time*: "The Canadian Language"
- 1967, *Kingston Whig-Standard*: "Canadians Have Own Language"
- 1979, *Globe and Mail*: "Canadian English is haphazard enough"
- 1985, *Montreal Gazette*: "Man the barricades. *Canadian English* is our very own hybrid, recognizable perhaps only to ourselves but precious, nonetheless"
- 1993, *Ottawa Citizen*: "New dictionary embraces Canadians, eh!"
- 1998, *The Record* (Kitchener, Ont.): "Canada finds its tongue"
- 2000, *National Post*: "We may speak English, but have we found our voice?"

In 1957, the idea of "Canadian language" was punctuated with a question mark. The year after, the question seemed settled. But not so quick: it takes a long time for ideas to trickle down from the ivory tower of learning to the people at large. So, in 1967, the *Kingston-Whig Standard* titled that Canadians had their own language, which seemed fitting for the centennial. But then, in 1979, the idea of a "haphazard", somewhat inconsistent language, referring to spelling, showed some unease with the varying Canadian linguistic practices – varying by province (BC more "British" than Alberta, for instance), medium (newspaper had a special role, spelling more "American" till *c.* 1990), and, indeed, speaker bio (personal idiolect and preference).

In 1985, humour was injected in the *Montreal Gazette*'s "Man the barricades" and the idea is brought forth that maybe the differences are only noticeable to Canadians (funnily enough, Canadians are the only people who matter in this regard, so this statement might be a sign of a growing linguistic awareness). When, in 1993, a Merriam-Webster title was adapted for Canada, it could be taken as a sign that the US company smelled the opportunity to make some money "up here" (as The Tragically Hip entitled one of their albums). Remember, Oxford University Press did not miss this opportunity but decided, to their credit, to invest more, with a reference unit of their own.

Then, in 1998, the Waterloo-Kitchener region *Record* declares the linguistic arrival of Canadian English, and in 2000 the *National Post* questions this arrival in Charles Foran's comparison of Canadian English with Irish English or French, whose speakers, in contrast to those of Canadian English, treat their languages "as though they inhabit them" (Foran 2000: A16). The last two headlines attest to a kind of attitudinal change. Even then there were doubts, but the level of discussion was perhaps more sophisticated than just a decade earlier.

A little later, starting around 2005, one can notice a real change in attitude – the reaching of a new level of linguistic awareness, it seems. I did not notice it at the time and it is only now, with the luxurious hindsight of a dozen years, that a trend in the news reporting over the early 2000s emerges. At about that time, *Globe and Mail* writer Russell Smith answered the fundamental question about Canadian English himself in the very same headline:

- 2006, *Globe and Mail*: "Why is our variety of English important? Because it's ours"

From that point on, the discussion has been more about how Canadian English is changing and less about debating its existence. Canadian English is, for the first time, defined on its own terms and not constantly pitched in comparison to bigger varieties. Suddenly, it is not about becoming more American, as in the 1980s and 1990s, anymore. Could this be a new phase in the evolution of

Canadian English? While the variety as such now seems beyond question, its specific details are discussed:

- 2012, *Ottawa Citizen*: "Canadians change the way they say A, eh?"
- 2017, *Daily Gleaner* (Fredericton, NB): "Canadian English accent surprisingly uniform coast to coast: Researchers"
- 2017, *Globe and Mail*, "Canadianisms dictionary is 'tabled' and 'all-dressed': New edition for the country's sesquicentennial owes some thanks to Austrians"

In 2012, we have a headline that alludes to the major Canadian pattern on foreign <a> rendering in English: will *Iraq*, *Stefan*, and *origami* be pronounced with the "ah" of father or the "a" in cat?

The year 2017 saw more coverage, in keeping with the sesquicentennial celebrations. The Fredericton *Daily Gleaner* reports on the homogeneity hypothesis, which I think would better be interpreted as the effects of ongoing standardization. In that year, veteran writer Michael Valpy penned a personal favourite of mine, when he showcased the seed funding of *DCHP-2* by the Austrian government, when little could be had from Canada, in the headline of his *Globe and Mail* article. Most impact came, however, from Jesse Sheidlower's (2017) very fine article in *The New Yorker* on a "delightful" dictionary of Canadian English.

Overall though, a different tone is discernible in the media since about 2005/ 06. There are, of course, more negative voices too, but they seem to be less numerous than before. Public outreach, for which linguists (in comparison to scientists, archaeologists, historians, economists, psychologists – you name it, really) are not famous, seems to have paid off. The idea of "Canadian English" has finally arrived in real life, with real-life speakers of Canadian English, as it were. Precisely at this point, we do have an up-to-date Canadian English grammar (Fee and McAlpine 2011) but no up-to-date dictionary.

But not all that glitters is gold. Despite this (qualitative) indicator for more positive attitudes towards Canadian English, counter-evidence is also to be found. If you go back to Figure 20 in Chapter 5, you will see a line plotting the frequencies for the phrase "Canadian English" in the Canadian press. Figure 38 offers a close-up, an extension to 2017, and better periodization of the data.[2]

So, what are we to make of this? It is very good evidence for concluding that, despite intermittently intense media coverage on Canadian English *words*, there is usually no connection made explicitly with an entity called "Canadian English". Such a connection was made much more explicit in the 1970s, when the old generation, the Big Sixers, were giving their interviews. As Figure 38 shows, the idea of a Canadian English was also more discussed in the early 1990s, probably in connection with a new world order in the lead-up to the NAFTA period that triggered discussion about Canada in relation to the USA.

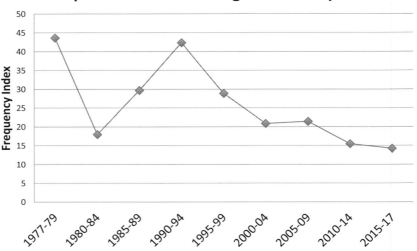

The phrase "Canadian English" in the press

Figure 38 The phrase "Canadian English", 1977–1979 to 2015–2017

Figure 38 gives us a good idea, but does not tell the whole story. The most recent year, 2017, lists, for instance, a mere forty-three mentions of the term *Canadianism(s)* and forty-five hits for *Canadian English*.[3] Cleaned for references that exclusively refer to the variety of English and not to Canadian English actors vs Canadian French actors, in all of 2017 there were a mere thirty-two mentions for "Canadian English" in *Canadian Newsstream*, which captures more than 300 newspapers nationwide. Considering that Canadian vocabulary, limited to words, is only one part of Canadian English – although an important one – it shows that in the discussions about Canadian words a big part of the overall message is lost.

There is, however, mounting evidence today that Canadian English has become a reality for many of its speakers. Imagine if the concept of Canadian English had been communicated more effectively? The anecdotal evidence of non-linguists who have an ear to the ground, such as *Globe and Mail* fashion writer Russell Smith perhaps (whose words we've seen above), are of a different quality than the quantitative data shown here. Or, maybe, this Canadian English is not that important at all. Maybe it's just ... weird?

Canadian What? Must Be Weird ...

This brings us to the second reporting angle on Canadian English that has established a veritable pedigree over half a century. The "weirdness" angle in

Canadian English goes back at least to Orkin's 1973 jocular book and best-seller *Canajan, Eh?* which is, with far over 100,000 copies sold (on the cover of the 1988 third edition, or the 1997 reprint), probably the most widely circulated book on Canadian English that is not a dictionary.

There is nothing wrong with being funny – far from it – but there is something wrong if a legitimate claim to a variety is downgraded to something obtuse, weird, or not a "real" variety. (This is precisely the tack that conservative German speakers take for Austrian German and Swiss German, for instance – see Dollinger in press.) The problem is that the variants of non-dominant varieties are generally perceived as "weird" by speakers of dominant varieties: "*Toque?* Weird! It's of course *a hat.*" There will be many Canadians who have had such an experience. But it is, actually, the ignorance of the others that is the real problem. "What, you spelled *color* with a *u*? That is wrong!" – I remember these words from an American friend. We all have a story like that.

There are traces of this in news reporting, of course. We have seen the 1985 quotation from the *Montreal Gazette* above ("Man the barricades!"). Recently, however, it has become much harder to produce examples from the weirdness stream. But here is a somewhat recent one:

- 2007, *Harbour City Star* (Nanaimo): "Only people fluent in Canadian would understand if you told them to put on a toque and dump a two-four of empties into their blue bin."

Such artificial sentences are, however, a very long shot from denigrating the variety. What is today more frequently found is the limitation of Canadian English to Canadian slang, generally meaning the informal, sometimes somewhat rude, un-genteel way of talking:

- 2017, *Toronto Star*: "Your knowledge of Canadian slang may start and stop with Bob and Doug McKenzie, but our language is littered with Canadianisms that our neighbours to the south would be hard-pressed to understand. Here are some examples of Canadian English that might reveal you're more of a keener than you realized."

But even in that area, some more sober voices are increasingly being heard:

- 2015, *Montreal Gazette*: "Indeed, to generalize wildly, Canadian slang is a lot more polite than American, British or Australian. We don't get mad and say new things. We have our own words for foods – but not for emotions."

In that last quotation, from an article by Mark Abley, we can actually hear a new story in the public discourse. We are told that the weirdness is not an internal characteristic of Canadian English, far from it, but the projection of the non-Canadian or the insecure Canadian (which is, I suspect, Lilles' unacknowledged point of departure: colonial cringe). Abley speculates about intrinsic qualities of Canadian English slang – far beyond the "weird", and fair and square in the area of . . . beauty:

I'm intrigued that nearly all these Canadian terms refer to objects. Lists of British idioms are full of verb phrases that North Americans find baffling – expressions like chat up, send up, knock off and put paid to. There are also countless adjectives that are scarcely known outside Britain: gutted, knackered, squiffy and so on. Colloquial British English also features many unique nouns, of course, but its uniqueness is not defined by objects. Without objects, an English-Canadian dialect would hardly exist. (Abley 2015: B5)

Abley's attitude seems indeed encouraging and it gives me hope that the *Groundhog Day* Loop of Canadian English might one day be a thing of the past: that the country is allowed one day to wake up, like Bill Murray, at 6 a.m. and *not* repeat the same news coverage. The question is what Canadians would have to do to achieve that.

That is, of course, until the next rookie journalist phones me up, in which case I can refer them to this chapter. The increasing appreciation by Canadians of their English seems evident. Don, apparently a long-time visitor to Canada, posted an insightful comment on a book website that may capture this change of linguistic attitudes:

Purchased this book [Orkin's *Canajan, Eh?*] while in Canada in 1976.
    Found it enjoyable then.
    Not sure how it would go now.[4]

This brings us to the all-important issue of identity, of which linguistic identity is only one part, a part that is becoming increasingly important in a globalizing world.

Linguistic Identities and "Ownership" of Language

In Chapter 1, we first discussed Kachru's Circle Model of English and the acceptance of the Outer Circle and, now increasingly so, Lingua Franca varieties of English. The central question in this long struggle for linguistic autonomy and self-determination of speakers of less dominant varieties is the question of "ownership".

We as individuals all have multiple identities. We can be a Finnish-Chinese Canadian, born in Canada, with a Finnish parent and a Cantonese parent and a Canadian identity. Simultaneously, we can be a surfer who lives the boarder lifestyle – which includes trips to Tofino on the west coast of Vancouver Island for surfing whenever the waves promise to be very high (and the weather bad) – eats vegan, and studies electrical engineering towards a BA at UBC. We can also be a young parent and an avid indoor climber and stand-up paddle (SUP) boarder at the same time. These identities – and the line between hobby and identity is blurry – are not exclusive of one another. Very few are, indeed. At least six of these (skateboarder, surfer, student, Finnish, Cantonese, and Canadian) are identities that will have a significant linguistic expression. If a parental role is added, it will show linguistically too. All these identities, or roles, co-exist. The Canadian, Chinese, and Finnish ones will come in handy in a globalizing world – and increasingly so, as it'll help people whom we meet to "make sense" of us to some degree, right after saying "Hello". Oh yes, you're the Canadian. The conversation usually starts there.

But who "owns" a particular language or variety and who has the "right" to set its standard(s)? With linguistic varieties that are associated with countries, we enter the sphere of standard varieties. One of my teachers in Vienna, H. (Henry) G. Widdowson, had a thing or two to say about the issue, long before others addressed it. Henry, who is one of the most important linguists today (and I'm not saying this as his student but as his colleague), found himself in the position to pen the key paper in that area in 1994. He had delivered that paper the year before at a conference of teachers of English as a Foreign Language – that particular subgroup of English teachers that have had a great investment of time, money, and effort in reaching a native speaker or native speaker-like target norm.

Widdowson set out some highly stimulating and, at the time, highly contested thoughts. By now, it has become clear that Widdowson was right with his reasoning. To walk you through the argument, let me start with what many of us have been taught, either expressly or in a more implied manner, about language. Language is compared with beverages, which drives home an essential point in the discussion:

As an analogy, consider a certain kind of beverage. There are all kinds of cola, but only one which is the real thing. Or, further afield, an analogy, from the French. They have, until just recently, successfully denied others the right to use the appellation *Champagne* for any wine that does not come from the region of that name where Dom Perignon first invented it. There may be all kinds of derivative versions elsewhere, excellent no doubt in their way, but they are not real or proper Champagne, even though loose talk may refer to them as such. Similarly, there is real English, Anglais real [*sic*], Royal English, Queen's English, or (for those unsympathetic to the monarchy) Oxford English. The vintage language. (Widdowson 1994: 378)

The way Widdowson presents the argument above almost sounds ridiculous, undemocratic, arrogant, posh, but this very line of thought is, in a different guise (one might say in "sheep's clothing"), still a very powerful force. We usually are taught in school the above assurance in a different form: that there is only one good English (either Standard British, or, for some, Standard American English). There is also a shorthand that these thoughts are usually presented with, which is the quality criterion that is bestowed upon Standard

British English, or Standard American English, in response to the question of why that variety is "better":

> The usual answer is: quality of clear communication and standard of intelligibility. With [British, as HGW writes from the UK perspective] standard English, it is argued, these are assured. (Widdowson 1994: 379)

By following the trail of evidence, as it were, Widdowson unearths in Inspector Columbo-like manner the important point in the discussion about which standards should be used in language. A frequent answer is that the standards must necessarily be set by those *born to the language*, the "native speaker". These are supposed to control the standard. So all native speakers, collectively, "guard" the standard? Widdowson continues to clarify:

> Not all native speakers, you understand. In fact, come to think of it, not most native speakers, for the majority of those who are to the language born speak nonstandard English and have themselves to be instructed in the standard at school. We cannot have any Tom, Jane, and Harry claiming authority, for Tom, Jane, and Harry are likely to be speakers of some dialect or other. So the authority to maintain the standard language is not consequent on a natural native-speaker endowment. It is claimed by a minority of people who have the power to impose it. The custodians of standard English are self-elected members of a rather exclusive club. (Widdowson 1994: 379)

Suddenly, we are left with the few members of an "exclusive club", usually with some very limited characteristics (to continue our crime-novel theme, think about another curmudgeon, this time Inspector Morse and his ilk – or rather the ilk he would have joined had he more conventionally used his Oxford degree). In the case of the UK, there have traditionally been Oxbridge (fe)males, but much more often male academics with bow tie and buttoned shirt, and tweed jacket with elbow patches. This sartorial style is reminiscent of the old-school lexicographer, which is no complete coincidence. Others might say that dictionaries have "come to be such arbiters" for vocabulary, though they "certainly did not always function that way" (Curzan 2014: 93) prior to the 1700s or so. Who writes these dictionaries? Here is where the circle is closed around lots of men with bow ties.

It is a very strange thought indeed that some small socially elite "in" group in England would be able to set a standard that is intelligible to everyone, globally. "By hook or by crook" is a phrase they might use. But who really knows what it means beyond that lustrous circle? (It means "by any and all means" and goes back to the Middle English period.) They are, in fact, setting a standard that is intelligible and comes easily to . . . them. But why would and should the entire planet have to follow their model? This is the point that Widdowson drives home in his landmark paper.

Luckily, the linguistic world is no longer uniquely organized along those lines, although the stuffy Oxbridge types still hold *some* clout. That more and more speakers the world over are now demanding that their own uses are codified in dictionaries and grammar books is seen in the Canadian press as well. In the late 1990s, the issue of an American spelling book purchased by Ontario schools was discussed in the provincial legislature (the parliament) in Toronto. The opposition critic accused the minister of education of cheating Canadian students out of learning English the way it is used in Canada, citing the difference in the pronunciation of *lieutenant*'s first syllable of "loo" in the USA and "lef" in Canada. The *Ottawa Citizen* reported:

Ontario Education Minister Dave Johnson was put on the spot in the legislature yesterday by NDP Leader Howard Hampton, who pointed out the new Grade 5 speller is teaching students the U.S. pronunciation of lieutenant. Mr. Hampton accused the Harris government of "Americanizing and propagandizing" Ontario textbooks. "Canadian children should be taught Canadian facts of language, spelling and pronunci- ation. We're our own people, not a branch plant of the U.S.A.," Mr. Hampton said. . . . Mr. Johnson said he would take steps to correct the situation. "We'll send an advisory to all the school boards to ask teachers to pronounce it as 'leftenant' because that's the proper way here in Canada," Mr. Johnson said. (Brennan 1998: A10)

The opposition critic alluded to one aspect that I have called the "birthright" of Canadians, by which we understand the right to be taught authentic infor- mation about the language(s) and varieties of the land, which would include information on Indigenous languages, besides Canadian English and, as per Canadian law, Canadian French.

Does this make me a nationalist? Some might say so, but everyone who knows me will understand that the issue is not nation but identity. Identity manifests itself on multiple levels, and such identity affiliations are constructed by cultural means, clothing, music, food, you name it – and include language. And here is why I think the national dimension is getting more and more important, but in a different way than it was (abused) in the nineteenth and first half of the twentieth centuries, or is currently abused in some countries. This leads us to the question of the usefulness, perhaps "essentialness", of Canadian English in the life of most Canadians.

"Gift to the Nation" or the "Narcissism of Small Differences"?

The question that headlines this section is at the very core of Avis' legacy. Is the work by Avis still relevant in a globalized world? I think yes – more so than ever actually, for reasons I'll lay out in this section. The media – at least part of them – are still receptive and attuned to the national angle. For Canada Day 2017, the *Toronto Star* penned an editorial in which it termed *DCHP-2* a "fine birthday gift to Canada". But what was meant by that phrase? Are we still limited by nationalistic jingoism and lines of thought, those lines that have enflamed Europe and the world for much of the twentieth century in unimagin- ably horrible ways? Listening to Mr Trump, the Brexiteer Farage, and the

Hungarian Prime Minister Victor Orbán might make us think so, but not so quick! There is more to the story.

First, one needs to know that scholarly communities, among the first truly international communities starting in the Middle Ages, have generally been sceptical of national angles. That scepticism is, first and foremost, a good thing. But when the scepticism becomes an end in its own right, it fails its purpose. The "narcissism of small differences" is a phrase attributed to Sigmund Freud and has been used to refer to Canada post-World War II:

> Between the release of the final report of the Royal Commission on National Development in the Arts, Letters and Science, chaired by Vincent Massey, in 1951 and Canada's centenary in 1967, the idea of "Canada" came to take on new meaning. The heady anti-Americanism of these decades was, in part, a reaction to the perceived economic and cultural invasion of Canada by the United States. Nationalist sentiment ran particularly deep in the lead up to 1967, when English-speaking nationalists . . . set out to Canadianize the country's economy, culture and universities. The desire to differentiate Canada from Great Britain and the United States led to the invention of "Canadian English". (High 2008: 89)

There we have it: academic critique levied at projects with a national dimension. I'm not saying that Steven High, who penned a wonderfully complex article that I recommend for reading, surmised this, but the ghosts of nineteenth-century nationalism, which led to World War I and then World War II, are in the room.

Yet there is a whole different level of "nationalism", a friendly one, that has nothing to do with the discriminatory, racist, colonial baggage that is inextricably linked with basically all of the nineteenth and much of the twentieth centuries, and that seems to be, sadly, in the Age of Trump and Brexit, returning through the back door. My point is that these developments are only possible because people do not find themselves reflected in public discourse, discourse that has neglected the level of identity, and this is how I see national dimensions: as one level of identity that is sometimes more, sometimes less important, but is often there.

And here is how things can go sideways rather quickly. If EU technocrats tell the people that nations in the EU no longer play a role, they are confounding their wishful thinking with realities. They declare their wishes *de facto* as dogma. In reality, it would take a good deal of effort and a few decades of real integrationist work in Europe to make that vision happen. Any dogmas are counterproductive in that process, in which EU citizens will want to express their multiple identities. Just pushing through European integration in a bureaucratic manner, as appears to be the usual modus operandum in Brussels, is outright dangerous, as the many destructive parties in the EU now attest to. Blaming the Austrian FPÖ, German AfD, French Front National, or the former Belgian Vlaams Blok is easy but misses the point: ask instead what happened to enable these anti-democratic and authoritarian parties to get a foothold in liberal democracies.

Not just politicians but also academics are prone to this mistake. Rutherdale and Fahrni (2008) consider the *DCHP-1* a product of nationalist zeal. While this stance is logical, I wonder whether nationalist zeal was the real driving force behind the Big Six's motivations. After all, Lovell, an American, can only with some qualifications be accused of pushing the Canadian nationalist case. Avis, likewise, seems to have cared much more about the real and precise description of the people's vernacular, the language they really use, than about any prescribed language use. For that reason, Avis is rightly termed a spokesperson for linguistic autonomy, as McDavid wrote.

I think it is quite clear that Avis was not a nationalist – at least not in the usual sense of the word of someone exercising a blind, fanatical one-sidedness. But he did wrestle Canadian English from the fangs of American and British English stakeholders, so to speak. I too have, not often and not too loudly, been called a nationalist – if not in the Canadian context then in the Austrian, where Austrians have been facing increasing pressures from Germans in the past ten years or so *against* their own Standard Austrian German, which is different from Standard German German. The nationalist accusation is a very powerful one. Many are silenced for fear of it. I won't be, because I care about the teaching in schools of what children and young people need to know about language. And to that purpose, we need to introduce in a new form the concept of the nation. Is that nationalism? Surely not. I prefer to call it an issue of language and identity that takes the state's role seriously – rather than ruling it out to begin with or belittling it.[5]

There are other critics. In the year 2000, an Ontarian English Literature MA graduate and, at one point, financial securities trader published an article in the general-audience journal *English Today*. This person, Jan Lilles, entitled his paper "The myth of Canadian English" and, as the provocative title states, it says nothing good about the concept. I have called Lilles' paper in my lectures – poignantly, but quite seriously – the "worst paper on Canadian English". That is because the paper is not a paper based on any data or other new information but more of a pamphlet – so much so that it should not have been published without a public critique. The paper is insightful for different reasons: it is a powerful testimony of personal anecdote and opinion, the kind of strong opinion that often steers public debate in one and not another direction. As an opinion piece, it offers a good debating case.

One of the basic problems in Lilles' paper is that it essentializes a prior state, before Canada was an independent political entity. That prior state is considered as a "gold standard". If Lilles were to go on and study the emergence of Standard British or Standard American English – or, many centuries earlier, the English language as such – he would see that his categorical distinction between England, France, and Canada does not hold water. And neither will his idealization of England and France as countries that speak nothing but their dominant languages. There are erroneous assumptions in his piece that have not been given proper thought.

Occasionally, one finds critique that is based – much like Lilles' but put forth more consistently – in what might be called 'apparent' intellectual rigour. Using Boberg's (2000) phrase on cross-border differences, "neither many nor large", High reasons that "one is struck not so much by the differences between American and Canadian English today as by its similarities" (High 2008: 104). They are varieties of the same language, so of course there must be many more similarities than differences. The real question, however, must be: why are there *any* differences at all? And, more importantly, why do they persist for the most part, and why are new ones being created?

High's statements can, moreover, easily be challenged for their interpretation of the literature. He concludes his paper on the "invention of Canadian English", calling the claims to a Canadian English "exaggerated", in the past more so than today:

> Yet not so very long ago, these linguistic differences loomed larger than life. One can conclude that these small differences were exaggerated to serve as markers of national distinctiveness at a time of intense national anxiety and nation building. (High 2008: 104)

While it is everybody's right, and every thinker's duty, to assess academic works with their own list of criteria, in High's case there seems to be a clear scepticism in linguistic, dialectological, and lexicographical methods. What we hear is High's opinion, as no data on language attitudes or the like are presented. And it is here, I think, where High captures only a small part of the Canadian population's feelings – that of some of the elite who, for whatever reason, consider the creation of a Canadian dimension in language as "petty", as the key thought of his paper, the "narcissism of small differences", announces to the world. High and Lilles have every right to their opinions about Canadian English, though it becomes clear from a reading of their texts that they are just that: personal opinions. As such, there are about 38 million opinions in the country. The only way to go beyond personal interpretations is to use data on the feelings that Canadians have, share, and purport about Canadian English.

So, is there a chance that the differences between, say, *parkade* and *parking garage* or *car park* are "too small"? Or that the narrow semantic differences between *take up* #9, which is limited to the school/university context, within the many other meanings of *take up* are too? The *OED*, for instance, lists under **take up** *verb* in meaning (93c) a similar meaning described as "With special obj[ect], implying a purpose of using in some way, such as in *to take up a book* (i.e., with the purpose to read)"? Are not these differences – as High (2008) says, with Freud – a narcissistic thing and a psychological disturbance of perception? Something that is irrelevant?

In any case, there is no doubt today that there *are* systematic differences between the US and Canadian varieties. Not everybody may be sufficiently alert to notice them, but they are a fact. As Boberg puts it for the forty lexical variables that he studied in the North American context:

Despite the massive influence of American English over the last half-century ... , regional linguistic variation remains one of the few ways in which Canadians can still be reliably distinguished from Americans, at least in most parts of the continent. (Boberg 2010: 25)

This is powerful stuff and clearer than most people would guess. Against the odds, Canadians have developed a system that is statistically different from the one used in the USA. Boberg's study, originally published in 2005, was the first to prove with statistical means what the Big Six and others have been saying all along. But are the differences relevant? Aren't they just "too small", anyway?

In order to answer the question of the sanity or insanity of interpretations of "small" linguistic differences, we need to see how the bulk of Canadian speakers feels about such differences. Very few things are absolute in language per se and a lot is in the hands of the users: it's all relative to what speakers make of it. For that reason, we will look at attitudinal data, especially in contrast to older data from thirty or forty years ago. In the end, it is the collective cumulative perception of Canadian English, its differences from other varieties, and, more importantly, its *perceived* differences and frequencies that matter; they are the only benchmark of "nonsense" or "a lot of sense".

What Do Canadians Think?

Yes, what *do* Canadians think? This is the key question if one wishes to prove (or falsify) that Canadian English is not "ridiculous" but a creation deeply rooted in the behaviour and awareness of its speakers. There are voices out there that seem to "know", unless they're shown otherwise:

Get over it, gals. There may, indeed, be a few genuinely native English-Canadian words. However, the idea that there is a language called Canadian English is ridiculous, a fantasy spun by bureaucrats. (Aminhotep, cbc.ca online forum, 2008, qtd in Dollinger 2011a: 7)

Aminhotep, using the name of Ancient Egypt's most powerful pharaoh, is obviously highly sceptical about Canadian English. The pharaoh aficionado s/he probably is might be interested in reading the present chapter, starting with Figure 39, which shows the responses of 429 Canadians from the Metro Vancouver area who were asked:

Is there a Canadian way of speaking?
Strongly agree Agree Somewhat agree Somewhat disagree Disagree Strongly disagree

"Canadian Way of Speaking" & Education

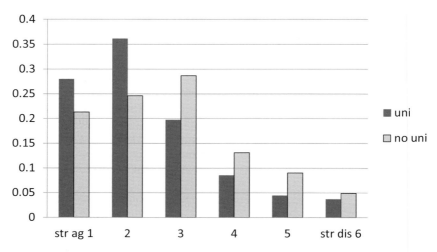

Figure 39 Perceived differences in Canadian English, Vancouver, 2009
($n = 429$)

They were quite clear in their answers. Split by level of education, the results are shown in Figure 39 for those with some schooling at a university or community college (completed or in progress) and those who do not have any post-secondary education. The chart shows that, among the university-educated, 28 per cent "Strongly agree" and 36 per cent "Agree" – a two-thirds majority of 64 per cent in total – that there is "a Canadian way of speaking".

Those without any university education are on the fence, with 47 per cent combined of "Strongly agree" and "Agree". If we include the "Somewhat agree" in both classes, however, we reach an overwhelming majority of about 80 per cent in both cases that are in agreement. But maybe we shouldn't include the "Somewhat agree" at this point. That's one of the tricks of offering no "neutral" category. People need to take sides and there is quite a difference between "Somewhat agree" and "Somewhat disagree" – of about 20 per cent – in both educational classes. This suggests that some folks see differences, though they may, only for these individuals, be considered as "small" and not important. Steven High appears to fall into that category.

We have reason to assume that the adherents of a "Canadian way of speaking" (about 80 per cent of them) may be under-reported nationally. That is because the survey was carried out in a Western Canadian location, whose dialects are considered to be quite similar to the adjacent American ones.

If you asked this question in the Maritimes or in Montreal, you might get even more than 80 per cent in total for responses one to three.

The "Miracle" of Canadian English

The qualitative analysis of press coverage over the years has suggested that, in the last decade or so, subtle adherents of Canadian linguistic autonomy have become more prominent. The best evidence of such attitudinal change in favour of Canadian English will be presented next – a change that has taken place in the past thirty to forty years, with some ups and downs. In 1979, Brigitte Halford (under maiden name Gulden) surveyed the language attitudes of University of Victoria students: once more in a Western Canadian location, once more with young Canadians in their late teens and early 20s but this time only. Henry Warkentyne summarized Halford's findings and came to the conclusion that in the 1979 data the students rated Canadian linguistic identity and Canadian national identity as very low, leading to the assessment that the low scores "should allay any fears that nationalism may be carried to extreme in British Columbia" (Warkentyne 1983: 73).

If we spin ahead the wheel of time by thirty years, from 1979 to 2009, when my ENGL 323A – Varieties of English class-collected data, the young adults in the 1979 study were then in their early 50s or late 40s. If 1979's teens and 2009's mature adults had stuck by their assessments of Canadian English, we would expect in that age group a dip, perhaps just like in the older age groups in general. And here is the "miracle" of Canadian English: despite a lack of consistent news coverage on the variety, despite the domestic linguists' general unwillingness to work on questions of language use (with some notable exceptions, especially the Canadian usage grammar of Fee & McAlpine 2011 [2007, 1997]), despite its relative neglect in schools, the sceptical young adults from 1979 appear to have changed their minds on Canadian English. As Figure 40 shows, there is no dip whatsoever among those in their 50s. Among those in their 40s, on the contrary, there is even a minor "bump", so those who were 18 or 19 in 1979 would indeed be in that age cohort.

Remarkably, down to those in their 80s (and better), a resounding 80 per cent *across all age groups* believe (categories Strongly agree, Agree, and Somewhat agree) that there is "a Canadian way of speaking".

Now that these data have been collated in different ways, a puzzling picture that has been full of apparent ambiguities emerges. With the interpretation of an attitudinal change between the late 1970s and the end of the first decade of the 2000s, letters to the editor such as the following make sense in the bigger picture: the writer mutates then not into an outlier but into an avant-garde aficionado of Canadian English. The letter was only one of a handful of "best"

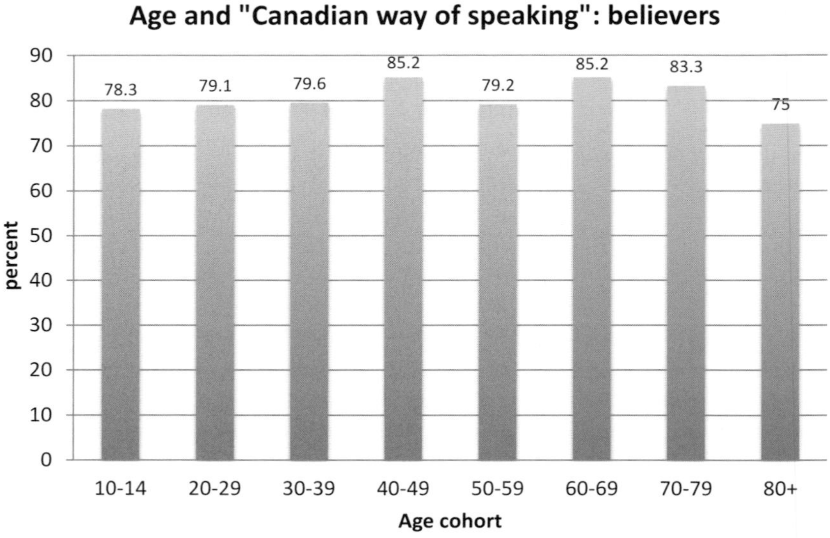

Age and "Canadian way of speaking": believers

Figure 40 "Believers" in Canadian English in Vancouver by age group ($n = 429$)

letters to the editor that year, selected by Naomi Lakritz. In response to the *DCHP-2* project's coverage in the *Calgary Herald* titled "Eh to zed, je suis Canadien!", the letter closed with the following line:

The dictionary [*DCHP-2*] is a boon to Canada. It makes a statement all Canadians should echo, the same one screamed by Joe in another famous commercial: I am Canadian! (*Calgary Herald*, editorial, 26 June 2007: A14)

Note that this was a full decade before the *DCHP-2* would be available. Clearly, the *Calgary Herald* editorial team at the time (perhaps even now) appreciated the *DCHP-2*. Then, Graham Kinmod from Sundre, Alberta, wrote this letter to the editor, which got published on Canada Day, 1 July 2007:

Lexicon - Re: "Eh to zed, je suis Canadien!," Editorial,
    June 26
    With the new Dictionary of Canadianisms, I recommend the following:

– No reference to "awesome."
– No reference to "thinking out of the box."
– No reference to "red-necks." We are Albertans.
– No reference to Ed Stelmach. This is only a bad dream.
– Ditto Henry Burris.

    Graham Kinmod, Sundre (Kinmod 2007)

Back in the day, I was not quite sure what to make of this letter: was it critique? With the benefit of a decade of hindsight and the data just presented above, I think Mr Kinmod presented a new kind of humour about Canadian English: it seems that Kinmod accepts Canadian English as an entity and is cracking a different kind of joke about it than the "weirdness" stream that had been pervasive. For the non-Albertans: Ed Stelmach was a short-time premier of the province, and Henry Burris a CFL footballer playing for the Calgary Stampeders – quite successfully, but *not* when Graham wrote his letter. To summarize, the humour is constructive, no longer destructive or demeaning as in Lilles' denial – not at all. It looks like Canadian English has finally really grown up.

Why Not Teach it in Elementary School?

Whenever I think about it, I'm surprised at *how ridiculous* the idea of "Canadian English" must have seemed to the 1950s Canadian. To prove the point, consider the following quote from one of Avis' letters to Charles Lovell, sent in 1954, which was around the time Avis was finishing his Ph.D. dissertation. By then, Avis must have had an idea what to look for that would define Canadian English. Yet Avis' words are really surprising, especially considering that a dozen years later he produced a book with nearly 10,000 terms that all had a legitimate claim to being Canadian, one way or another. This is what Avis wrote to Lovell:

> The problem of Canadianisms is a very real one. I find it extremely difficult to discover anything that can be clearly labelled Canadian as opposed to British or American.... I did give him [Henry Alexander] one or two, including import, home brew, and ex-import. These terms refer to Canadian professional footballers as you know. The last is rather interesting and of recent (1953–54) vintage. (Avis to Lovell, 9 Dec. 1954, University of Victoria Archives, 90–66, Box 4 File 6)

This, more than anything, is the most stunning fact about *DCHP-1*: in a little more than a decade, the Big Six literally "created" Canadian English as an empirically tested entity by describing it in such sophisticated ways – measured by the standards of the day and far beyond. That the concept was ridiculed once more by folks like Lilles and other opinionated Canadians – but also some linguists – is equally stunning. Had Avis had a few graduate students of his own – which he didn't have, as a result of his working at RMC – the situation would have looked differently. So much so that there might have been no need to write the present book.

It is no overstatement, despite the good work of my Canadian colleagues today, that an entire tradition of Canadian dialectology was laid to rest with

Avis' passing. The biggest travesty is that none of those who was around or came later seriously continued it. This is a case of how not to discontinue a particular approach, with little or no objective reason. If you drop an established research stream, say so clearly and say why you think what you're doing is more important and relevant. Or perhaps Avis' shoes were just too big and too daunting to fill. The good news is that, with a delay of a generation, we are once more in a position to continue the work that Avis and his generation started. Or, as I tried to show, that Lovell started – Charles J. Lovell, the unsung hero for all of us working on Canadian English. Sidelining him as a guy interested in words would be a fatal mistake: few were interested in Canadian words then. You've got to start somewhere and Lovell did, like any true pioneer.

I have always wondered why Canadian English is not taught upfront, consistently and positively, as an identity-confirming cultural artefact in the school system. Canadian elementary and high schools take Canadiana very seriously, Terry Fox[6] and all, which is taught in kindergarten (much to the surprise of some parents; Terry did die after all, which is hard to grasp for KGers). I have been asking English teachers over the past one and a half decades how they treat Canadian English and I've gotten all kinds of answers. For dictionary use, for instance, there is no consistent answer; they are all over the board. One teacher, in East Vancouver, said she accepts any dictionary that includes etymologies: Webster's, Oxford types, but I guess not the Gage school dictionaries, as they don't have that. Then again, the Gage series has been the bestselling school dictionary.

At this point in the game, sixty years after its "invention", there is still an unfulfilled prerogative to teach Canadian English in schools. This is a birthright. Such knowledge will help students to root themselves in a changing world, in a globalizing world, and will help them become better citizens, Canadians, hyphenated Canadians, North Americans, global citizens – take your pick. Figure 41 visualizes the "semantic domains" that comprise the new content in *DCHP-2*. It lists all "meanings" (senses), which are individually categorized.[7]

The chart shows the thirty-eight semantic domains in the new content in *DCHP-2* ("*DCHP-2* Update" – thirty-seven are shown in Figure 41, where two aboriginal labels are combined).[8] It might surprise the reader that, of 1,248 new meanings, 377 meanings – or 30 per cent – are from the top three domains: Food & drink (138), Administration (130), and Politics (111).

So, what are some of these Food & drink terms, one might wonder, beyond *poutine*? They include *all-dressed*, *Cheezies*, *double-double*, *frissant*, *icing* 'US: frosting, on cakes etc.', *Kraft Dinner* 'mac and cheese', *Montreal smoked meat*, *Nanaimo bar* 'type of dessert',[9] *pop* 'fizzy drink', *stubby* 'the old, stubby beer bottle', *toupie* 'a ham', *vang* 'Newfoundland delicacy', or *Vi-Co* . . . folks

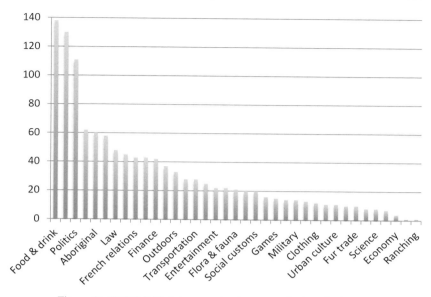

Figure 41 *DCHP-2* Update, meaning by semantic domain (n = 1,248)

from the province of Saskatchewan will tell you. Administrative terms are also frequent; some are *BDC* 'Business Development Bank of Canada', *blood donor clinic*, *CPP*, *First Minister*, *GST*, *home language*, *HST*, *Indian Register*, *isolation pay*, *make-work*, *National Film Board*, *New Canadian*, *postal code*, *RRSP*, *SIN*, *T4*, *unemployment insurance*, and *vacation pay*. Finally, political terms are numerous. While the Canadian parliamentary system is based on the Westminster system, it has evolved since, creating its own terms or adapting old ones: *acclaim* 'elect without opposition', *Big Blue Machine*, *Bloqiste*, *Fat City*, *fuddle duddle*, *mainstreeting*, *prorogue*, *Rest of Canada*, *scrum*, *separatism*, *sovereignist*, *Trudeaumania* (in 2015 for Version 2.0), and *upload* 'a higher governmental level foots the bill'. Details for all terms are found at www.dchp.ca/dchp2.

While such stats are important and nice, they do not nearly illustrate the diversity of the distinctly Canadian lexis in English: *playoff beard*, for instance, did not make the top three but is, along with *Game 7* or *dipsydoodle*, still in sixth position among the many hockey terms in and beyond the sports context. Not all hockey terms come from NHL[10] terminology, as the term *shinny*, which is an informal (pick-up[11]) game, illustrates (see Figure 42). While Hayley Wickenheiser's (women's hockey) many successes, Sidney Crosby's ("Sid the Kid", as he was once called) overtime goal in the Vancouver Olympics' final against Team USA, or The Great One's[12] scoring records

Figure 42 Playing *shinny* in the setting winter sun
(Ponsibili on Wikimedia Commons, used under CC by 2.0; photo: Dean Jarvey)

are important, the real *hockey* is found with the *hockey moms* and *hockey dads* at local rinks throughout this vast land. The latter are the true heroes and heroines of the Great (Traditional) Canadian Game.

Hockey, whether in sports or non-sports (e.g., "The hiring process came down to a Game-7 scenario"), professional or *shinny* contexts, provides only the tip of the iceberg of the distinctly Canadian vocabulary. But if Canadian girls and boys play hockey well, they may go on to play for Team Canada in the Olympics, as did five-time Olympian, four-time Olympic-gold medallist Hayley Wickenheiser, playing for the Canadian women's hockey team for twenty-three years, from 1994 to 2017. Hayley is the Gretzky of professional women's hockey. Since we have the word *Gretzky effect*, signifying the popularization of hockey in the USA because of Wayne Gretzky, one may wonder when the *Wickenheiser effect* will be named. Hayley is shown in action in Figure 43 in her last Olympic Games in Sochi.

While hockey holds a special place in many Canadians' hearts, recent decades have seen a diversification not just in the sports played but also in other activities. *May long* 'long holiday weekend in May' is used by the younger speakers, while some older ones stick to *May two-four* (it happens around 24 May, Victoria Day) or simply *May long weekend*. There is also *zunga* 'rope swing' in Powell River, BC, and environs, which has a Swedish legacy and demonstrates the best of Canadian culture: you have a name for something we didn't have, we'll keep the name, including a pronunciation and spelling that we can get away with. Unfortunately, such tolerance has not always been the norm. Then, there are words like *idiot string* 'string connect-ing two mittens'; one wonders if it will stick around, given that it oscillates

Figure 43 Hayley Wickenheiser *stickhandling* for Team Canada at the Sochi
Olympics
(Photo: Dave Holland, kindly provided by Hayley Wickenheiser)

between the self-ironic and the abusive. Like the terms behind the domains in
Figure 41, all these words are at your fingertips in *DCHP-2*.

Another advantage of teaching Canadian English from the ground up in
schools – indeed, a pressing need – would be preventing the misuse of the term
in a light that is sadly reminiscent of twentieth-century nationalism:

> In September, I nearly lost my daughter. I had driven her to the Golden Mile shopping
> centre in Regina to attend a social drop-in group for adults with autism. As we were
> walking toward the mall entrance, a car, whose driver had clearly seen us, came
> speeding in our direction. If I hadn't grabbed my daughter and pulled her to safety,
> the car would have hit her.
>
> The driver, an older white man, parked close by, so I decided to speak to him. "Why
> did you do that?" I asked. He replied, "Canadian English please," and proceeded
> towards the mall.
>
> In case you're wondering what I look like, I cover my hair with a scarf in order to affirm
> my identity as a Muslim woman. (*Star-Phoenix*, Saskatoon, SK, 27 Oct. 2017: A10)

The question seems to be: do we want to fill Canadian English with "positive"
content, its features and innovations, or do we leave the term to folks as
described above: a "discriminatory kind of Canadian English"? It's up to you.

Tuum est: It's Up to You

It's up to you indeed! In case your Latin, just like mine today,[13] is a bit rusty,
tuum est is a phrase that is particularly witty. It happens to be UBC's motto and
aptly demonstrates that West Coasters in the 1910s did have great knowledge
and a good kind of humour and wit. It means either "It is yours" or – and this
is, in my mind, more important than the first reading – "Make it yours."

In Latin, the indicative mood (which expresses the "normal", statement-of-fact way of speaking and is behind the first translation to "It is yours") and the imperative mood of giving commands (so, in English, "Be brave!" or "Go away!", which is behind the second translation to "Make it yours") are identical.

Now think about the phrase again: *tuum est*. I can't think of a better motto for a university that strives to discover new knowledge and to pass on this knowledge and discuss it in general. I also can't think of a better motto in relation to the term *Canadian English*. Because, if you see yourself as Canadian, it *is* yours. As the work over the past six decades has shown, you also need to *make it yours*. This is just as the British had to create their own standard English, starting with the late Middle English writers (think Chaucer, Gower, . . .) and the printing press in the late fifteenth century. Or the Americans, who had, fitting with their purported traits, a vocal proponent named Webster in the field of linguistics, which is why the Americans were, propped by their increasing political and economic clout, relatively quick at creating their own standard. Nothing comes from nothing, not even a standard variety, and my friend Jan Lilles and other critics who "don't like" the idea would do well to appreciate the "creation aspect" that is behind a lot of language use. Nothing comes from nothing, and if you believe that, say, the French had it so much easier in the codification of their standard variety, you can't know a lot about French (linguistic) history. In the American case, for instance, the creation of Standard American English still took a century and a half until Americans and the world would accept American English as another standard of English.

At a Canadian Studies conference in Canada House in London in 2017, Guy Laforest informed the audience that the twenty-first century would be "Canada's century". Sure, there is always China but I do think that Canada, not having gone down the equivalent route of the Brexit fiasco or the Trump detour, does have a good shot at coming out a winner in 2100. Maybe we can make the world a better place, as I don't think many Brexiteers or Trumpists will be in the position to do so. It's a crazy world we live in. What role will Canadian English play in 2100? Domestically? Regionally? Globally?

As Russell Smith, the culture columnist, put it some years ago in the *Globe and Mail*: "Nothing that I write gets as big a response as my ramblings on language" (Smith 2007: R1). I think we linguists owe it to the people to share the word on Canadian English and, I hope, this book will go some way towards that goal. Canadian English: *tuum est*! I almost feel that my team and I did our part for Canadian English by including *fuddle duddle* in *DCHP-2*. It's a most interesting entry in *DCHP-2*, a long one, with video links showing the sequence of events that took place in 1971 and involved Trudeau the Elder:

Pierre Elliott Trudeau. Justin Trudeau was just a twinkle in his dad's eye at that point, as they say. The *Toronto Star*'s Harry Bruce would be pleased, as in 1986 he bitterly complained that neither the *Gage Canadian* nor the *Concise DCHP-1* (or the big one, for that matter) included *fuddle duddle*, which is Canuck politics talk for *f*** off*:

We need all the proof we can muster that English-speaking Canada has a unique culture, and what other nation can boast fuddle-duddle as a substitute for a common, four-letter, Anglo-Saxon word, followed by off? But, alas, neither the *Gage Canadian Dictionary* (1983) nor *A Concise Dictionary of Canadianisms* (1973) makes any mention of fuddle-duddle. (Bruce 1986)

Rather than using the crude *F*-word and preposition *off*, we say *fuddle duddle*. Very polite, isn't it? You can of course look up *fuddle duddle's* prime-ministerially mouthed history at www.dchp.ca/dchp2. The proof is right there. But is it . . . *enough*?

You be the judge. If you are either a user of Canadian English or in one way or another connected to it, you *must* judge. It's like in the presidential elections in Austria:[14] if you have the right to vote, you must vote. Not voting is illegal and may be punished with a fine. As someone interested in Canadian English – and why else would you be reading these lines? – you have a vote. I stated the facts and told you the story of how Canadian English became a concept and a term. Now over to you! Were the Big Six nationalists who created something where there was and still is nothing, or were they visionaries who sensed a need for something and created guidelines in the form of dictionaries based on what Canadians did with their English?

It's always useful to look for parallels in history for any difficult question. We can then decide whether we agree with the previous path of action or not. In the case of the diversification of English into various national varieties, H. L. Mencken offers us a view from 1936 for his "battle front", the acceptance of Standard American English on a par with Standard British English:

The American people now constitute by far the largest fraction of the English-speaking race [in today's parlance: people], and since the [First] World War they, have shown an increasing inclination to throw off their old subservience to English precept, for example. If only by the force of numbers, they are bound to exert a dominant influence upon the course of the common language hereafter. (Mencken 1936: vi)

Should Canadians, as Lilles (2000) and others have basically claimed, remain "subservient" to English or American "precept"? Should they, because the Canadian "force of numbers" is not nearly as big as in the American case? If so, we'd pursue the 1930s race of hegemony in the linguistic realm. That aspect, in my opinion, is not desirable today. But would the acceptance, once and for all, of Standard Canadian English be a good thing? What would be the possible downsides, I wonder?

Regardless of your decision, it is my hope that this book will help put the legacies of Wally Avis and Charlie Lovell, two "worker[s] in the vineyard" of Canadian English in this chapter's epigraph, back in the intellectual context, and with it the legacies and achievements of Charles Crate, Doug Leechman, and, last but not least, Paddy Drysdale and Harry Scargill. The Big Six ought to be recognized – because a field that forgets its history is doomed to repeat previous mistakes, reinvent the wheel, and add more errors. We should not and cannot afford such folly. And we don't have to, because *Tuum est*.

Notes

1 What is Canadian English?

1 Avis (1966: 17).
2 A digitized edition can be accessed free of charge at www.dchp.ca/dchp1. If you'd like to consult the 2017 *Second Edition* and update, you can do so for free at www .dchp.ca/dchp2. Because work was started before phones were as smart as they are now, it's best to do so on a bigger screen.
3 My count is based on the 2016 Census, Languages Spoken at Home, see www12.statcan.gc.ca/census-recensement/2016/rt-td/lang-eng.cfm.
4 Chambers and Trudgill (1998: ch. 1) drives home that point more fully.
5 Rice (2016).
6 See Keddie (2003), especially the map on p. 48.
7 The linguistic situation in the area is wonderfully complex but sadly deprived of speakers, so that we are dealing with languages and dialects that are either already sleeping or close to extinction. In the following, I introduce the family tree (like English is part of Low West Germanic, of West Germanic, of Proto Germanic, of Proto Indo-European) of the Lekwungen language, based on Mithun (1999: 485, 488). The underlined parts mark the branches of the family tree that lead down to LEKWUNGEN, which was spoken on what is now Oak Bay. Lekwungen is part of the language family that is called the SALISHAN family. The SALISHAN language family is comprised of three groups: the BELLA COOLA language, the COAST languages, and the INTERIOR languages. The COAST languages are divided into two subgroups, the CENTRAL SALISH group and the TSAMOSAN (OLYMPIC) group. The CENTRAL SALISH group is further subdivided into a NORTH GEORGIA branch (named after the Strait of Georgia, which is part of the Salish Sea) and a SOUTH GEORGIA branch. In the SOUTH GEORGIA branch, there are four subdivisions on the next level: the SQUAMISH language, the HALKOMELEM language (in at least three dialects), the NOOKSACK language, and the STRAITS languages. The latter are also called the LKUNGEN GROUP, not to be confused with the Lkungen (= Lekwungen) language as such. The Lkungen Group (also spelled Lekwungen Group), is subdivided into the NORTHERN STRAITS languages and the KLALLAM language (= CALLAM, KALLAM). There are six Northern Straits languages: the SOOK language, the LEKWUNGEN language (= LEKUNGEN = SONGHEES = SONGISH), the SENĆOŦEN language (spelled in upper case with special characters, formerly called SAANICH), the SAMISH language, the LUMMI language, and the SEMIAHMOO language. The language traditionally and ancestrally

spoken in Oak Bay was the Songish language, which is today most often called the Lekwungen/Lkungen language (not to be confused with the Lkungen group).

8 Mitchell (1968) is an unpublished dictionary of Lekwungen that was supported if not initiated by Scargill (Mitchell 1968: 4). It transcribes *ȼċés* as *tl'chés*, which is very close to the ASCII-only character version used in the present book.

9 Keddie (2003: 14).

10 Conference Programme of the Symposium "First Nations, Land, and James Douglas: Indigenous and Treaty Rights in the Colonies of Vancouver Island and British Columbia, 1849–1864". Symposium at the Songhees Wellness Centre, 24–26 February 2017, p. 3.

11 This quotation, as well as the immediately preceding one from the Chilcowitch treaty, is from the copy at the Oak Bay Archives. Also accessible at BC Archives, MS-0772 Vancouver Island treaties 1850–1854.

12 Quote from the Conference Programme of the Symposium at the Songhees Wellness Centre, 24–26 February 2017, p. 2.

13 The distortion is, of course, not limited to the historical background. Travel the world in English with Lonely Planet guides and other English-language resources and you'll miss out big time without even noticing it.

14 The rationale may have been that the use of Indigenous language and names without explanations is an act of resistance. It is, after all, not the responsibility of the Indigenous population to teach the settler population about colonization. They may do so, but they do not have to.

15 Standard British English is a construct that prominent sociolinguists do not adopt, preferring the concepts of Standard English English and Standard Scottish English instead. For simplicity's sake in the global and Canadian cases, I will use the first term, though this should not be interpreted as rejecting the English–Scottish split in relation to Standard English.

16 The low percentage for native standard speakers in the UK is based on Trudgill and Hannah (2017: 2), which is an excellent resource for the international character of Standard Englishes. See Dollinger (2011a) for the mathematical equation based on the 2006 census, when 36 per cent of Canadians spoke Standard Canadian English. That share has gone up since. Kretzschmar (2008) informs us about Standard American English. Hickey (2013) is a treatment of Standard Englishes.

17 For two interesting papers on the shift's spread in Canada, see Roeder (2012) and Roeder and Gardner (2013). For a cross-border perspective, see Swan (2016).

18 Haugen (1966) is still the standard work, distinguishing four stages of standardization: selection of a variety (the king's?), codification (in dictionaries and grammars), elaboration (are there any words, etc., missing?), and, finally, acceptance by the speakers in general.

19 Referring to denim bottoms and denim top, originally used in jest but now quite an established style (see http://dchp.ca/dchp2/Entries/view/Canadian%252520tuxedo).

20 Note that it is special only in the context of industrialized nations, where L2 speakers are usually in the minority: German, Russian, Italian, even Japanese and many other languages have more L1 speakers than L2 speakers. If that is not the case – that is, if more non-native speakers exist – one speaks of a *Lingua Franca*. Vulgar Latin was a Lingua Franca in the Roman Empire, German in the Austrian Empire, and today English is one in the global context. In Southeastern Africa,

Kiswahili is another Lingua Franca with many more non-native than native speakers.

21 David Crystal (2003, 2013), one of the world authorities on the English language, is one of the few who can provide a comprehensive picture. He is the man who keeps track of this ratio, among many other things. In 1997, he considered it 2:1, in 2003 it was 3:1 (Crystal 2012 [2003]: 69), and in 2013 he estimated 5:1. With population growth being at least two and a half times as much in developing countries and with access to English learning increasing, I'm proposing that today we are at 6:1.

22 Kachru (1985) introduces what has become known as the "Circle Model" of World Englishes.

23 David Crystal's (2012 [2003]) book tells that story brilliantly and succinctly.

24 See Edgar W. Schneider (2007), especially pages 21–70.

25 See Chambers (2010).

26 Akrigg (1980: 10), quoting Professor Woodhouse, who "repeatedly" described Sedgewick as such.

27 See Chambers (2004) on Canadian Dainty.

28 Irving Layton, "Anglo-Canadian", a poem published in 1956.

29 See Geikie (2010 [1857]).

30 See *DCHP-1*, under *Canadian English* in Avis *et al.* (1967) or online at www.dchp.ca/dchp2/Entries/view/Canadian%252520English.

31 As indeed the story has been written in Bonnie Lovell's (2011) unpublished memoir entitled "The Lexicographer's Daughter".

32 Lovell was born in 1907 (B. Lovell 2011: 138). See also *ibid.*: 48.

33 Claire Cassidy's (2002) obituary is a testament to her father, one of the true pioneers of dialectology and lexicography.

34 See *DCHP-2*, s.v. "Meech Lake Accord", or www.dchp.ca/dchp2/Entries/view/Meech%252520Lake%252520Accord.

35 See Joos (1942) for a description of this phenomenon, which many years later would be called Canadian Raising by J. K. Chambers. See Onosson (2018) for a recent account.

36 For an overview of what we know about that process, see Dollinger (2017a).

2   THE HERITAGE OF CANADIAN ENGLISH

1 Romaine (1982) and Devitt (1989) were two early trailblazers in historical sociolinguistics.

2 See Brown (2015: ch. 1).

3 Note that *ice-road* is an outdated *DCHP-1* entry, left there awaiting revision, while *ice road* is up to date.

4 See Henry Alexander's (1939) short text on his fieldwork in Nova Scotia, which was to be complemented in the 1940s and early 1950s with scattered work in central Canada, of which Raven I. McDavid's recordings of some 100 speakers in Ontario are by far the most substantial Canadian records for *The Linguistic Atlas of the United States and Canada*. The atlas petered out, incomplete but with a substantial data set, in the 1980s (Kretzschmar 2009 introduces some of the data, which can now be accessed at www.lap.edu).

5 See Thomas (1991).

6 Fortunately, Charles Boberg has devised written questionnaires and analyzed them in innovative ways to tell us which Canadian regions are more similar to one another and how they compare with adjacent regions in the USA. As this work was only carried out after 2000 (see Boberg 2005, 2008), we'd been pretty much in the dark till then, beyond educated guesses, of which we have had many (such as Chamberlain 1890 and Bailey 1991, a full century apart).

7 Doherty (2019) has recently shed light on Sandilands.

8 Lovell was not happy with how Craigie had proceeded. In a letter dated 2 Dec. 1954, he expresses to Avis his disappointment over Craigie's reading programme, which was carried out by 400 people *unfamiliar* with the subject matter and not up to standard. We can see Lovell's high expectations, which reflect the scholar he was (University of Victoria Archives 90–66, Box 4 File 6).

9 Read the epigraph at the beginning of Chapter 1 in this context.

10 Avis' MA thesis is today still inspiring in its historical treatment of fictional speech (see Avis 1950, which is only available in microfiche of bad quality, not in hard copy).

11 See Avis' (1957/58) critical review of American dictionaries, emphasizing the point that Canadian English needs its own dictionaries and that using American or British ones will no longer do.

12 See Pratt (2004) and its discussion of *skid road* (*skid row*).

13 See Bloomfield (1948: 66, final paragraph).

14 See Avis (1954, 1955a, and 1956) for these (short but important and empirically sound) papers.

15 The report was the result of the Royal Commission on National Development in the Arts, Letters and Sciences, which was headed by Vincent Massey, later to become the eighteenth Governor General of Canada. The report led to a number of significant improvements and strategic planning that had not been seen before.

16 The thesis, Davis (1948), is hard to obtain, but I summarize it in some detail in Dollinger (2015a: 30–34) for its historical importance in a methodological dispute and an ensuing bias that was to develop in the latter half of the twentieth century. Davis' (1948) thesis showed that scepticism regarding written questionnaires was unwarranted and exaggerated, a result that was not widely well received.

17 The earliest comprehensive overview is Avis (1973), written around 1971. It is still a useful text.

18 Queen's University Archives, Avis Fonds. Typed letter from J. K. Chambers to W. Avis.

19 The second real textbook, with exercises, would only come forth almost half a century later (Walker 2015).

20 The image is archived at https://babel.hathitrust.org/cgi/pt?id=uiuo.ark:/13960/t18k8kt7m, the repository of choice for University of Illinois Libraries (William Schlaack, 16 May 2018).

21 It is interesting to note that Louise Pound (1872–1958), BA 1892, MA 1895, Ph.D. 1900, and promoted to full professor *c*. 1915 (Krohn 2008: 124), must be considered a feminist pioneer in the field, two generations or more ahead of other women. When American universities would not admit her for a Ph.D. because she was a woman, Pound went to Heidelberg, Germany, then a hot spot for English

historical linguistics. She became co-founder of *American Speech* in 1925, at a time when she was Professor of English Language at the University of Nebraska. This was a smart move, because at the more established universities women had a very restricted role to play for quite some time longer (the first female full university professor at Oxford University, for instance, was appointed after World War II, in 1948). In 1955, Pound became the first female President of the Modern Language Association. She was the "poster woman" and trailblazer long, long before others were to follow her. In Pound's case, it was a combination of the laxer western US academic rules, a professor father (which surely helped), and her drive to make something of herself beyond the path set forth by the society of the day and beyond all obstacles thrown at her. In other words: she was a linguistic heroine.

22 Janice McAlpine, then director of the unit, was in charge of that project, which offered some rare quotations for *DCHP-2* from the Avis files.

23 *The Walrus*, December 2017, p. 74.

24 *Ibid.*

25 See https://archie.library.carleton.ca/index.php/faith-avis-wally-avis-and-h-m-tory-greeting-people-as-they-enter-building-for-social-gathering-1945–1946.

26 At the Fourth International Conference of English as a Lingua Franca in 2011 in Hong Kong, Andy Kirkpatrick used the phrase to refer to Jennifer Jenkins (Southampton), Barbara Seildhofer (Vienna), and Anna Mauranen (Helsinki) as the "three mothers" of English as a Lingua Franca research (Wang 2012: 2).

27 See Seidlhofer (2007) for a key paper and the full rationale for the argument.

28 For a digitized version, see www.dchp.ca/DCHP-1/files/DCHP-1_Copyright.pdf.

29 As we will discover in Chapter 8, there *might* possibly be a yet darker spot on *DCHP-1*'s record, but, lacking evidence beyond a striking similarity of names between contributor Charles Crate and a Canadian fascist from the mid-1930s, we are almost certainly just dealing with an unfortunate coincidence. More of that in Chapter 8.

30 The returns are astonishingly good for very little money, not just by international comparison but also in actual dollar figures. I am adding this note to dispel occasional Canadian rumours that the humanities are a waste of money. Anything but: the humanities provide among the best returns on research investment you can get.

31 By 1934, Americans had finally converged on an authoritative dictionary, the (very thick) *Second Edition* of *Webster's New International Dictionary*, which had become "an authoritative source" (Finegan 2001: 403) – so much so that the *Third Edition* from 1961 was rejected as too "modern" by almost all public voices in the USA (see ibid: 404–11). In that climate, the Big Six and Robert J. Gregg set about writing their four dictionaries of Canadian English for Gage.

32 This remarkable story was first brought to the attention of expert circles in Knowles (1990), popularized by Winchester (1998), and woven into a more comprehensive context in Gilliver's (2016) most impressive history of the *OED*.

33 See Gilliver (2016: 201), who explains why Minor's absolute figures of quotations are "dwarfed" by contributors who just sent in quotations at random. Minor's quotations were targeted in response to editors' queries and therefore of the highest quality. Note that Knowles (2000) must be credited for unearthing most details about William Chester Minor.

34 Lovell to Avis, 2 Dec. 1954, University of Victoria Archives 90–66, Box 4 File 6.
35 Examples include Crystal (2005, 2017). Other effective titles for the general reader are, e.g., Curzan (2014) or Tagliamonte (2016a); such books are rare in the big picture of linguistic writing.

3 Avis Pulls It Off

1 McDavid (1981: 125).
2 High (2008: 93).
3 See https://slmc.uottawa.ca/?q=org_can_lexico_en_1962–73_avis.
4 It might well be true that only the good die young. Alexander Kautzsch of Regensburg, Germany, colleague in English historical linguistics, died utterly unexpectedly in March 2018, not yet 50, leaving behind a young family. Lovell was about the same age when he died of the same cause, leaving his own family behind.
5 See Harris' (1995) account of one type of linguistic war.
6 See www.lap.uga.edu to access the data.
7 I am grateful to Professor Herbert Schendl, Chair Emeritus in English historical linguistics at Vienna University, for sharing this information about Ernst Pulgram with me and granting permission to use it here.
8 I am unaware of any history of the CLA in the same detail that Adams (2017) has unearthed for the DSNA (Dictionary Society of North America). Such an enterprise would throw into relief the early fault lines in Canadian linguistics.
9 Thanks go to Michael Montgomery for sharing this information with me at the 2011 American Dialect Society meeting, and to John Kirk for sending some of Gregg's key Ulster texts to the University of British Columbia Canadian English Lab for safekeeping.
10 E.g., Winchester (2003: 98–103), Gilliver (2016: 53–54 and passim).
11 University of Victoria Archives, 90–66, Box 4 File 2.
12 In Canada, the sport is invariably called *hockey*. If one speaks of a sport on grass or the street, it's *field hockey* or *ball hockey*, never *hockey*. *Ice hockey* is a foreign term only, but used for that reason in certain international contexts in Canada.
13 Drysdale (pers. correspondence, 26 May 2018) independently confirmed that Hall probably moved from Calgary to Victoria with the project.

4 The "Technology": Slips, Slips, and More Slips

1 Thanks to Professor Niki Ritt for introducing us to the film at a Vienna University English Department movie night.
2 The report, which relied on some of the best experts at the time, was a departure from previous governmental policies towards First Nations people, which had become increasingly criticized for failing to improve the situation of BC's First Nations, as "Indian affairs administrators selectively interpreted the conclusions of social science scholarship to suit particular bureaucratic and political ends" (King Plant 2009: 7). Some of its recommendations were progressive, such as the increase of funding for the "purposes of promoting Indian enterprise, employment diversification, job training and placement, and the creation of a community development

program" (*ibid.*: 22). But, like so many policy steps in the right direction, they were not taken.
3 Kytö and Walker (2006) or the pioneering work of Kytö (1991).
4 Dollinger (2008a) and Reuter (2017).
5 For that, see, for instance, Durkin (2009) or Sledd (1978).
6 A suggestion I put forth in Dollinger (2006), based on Sledd's (1978) legwork and connection of *kanaka* with East Coast whaling.
7 Leechman's files, labelled *C, M–Q*, include the following note: "FIRST DRAWER of LETTER "C" in OLD FORMAT It has been retyped in new format May 1965 DL" (MS-1290, Box 47 File 1).
8 Drysdale to Scargill, with copy to Avis, Crate, and Leechman, 19 April 1967 (BC Archives, MS-1290, Box 4 File 12).
9 Paddy Drysdale: pers. correspondence with author, 2 Dec. 2017.
10 Scargill in the preface to *DCHP-1*, see www.dchp.ca/DCHP-1/pages/frontmatter#preface.
11 The counts can be checked on the final version, which is online at www.dchp.ca/dchp1 (via the Browse function). We slightly inflate Avis' work with this method, as doubtless at later stages some additional headwords would have been entered.
12 All dollar conversions to 2018 dollars are in Canadian dollars, as calculated by the Bank of Canada's inflation calculator: www.bankofcanada.ca/rates/related/inflation-calculator.
13 Doughty and Martin (1929) remains the key edition, with Warkentin (1994) being a recent reprint without consultation of the manuscripts (1994: 1).

5 1967 – Excitement and Hype

1 Search it at http://no2014.uio.no/eNo/tekst/omoss.html.
2 Access the WNT online at http://www.inl.nl/onderzoek-a-onderwijs/lexicologie-a-lexicografie/wnt.
3 The 1937 edition of the *Winston Simplified* (Brown & Alexander 1937) is often given as the first Canadian dictionary. Examination of this very rare dictionary has proven that, while Henry Alexander edited from the 1927 US edition, the edits merely affected spelling variation (so, e.g., *honour*, not *honor*, or *centre*, not *center*, as main entries); no lexemes were added (e.g., no *chesterfield*, no *toque*). This sober result means that, although the book was edited for the Canadian market, it was done with as minimal a change in the book print plates as possible; so, Brown & Alexander (1937) is not the first Canadian English dictionary in any meaningful definition of the term. Also note that the book title does not contain the word "Canada" or "Canadian", as is sometimes purported.
4 See Meyerhoff and Niedzielski (2003: 543).
5 Queen's University Archives, letter from Jess Stein of Random House Inc. to Walter Avis, 1 Dec. 1967.
6 Nelson Education files on *DCHP-1*, accessed through David Friend, 2007.
7 BC Archives, MS-1290, Box 4.
8 BC Archives, MS-1290, Box 4 File 13. Translated from *Movoznavstvo (Linguistics)* 2 (March–April 1970), a publication by the Ukrainian Academy of Sciences, Kiev.

9 *DCHP-1* "prendra place parmi les ouvrages de référence auprès de l'Oxford English dictionary et du Dictionary of Americanisms dont il est le frère" (Elisabeth Hermite in *Bulletin des bibliothèques de France*, 14[2] [Feb. 1969]).
10 E. W. Holmes, "Review of *A Concise Dictionary of Canadianisms*, an abridgement of *DCHP-1*, Gage c1973" (1973), qtd from BC Archives MS-1290, Box 4 File 13.
11 Harvey Currell to P. D. Drysdale, W. J. Gage, 18 Apr. 1967; University of Victoria Archives, Centre for Lexicography Fond.
12 See Dresser (1968). Note that there apparently is no longer a public copy available anywhere. University of Victoria Interlibrary Loan inform us: "Regret, only 4 locations worldwide hold this title and none of them have the year and/or issue you need." I found this quotation in my old lecture slides but cannot locate the source of my source. This appears to be an orphaned quotation as of today.
13 David Love, quoted in Ray (2003: R9).
14 Donald Stainsby in *Vancouver Life*, Sept. 1968.
15 *Weekend Magazine*, 47 (1967): 33–34.
16 Winchester (2003: 219) writes that, in August 1897, Queen Victoria's private secretary "replied: yes, indeed, after due consideration the Queen had seen fit to accept. Oxford was duly delighted. Murray was well pleased that what was, indeed, a ploy to ensure continuance had worked."
17 The interested reader may still order copies of this softcover reprint of the 1967 edition (Cdn$44.45 plus shipping): Nelson Customer Service 1–800–268–2222 (order "*A Dictionary of Canadianisms on Historical Principles*, 0771519761"). All proceeds go to Nelson Education and have no connection with *DCHP-2* or myself. I am offering this information as it is the only way to obtain a new hard copy of *DCHP-1* today.
18 There was one predecessor, a trailblazer: published before 1900, Morris' (1898) dictionary of Australian English is in a league of its own.
19 Which is why when starting out on *DCHP-2*, student Brianna Laing looked at this section in *DCHP-1* with the funds from the 2007 DSNA Laurence Urdang Award, for which we are thankful. It is not easy to receive funds for this kind of detective work, as it promises no new patents, products, or monetizable information – at least, not right away.
20 Write to stefan.dollinger@ubc.ca or get in touch via Twitter @CanE_Lab.
21 As I said repeatedly elsewhere in a related linguistic context, the "Canadian dimension often remains undetected or underappreciated" (Dollinger 2017a: 100).

6 RIDING THE WAVE OF SUCCESS

1 David Friend: pers. conversation, 2007.
2 J. K. Chambers: pers. correspondence, 2010.
3 Schneider (2007). Note that Schneider's timing, based on older information, is a bit earlier than my dating here for Phase IV, "Endo-normative stabilization".
4 E. W. Holmes, "Review of *A Concise Dictionary of Canadianisms*, an abridgement of *DCHP-1*, Gage c1973" (1973), qtd from BC Archives MS-1290, Box 4 File 13.
5 Avis' rationale for *not* including *eh* in *DCHP-1* is found in Avis (1972).
6 There is today an international need for these materials. Raymond Hickey, interested in all things Irish and Irish diaspora, inquired about the Pringle/Padolsky material as early as 2005, yet its location is unknown.

7 Scargill to J. McClelland, 30 April 1980 (University of Victoria Archives, 90–66, Box 1).

8 *Ibid.*

9 Mencken to Leechman, 2 April 1940 (BC Archives, MS-1290, Box 6 File 26).

10 The *OED*, however, was not the only lexicographical project of Leechman's post-*DCHP-1* time; he also helped Partridge with his *Dictionary of Catch Phrases* (Burchfield to Leechman, 26 Nov. 1968).

11 We don't know whether Leechman kept any copies of the 20,000 quotations for the *DCHP-1* or of the 25,000 for the *OED*.

12 The material is found in the Avis Fonds at Queen's University's archives.

13 A detailed account of this problem, on the "regrettable dichotomy between philology and linguistics", is Dollinger (2016).

14 See, e.g., Chambers (1975, 1994, 1998, 2002, 2006, 2009a, 2012).

15 Clarke (2010) is an introduction to Newfoundland and Labrador English, Kirwin (2001) a classic short article on the variety.

16 Jack Chambers: pers. correspondence, 7 Dec. 2017.

17 One of the problems of NWAV reviewing is that it is carried out by self-declared experts with basically no conference organizer oversight, veto, or corrective. Everyone who went to NWAV can self-identify their areas of expertise and significantly affect the inclusion or rejection of a given paper. This ensures that "bandwagon" ideas – fashionable ideas – have the best chance of acceptance. Like in other "families", plurality is today not one of NWAV's strengths.

18 Quoted from Chambers (1986: 1).

7 A Global Village and a National Dictionary War

1 *Globe and Mail*, 8 Aug. 1998: D10.

2 Personal conversation with David Crystal, Ashmolean Museum, Oxford, April 2013.

3 Readers interested in this dispute between Popper and Wittgenstein, which involves the use of a fire poker, may want to read the brilliant book by Edmonds and Eidinow (2001), fittingly – and in a double entendre – entitled *Wittgenstein's Poker*.

4 I was recently told that Popper was the "wrong philosopher". Unlike other theoretical areas, however, science and knowledge theory is not a subjective domain in which one can "choose" one's favourite philosophers.

5 See Chambers (1980) or, for the whole story in hindsight, Dollinger and Clarke (2012).

6 An increase of American-like linguistic forms was attested in Chambers (1980, 1998), Clarke (1993b), Woods (1993), Nylvek (1992, 1993), and Zeller (1993).

7 See Dollinger (2012), the case of Mario.

8 I wrote my own short piece on the question a few years ago, using Chambers' paper as a springboard (Dollinger 2011a); like Chambers', my paper has not found a significant academic audience.

9 Story (1986: 43).

10 Only a few copies of this 629-page dictionary, which was edited by Thomas Kite Brown (its general content) and Canadianized by Henry Alexander, exist.

11 McCune (1992) is one of the first news items, in Nov. 1992, on a dictionary that would not appear for another six years.

12 Leaving aside *Collins Gage Canadian* reprints and minor Canadian adaptations of existing Collins titles.

13 The full title is *ITP Nelson Canadian Dictionary of the English Language: an Encyclopedic Reference* (see Friend *et al.* 1997).

14 The following counts are based on our conference paper Dollinger and Gaylie (2015).

15 See Oxford University Press Canada website: www.oupcanada.com/catalog/9780195418163.html.

16 Considine (2017) shows that Type 5 – Frequency is correct, while *DCHP-2*'s primary assessment of Type 1 – Origin is not borne out. The term was originally coined in the USA.

17 In this respect, ownership of linguistic resources is not unimportant. The main dictionary of Austrian German, the *Österreichisches Wörterbuch*, has been produced by the Österreichische Bundesverlag (ÖBV) since 1951. ÖBV was owned by the Republic of Austria and, in 2003, was sold to Ernst Klett Verlag, a German publisher, to help balance the budget. As the Oxford University Press involvement in Canadian English has shown, foreign ownership complicates the picture and at times interferes in unimagined ways in endo-normative processes.

8 Decolonizing *DCHP-1* and *DCHP-2*

1 Dollinger, Brinton, and Fee (2013).

2 For two reports on the problem, see www.nunatsiaqonline.ca/stories/article/65674 respected_cp_stylebook_replete_with_errors_about_inuit and www.cbc.ca/news/canada/north/errors-cp-stylebook-inuit-1.4449665.

3 J. K. Chambers: pers. correspondence, *c.* 2015.

4 Crate's birth registration is located in the Archives of Ontario, MS931 – Reel 29, reading "CRATE CHARLES BRANDEL", identity # 901423, Yr Rg 37, Place of event Weston, G.O.C.I. 70, Sex M and CONT. 11.

5 McBride (1997: 57), Principe (1999: 246, footnote 50).

6 Wikipedia, s.v. "Mackenzie North": https://en.wikipedia.org/wiki/Mackenzie_North.

7 Indian Residential School History and Dialogue Centre. Official Opening, 9 April 2018. Watch the archived video at https://ceremonies.ubc.ca/irshdc-opening. Coincidentally, the video includes the UBC president's apology to the First Nations for UBC's role in the cultural genocide. The acknowledgement of Harry Hawthorn by Grand Chief Edward John is found at 1h 04min 00sec into the video.

8 From the Indigo Books website: www.chapters.indigo.ca/en-ca/books/the-indians-of-canada/9780802063267-item.html.

9 *Canadian Encyclopedia*, s.v. "Diamond Jenness": www.thecanadianencyclopedia.ca/en/article/diamond-jenness.

10 *Canadian Encyclopedia*, s.v. "Diamond Jenness", www.thecanadianencyclopedia.ca/en/article/diamond-jenness.

11 The 2018 O'Hagan Annual Essay on Public Affairs in *The Walrus* offers a most interesting look at what might well be one of the watershed years in Canada's language policies: can the stalemate between French and English be overcome? See Abley (2018) for some answers and yet more questions.

9 Is There Really a Canadian English?

1 *Yeh* is a historically and regionally documented variant of *yeah* in English varieties.

2 What Figure 38 shows is only at first glance different from what is shown in Figures 20 and 21 in Chapter 5: by dividing the first period of the original graphs, which goes from 1977 to 1984, into two periods, 1977–79 and 1980–84, we see how the actual drop and climb appear as an increase in Figure 20. More recent periods have also been added.

3 Forty-five hits for "Canadian English" translates to 15 index points when put in relation to the size of the corpus in that period (see Dollinger 2016).

4 www.goodreads.com/book/show/130037.Canajan_Eh.

5 My stand on Austrian Standard German and German Standard German is summarized here: www.academia.edu/35962423; see Dollinger (in press) for the full argument.

6 Terry Fox was a university student from British Columbia when his right leg had to be amputated just below the hip because of cancer. Terry then decided in 1980 to run across Canada on an artificial leg to raise funds for cancer research for his "Marathon of Hope". He ran from Newfoundland to just outside Thunder Bay, when he was re-diagnosed with cancer. He died in 1981 but started a legacy that is rivalled by few Canadians. Every year in September, the annual Terry Fox Run raises millions of dollars towards finding a cure.

7 If you'd like to check for yourself, go to www.dchp.ca/dchp2, select "Search Entries", and then click on "DCHP-2 Update only". This lets you search only the new content. Then jump to "Usage notes", where you'll find the mark-up with semantic domains.

8 It is noteworthy to point out that the vocabulary in a dictionary of -isms has likely different properties than the vocabulary in a general language dictionary. For instance, Zipf's law probably does not apply (Hanks 2013: 31–32). This law states that the frequency of a given type is roughly inversely proportional to its rank, so the second most frequent word is only half as frequent as the most frequent word, the third most frequent only one third as frequent as the most frequent one. This is because -isms are not distributed in the same way that an entire natural language is distributed – e.g., they are heavier on the noun side and leaner on the adverb, verb, etc., side.

9 *DCHP-2* defines Nanaimo bars as "a dessert square with three layers: a crumb base, a layer of buttercream, and melted chocolate icing", with a first quotation from 1953.

10 The abbreviation for the North American National Hockey League, governing the sport of (ice) hockey in that region. Note that "national" refers to Canadian.

11 Meaning that teams are formed ad hoc from the players that show up at playtime.

12 The bona fide moniker of Wayne Gretzky, to date the greatest hockey player of all time. The term has existed since at least 1981; Gretzky would go on to play until the end of the 1998–99 season (see www.dchp.ca/dchp2/entries/view/The%252520Great%252520One).

13 I have very few chances to write about my Latin teacher, Professor Johannes Divjak (University of Vienna), who taught us in amazingly refreshing classes a great deal about Latin, ancient Roman culture, and more. That he is an international authority is something we discovered only years later. It was true: *magister bonus est*, 'the teacher is good' – the first sentence he ever had us translate.

14 For the presidential election, electoral law stipulates that one must vote, even under threat of penalties, though they have never been enforced. The 2016 election produced the world's first Green president, by the way.

Further Reading

The reader will find many references in the footnotes throughout this book, so much so that in this section I will offer only the most important springboards for those who'd like to get more intricately involved with the topic. I will proceed by chapters.

Introductions to Canadian English (Chapter 1)

... are available in McConnell's (1978) classic textbook, which is still worth a read. Boberg's (2010) monograph offers a very detailed overview of the features of Canadian English, which can be complemented with Tagliamonte's (2013) book that includes the morphosyntax more fully, yet with a trans-Atlantic, rather than a purely Canadian, focus. Morphosyntax is also dominant in Walker's textbook (2015). Dollinger (2015a) is a textbook for the study of linguistic variation, with a very simple yet effective method using examples exclusively from Canadian English. For historical reasons, a glance at Orkin (1970) is still a good idea.

The History of Linguistics (Chapter 2)

... is a fascinating field, to which Campbell (2017) is one of the most practical introductions. Hanks (2013: ch. 11) is a most concise introduction to the philosophy of language from Aristotle to the present. Law (2003) is a general introduction from antiquity to Shakespeare's time, while Waterman (1970) covers the nineteenth and twentieth centuries. More substantially, Joseph, Love, and Taylor (2001) survey the issues of twentieth-century linguistics, with a predecessor volume – Harris and Taylor (1997) – covering the western tradition of linguistics from antiquity to Saussure in the early 1910s. For a subjective yet reasoned choice of fifty "key thinkers" in linguistics, see Thomas (2011). For an easy and witty read on the USA–UK split in English, which was the precondition for the "Canadian split", see Murphy (2018).

The Dictionary-making Process (Chapter 3)

... is introduced and contextualized in its traditional guise in an excellent textbook by Landau (2001), which is a perfect place to start. If the history of the *OED* is of interest, Gilliver (2016) offers the most authoritative account and is the go-to source. Winchester's books (1998, 2003) are an easier read, well researched, but not nearly as detailed as

Gilliver's. John Considine (2008) is the best source on Early Modern dictionaries. For those who really would like to know, Hausmann et al.'s (1989–91) three-volume handbook is, while not the newest, still a compelling source. The journal *Dictionaries*, published twice a year by the Dictionary Society of North America, includes many pertinent topics. Fuertes Olivera (2018) and Durkin (2016) offer up-to-date accounts of the field.

Dictionary Making in the Paper Age and Beyond (Chapter 4)

... is, once more, best introduced in Landau (2001). Brewer's (2007) book on the *OED* offers lots of insights into the process. A history of *DARE* (Cassidy and Hall 1985–2013) would need to present the massive computer effort for *DARE* as of the late 1970s (see www.daredictionary.com), as would a history of the *Dictionary of Old English* (*DOE*) (Healey, Wilkin, and Xin, 2009), which had already gone digital in the early 1980s (see www.doe.utoronto.ca/pages/index.html). Unfortunately, no monograph accounts of these two important dictionaries are available, but see Adams (2013) and the *Dictionary of Old English* 2017 Progress Report. Stamper (2017) is a personal, entertaining look at the world behind the scenes of one of the US' biggest dictionary publishing houses.

The Canadian Centennial Excitement (Chapters 5 and 6)

... is captured in a number of publications. Fahrni and Rutherdale (2008) offers a critical look back at "the making of modern Canada", in which the *DCHP-1* played a role too. Hawthorn (2017) offers a more entertaining look at what he calls "that fun, exciting year" that was the sesquicentennial of Canadian confederation in 2017. Leechman's connection to Burchfield and the *OED* is one of the unexpected findings of this book. Burchfield's tenure at the *OED* is covered in both Gilliver (2016) and Brewer (2007).

Global Englishes and English as a Lingua Franca (Chapter 7)

... can be explored in Jenkins' (2015) textbook – which offers the best starting point – Mufwene (2001), and the new edition of *The Handbook of World Englishes* (Nelson, Proshina, and Davis in press). The *OED* in the global context is very favourably viewed in Ogilvie (2013), a point that can be challenged. Those interested in English as a Lingua Franca, perhaps the most frequently used form of English globally, will find food for thought in Seidlhofer (2011).

Decolonization and Reconciliation (Chapter 8)

... has become a very important topic in Canada today. Warrior (2015) covers a wide range of issues that Native North Americans are currently faced with. Fee (2015) offers decolonization perspectives in relation to land, one of the key issues in reconciliation. A slightly unusual approach is Justice's (2015) cultural history of the badger, which is consistent with the appreciation of all living things in many Indigenous cultures, and thus decolonizing.

Making Up One's Mind (Chapter 9)

... is no easy task. I hope the information offered in this book gives enough food for thought. If not, see Haugen's (1966) trailblazing study of the creation of Norwegian out of Danish and Swedish dialects. Havinga (2018) is an interesting historical look at a parallel scenario on "invisiblizing" Austrian German (vs German German), while Dollinger (in press) is on the greater issue of linguistic autonomy, which should not be confused with raging nationalism, which we all reject. Those who read German may also wish to consult Davies et al. (2017), an up-to-date collection of essays on the issue of standard languages, which is, after all, at the core of the present book. For language change in English more generally, which the present book has been all about in terms of Canadian English, McWhorter (2016) offers an entertaining look, as does Adams (2009). If you prefer to listen to smart and witty talk about language, try out www.waywordradio.org (Barnette and Barrett 2018), which must be the longest-running radio show on linguistics. Sometimes, quality does prevail.

Bibliography

Abate, Frank. 2008. Laurence Urdang 1927–2008. *DSNA Newsletter*, Fall, 32(2): 4–5 and 10. http://dictionarysociety.com/wp-content/uploads/2018/04/2008–32-2-68-DSNAN.pdf.

Abley, Mark. 2015. Canadians eat poutine and butter tarts on the chesterfield; many nouns in daily use would sound odd to English-speakers elsewhere. *Montreal Gazette*, 9 May: B5.

    2018. Beyond bilingualism: the Official Languages Act will soon turn fifty. Have we outgrown it? *The Walrus*, June: 30–39.

Adams, Michael P. 2009. *Slang: the People's Poetry*. Oxford University Press.

    2013. Review of *Dictionary of American Regional English* Vol. V: Sl–Z and Vol. VI: Contrastive Maps, Index to Entry Labels, Questionnaire, and Fieldwork Data. *American Speech*, 88: 168–95.

    2017. The Dictionary Society of North America: a history of the early years (part II). *Dictionaries*, 38(1): 1–46.

Aitken, A. J. 2004. Craigie, Sir William Alexander (1867–1957). In *Oxford Dictionary of National Biography*, rev. entry. Oxford University Press. www.oxforddnb.com/view/article/32614.

Akrigg, G. P. V. 1980. *Sedgewick: the Man and his Achievement*. Eleventh Garnett Sedgewick Memorial Lecture. Vancouver: University of British Columbia, Department of English.

Alexander, Henry. 1939. Charting Canadian speech. *Journal of Education (Nova Scotia)*, 10: 457–58.

    1962 [1940]. *The Story of Our Language*. 2nd edn. Toronto: Nelson.

    1951. The English language in Canada. In *Royal Commission Studies, "Massey Report"*, 13–24. Ottawa: King's Printer.

Algeo, John (ed.) 2001. *The Cambridge History of the English Language*. Vol. VI: *English in North America*. Cambridge University Press.

Anon. 1920. "The Canadian Language?" *Canadian Bookman*, December: 4–5.

Aronoff, Mark, and Janie Rees-Miller (eds.) 2017. *The Handbook of Linguistics*. 2nd edn. Malden, MA: Wiley-Blackwell.

Avis, Walter S. 1950. The speech of Sam Slick. MA thesis, Queen's University, Kingston, Ontario.

    1954. Speech differences along the Ontario – United States border. I: Vocabulary. *Journal of the Canadian Linguistic Association*, 1(1, Oct.): 13–18.

    1955a. Speech differences along the Ontario – United States border. II: Grammar and syntax. *Journal of the Canadian Linguistic Association*, 1(1, Mar.): 14–19.

1955b. The mid-back vowels in the English of the eastern United States: a detailed investigation of regional and social differences in phonic characteristics and in phonemic organization. Unpublished Ph.D. dissertation, University of Michigan.

1956. Speech differences along the Ontario – United States border. III: Pronunciation. *Journal of the Canadian Linguistic Association*, 1(1, Mar.): 41–59.

1957/58. Review of a Dictionary of Americanisms. Ed. Mitford M. Mathews. *Queen's Quarterly* (Kingston, ON), 64: 147–48.

1960. Secretary's Report, 1959–60. *Canadian Journal of Linguistics*, 6(2): 103–104.

1961. The "New England Short o": a recessive phoneme. *Language*, 37(4): 544–58.

1966. Canadian spoken here. In Scargill and Penner (eds.), 17–39.

1967. Introduction. In Avis *et al.* (eds.), xii–xv. Online in: Dollinger, Brinton, and Fee (eds.) (2013).

1969. Problems in editing *A Dictionary of Canadianisms on Historical Principles*. Presented to Section 13, Modern Languages Association, 28 Dec. 1969, Denver, Colorado. Typed version available through University of Queen's Archives, Avis fonds.

1972. So Eh? is Canadian, Eh? *Canadian Journal of Linguistics*, 17(2): 89–104.

1973. The English language in Canada. In *Current Trends in Linguistics*. Vol. X(1), ed. Thomas Sebeok, 40–74. The Hague: Mouton.

Avis, Walter S. (Chief Editor), Charles Crate, Patrick Drysdale, Douglas Leechman, Matthew H. Scargill, and Charles J. Lovell (eds). 1967. *A Dictionary of Canadianisms on Historical Principles*. Toronto: W. J. Gage.

Avis, Walter S., and A. M. Kinloch (eds.) 1977. *Writings on Canadian English, 1792–1975: An Annotated Bibliography*. Toronto: Fitzhenry & Whiteside.

Barber, Katherine. 2007. *Only in Canada, You Say: A Treasury of Canadian Language*. Oxford University Press.

Bailey, Richard W. 1991. Dialects of Canadian English. *English Today*, 27: 20–25.

2012. *Speaking American: A History of English in the United States*. Oxford University Press.

Barman, Jean. 2007. *The West Beyond the West: A History of British Columbia*. 3rd edn. University of Toronto Press.

Barnette, Martha, and Grant Barrett. 2018. A Way with Words. [Independently produced, syndicated radio show on language matters, since 1998.] http://waywordradio.org, San Diego, CA.

Bloomfield, Morton W. 1948. Canadian English and its relation to eighteenth century American speech. *Journal of English and Germanic Philology*, 47: 59–66.

Boberg, Charles. 2000. Geolinguistic diffusion and the U.S.–Canada border. *Language Variation and Change*, 12: 1–24.

2005. The North American Regional Vocabulary Survey: new variables and methods in the study of North American English. *American Speech*, 80: 22–60.

2008. Regional phonetic differentiation in Standard Canadian English. *Journal of English Linguistics*, 36(2): 129–54.

2010. *The English Language in Canada: Status, History and Comparative Analysis*. Cambridge University Press.

Boyd, Sally, Michol F. Hoffman, and James A. Walker. 2015. Sociolinguistic practice among multilingual youth in Sweden and Canada. In *Language, Youth and Identity in the 21st Century*, ed. Bente Ailin Svendsen and Jacomine Nortier, 290–306. Cambridge University Press.

Brennan, Richard. 1998. Ontario speller has U.S. accent. *Ottawa Citizen*, 18 Dec.: A10.

Brewer, Charlotte. 2007. *Treasure-House of the Language: The Living OED*. Yale University Press.

Brown, Beth. 2017. Respected CP Stylebook replete with errors about Inuit. *Nutasiaq Online*, 14 Dec., www.nunatsiaqonline.ca.

Brown, Brandon R. 2015. *Planck: Driven by Vision, Broken by War*. Oxford University Press.

Brown, Thomas Kite, and Henry Alexander (eds.) 1937. *The Winston Simplified Dictionary: For Home, School and Office. 1100 Pictorial Illustrations*. Toronto: John C. Winston Co. Limited.

Bruce, Harry. 1986. Just watch my lips if you want to know. . . *Toronto Star*, 24 May: M2.

Buschfeld, Sarah, Alexander Kautzsch, and Edgar W. Schneider. In press. From colonial dynamism to current transnationalism: a unified view on postcolonial and non-postcolonial Englishes. In Deshors (ed.), 15–44.

Campbell, Lyle. 2017. The history of linguistics. In Aronoff and Rees-Miller (eds.), 97–117.

Casselman, Bill. 1995. *Casselman's Canadian Words: A Comic Browse through Words and Folk Sayings Invented by Canadians*. Toronto: Copp, Clark.
   1999, 2002, 2004. *Canadian Sayings 3, 2, 1*. Toronto: McArthur & Company.
   2006. *Canadian Words and Sayings*. Toronto: McArthur & Company.

Cassidy, Claire M. 2002. Memories of Frederic G. Cassidy. *DARE Newsletter* (Madison, WI), 5(4): 1–5.

Cassidy, Frederick G., and Joan Houston Hall (eds.) 1985-2013. *Dictionary of American Regional English*. Vols. I–VI. Cambridge, MA: Belknap Press of Harvard University Press.

Chamberlain, A. F. 1890. Dialect research in Canada. *Dialect Notes*, 2: 43–56.

Chambers, J. K. (ed.) 1975. *Canadian English: Origins and Structures*. Toronto: Methuen.
   1980. Linguistic variation and Chomsky's "homogeneous speech community". In *Papers from the Fourth Annual Meeting of the Atlantic Provinces Linguistic Association. University of New Brunswick, Fredericton, N.B., 12–13 December 1980*, ed. A. Murray Kinloch and A. B. House, 1–31. Fredericton: University of New Brunswick.
   1986. Three kinds of standard in Canadian English. In Lougheed (ed.), 1-19.
   1994. An introduction to dialect topography. *English World-Wide*, 15: 35–53.
   1997. Gage Canadian dictionary. *Books in Canada*, 26(2): n.p. (Proquest file).
   1998. English: Canadian varieties. In Edwards (ed.), 252–72.
   2002. Patterns of variation including change. In *The Handbook of Language Variation and Change*, ed. J. K. Chambers, Peter Trudgill, and Natalie Schilling-Estes, 349–72. Malden, MA: Blackwell.
   2004. "Canadian Dainty": the rise and decline of Briticisms in Canada. In Hickey (ed.) (2004), 224–41.

2006. Canadian Raising retrospect and prospect. *Canadian Journal of Linguistics*, 51(2&3): 105–18.

2009a. *Sociolinguistic Theory*. 3rd, revised edn. Malden, MA: Wiley-Blackwell.

2009b. Do language norms follow national boundaries? Paper presented at the International Prescriptivism(e) & Patriotism(e) Conference: Language Norms and Identities from Nationalism to Globalization. University of Toronto, 19 Aug.

2010. English in Canada. In *Canadian English: A Linguistic Reader*, ed. Elaine Gold and Janice McAlpine, 1–37. Kingston, ON: Strathy Language Unit. www.queensu.ca/strathy/apps/OP6v2.pdf.

2012. Homogeneity as a sociolinguistic motive in Canadian English. *World Englishes: Special Issue on Autonomy and Homogeneity in Canadian English*, ed. Stefan Dollinger and Sandra Clarke, 31(4): 467–77.

Chambers, J. K., and Peter Trudgill. 1998. *Dialectology*. 2nd edn. Cambridge University Press.

Cheshire, Jenny. 1991. Introduction: sociolinguistics and English around the world. In *English Around the World: Sociolinguistic Perspectives*, ed. Jenny Cheshire, 1–12. Cambridge University Press.

Clarke, Sandra. 1982. Sociolinguistic approaches to current languages: two current investigations. *RLS – Regional Language Study*, 10: 15–19. http://collections.mun.ca/cdm/ref/collection/rlsn/id/595.

1993a. *Focus on Canada*. Varieties of English around the World G11. Amsterdam: Benjamins.

1993b. The Americanization of Canadian pronunciation: a survey of palatal glide usage. In S. Clarke (ed.), 85–108.

2006. *Nooz or nyooz?* The complex construction of Canadian identity. *Canadian Journal of Linguistics*, 51(2 & 3): 225–46.

2010. *Newfoundland and Labrador English*. Edinburgh University Press.

2012. Phonetic change in Newfoundland English. *World Englishes: Special Issue on Autonomy and Homogeneity in Canadian English*, ed. Stefan Dollinger and Sandra Clarke, 31(4): 503–18.

Clyne, Michael (ed.) 1992. *Pluricentric Languages: Differing Norms in Different Nations*. Berlin: Mouton de Gruyter.

Considine, John. 2003. Dictionaries of Canadian English. *Lexikos*, 13: 250–70.

2008. *Dictionaries in Early Modern Europe: Lexicography and the Making of Heritage*. Cambridge University Press.

2017. Parkade: one Canadianism or two Americanisms? *American Speech*, 92(3): 281–97.

(ed.) in press. *Cambridge World History of Lexicography*. Cambridge University Press.

Curzan, Anne. 2014. *Fixing English: Prescriptivism and Language History*. Cambridge University Press.

Craigie, William, and James R. Hulbert (eds.) 1968 [1938–44]. *A Dictionary of American English on Historical Principles*. 4 vols. University of Chicago Press.

Crystal, David. 2003 [1997]. *English as a Global Language*. 2nd edn. Cambridge University Press.

2005. *Pronouncing Shakespeare*. Cambridge University Press.

2012 [2003]. *English as a Global Language*. 2nd edn reprint. Canto Classics. Cambridge University Press.

2013. Discussion contribution after opening session of the OED Symposium: Symposium on the Future of the Oxford English Dictionary. Oxford University Press, Oxford, 1 Aug.

2017. *Making Sense: the Glamorous Story of English Grammar*. Oxford University Press.

D'Arcy, Alexandra. 2017. *Discourse-Pragmatic Variation in Context: 800 Years of LIKE*. Amsterdam: Benjamins.

Davies, Winifred V., Annelies Häcki Buhofer, Regula Schmidlin, Melanie Wagner, and Eva Lia Wyss (eds.) 2017. *Standardsprache zwischen Norm und Praxis: theoretische Betrachtungen, empirische Studien und sprachdidaktische Ausblicke*. Tübingen: Francke.

Davis, Alva L. 1948. *A Word Atlas of the Great Lakes Region*. Ph.D. dissertation, University of Michigan.

DCHP-1. See Avis *et al.* (eds.).

DCHP-1 Online. See Dollinger, Brinton, and Fee (eds.).

DCHP-2. See Dollinger and Fee (eds.).

Denis, Derek and Alexandra D'Arcy. 2018. Settler colonial English are distinct from postcolonial Englishes. *American Speech* 93(1): 3–31.

Deshors, Sandra C. (ed.) in press. *Modelling World Englishes in the 21st Century: Assessing the Interplay of Emancipation and Globalization of ESL Varieties*. Varieties of English Around the World, 61. Amsterdam: Benjamins.

Devitt, Amy. 1989. *Standardizing Written English: Diffusion in the Case of Scotland 1520–1659*. Cambridge University Press.

Dictionary of Old English 2017 Progress Report. www.doe.utoronto.ca/pages/report.pdf.

Doherty, Alexandra. 2019. The Western Canadian dictionary and the making of the Canadian West. Paper presented at DSNA-22. Bloomington, IN, May 2019.

Dollinger, Stefan. 2006. Towards a fully revised and extended edition of the Dictionary of Canadianisms on Historical Principles (DCHP-2): background, challenges, prospects. *Historical Sociolinguistics / Sociohistorical Linguistics*, 6. www.academia.edu/4591720.

2008a. *New-Dialect Formation in Canada: Evidence from the English Modal Auxiliaries*. Amsterdam: Benjamins.

2008b. Review of "Barber, Katherine. 2007. *Only in Canada, You Say: A Treasury of Canadian Language*. Oxford: Oxford University Press." *American Speech*, 83(4): 472–75.

2008c. The canary in the coalmine? *Newsletter of the Dictionary Society of North America*, 32(2): 1 and 3. www.academia.edu/35460392.

2011a. Academic and public attitudes to the notion of "standard" Canadian English. *English Today* 27(4): 3–9. www.academia.edu/4049232.

2011b. The "Groundhog Day Loop" in Canadian English. Strathy Language Unit Blog, April/May 2011. 1,200 words, 14 April 2011. www.queensu.ca/strathy/blog/guest-column/stefan-dollinger.

2012. The written questionnaire as a sociolinguistic data gathering tool: testing its validity. *Journal of English Linguistics*, 40(1): 74–110.

2015a. *The Written Questionnaire in Social Dialectology: History, Theory, Practice.* IMPACT 40. Amsterdam: Benjamins.

2015b. How to write a historical dictionary: a sketch of The Dictionary of Canadianisms on Historical Principles, Second Edition. *Ozwords*, October, 24(2): 1–3 and 6. www.academia.edu/18967380.

2015c. The Dictionary of Canadianisms on Historical Principles, Second Edition and regional variation: the complex case of Newfoundland. *Regional Language Studies . . . Newfoundland*, 26: 9–20. www.academia.edu/16544684.

2016. On the regrettable dichotomy between philology and linguistics: historical lexicography and historical linguistics as test cases. In *Studies in the History of English VII: Generalizing vs. Particularizing Methodologies in Historical Linguistic Analysis*, ed. Don Chapman, Colette Moore, and Miranda Wilcox, 61–89. Berlin: Mouton de Gruyter. www.academia.edu/22416903.

2017a. Canadian English in real-time perspective. In *History of English*. Vol. V: *Varieties of English*, ed. Alexander Bergs and Laurel Brinton, 53–79. De Gruyter Mouton Reader Series. Berlin and New York: de Gruyter Mouton. www.academia.edu/35010966.

2017b. TAKE UP #9 as a semantic isogloss on the Canada–US border. *World Englishes*, 36(1): 80–103.

2018. How old is "eh"? On the early history of a Canadian shibboleth. In *Wa7 xweysás i nqwal'utteníha i ucwalmícwa: He Loves the People's Languages. Essays in honour of Henry Davis*, ed. Lisa Matthewson, Erin Guntly, and Michael Rochemont, 467–88. UBC Occasional Papers in Linguistics, 6. Vancouver, BC: University of British Columbia. www.academia.edu/34683420.

2019. *The Pluricentricity Debate: On Parallels, Differences and Distortions in German, English and other Germanic Languages.* Focus Series. London: Routledge.

Dollinger, Stefan, Laurel J. Brinton, and Margery Fee (eds.) 2013. *DCHP-1 Online: A Dictionary of Canadianisms on Historical Principles Online.* Based on Avis *et al.* (eds.). Online dictionary: www.dchp.ca/dchp1.

Dollinger, Stefan, and Sandra Clarke. 2012. On the autonomy and homogeneity of Canadian English. In *World Englishes: Special Issue on Autonomy and Homogeneity in Canadian English*, ed. Stefan Dollinger and Sandra Clarke, 31(4): 449–66.

Dollinger, Stefan (Chief Editor) and Margery Fee (Associate Editor) 2017. *DCHP-2: The Dictionary of Canadianisms on Historical Principles, Second Edition.* With the assistance of Baillie Ford, Alexandra Gaylie, and Gabrielle Lim. Vancouver: University of British Columbia. www.dchp.ca/dchp2.

Dollinger, Stefan, and Alexandra Gaylie. 2015. Canadianisms in Canadian desk dictionaries: scope, accuracy, desiderata. Paper presented at DSNA-20 & SHEL-9 Conference, Vancouver, 5 June.

Doughty, Arthur G., and Chester Martin (eds.) 1929. *The Kelsey Papers.* Ottawa: King's Printer.

Dresser, Norman. 1968. Centennial reader. *Voxair* (Winnipeg, MB), 2 Jan.: n.p.

Drysdale, Patrick. 1980. Walter S. Avis – a tribute. *English World-Wide*, 1(1): 125–28.

Durkin, Philip. 2009. *The Oxford Guide to Etymology.* Oxford University Press.

2016. *The Oxford Handbook of Lexicography*. Oxford University Press.

Edmonds, David, and John Eidinow. 2001. *Wittgenstein's Poker*. London: Faber.

Edwards, John (ed.) 1998. *Language in Canada*. Cambridge University Press.

Emenau, Murray B., Winfried G. Kudszus, Irmengard Rauch, Hinrich C. Seeba, and Frederic C. Tubach. 1995. Herbert Penzl, German: Oakland. In *University of California: In Memoriam, 1995*, ed. David Krogh, 145–48. Berkeley: University of California. www.cdlib.org.

Fahrni, Magda, and Paul Rutherdale (eds.) 2008. *Creating Postwar Canada: Community, Diversity and Dissent, 1945–1975*. Vancouver: University of British Columbia Press.

Fee, Margery. 1991. Frenglish in Quebec English newspapers. In *Papers from the Fifteenth Annual Meeting of the Atlantic Provinces Linguistic Association November 8–9, 1991, University College of Cape Breton, Sydney, Nova Scotia*, ed. William J. Davey and Bernard LeVert, 12–23. Sydney, NS: University College of Cape Breton.

2011. Academic accidents and the development of a usage guide. Strathy Language Unit Blog. www.queensu.ca/strathy/blog/guest-column/margery-fee.

2015. *Literary Land Claims: the "Indian Land Question" from Pontiac's War to Attawapiskat*. Waterloo, ON: Wilfried Laurier University Press.

Fee, Margery, and Janice McAlpine. 2011 [2007, 1997]. *Guide to Canadian English Usage*. 2nd edn., corrected reprint. Toronto: Oxford University Press.

Finegan, Edward. 2001. Usage. In Algeo (ed.), 358–421.

Foran, Charles. 2000. We may speak English, but have we found our voice? *National Post*, 1 July 2000: A16.

Friend, David, Julia Keeler, Dan Liebman, and Fraser Sutherland (eds.) 1997. *ITP Nelson Canadian Dictionary of the English Language: an Encyclopedic Reference*. Toronto: ITP Nelson.

Fuertes Olivera, Pedro A. (ed.) 2018. *The Routledge Handbook of Lexicography*. London: Routledge.

Garnett, Gale. 1996. Yes, Virginia, harbour has a "u". *The Globe and Mail*, 21 Dec. 1996: D14.

Geikie, Reverend A. Constable. 2010 [1857]. Canadian English. In *Canadian English: A Linguistic Reader*, ed. Elaine Gold and Janice McAlpine, 44–54. Kingston, ON: Strathy Language Unit. www.queensu.ca/strathy/apps/OP6v2.pdf.

Gilliver, Peter. 2016. *The Making of the Oxford English Dictionary*. Oxford University Press.

Görlach, Manfred. 1990. The dictionary of transplanted varieties of languages: English. In Hausmann *et al.* (eds.), Vol. II, 1475–99.

Gregg, Robert J. 1962. Canadian lexicography. *Canadian Literature*, 14: 68–69.

1993. Canadian English lexicography. In Clarke (ed.), 27–44.

2004. *The Survey of Vancouver English: A Sociolinguistic Study of Urban Canadian English*, ed. Gaelan Dodds de Wolf, Margery Fee, and Janice McAlpine. Strathy Language Unit Occasional Papers 5. Kingston: Queen's University.

Gulden, Brigitte K. 1979. Attitudinal factors in Canadian English usage. Unpublished MA thesis, University of Victoria.

Halford, Brigitte K. See Gulden.

Hanks, Patrick. 2013. *Lexical Analysis: Norms and Exploitations*. Cambridge, MA: MIT Press.

Harris, Randy Allen. 1995. *The Linguistics Wars*. Oxford University Press.

Harris, Roy, and Talbot J. Taylor. 1997. *Landmarks in Linguistic Thought: The Western Tradition from Socrates to Saussure*. 2nd edn. London and New York: Routledge.

Haugen, Einar. 1966. *Language Conflict and Language Planning: The Case of Modern Norwegian*. Cambridge, MA: Harvard University Press.

Hausmann, Franz J., Oskar Reichmann, Herbert E. Wiegand, and Ladislav Zgusta (eds.) 1989–91. *Wörterbücher: Dictionaries: Dictionnaires: An International Encyclopedia of Lexicography*. 3 vols. Berlin: de Gruyter.

Havinga, Anna D. 2018. *Invisibilising Austrian German: On the Effect of Linguistic Prescriptions and Educational Reforms on Writing Practices in 18th-century Austria*. Berlin: de Gruyter.

Hawthorn, H. B., C. S. Belshaw, and S. M. Jamieson. 1958. *The Indians of British Columbia: A Study of Social Adjustment*. University of Toronto Press.

Hawthorn, Tom. 2017. *The Year Canadians Lost Their Minds and Found Their Country: The Centennial of 1967*. Madeira Park, BC: Douglas & McIntyre.

Headland, Thomas N. 2004. KENNETH LEE PIKE: June 9, 1912–December 31, 2000. *Biographical Memoirs* 84: 287–306. www.nap.edu/read/10992/chapter/16.

Healey, Antonette diPaolo, John Price Wilkin, and Xin Xiang (eds.) 2009. *The Dictionary of Old English Corpus on the World Wide Web*. Toronto: Dictionary of Old English Project.

Hickey, Raymond (ed.) 2004. *Legacies of Colonial English: Studies in Transported Dialects*. Cambridge University Press.

  2013. *Standards of English: Codified Varieties around the World*. Cambridge University Press.

High, Steven. 2008. The narcissism of small differences: the invention of Canadian English. In Fahrni and Rutherdale (eds.), 89–110.

Hinrichs, Lars. 2015. Tropes of exile in everyday Caribbean-diasporic speech: the reindexicalization of dread talk in the Jamaican diaspora. In *Censorship and Exile*, ed. J. Hartmann and H. Zapf, 65–81. Göttingen: V&R unipress.

  2018. The language of diasporic blogs: a framework for the study of rhetoricity in written online code-switching. In *Analyzing Youth Practices in Computer-Mediated Communication*, ed. C. Cutler and U. Røyneland. Cambridge University Press.

Hoffman, Michol F., and James A. Walker. 2010. Ethnolects and the city: ethnic orientation and linguistic variation in Toronto English. *Language Variation and Change*, 22: 37–67.

Jenness, Diamond. 1977 [1932]. *The Indians of Canada*. 7th edn. University of Toronto Press.

Jenkins, Jennifer. 2015. *Global Englishes: A Resource Book for Students*. 3rd edn. New York: Routledge.

Joos, Martin. 1942. A phonological dilemma in Canadian English. *Language*, 18: 141–44.

Joseph, John E., Nigel Love, and Talbot J. Taylor. 2001. *Landmarks in Linguistic Thought II: The Western Tradition in the Twentieth Century*. London: Routledge.

Justice, Daniel Heath. 2015. *Badger*. London: Reaktion Books.

Kachru, Braj. 1985. Standards, codification and sociolinguistic realism: the English language in the Outer Circle. In *English in the World: Teaching and Learning of Language and Literature*, ed. Randolph Quirk and Henry G. Widdowson, 11–36. Cambridge University Press.

Keddie, Grant. 2003. *Songhees Pictorial: A History of the Songhees People as seen by Outsiders, 1790–1912*. Victoria: Royal British Columbia Museum.

Kelsey Papers. See Doughty and Martin (eds.).

King Plant, Byron. 2009. "A relationship and interchange of experience": H.B. Hawthorn, Indian Affairs, and the 1955 BC Indian Research Project. *BC Studies*, 163: 5–31.

Kinloch, A. M. 1980. Walter S. Avis: 1919–1979. *Canadian Journal of Linguistics*, 25(1): 108–109.

Kinmod, Graham. 2007. Defining moments omitted [letter to the editor]. *Calgary Herald*, 1 July: A9.

Kirwin, William. 2001. Newfoundland English. In Algeo (ed.), 441–55.

Knowles, Elizabeth. 1990. Dr. Minor and the Oxford English Dictionary. *Dictionaries*, 12: 27–42.

    2000. Making the OED: readers and editors. A critical survey. In Mugglestone (ed.), 22–39.

Kretzschmar, William A., Jr. 2008. Standard American English pronunciation. In *Varieties of English*. Vol. II: *The Americas and the Caribbean*, ed. Edgar W. Schneider, 37–51. Berlin: Mouton de Gruyter.

    2009. *The Linguistics of Speech*. Cambridge University Press.

Krohn, Marie. 2008. *Louise Pound: The 19th Century Iconoclast who Forever Changed America's Views on Women, Academics, and Sports*. Clearfield, UT: American Legacy Historical Press.

Kytö, Merja. 1991. *Variation in Diachrony, with Early American English in Focus: Studies on CAN/MAY and SHALL/WILL*. Bern: Lang.

Kytö, Merja, and Lucia Siebers (eds.) In press. *Earlier North-American Englishes*. Varieties of English Around the World. Amsterdam: Benjamins.

Kytö, Merja, and Terry Walker. 2006. *Guide to A Corpus of English Dialogues 1560–1760*. Studia Anglistica Upsaliensia 130. Uppsala: Acta Universitatis Upsaliensis.

Labov, William. 1972. *Sociolinguistic Patterns*. Philadelphia: University of Pennsylvania Press.

    2008. Triggering events. In *Studies in the History of the English Language IV: Empirical and Analytical Advances in the Study of English Language Change*, ed. Susan M. Fitzmaurice and Donka Minkova, 11–54. Berlin: Mouton de Gruyter.

Labov, William, Sharon Ash, and Charles Boberg. 2006. *The Atlas of North American English: Phonetics, Phonology and Sound Change*. Berlin: Mouton de Gruyter.

Landau, Sidney I. 2001. *The Art and Craft of Lexicography*. 2nd edn. Cambridge University Press.

Law, Vivian. 2003. *The History of Linguistics from Plato to 1600*. Cambridge University Press.

Leechman, Douglas. 1926. The Chinook Jargon. *American Speech*, 1(10): 531–34.

1957. *Native Tribes of Canada*. Toronto: Gage.

Lilles, Jaan. 2000. The myth of Canadian English. *English Today*, 62(16/2): 3–9, 17.

Lo, Katrina. 2012. (Re)Defining the "Eh": reading a colonial narrative in the *Dictionary of Canadianisms on Historical Principles*. Unpublished MA thesis, University of British Columbia, Department of English.

Lougheed, William C. (ed.) 1986. *In Search of the Standard in Canadian English*. Strathy Language Unit Occasional Papers, 1. Kingston, ON: Queen's University.

Lovell, Bonnie A. 2011. The lexicographer's daughter: a memoir. Unpublished Ph.D. dissertation. University of North Texas.

Lovell, Charles J. 1955a. Lexicographic challenges of Canadian English. *Journal of the Canadian Linguistic Association*, 1(1, March): 2–5.

1955b. Whys and hows of collecting for the Dictionary of Canadian English: Part I: Scope and source material. *Journal of the Canadian Linguistic Association*, 1(2, Oct.): 3–8.

1956. Whys and hows of collecting for the Dictionary of Canadian English: Part II: Excerption and quotation. *Journal of the Canadian Linguistic Association*, 2(1, March): 23–32.

1958. A sampling of materials for a dictionary of Canadian English based on historical principles. *Journal of the Canadian Linguistic Association* (now Canadian Journal of Linguistics), 4(1): 23–32.

Lutz, John Sutton. 2008. *Makúk: A New History of Aboriginal–White Relations*. Vancouver: University of British Columbia Press. [makúk: 'let's trade' in Mowachaht of Nootka Island & James Cook. Yuquot, called Nootka or Friendly Cove by James Cook – friendly welcome!]

Mathews, Mitford M. 1969. Review of *A Dictionary of Canadianisms on Historical Principles*. Walter S. Avis, ed.-in-chief. *Journal of English Linguistics*, 3 (March): 89–91.

Matthewson, Lisa (ed.) 2008. *Quantification: a Cross-linguistic Perspective*. Bingley, UK: Emerald.

Matthewson, Lisa, Erin Guntly, and Michael Rochemont (eds.) 2018 *Wa7 xweysás i nqwal'utteníha i ucwalmícwa: He Loves the People's Languages. Essays in Honour of Henry Davis*. Vancouver: University of British Columbia Press.

Mawani, Renisa. 2009. *Colonial Proximities: Crossracial Encounters and Juridical Truths in British Columbia, 1871–1921*. Vancouver: University of British Columbia Press.

McArthur, Tom. 1989. *The English Language as Used in Quebec: A Survey*. Strathy Language Unit Occasional Papers 3. Kingston, ON: Queen's University.

McBride, Michelle. 1997. From indifference to internment: an examination of RCMP responses to Nazism and Fascism in Canada from 1934 to 1941. MA thesis, Department of History, Memorial University of Newfoundland.

McConnell, Ruth E. 1978. *Our Own Voice: Canadian English and How it Came to Be*. [1979 reprint with new subtitle *Canadian English and How it is Studied*]. Toronto: Gage.

McCune, Shane. 1992. *The Province* (Vancouver, BC), 6 Nov. 1992: A6.

McDavid, Raven I. 1967. Review of *A Dictionary of Canadianisms on Historical Principles*, Walter S. Avis, ed.-in-chief. *Canadian Journal of Linguistics*, 13: 55–57.

1980. [Reviews of] Scargill, M. H. 1977. A short history of Canadian English and McConnell, Ruth E. 1979. Our own voice: Canadian English and how it is studied. *Journal of English Linguistics*, 14(March): 45–58.

1981. Webster, Mencken, and Avis: spokesmen for linguistic autonomy. *Canadian Journal of Linguistics*, 26(1): 118–25.

McGovern, Michael Thomas. 1989. Phonetic Aspects of CBC Newsreading 1937–1987. Unpublished MA thesis, University of Victoria, Department of Linguistics.

McLay, W. S. W. 1930. A note on Canadian English. *American Speech*, 5(4): 328–29.

McWhorter, John. 2016. *Words On the Move: Why English Won't – and Can't – Sit Still (Like, Literally)*. New York: Henry Holt.

Mencken, H. L. 1936. *The American Language: An Inquiry into the Development of English in the United States*. 4th, corrected, enlarged, and rewritten edn. New York: Knopf.

Meyer, Matthias L. G. (ed.) 2008. Focus on Canadian English. Special issue of *Anglistik*, 19.

Meyerhoff, Miriam, and Nancy Niedzielski. 2003. The globalisation of vernacular variation. *Journal of Sociolinguistics*, 7(4): 534-55.

Milroy, Lesley. 1987. *Language and Social Networks*. 2nd edn. Oxford: Blackwell.

Mitchell, Marjorie R. 1968. A Dictionary of Songish, a Dialect of Straits Salish. Unpublished MA thesis, University of Victoria, British Columbia.

Mithun, Marianne. 1999. *The Languages of Native North America*. Cambridge University Press.

Moore, Mavor. 1967. How we talk Canadian. *Saturday Night* (Toronto), November, 54–55.

Morris, Edward E. 1898. *Austral English: A dictionary of Australasian words, phrases and usages with those aboriginal-Australian and Maori words which have become incorporated in the language, and the commoner scientific words that have had their origin in Australasia*. London: MacMillan.

Mufwene, Salikoko S. 2001. *The Ecology of Language Evolution*. Cambridge University Press.

Mugglestone, Lynda (ed.) 2000. *Lexicography and the OED: Pioneers in the Untrodden Forest*. Oxford University Press.

Muhr, Rudolf, Carla Amorós Negre, Carmen Fernández Juncal, Klaus Zimmermann, Emilio Prieto, and Natividad Hernández (eds.) 2013. *Exploring Linguistic Standards in Non-Dominant Varieties of Pluricentric Languages – Explorando estándares lingüísticos en variedades no dominantes de lenguas pluricéntricas*. Österreichisches Deutsch – Sprache der Gegenwart, 15. Berne: Peter Lang.

Munroe, Helen C. 1929. Montreal English. *American Speech*, 5(1): 21.

1930. Bilingual signs in Montreal and its environs. *American Speech*, 5(3): 228–31.

1931. "Raise" or "rise"? *American Speech*, 6(6): 407–10.

Murphy, Lynne. 2018. *The Prodigal Tongue: The Love–Hate Relationship between American and British English*. New York: Penguin RandomHouse.

Nelson, Cecil, Zoya Proshina, and Daniel Davis (eds.) In press. *The Handbook of World Englishes*. 2nd edn. Malden, MA: Wiley-Blackwell.

Newell, Kristan M., 2019. Redefining the Acadian French lLexicon: The Role of English Loanwords in Two Acadian Villages. Unpublished MA thesis, UBC English.

Nylvek, Judith A. 1992. Is Canadian English in Saskatchewan becoming more American? *American Speech*, 67(3): 268–78.

1993. A sociolinguistic analysis of Canadian English in Saskatchewan: a look at urban versus rural speakers. In Clarke (ed.), 201–28.

Ogilvie, Sarah. 2013. *Words of the World: A Global History of the Oxford English Dictionary*. Cambridge University Press.

Onosson, D. Sky 2018. An acoustic study of diphthong-raising in three dialects of North American English. Unpublished Ph.D. thesis, University of Victoria.

Orkin, Mark M. 1970. *Speaking Canadian English: An Informal Account of the English language in Canada*. Reprint. New York: McKay Company.

1973. *Canajan, Eh?* Don Mills, ON: General Publishing.

1988 [1982, 1973]. *Canajan, Eh?* 3rd edn. Don Mills, ON: General Publishing.

Paddock, Harold J. 1981. *A Dialect Survey of Carbonear, Newfoundland*. Publications of the American Dialect Society, 68. University of Alabama Press.

Padolsky, Enoch, and Ian Pringle. 1981. *A Historical Source Book for the Ottawa Valley: A Linguistic Survey of the Ottawa Valley*. Ottawa: Carleton University, Linguistic Survey of the Ottawa Valley.

Partridge, Eric, and John W. Clark (eds.) 1968 [1951]. *British and American English since 1900. With Contributions on English in Canada, South Africa, Australia, New Zealand and India*. New York: Greenwood Press.

Pratt, T. K. 1986. A response to G. M. Story. In Lougheed (ed.), 54-64.

1993. The hobgoblin of Canadian English spelling. In *Focus on Canada*, ed. Sandra Clarke, 45-64. Amsterdam: Benjamins.

2004. Review of DARE, Vol. IV: P–Sk. *Canadian Journal of Linguistics*, 49: 127–30.

Priestley, F. E. L. 1968 [1951]. Canadian English. In *British and American English since 1900*, ed. Eric Partridge and John W. Clark, 72–84. New York: Greenwood Press.

Principe, Angelo. 1999. *The Darkest Side of the Fascist Years: The Italian-Canadian Press 1920–1942*. Toronto: Guernica.

Quirk, Randolph, Sidney Greenbaum, Geoffrey Leech, and Jan Svartvik. 1985. *A Comprehensive Grammar of the English Language*. London: Longman.

Ray, Randy. 2003. Obituary of Gage Love 1917–2003: making the world a better place. *The Globe and Mail*, 30 Oct.: R9.

Reuter, David M. 2017. *Newspaper, Politics, and Canadian English: A Corpus-Based Analysis of Selected Linguistic Variables in Early Nineteenth-Century Ontario Newspapers*. Heidelberg: Winter.

Rice, Keren. 2016. Indigenous languages of Canada. *Canadian Encyclopedia*. www.thecanadianencyclopedia.ca/en/article/aboriginal-people-languages.

Richler, Howard. 1996. Questions of survival and Canadian language. *Toronto Star*, 30 Nov.: L7.

Roeder, Rebecca V. 2012. The Canadian Shift in two Ontario cities. *World Englishes: Symposium Issue on Autonomy and Homogeneity in Canadian English*, ed. Stefan Dollinger and Sandra Clarke, 31(4): 478–92.

Roeder, Rebecca V., and Matt Hunt Gardner. 2013. The phonology of the Canadian Shift revisited: Thunder Bay & Cape Breton. *University of Pennsylvania Working Papers in Linguistics* 19(2, Selected Papers from NWAV41): 161–70.

Romaine, Suzanne. 1982. *Socio-historical Linguistics: Its Status and Methodology.* Cambridge University Press.

Sandilands, John. 1977 [1913]. *Western Canadian Dictionary and Phrasebook: Facsimile Edition of the 1913 [2nd] edition, with an introduction by John Orrell* [1912 1st edn]. Edmonton: University of Alberta Press.

Scargill, Matthew H. 1957. Sources of Canadian English. *Journal of English and Germanic Philology*, 56: 611–14.

  1967. Preface. In Avis *et al.* (eds.) www.dchp.ca/DCHP-1/pages/frontmatter#preface.

  1977. *A Short History of Canadian English.* Victoria: Sono Nis.

Scargill, Matthew H., and P. G. Penner (eds.) 1966. *Looking at Language: Essays in Introductory Linguistics.* Toronto: Gage.

Scargill, Matthew H., and Henry J. Warkentyne. 1972. The survey of Canadian English: a report. *The English Quarterly. A Publication of the Canadian Council of Teachers of English*, 5(3, Fall): 47-104.

Schneider, Edgar W. 2007. *Postcolonial English: Varieties Around the World.* Cambridge University Press.

Seidlhofer, Barbara. 2007. English as a lingua franca and communities of practice. In *Anglistentag 2006 Halle: Proceedings*, ed. S. Volk-Birke and J. Lippert, 307–18. Trier: Wissenschaftlicher Verlag.

  2011. *Understanding English as a Lingua Franca.* Oxford University Press.

Sheidlower, Jesse. 2017. A delightful dictionary for Canadian English. *The New Yorker*, online 23 March 2017. www.academia.edu/32007636.

Simpson, John. 2016. *The Word Detective: Searching for the Meaning of It All at the Oxford English Dictionary: A Memoir.* New York: Basic Books.

Sledd, James. 1978. What are we going to do about it now that we're number one? *American Speech*, 53: 175–94.

Smith, Russell. 2007. Who knew "nooz" was about morality? *The Globe and Mail*, 20 Dec. 2007: R1.

Stamper, Kory. 2017. *Word by Word: The Secret Life of Dictionaries.* New York: Pantheon.

Story, George M. 1986. The role of the dictionary in Canadian English. In Lougheed (ed.), 41-53.

Story, George M., and William Kirwin. 1971. National dictionaries and regional homework. *RLS - Regional Language Studies*, 3: 19–22.

Swan, Julia. 2016. Canadian English in the Pacific Northwest: a comparison of Vancouver, BC and Seattle, WA. *Proceedings of the CLA Conference*, ed. Lindsay Hracs. http://cla-acl.ca/wp-content/uploads/actes-2016/Swan_CLA2016_proceedings.pdf.

Swanky, Tom. 2012. *The True Story of Canada's "War" of Extermination on the Pacific plus The Tsilhqot'in and other First Nations Resistance.* Burnaby: Dragon Heart.

Tagliamonte, Sali A. 2013. *Roots of English.* Cambridge University Press.

  2016a. *Teen Talk: The Language of Adolescents.* Cambridge University Press.

2016b. *Making Waves: The Story of Variationist Sociolinguistics*. Malden, MA: Wiley-Blackwell.

Telfer, Geordie. 2009. *Dictionary of Canadianisms: How to Speak Canadian, Eh*. Edmonton: Folklore.

Thay, Edrick. 2004. *Weird Canadian Words: How to Speak Canadian*. Edmonton: Folklore.

Thoma, Sonja C. 2016. Discourse particles and the syntax of discourse-evidence from Miesbach Bavarian. Unpublished Ph.D. dissertation, University of British Columbia Linguistics.

Thomas, Eric R. 1991. The origin of Canadian Raising in Ontario. *Canadian Journal of Linguistics*, 36: 147–70.

Thomas, Margaret. 2011. *Fifty Key Thinkers on Language and Linguistics*. London and New York: Routledge.

Tieken-Boon van Ostade, Ingrid M. 2010. *The Bishop's Grammar: Robert Lowth and the Rise of Prescriptivism*. Oxford University Press.

Toon, Thomas E. 1981. Making a North American dictionary after Avis. *Canadian Journal of Linguistics. Special Issue. Lexicography and dialectology: Walter S. Avis in memoriam*. 26(1): 142–49.

TRC Final Report. 2015. *The Survivors Speak: A Report of the Truth and Reconciliation Commission of Canada*. www.trc.ca/websites/trcinstitution/index.php?p=890.

Trudgill, Peter. 1974. *Sociolinguistics: An Introduction*. Harmondsworth: Penguin (today available in 4th edition from 2001).

2004. *New-Dialect Formation: The Inevitability of Colonial Englishes*. Edinburgh University Press.

Trudgill, Peter, and Jean Hannah. 2002. *International English: A Guide to Varieties of Standard English*. 4th edn. London: Arnold.

2017. *International English: A Guide to Varieties of English Around the World*. 6th edn. London: Hodder.

Vallance, Neil. 2015. Sharing the land: the formation of the Vancouver Island (or "Douglas") treaties of 1850–1854 in historical, legal and comparative context. Unpublished Ph.D. dissertation, University of Victoria, Faculty of Law. http://hcmc.uvic.ca/songheesconference/pdf/Vallance_Neil_PhD_2016.pdf.

Van Herk, Gerard. 2011. Except Newfoundland English. Which is unique. And endangered. Or not. Guest Column, Strathy Language Unit, 26 May. www.queensu.ca/strathy/blog/guest-column/gerard-van-herk.

Vinay, Jean-Paul. 1981. Note sur l'élargissement possible du terme canadianisme. *Canadian Journal of Linguistics: Special Issue on Lexicography and Dialectology. Walter S. Avis in Memoriam*. 26(1): 150-59.

Vincent, Thomas, George Parker, and Stephen Bonnycastle (eds.) 1978. *Walter S. Avis: Essays and Articles. Selected from a Quarter Century of Scholarship at the Royal Military College of Canada, Kingston*. Kingston: Royal Military College of Canada.

Walker, James A. 2015. *Canadian English: A Sociolinguistic Perspective*. London: Routledge.

Wanamaker, Murray G. 1965. The language of King's County, Nova Scotia. Unpublished Ph.D. thesis, University of Michigan.

1981. Walter S. Avis: gōd wīs secg. *Canadian Journal of Linguistics: Special Issue on Lexicography and Dialectology. Walter S. Avis in Memoriam.* 26(1): 87-89.

Wang, Ying. 2012. Chinese speakers' perceptions of their English in intercultural communication. Ph.D. thesis, University of Southampton. https://eprints.soton.ac.uk/367398/1/Ying%2520Wang%2520PhD%2520thesis.pdf.

Warkentin, John (ed.) 1994. *The Kelsey Papers: A Reproduction of the 1929 Edition by Arthur G. Doughty & Chester Martin.* University of Regina, Canadian Plains Research Centre.

Warkentyne, Henry J. 1983. Attitudes and language behavior. *Canadian Journal of Linguistics,* 28: 71–76.

Warrior, Robert (ed.) 2015. *The World of Indigenous North America.* London: Routledge.

Waterman, John T. 1970. *Perspectives in Linguistics.* 2nd edn. University of Chicago Press.

Weinreich, Uriel, William Labov, and Marvin Herzog. 1968. Empirical foundations for a theory of language change. In *Directions in Historical Linguistics,* ed. Winfried P. Lehmann and Yakov Malkiel, 95–195. Austin: University of Texas Press.

Whitney, William D. 1971 [1884]. On the narrative use of imperfect and perfect in the Brahmanas. In *Whitney on Language: Selected Writings of William Dwight Whitney,* ed. Michael Silverstein, 306–35. Cambridge, MA: MIT Press.

Widdowson, Henry G. 1994. The ownership of English. *TESOL Quarterly,* 28(2): 377-89.

Wilson, H. Rex. 1958. The dialect of Lunenburg County, Nova Scotia: a study of the English of the county, with reference to its sources, preservation of relics, and vestiges of bilingualism. Unpublished Ph.D. thesis, University of Michigan.

Wiltschko, Martina. 2014. *The Universal Structure of Categories: Towards a Formal Typology.* Cambridge University Press.

Winchester, Simon. 1998. *The Professor and the Madman: A Tale of Murder, Insanity, and the Making of the Oxford English Dictionary.* Moosic, PA: Harper Collins. Appeared in the UK as *The Surgeon of Crowthorne: A Tale of Murder, Madness and the Love of Words.* London: Viking.

2003. *The Meaning of Everything: The Story of the Oxford English Dictionary.* Oxford University Press.

Woods, Howard B. 1993. A synchronic study of English spoken in Ottawa: is Canadian English becoming more American? In Clarke (ed.), 151–78.

1999 [1979]. *The Ottawa Survey of Canadian English.* Kingston, ON: Strathy Language Unit, Queen's University.

Wright, Robert. 2008. From liberalism to nationalism: Peter C. Newman's discovery of Canada. In *Creating Postwar Canada: 1945–1975,* ed. Magda Fahrni and Robert Rutherdale, 111–36. Vancouver: University of British Columbia Press.

Yu, Skylet. 2018. Caradianisms in the *Collins Canadian Dictionary* (2010, 2011, and 2016): representativeness, comprehensiveness, and accuracy. UBC English 507A graduate term paper.

Zeller, Christine. 1993. Linguistic symmetries, asymmetries, and border effects within a Canadian/American sample. In Clarke (ed.), 179–200.

Zimmer, Ben. 2010. On language: optics. *The New York Times,* 4 March, Sunday Magazine MM14. www.academia.edu/36659992.

General Index

Abley, Mark, 225, 254
acclaim (v.), 239
Adams, Michael P., 206, 250, 257–59
Alexander, Henry
  Avis' teacher, 71
  Canadianisms, 237
  fieldwork, 41, 150, 247
  lex committee, 77
  Massey Report, 44
  Queen's University, 43
  textbook, 30
  Winston Simplified, 173, 251, 253
all-candidates meeting, 192
all-dressed, 238
American Dialect Society (ADS), 42, 156
Americanization, 165–66, 168–69, 171
Anishnabe, 96–97 *See* Ojibway
attitudes, linguistic, 223, 226
Atwood, Margaret E., 46, 99
Auer, Anita, 48
Australian English, 252
autonomy, linguistic, 226, 231, 235,
  258
Avis, Faith, 46–47, 50, 71–72, 112–13
  Carleton University, 71
  education, 71
  picture, 47
Avis, Walter S.
  army, 25, 70, 156
  Beginning Dictionary, 26, 67
  Big Six, 21, 25, 66
  Calgary 1963, 81
  Canadian English, 40–41, 44, 57–58, 62, 69,
    72, 74
  Canadian quotations, 74, 84, 208
  career, 70, 76
  Chambers, J. K., 44
  CLA, 48, 66, 76
  cross-border research, 76
  cross-country travel, 79
  death, 21, 44, 65–67, 155–56
  dialectology, 159

dictionary plans, 74
dissertation, 74
early years, 70
editor, 78–79
editorial principles, 140
education, 43, 71
fame, 163
friendship, 67, 75
funding, 67–68
Gage, 68
health, 44, 74, 80, 85
historical linguistics, 43–44, 72
job prospects, 81
Kingston, 21
legacy, 21, 36, 43, 63, 66, 79, 155
lexicographical committee, 77
linguistic fashions, 69–70, 76, 156,
  165
linguistics, 65, 76
Lovell, 51
Mathews, 121
McConnell, Ruth, 44
Michigan, 73
MLA, 48
obituary, 66–67, 77, 155, 264
perfectionism, 68
picture, xv, 47, 64
predecessor, 41, 43–44
Queen's University, 41, 71
quotation slips, 79–80, 92
quotes, 28, 87, 245
recent graduate, 77
RMC, 20, 44, 66, 78, 82
role, 80
Sam Slick, 41, 43
scope creep, 68
successor, 62
teacher, 44, 49, 67, 73
teaching, 14, 43, 70
veteran, 71
Vinay, 155
workaholic, 62, 74–75, 80

274

Lovell, Charles J. (cont.)
  workaholic, 56, 61, 67, 74–75
  worries, 99
  young adult, 24
Luick, Karl, 73, 159
Lunenburg dory, 130

make-work, 239
Mathews, Mitford M., 40, 55–56, 60, 69, 75,
      120–21, 129–30, 140
  on *DCHP-1*, 130
  on Lovell, 56–57
Mauranen, Anna, 249
Mawani, Renisa, 5
May, Bryan (guitarist in Queen), 44
May long, 240
May long weekend, 240
May two-four, 240
McClelland & Stewart, 99
  publisher for *DCHP-1*, 99
McDavid, Raven I., 231, 247
  army, 156
  *Linguistic Atlas of the United States and
      Canada* director, 66, 71, 73
  on Avis, 65–66, 69, 78, 138
  on Scargill's late work, 144
  quote, 138, 154
  review of *DCHP-1*, 130, 140
  tribute to Avis, 70, 76, 130, 154
Memorial University, 45, 67, 100, 139, 158
Mencken, H. L., 33, 46, 55, 75, 115, 152, 154,
      253
  Avis, 65
  death, 66
  household name, 70
  life, 69
  linguistic autonomy, 69
Merriam-Webster, 161, 174
Messner, Reinhold, 54
Meyerhoff, Miriam, 251
Middle English, 29, 72, 84, 228, 242
Minor, W. C., 56, 84, 101, 249
moccasin, 84
Modern Languages Association (MLA),
      41–42, 48
Montgomery, Michael, 250
Montreal smoked meat, 238
mountaineering, 21, 24, 54
Mountie, 199
multilingualism, 176, 180
Munroe, Helen C., 45–46
Murray, Bill (actor), 221, 226
Murray, James A. H., 52, 252
  character, 80
  death on the job, 104

link to Lovell, 40
outsider status, 24, 52
parallels with Lovell, 52
Philological Society, 55
quotations, 79
Scot, 58
W. C. Minor, 56, 84, 101
muskeg, 37, 95

Nanaimo bar, 238
National Film Board, 239
nationalism, 69, 124, 127, 166, 230–31, 235,
      241, 258
native speaker, 4, 18–19, 164, 182, 217,
      227–28
Nelson Ltd, 161
Neufeldt, Victoria, xv
New Canadian, 239
new-dialect formation, 12, 26
New-Dialect Formation Theory. *See* Trudgill
Newfoundland English, 167, 172, 253
  ballicater, 139
  COD-2, 188
  critique of *DCHP-1*, 139
  Drysdale, 100
  in *DCHP-1*, 129
  linguistic enclave, 172
  nose (Grand Banks), 187
  present-day change, 173
  Story, 77
  variation studies, 158
  wreckhouse winds, 187
  yod-dropping, 169
Newfoundland terms, in *DCHP-1*, 129
non-native speaker, 18, 48, 164
non-native/native speaker ratio, English,
      18–19, 92, 152, 247
Norwegian, 258

OED. See *Oxford English Dictionary*
Ojibway, 96–97
Old English, 16, 29, 257, 266
Orkin, Mark M., 67, 149, 169, 225–26, 256
Orkneyman, 186
Outer Circle, 19, 163–64, 226, 267
ownership, linguistic, 18, 226, 254
Oxford English Dictionary
  before 1879, 82
  Canadian data, 153
  Canadian quotations, 153
  CD-ROM, 180
  Chicago, 38, 99
  Chief Editor, 90
  DCHP-1 connection, 38, 152–53, 253, 257
  earlier fascicles, 140